CASINO GAMBLING SECRETS

CASINO GAMBLING SECRETS

MARTEN JENSEN

CARDOZA PUBLISHING

ABOUT THE PUBLISHER

Cardoza Publishing is the foremost gaming and gambling publisher in the world with a library of over 100 up-to-date and easy-to-read books and strategies. These authoritative works are written by the top experts in their fields and with more than seven million books in print, represent the best-selling and most popular gaming books anywhere.

FIRST EDITION

Library of Congress Catalogue Card No: 2003100599
ISBN: 1-58042-107-5

Visit our web site (www.cardozapub.com) or write for
a full list of books, advanced strategies and computer games.

CARDOZA PUBLISHING

P.O. Box 1500, Cooper Station, New York, NY 10276
Phone 1-800-577-WINS
email: cardozapub@aol.com

TABLE OF CONTENTS

TABLE OF CONTENTS

TABLE OF CONTENTS

♦1♦
INTRODUCTION

This book covers fifteen of the most widespread table games currently banked by casinos across the United States. It also includes extensive information on video poker, slot machines, and keno. Thus, it is no longer necessary to purchase a separate book for every game of interest. This one volume gives you all the information you will need to play these games like an expert.

Each game is described in full detail, including the complete rules of play, the best wagers to make, and the best playing strategies. Numerous charts and tables display information on the various bets, payouts, and bonuses.

The very best playing advice is given for every game to maximize your chances of winning. This expert strategy advice will also help you to reduce the house edge to the bare minimum. In some cases, simplified but effective strategies have been devised especially for the casual and recreational player.

ALL THE LATEST GAMES
The traditional table games offered by most casinos were invented hundreds of years ago and have evolved over time to reach their present form. The modern casino-banked versions of blackjack and craps have been around for almost 100 years, and games such as roulette, baccarat, and keno are more than 150 years old.

Over the past twenty or thirty years, many new and different games have appeared in the casinos. Games such as Caribbean Stud Poker, Let It Ride, and Spanish 21 are now mainstays in most places, along with modified Asian games such as Pai Gow Poker and Sic-Bo. During the same period, the ubiquitous Slot Machine has evolved into a high-tech marvel, along with its popular cousin Video Poker.

All of these games, old and new, are described in complete detail on the following pages. The playing strategies are the best that contemporary gaming experts, statisticians, and mathematicians, along with their computers, can devise for maximizing your chances of winning. You cannot find better gambling advice anywhere.

If you enjoy playing the wide variety of games that are available today, you would be hard pressed to find a game in a U.S. casino that isn't thoroughly described within these pages. For the average gambler, this is the only book you will ever need. It is, essentially, a whole library in one volume.

ACKNOWLEDGEMENTS

The major strategies in this book were devised and tested by the most respected specialists in the field. My special thanks to mathematical geniuses Michael Shackleford (*The Wizard of Odds*) and Stanford Wong for allowing me to publish their work. I would also like to acknowledge the late Julian Braun and the late Lenny Frome for their major contributions to the knowledge base of gambling, which I have freely tapped.

Many people who take a vacation at a gambling venue, simply walk into the casino, find an empty seat at their game of choice, sit down, and begin to play. Or they look at a dozen slot machines and arbitrarily sit down at one that looks interesting.

A better approach is to survey most of the tables or most of the slot machines in the casino first, in order to find the most suitable game. Of course, you can't do this if you don't know which games are the most suitable. Some of what you should look for is explained in the following sections. The rest is covered in the chapters on the specific games.

The first time you ever attended a formal banquet dinner, you were probably intimidated by the number of forks of various shapes and sizes that were sitting to the left of your plate. To avoid embarrassment, the best advice at that time was to carefully watch what the other diners were doing. The same advice applies if you are new to a particular table game. Just watch what the other players are doing and follow their lead. If you do make a mistake, the dealer will correct you. Nowadays most dealers are trained to do this in a polite and unobtrusive way.

TABLE LIMITS

It can be more than a little embarrassing to plop down at a table, throw out a fifty, ask for nickels ($5 chips), and then find out that the table has a $100 minimum bet limit. Every table game has a little placard that gives the betting limits, and you should inspect those signs before you select a table. The table limit sign usually looks like the following illustration.

```
TABLE LIMIT
Min  $10
Max  $1000
```

In many casinos, the minimum bet can be quickly determined by the color of the sign. Red indicates a $5 minimum, yellow is $10, green is $25, and black is $100. Sometimes the placard may also post one or more specific rules for that table.

Although every slot machine has its denomination posted, it is not always obvious. A simple way is to glance at the service lights on top of the machines.

These lights are color-coded according to denomination, which can be a big help in locating your favorite games. Most casinos use the following colors.

```
RED = nickel
GREEN = dime
YELLOW = quarter
ORANGE or GOLD = half dollar
BLUE = one dollar
PURPLE = five dollar
```

Before you can intelligently decide which table or which denomination of machine to play, you need to determine how much you can afford to bet. The next chapter on Money Management will give you some guidelines.

CASINO CHIPS

Table games are played with casino chips. At most table games, you can throw a bill on the table and say, "Cash plays," but you will be paid off with casino chips. The accepted procedure is to drop some currency in front of the dealer and ask for chips. The dealer will ask what denomination you want and will then place a stack in front of you. Your money will be converted entirely into chips; the dealer cannot make change. When you quit playing and are ready to change your chips back into cash, you can do so at the cashier's cage.

In most casinos, $1 chips are white, $5 chips are red (called nickels or reds), $25 chips are green (called quarters or greens), and $100 chips are black. In the few casinos that modify this color scheme, the differences will quickly become apparent. The minimum denomination used in most casinos is $1.

The terms **check** or **cheque** (pronounced *check*) are used by casino personnel, high rollers, and professional gamblers. The term **chip** is used everywhere else, including in this book. The two terms are synonymous.

ROULETTE CHIPS

The game of roulette uses special colored chips, which are sold by the dealer in stacks of 20. Since all of the players at the table intermingle their bets on the same betting layout, each person is issued chips of a different color to avoid mix-ups. The value of each roulette chip depends on how much you paid for the stack. In Nevada, the minimum price for a 20-chip stack will be between $10 (50 cents per chip) and $100 ($5 per chip), depending on the casino and the time of day. If you pay more than the minimum, the dealer will place a special marker, called a **lammer**, on the rim of the wheel to remind her of what your particular chips are worth.

Roulette chips may be bought with cash or with regular casino chips (from that casino). When you are finished playing, the dealer will exchange your remaining roulette chips for regular casino chips. You are not allowed to remove the colored roulette chips from the roulette table—they cannot be used anywhere else and only the dealer you bought them from knows what they are worth.

GAME RULES

Once you have determined your betting limits, the next step is to find a table with good playing rules. The rules for some games can change from table to table. This is especially true of blackjack and all its variations. For other games, the rules can change from casino to casino. Be sure to carefully read up on your games of choice before you begin to play.

People are often unaware of how many different types of video poker and slot machines can be found in a single casino. There is considerable variability in the payout schedules, and you should know what they are. Some machines are much easier on your bankroll than others, and some are even beatable. Be sure to read those chapters to get the inside scoop.

FINDING A SEAT

Now that you've found a table with suitable betting limits and reasonable playing rules, take a seat. Except for some advanced playing techniques, which are beyond the scope of this book, it doesn't matter which seat you take.

During the busy times, you won't have much choice. Unless you are sitting down at a high-limit table, there will often be only one or two unoccupied seats to choose from. If you are a relative beginner and need extra time to decide how to play your hand, find a seat as close to third base (the dealer's right) as you can.

WAGERING ETIQUETTE

Casino table games have unwritten rules of behavior that are followed as a matter of courtesy to the dealer and to the other players. These rules are primarily designed to avoid misunderstandings and to keep the game moving smoothly.

When you first sit down at a table, you will need to **buy in**. If you brought chips from another game at that casino, you can play with those; however, you cannot use chips that you brought in from a different casino. In Nevada, real currency can be played at most table games. If you toss a bill on the bet circle, the dealer will call out (for the floor person to hear), "Money plays." If you win your money bet, you will be paid off with casino chips.

To buy in, place your money on the layout; never hand it to the dealer. The dealer will not convert your cash until the current hand is concluded, so don't think she is ignoring you. If you lay out a large bill, it will be converted entirely into chips; the dealer cannot make change. You may, however, ask for specific denominations of chips. When you quit playing and are ready to change your chips back to cash, you can do so at the cashier's cage.

No matter which game you are playing, at the start of each hand you need to put up one or more bets. If you are slow in doing this, the dealer will gently remind you, but it will also hold up the game. In some games, such as baccarat, you are not expected to bet every hand.

Once the dealer starts distributing the cards, you may not touch your original bet. If you do, you will be admonished. This is because one method of cheating is to change the amount of the bet after seeing how good a hand was dealt.

The above rules are general and apply to all table games. Every different type of game also has some unique rules of its own. These additional rules are covered in the chapters on the specific games.

OBTAINING CREDIT

If you are a serious table player and would rather not carry around large sums of cash, you may wish to establish a line of credit at the casino. To obtain credit, you first have to stop at the cashier's cage and get rated. You will have to fill out a credit application, so they can check your credit history. If you already have credit at another casino, it won't take very long because all casinos use the same credit agency. If you have never established credit at a casino before, they will have to check with your bank, which could take a day or two—and even longer on a weekend. In any case, the casino is not likely to give you more credit than 75% of your average checking account balance as they expect you to settle any losses by writing a check before you leave.

Once your credit is established at a casino, you can step up to a gaming table and ask for a **marker** for a specific amount. (Bear in mind that few casinos will write markers for less than $500.) The dealer will pass your request to a floor supervisor, who will ask you for identification. He will either check his computer or call the cashier to verify that you have adequate unused credit. He will then ask you to sign a marker (which is a simple IOU), and instruct the dealer to give you chips in the requested amount.

If you have a large number of chips when you are finished playing, you will be expected to redeem your marker before you leave the table. In any case, you should settle up at the cashier's cage before you leave the casino.

TIPPING

Let me say at the outset that I don't believe in tipping unless a service has been rendered in an efficient and pleasant manner. In a casino, tipping is never required. You are in total control as to when, where, and how much to tip.

In a restaurant, the tipping situation is well defined. The 15 to 20% tip has become so standardized that many patrons leave 15 or 20% whether the service was good, bad, or mediocre. In a casino, however, there are large gray areas—so much so that many people over-tip when tipping isn't even indicated.

When it comes to casino dealers, the terminology changes so that a tip becomes a **toke**. Something many people are unaware of is that if you give a dealer a generous toke, that toke will be shared with other dealers on that shift. To comply with IRS regulations, the tokes are usually pooled and taxes withheld by the casino before the remaining money is divided among the other dealers. So your big toke is first taxed and then the balance is split up evenly between all the dealers in that pit.

Since tipping is strictly optional, why would you toke dealers? As employees of the casino, you would expect them to look out for the interest of the casino before they look out for yours. Actually, most dealers look out for your interest first, letting the pit supervisors take care of the casino. They do this because they earn a relatively low base wage and are heavily dependent on tokes from satisfied customers.

Expert and professional card players toke dealers for good will and for extraordinary services. These services might include dealing a deck down further than usual to benefit a card counter or might be in the form of subtle hints on whether or not to take a hit. In other words, they toke because the dealer actually helped them to win money.

The pros aren't the only players who benefit from toking, however. Novice players need all the help they can get. Thus, if you are a newbie, toking a dealer early on will demonstrate that you are not a stiff, and will usually insure you of getting good advice. I would also toke a dealer after a run of good luck, but only if she was pleasant and helpful and I enjoyed playing at her table. Toking often pays for itself, especially if the dealer gives you some helpful advice or points out a betting mistake that would have cost you money.

Some people wonder if they should tip the employee who is paying them their winnings at a slot machine. If the amount is only a few hundred dollars, I would avoid tipping because you are probably only recouping what you have already lost. For a jackpot payout of $1000 or more, a tip is customary, even if you lost more than that earlier.

The other service provider that you encounter while playing at a table or a machine is the cocktail waitress. This is a no-brainer. You normally tip her a dollar or so per drink, depending on her efficiency and the complexity of the drink you order. If you are playing at a $25 table, tip at least two dollars if you don't want to look like a cheapskate.

A FEW WORDS ABOUT STRATEGY

Information on the best playing strategy is provided for each of the games covered in this book. For those games where the strategy is complex, both a simplified strategy and a perfect or best strategy are provided. The simplified strategies give results that very closely approximate the perfect strategies and, in any case, are better than using no strategy at all. If you would rather play by intuition, you don't really need this book; you will, however, need a fat wallet.

The purpose of the strategies is to keep you playing as close to the theoretical minimum house edge as possible. In other words, if the house edge for a particular game is given as 3% and you correctly apply the strategy, you should lose $3 for every $100 that you risk. This is a *long-term average,* and may not apply to short playing sessions. During short playing sessions, ordinary luck is usually the dominant factor.

If you sit down at a table and start losing hand after hand, you may think, "This strategy is not working for me—I need to do something different." As bad as it looks, you will probably be worse off if you stray from the correct strategy. The smartest move is to leave the table or the machine.

Of course, the reverse could also happen: your first few hands could all be winners. This, also, cannot be attributed to the playing strategy, but is the result of normal fluctuations. Regardless of short-term vacillations, in the long run, you are always better off when you stick to the statistically correct strategy.

◆3◆
MONEY MANAGEMENT

After you have won a sum of money as the result of diligent and intelligent play, you should reap the rewards that those winnings can provide. Too many gamblers win a pile of money just to lose it back to the casino or give it to the IRS. The purpose of money management is to retain as much of that money as possible. Hopefully, the following advice will help you to evade these money traps.

CONTROLLING YOUR BANKROLL

Before you step up to any table game or slot machine, be sure you have first designated a specific sum of money to risk for your playing session. Otherwise, you may end up like some impromptu gamblers who, after sustaining a losing streak, continue to dig for more money in an attempt to recoup their losses. By doing this, they may lose their entire bankroll on the first day of a gambling trip, and then wonder how they might spend the rest of their time. Some will head for the nearest ATM and start using money that was never intended for gambling. This is a trap that you don't want to fall into.

To avoid such a situation you must take precautionary measures. Let's say you are on a two-day gambling junket and have allocated $1000 that you can afford to lose. Divide that bankroll into two $500 stakes, one stake for each day. Whatever you do, don't gamble away more than $500 in any single day, and stay away from the ATMs. You must be disciplined about this.

IMPORTANT NOTE: *If you can't maintain that kind of money discipline, you have a problem and should seek out help. Although they would rather not, most casinos will tell you where to go or who to call to get the necessary help. If you don't do this, you can ruin your life.*

If your discipline is marginal, bring only the designated $500 with you into the casino. Leave the rest of it with someone you trust or lock it up in the room safe. If you lose the entire $500 stake, quit gambling for the day. Go sightseeing, see a show, have dinner, but don't gamble another cent until the following day.

The next day, repeat the procedure with the second $500, but try carefully not to lose it all. If you lost your daily stake on the first day, you should carefully read the following section on When to Quit. By dividing your allocated gambling funds into daily stakes, you are maintaining a measure of control over your bankroll. Even if you do eventually lose it all, this form of monetary discipline will assure that you can do some gambling every day, which is the reason you went on the trip in the first place.

Now that you've determined your daily bankroll allocation, you should break that stake down for your individual gambling sessions. If you have decided that you will probably hit the tables or the machines twice a day, divide that $500 daily allocation in half and don't step up to a table with more than $250 in your pocket. If you lose that amount and don't dig for more, you will be assured of having another playing session that day—and this time you may come out ahead.

PERSONAL BETTING LIMITS

You should determine ahead of time how much you can afford to bet. Many casino games are rather volatile, which means you may lose several hands or spins before you start winning (or vice versa). If you want to stay alive for any length of time, you should not sit down at a

$25 minimum table with only $200 in your pocket. In blackjack, a losing split and a couple of bad double downs will break you very quickly. In craps, a couple of seven-outs will do the same. How much, then, do you need to weather the ups and downs?

As a general rule of thumb, you should have a gambling bankroll of 20 to 40 times your basic wager for every hour you intend to play, or at least for your initial playing session. Why such a wide range for the bankroll? Because some people are more conservative than others, and this is just a guideline. You will have to determine the exact risk for yourself.

If, for instance, you have allocated $400 for a gambling session, then a conservative wager would be $10 ($400 ÷ 40). Thus, with a $400 bankroll, you shouldn't place an initial bet of more than $10 a hand. If, during your first playing session, you come out ahead, you can then re-adjust your betting level.

The same ratio can be applied to slots and video poker. If you allocate $200 for a four hour playing session, your betting rate is $50 per hour. The indicated betting level would then be $1.25 ($50 ÷ 40) per spin. Thus, if you are betting five coins per spin, you should stick to quarter machines.

WHEN TO QUIT

The gambler who doesn't know when to quit will never come out ahead, no matter how well he or she plays. A commonly heard piece of advice is: "Quit while you're ahead." That's good advice, except that many people misinterpret it to mean: "Quit while you are winning." No, no, no! The correct rule is:

NEVER QUIT WHILE YOU ARE WINNING!

When you are on a hot winning streak, you should always stick with it and slowly increase your bet size. Of course, you never know in advance when the streak will end, but sooner or later, it will. When you do start losing, cut the size of your bets right down to the minimum, and if you continue to lose, quit playing.

SET A LOSS LIMIT

The best way to handle a winning streak is to set a **loss limit** and *stick to it*. When you first get ahead, quit playing when you have lost 25% of your total winnings—because the streak is over. If you keep winning and have doubled or tripled your bankroll, reduce the loss limit to 20%, and then 15%. The more you win, the tighter the loss limit. The idea is to protect your profit.

For example, shortly after you start playing a machine or a table game with a $300 bankroll, you find that you are $200 ahead. Mentally set a stop loss at $150 of your winnings. That is, if your $200 winnings dissipate down to $150, quit playing. You are down $50, which is 25% of your $200 winnings, and you walk away $150 richer.

If you keep winning, however, keep resetting the loss limit. When your winnings double your bankroll, start reducing the loss limit percentage. At $600, your stop loss should be $480 (20%), and at $1000, your stop loss should be $850 (15%). This, of course, is just a guideline, but wherever you set your personal loss limit, stick with it.

MINIMIZING LOSSES

What if you win a few and lose a few, and find that the house is slowly grinding down your bankroll? Once you realize what is happening, take a break, or at least change tables or machines before you lose your entire daily stake. If you maintain the proper discipline, whenever you have gone through your daily gambling allotment, you are through gambling for the day.

Whatever you do, never try to recoup losses by increasing your bet size. Risking more money will not change your luck or change the inherent odds of the game you are playing. If you are on a losing streak, bigger bets will only cause you to lose faster.

You need to recognize those specific situations when your best option is to quit playing. Although there are some situations that you will have to determine for yourself, the following list covers most of them:

Quit playing

- When you are losing.

- When you reach your loss limit.

- When you try to recoup by increasing your bet size.

- When you try to recoup by making long-shot bets.

- When you are unhappy with the dealers.

- When you are unhappy with other players.

- When you are angry (for whatever reason).

- When you are not feeling well.

- When you are depressed.

- When you are tired.

- When you have sucked down too many free drinks.

If you are on a winning streak, however, grit your teeth and stick with it, even if you are unhappy, angry, or tired. Remember: *Never quit while you are winning!*

MONEY MANAGEMENT REMINDERS

- Never play with money that you can't afford to lose—your chances of losing are greater than your chances of winning.

- Never step up to a table or a machine without first having designated specific funds for your gambling session.

- If you lose your allocated stake for the session or for the day, never change your pre-established bankroll rules and dig for more money. Instead, quit playing.

- Never deviate from smart playing strategy.

- Never try to chase your losses.

- When you are winning, always set a loss limit.

DEALING WITH THE IRS

The relationship between gambling and the IRS is a complex subject that can even confound lawyers and accountants specializing in taxes. In this section, I am not giving you any specific tax or legal advice. I am only making you aware of certain IRS requirements. It is valuable to know about some of these things before encountering them in a real situation.

If you engage in casino transactions of more than $10,000, you should consult an accountant familiar with gaming laws. Casinos must report all cash transactions in excess of $10,000 to the IRS. They must also report an aggregate of cash transactions that occur within a 24-hour period and total more than $10,000. If you place a large bet at a sports book, cash-in chips, or even cash a check larger than $10,000, it must be reported. This is just a reporting requirement (presumably to control money laundering) and doesn't mean that you have to pay taxes on the transaction. The state of Nevada has a similar reporting requirement.

The IRS rule that is most important to gamblers is the requirement for the casino to report any lump sum win of $1200 or more by submitting a W-2G form. This, of course, refers mainly to slot machine jackpots, bingo prizes, and the like. Most table players don't have to worry about this requirement. For some inexplicable reason, the reporting requirement for keno is $1500 or more.

If you won a lump sum during a tournament, however, the IRS reporting requirement drops to $600. For this kind of a win, the casino has to submit a 1099-MISC form.

Gambling winnings are considered ordinary income by the IRS and must be reported under "Other Income" on your 1040 tax return. If you are unfortunate enough to have a casino report your winnings, be sure you attach a copy of the W-2G or 1099-MISC to your return, or you will eventually get a letter from the IRS asking where it is.

If you are saddled with reported wins, you can reduce the tax burden (up to the amount of your winnings) if you can prove that you had offsetting gambling losses in the same year. Such losses cannot be subtracted from itemized winnings, but must be listed separately on Schedule A under "Miscellaneous Deductions." However, if your itemized deductions don't exceed the standard deduction, your gambling losses will not be useful as an offset. Also, keep in mind that you cannot reduce your overall tax by taking a *net* gambling loss—you can only offset winnings.

How do you prove that you had gambling losses? By keeping a detailed dairy of all your gambling activities. How detailed? The IRS recommendation is that you record the date, the time, the amount of your wins and losses, and the type of game. You should also record the name and location of the casino, and the names of any people (witnesses) with you at the time. Supporting documentation such as airline ticket receipts and hotel bills will help to convince an IRS auditor that you were actually there. However, unless you are a professional in the business of gambling *and* your trip was primarily for business purposes, do not try to deduct expenses such as transportation, hotel rooms, or restaurants.

Once you get used to the idea, you will see that keeping a diary is not as daunting as it first appears. How you actually deal with it, that is, what you put in and what you leave out, is entirely your decision. Just keep in mind that if the entire diary does not appear to be reasonable, an auditor may judge that it is inaccurate and disallow it.

◆4◆
UNDERSTANDING
THE ODDS

The statistical term for describing the chance of an event occurring is **probability**. Mathematicians use this term because it is clear and unambiguous. In a gambling situation, such as the flip of a coin or the roll of a single die, where all possible outcomes are equally likely, it can be defined as follows:

The probability of winning is equal to the number of ways to win divided by the number of possible outcomes.

Probability is always a number between 0 and 1 that can be stated as a fraction or a decimal. Sometimes the decimal is multiplied by 100 and expressed as a percentage.

Most gamblers, however, prefer to use the term **odds**. The trouble with this term is that it can be stated in several different ways, leading to confusion and misinterpretation by newcomers. The confusion arises from the use of the modifiers against, to, for, and in.

For example, a die is a six-sided cube with a different number of spots on each side, from 1 to 6. Thus, there is one way to roll any particular number and there are five ways to not get that number. If you are betting that a 4 appears on the next roll, there is one way to win and five ways to lose. The total number of possibilities is six, which is the sum of the ways to win and the ways to lose. This situation can be described in the following ways.

- The odds of winning are 1 *in* 6. This means that there is 1 chance of winning out of a possible 6 chances.
- The odds *for* winning are 1 *to* 5. This means that there is 1 chance of winning and 5 chances of losing.
- The odds *against* winning are 5 *to* 1. This means that there are 5 chances of losing and 1 chance of winning.

In the first of the above examples, a fraction bar can be substituted for the word "in." For instance, 1 in 6 is often written as 1/6. In the second and third cases, a colon can be substituted for the word "to." For instance, 1 to 5 is often written as 1:5.

No matter how the odds are stated, they are all mathematical ratios. You have to be careful, however, to ascertain what the ratio is. In particular, be sure you know (1) if the ratio is chances of winning vs. chances of losing or (2) if the ratio is chances of winning vs. all possible chances (winning plus losing).

CALCULATING THE ODDS

The simplest way to compute odds is by using the following formula:

$$\text{Odds for winning} = \frac{\text{ways to win}}{\text{ways to lose}}$$

Using the single die example, the result is:

$$\text{Odds for winning} = \frac{1}{5}$$

This says that the odds for winning are 1 to 5, or 1:5, which means that there is one chance to win and five chances to lose.

Another place people get confused is when the odds are stated in reverse. For instance, if the odds *for* winning are 1:5, then the odds *against* winning are 5:1 and the odds formula is inverted:

$$\text{Odds against winning} = \frac{\text{ways to lose}}{\text{ways to win}}$$

In the above example, the distinction between *odds for* and *odds against* is obvious, but when the odds are close to even, it can be more subtle. For instance, when the odds for winning are 4:5, then the odds against winning are 5:4. While the seasoned gambler has no problem with this, the newcomer can be easily misled by interchanging the words *for* and *against*. Although not as technically correct, some people think it is clearer to say "winning odds" instead of odds for winning and "losing odds" instead of odds against winning. They have a point.

PAYOFF ODDS

The above discussion has been about **true odds** or **correct odds**. When a casino pays off a winning bet, however, they don't pay correct odds because they expect to make a profit. Instead, they pay **house odds**, which are slightly poorer than the true odds. The difference is the **house edge**.

House odds or odds paid are the inverse of winning odds, that is, the lower the chances of winning, the higher the payoff. In the example of a single die, the odds for winning are 1:5 and the odds against winning are 5:1. Since the house is betting against the player, the odds paid are the same as the odds against winning, assuming the house does not take a cut. On an even playing field, if a 1-unit bet wins, the amount won should be 5 units. In actuality, the house odds will always be a little less than the odds against winning. This gives the casino its profit margin.

A subtle trick is sometimes used to make house odds look better than they are—by stating the odds as 5 *for* 1, instead of 5 *to* 1. If you win a payoff of 5 *to* 1, you are paid 5 units *and* get to keep your original 1-unit bet, whereas a payoff of 5 *for* 1 means you are paid 5 units, but lose your original bet. Odds of 5 for 1 is equivalent to odds of 4 to 1. Again, the professional gambler has no difficulty with this, but less experienced players can easily get confused.

THE HOUSE EDGE
In many cases, the casino's edge is not unreasonable; however, to get the house percentage down as far as it will go requires the use of proper playing strategy. The following chart shows how all of the games described in this book compare to each other.

HOUSE PERCENTAGE FOR CASINO GAMES

Game	Conditions	House Edge
Baccarat	banker (5% comm. on win)	1.06%
Baccarat	player	1.24%
Baccarat	tie bet	14.4%
Big Six Wheel	varies with bet	11.1% to 24.1%
Blackjack	card counting	-0.2% to -1.2%
Blackjack	basic strategy, single deck	0.1% to 0.2%
Blackjack	basic strategy, AC rules	0.43%
Caribbean Stud	perfect strategy	5.22%
Casino War	go to war on ties	2.88%
Casino War	tie side bet	18.7%
Craps	pass, come, no odds	1.41%
Craps	pass, come, full double odds	0.57%
Craps	place 6 or 8	1.52%
Craps	field	2.8% to 5.6%
Crapless Craps	pass, come, no odds	5.4%
Keno	varies with casino and bet	24% to 30%
Let It Ride	perfect strategy	3.51%
Pai Gow Poker	banker (5% comm. on win)	-0.4 to 0%
Pai Gow Poker	player (5% comm. on win)	2.85%
Red Dog	perfect strategy	2.8% to 3.2%
Roulette	single-zero wheel	2.70%
Roulette	double-zero wheel	5.26%
Sic-Bo	varies with bet	2.8% to 33.3%
Slot Machines	max coins for some types	2% to 15%
Spanish 21	dealer stands on soft 17	0.4%
Spanish 21	dealer hits soft 17	0.8%
Super Fun 21	perfect strategy	0.94%
Three Card Poker	Pair Plus side bet	2.32 to 7.28%
Three Card Poker	perfect strategy	3.37 to 4.28%
Video Poker	perfect strategy	0.5% to 6%
Wild Hold'em Fold'em	perfect strategy	6.86%

For those games where players can make strategic choices, the house percentages shown above are largely based on mathematically-perfect playing strategies. The negative percentages shown for blackjack (when counting cards) and pai gow poker (when acting as banker) indicate that they can have a positive expectation of winning for the player.

The house percentage or house edge is the profit the casino makes on the money that a player risks on a game. For instance, if the house edge is 5%, you will lose $5 out of every $100 that you bet. Over the long-term, this is a statistical certainty and the percentages listed above only apply if you play the game using the best strategy. If your playing strategy is poor, the house will get a lot more.

◆5◆
BACCARAT

Although most experts agree that baccarat originated in Italy, it is generally considered to be a French game. The standard casino-banked game in Europe is actually called *Baccarat en Banque*, and the version where the players take turns banking the game is called *Chemin de Fer*. In most European casinos, these big-money games are only played by the very wealthy.

This chapter deals with the version of baccarat that is played in the United States. It is a watered-down adaptation of the games played in European casinos and is sometimes called American Baccarat or Nevada Baccarat. Strangely, the insipid American version is beginning to catch on in Europe, where it is called *Punto Banco*.

Most people are reluctant to play baccarat because the elaborate rituals and lavish trappings intimidate them. The game is almost always located in a separate room or roped-off area, the dealers wear dinner jackets, and the players seem better dressed than most gamblers in the casino. Often there are attractive women seated around the table, but most of them are *shills*. The **shills** (the casinos call them "game starters") play with house money and give the appearance that the game is popular and active in order to attract those persons who don't like being the only player at the table.

Many people are also afraid that the high minimum bet requirement is beyond their means. Although most minimums run $25 to $100 and higher, a few baccarat tables in Nevada have minimums as low as $5 or $10.

Although it is a very simple game to play, it seems complicated to the uninitiated. The fact is that you don't need to know anything except that there are three bets to choose from. You can bet on the Player, you can bet on the Banker, or you can bet that there will be a tie. Like roulette, other than selecting the bet, there is no playing strategy, and the actual mechanics of the game are entirely handled by the dealers.

The game is dealt from an eight-deck shoe, which can last for as many as 75 hands. This is because each hand consists of only four to six cards. Two cards are dealt for the Player's hand and two cards are dealt for the Banker's hand. Each of these hands may or may not get a third card.

Although this sounds similar to blackjack, in baccarat, the Player's hand is a community hand for which the players have no say in whether or not a third card is drawn. In baccarat, the best hand is a 9 and the play of the game is significantly different than that of blackjack.

First, there is only one Player hand and one Banker hand, and the players can bet on either one. Second, only one additional card may be drawn on either hand. Whether the draw is permitted is determined by a fixed set of rules, which will be explained later. Third, a hand cannot be busted. For any total over 9, only the units (right-hand) digit is significant. Consequently, a total of 10 has a value of 0, a total of 11 has a value of 1, a total of 12 has a value of 2, etc.

When the draws (if any) are completed, the hand with a value closest to 9 is the winner. If the winning hand is the Banker's, all players who bet on the Banker win even money and vice-versa. Should both hands have exactly the same value, players who bet on a tie get paid 8 to 1, while all others push.

FUNDAMENTALS OF PLAY

THE PLAYING TABLE

Baccarat is played on a long double-ended table with six or seven player positions at each end. Thus, there may be as many as twelve or fourteen players, depending on the size of the table (see illustration). Two dealers are seated at one of the long sides of the table, each one handling the wagers at their end. A third dealer, known as the caller, stands at the center of the table on the opposite side of the seated dealers.

Each player position has three betting boxes. The nearest is for a bet on the Player's hand, the next is for the Banker's hand, and the third is for a tie bet. In front of the dealers is a row of numbered boxes. This is where the dealers keep track of owed commissions that accumulate in the course of a shoe. In front of the caller is a space marked BANKER'S where the Banker's hand is placed, and a space marked PLAYER'S where the Player's hand is placed.

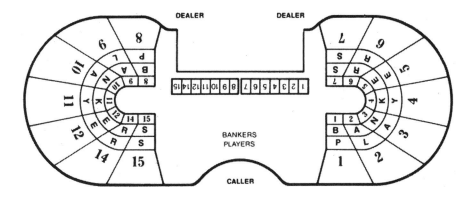

Baccarat Table

THE PERSONNEL

The seated dealer at your end of the table handles all of your transactions. This is the casino employee who changes your money into chips, collects losing bets, pays winning bets, and keeps track of any commissions (explained below) that may be owed by you or other players at that end of the table.

The third dealer, or caller, stands opposite the two seated dealers, at the center of the table. This dealer is in charge of the table. The caller controls the play of the game by calling for bets, informing the player with the shoe when to draw cards, and announcing the winner.

The fourth employee in the baccarat room is the supervisor. The supervisor, who sits in an elevated chair and oversees all of the action on the table, makes certain that the game is being run properly and settles any monetary disputes that may arise.

HOW THE GAME IS PLAYED

Once seated at the table, the dealer will convert your cash into chips. Before you put chips in one of the bet boxes, wait for the caller to announce, "Place your bets." You may wager on the Player (nearest box), on the Banker (next box), or on a tie (farthest box). Be sure that you wager at least the table minimum.

When the bets have been placed, the caller declares "No more bets," and the ritual of drawing the cards begins. The caller says "cards," or simply nods his head and the player who is acting as the Bank (more on that, later) draws one card from the dealing shoe and slides it, face down, over to the caller. This is the first of the two Player's cards. The dealer then draws a second card and slips it, face down, under the front corner of the shoe. This is the first Banker's card. A third card is slid over to the caller, which is the second Player's card, and a fourth card is slipped under the corner of the shoe, which is the second Banker's card.

The caller gives the two Player's cards, still face down, to the person with the highest wager on the Player's hand. This person turns over the cards and flips them back to the caller, who announces the total and places them on the space marked PLAYER'S. The dealer now turns over the two Banker's cards and slides them over to the caller, who announces the total and places them on the space marked BANKER'S.

The Player's hand is acted on first and a third card may or may not be drawn, as dictated by the fixed rules of the game. The same is true for the Banker's hand. If a third card is required, the caller instructs the dealer, "Card for the Player," or, "Card for the Bank." When the hands are complete, the caller announces the winner.

The seated dealers now collect the losing bets and pay off the winners. Winning bets are paid even money, except for a tie, which is paid 8 to 1. If the Bank won, then players who bet on the Banker's hand have to pay a 5% commission. This payment is not made at that time, but is accumulated and finally collected at the end of each shoe. Whenever a player leaves the game, owed commissions must be settled. The dealers keep track of all commissions due on the row of numbered boxes that runs across the center of the table.

THE RULES OF PLAY

Baccarat is usually played with eight standard 52-card decks. Each card is worth its face value except tens and face cards, which are counted as zero. Aces are counted as one, and the suits are immaterial.

The value of a hand is the right-hand digit of the total count. That is, if the total is greater than one digit, the first digit is ignored. For instance, a hand consisting of an 8 and a 9 adds up to 17, but the hand value is 7. Thus, a hand cannot have a value greater than 9, and the closest to that number is the winner.

EXAMPLES OF HAND VALUES	
Cards	Hand Value
4, 4	8
4, 9	3
4, K	4
7, 7	4
7, 10	7
A, 2, 3	6
J, 2, 3	5
A, K, Q	0
3, 8, 8	9

A two card hand with a value of 8 or 9 is called a **natural** and cannot draw a third card. Other two card hand values may or may not draw a third card as shown in the following charts.

RULES FOR PLAYER'S HAND	
Total	Action
0, 5	Draw one card
6 or 7	Stand
8 or 9	Stand

RULES FOR BANKER'S HAND		
IF PLAYER DOES NOT DRAW, then Player rules are applied to Banker's hand.		
IF PLAYER DRAWS A THIRD CARD, then Banker rules are as follows:		
Two card total of Banker's hand	**DRAW when Player's third card is:**	**DO NOT DRAW when Player's third card is:**
0 – 2	Always draw	—
3	0 – 7, 9	8
4	2 – 7	0, 1, 8, 9
5	4 – 7	0 – 3, 8, 9
6	6, 7	0 – 5, 8, 9
7	—	Always stand
8, 9	—	Always stand

DEALING WITH THE SHOE

Even though the casino banks the game, passing the dealing shoe from player to player is part of the baccarat ritual in the United States. The shoe rotates around the table in a counter-clockwise direction, and the player who has it is considered to be the Bank. This is strictly an honorary title because the casino actually banks the game. When the shoe reaches you, you have the option of dealing or passing it to the player on your right. There is no advantage gained or lost by acting as the Bank.

Should you decide to keep the shoe, the procedure is very simple. Just follow the directions of the caller, who will tell you when to begin drawing cards. You start by removing a card from the shoe for the Player's hand and sliding it over to the caller. Then draw a second card for the Banker's hand and slip it under a corner of the shoe. The third card should go to the caller and the fourth is put under the shoe with the second card. If you are new at this, do it slowly and methodically so as not to fumble the cards.

Don't look at any of the cards and keep them face down. When the caller is ready for them, turn over the Banker's hand and toss it over to the caller. The caller will then let you know if an additional card is needed for either the Player's or Banker's hand.

Before you take on this duty, however, it would be prudent to watch how the other players handle the shoe. When you are acting as the Bank, you are expected (but not required) to wager on the Banker's hand. Consequently, players who would rather bet on the Player's hand turn down the opportunity to be the Banker.

The player acting as Banker keeps the shoe until a Player's hand is won. When that occurs, the shoe is offered to the next player in the rotation.

TABLE ETIQUETTE

Seeing how formally the dealers are dressed, it should be no surprise that the casino expects baccarat players to be dressed decently. If you try to enter a baccarat room wearing cutoffs or a muscle shirt, you might be politely refused.

When you enter the room, you should already know the minimum bet requirement. Asking this question will peg you as someone who is in the wrong place and probably over his or her head. Most experienced players do not sit down without first observing the games for a few minutes, if for no other reason than to find a shoe that is almost finished or one that has just begun. Methodical players don't sit down in the middle of a shoe, and the shift supervisor knows that.

If other players nod or smile when you take a seat, just nod or smile back. Don't introduce yourself by name. The closest anyone comes to using a name is when a well-known player is referred to as Mr. J.

Wait until the caller says, "Place your bets," before putting out your chips. If you win a hand, don't pull back your chips until everyone is paid or the payoffs are well past you. The game moves slowly so you have plenty of time. When you are offered the shoe, pass up the opportunity until you feel confident that you can handle it properly.

If you have to go to the rest room or just want to take a short break, leave your chips in place. They will be safe. Many players take breaks when a shoe is finished and the cards are being shuffled, which is a lengthy procedure.

If you are winning and feel generous, tipping the dealers is appropriate. You can also make a side bet for them, as is done in other table games.

PLAYING STRATEGY

THE HOUSE EDGE

In terms of the house edge, baccarat is one of the best games offered by any casino. The only way you can get a lower edge is by making a pass line or come bet with odds in the game of craps, or playing blackjack with favorable rules.

The house edge on the Player's hand is 1.36% (or 1.24%, depending on whether or not you ignore ties in the calculation). Conversely, betting on the Banker's hand gives the *player* an edge of 1.36%. If the casino allowed this to stand, it would go bankrupt very quickly. To keep its advantage on both sides of the wager, the casino charges a 5% commission on winning Banker bets, which alters the edge so that it favors the house. With the commission factored in, the house edge on the Banker is 1.17% (or 1.06%). If more people knew about this low house edge, baccarat would certainly be a more popular game.

The only bad wager in baccarat is the tie bet. Although it pays 8 to 1, the correct odds are 9.5 to 1, giving the house an edge of more than 14%.

BETTING STRATEGY

The best wager in baccarat is a bet on the Banker's hand, and there is nothing wrong with making all bets on the Bank, just as there is nothing wrong with making all bets in craps on the pass line with odds. This is a mathematically-sound approach, but it will get boring after a while.

The next best wager is a bet on the Player's hand. The slightly higher house edge will have little effect in the short run. The worst wager is to bet on a tie. Although this is a poor bet from a mathematical standpoint, you will find many players making it.

SCORECARDS

Most baccarat players keep track of the results on a scorecard. (Blank cards and pencils or pens are available at every table.) These players watch for trends and have various theories as to when to bet into a winning sequence and when to bet against it. Just remember that the fall of the cards is as random as the elaborate shuffling ritual can make it.

Today, most score cards are about 4 inches high by 14 inches long. They consist of a matrix of squares, typically 46 or 48 vertical columns wide, with each column containing two groups of 6 squares. The layout of the card consists of two series of columns, one above the other, for a total of 92 or 96 columns, each with six squares. The illustration on the next page shows only a portion of one of these cards because the book page isn't big enough to show the entire card.

The card can be marked in various ways. One way is to write in a "B" for a Bank win and a "P" for a Player win as shown in the illustration. Another way is to alternately write Bs and Ps above the columns and then put an "X" in each square. Some casinos provide you with pens that have black ink at one end and red ink at the other end. Then you can mark Bank wins in red and Player wins in Black.

The main purpose of the scorecard is to keep track of runs. Suppose the Banker wins the first three hands. You would then show three Bs down the first column. If the Player won next, put a P in the top square of the second column. If the Player won again, put a P in the second square of the second column. Keep adding Ps to the second column until the Banker wins again and then start a third column.

If the card is made out properly, you can see at a glance the history of long and short runs. This information is used by many players who like to play trends. One method is to wager that a run of two wins will not turn into a run of three.

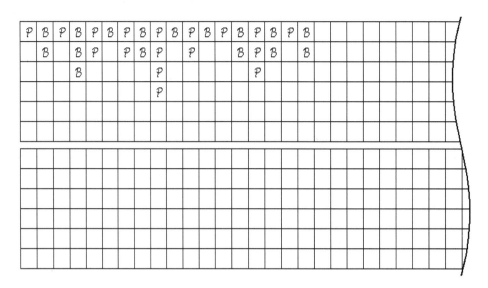

Part of a Baccarat Scorecard

A way to do this is to bet one unit on the opposite hand after a run of two. That is, if the Bank won twice in a row, bet on the Player, or vice-versa. If you lose that wager twice in succession, increase your bet to two units. If you lose that bet, start over. In this method, you only place a bet if there has been a run of two, otherwise, you don't bet.

There are many other betting schemes based on trends, but they are beyond the scope of this chapter. More comprehensive coverage of this subject may be found in *Secrets of Winning Baccarat* by Brian D. Kayser.

THE CLASSICAL SYSTEMS

Some players apply one of the classical betting systems such as the Martingale, the D'Alembert, or the Labouchere. These systems are fully described in the chapter on roulette. They work best with even-money wagers and are perfectly suited to baccarat if you have a big enough bankroll.

In baccarat, you are not expected to wager on every hand. Many systems players hold off betting for several hands until a favorable series occurs. Thus, you can easily apply one of the systems mentioned above, where you wait for a run, before starting the sequence. When using an even-money betting system, it is recommended to bet on the Banker's hand because of the lower house percentage.

If you want to play a system, it is not advisable to be the only player at the table because the cards won't be dealt until you make a wager. Of course, this can happen inadvertently when the only other player leaves. If this occurs when you are in the middle of a sequence, and you would rather skip the next hand, there is a way to do this. You can wager on both the Player's and Banker's hands simultaneously which, with the low house edge, is close to a wash. Of course, the dealers will give you strange looks, but it is legal. If they ask, just explain that it's required by your system.

MINI-BACCARAT

Mini-baccarat is essentially identical to the game played on the big table. The main difference is that all of the rituals have been eliminated to speed up the action. It is played on a blackjack-like table and requires only one dealer. All you have to do is place your bet and the dealer does the rest.

Although the minimum bet requirements are much lower in mini-baccarat (typically $5 to $10), the game moves so quickly that you will lose money at a faster rate. You will also find mini-baccarat to be very boring. It is amazing how the elaborate baccarat rituals can turn a rather bland game into an interesting experience.

◆6◆
BIG SIX WHEEL

A big six wheel can be found in almost every large casino and many smaller ones. It is essentially the same as the wheels used in the small carnivals that traveled around the Midwest and the South, where they were called *wheel of fortune*. The only difference is that the wheels in legal casinos are not gaffed (fixed). With the house edge ranging from 11.1% to 24.1%, they don't need to be.

The big six is a large vertical wheel, about five feet in diameter, which stands almost eight feet tall. Around the circumference of the wheel are inlaid bills of various denominations, thus it is also called a *money wheel*. The name "big six" dates back to the beginning of the twentieth century when similar wheels had groups of six numbers around the rim. For some reason, the term stuck.

Another version is called a *dice wheel* because it is inlaid with dice instead of currency. The wheels are very similar, however, in that they both have 54 positions and the same high house edge. The lack of a counter-rotation characteristic, such as in a roulette wheel, makes these wheels easy to rig, which is why the carnies liked them.

In front of the wheel is a table where the players sit and make their wagers. The game is normally handled by a single dealer who spins the wheel, collects the losing bets, and pays the winning bets.

FUNDAMENTALS OF PLAY

After the players lay down their bets on the surface of the table, the dealer spins the wheel. When it stops, the dealer pays the winners according to the following charts:

BIG SIX PAYOUTS — MOST CASINOS			
Wager on	Pays	No. of Wheel Positions	House Edge
$1	1 to1	24	11.1%
$2	2 to 1	15	16.7%
$5	5 to 1	7	22.2%
$10	10 to 1	4	18.5%
$20	20 to 1	2	22.2%
Joker	40 to 1	1	24.1%
Logo	40 to 1	1	24.1%

The above chart applies to most casinos in the United States. In Atlantic City, however, the payouts are slightly different, as shown below.

BIG SIX PAYOUTS — ATLANTIC CITY			
Wager on	Pays	No. of Wheel Positions	House Edge
$1	1 to 1	24	11.1%
$2	2 to 1	15	16.7%
$5	5 to 1	7	22.2%
$10	10 to 1	4	18.5%
$20	20 to 1	2	22.2%
Joker	45 to 1	1	14.8%
Logo	45 to 1	1	14.8%

BIG SIX STRATEGY

Big six is obviously a losing game, but if you must play it, do so in Atlantic City and try for the 45 to 1 payouts. For comparison, however, you should remember that a single-number win at roulette pays 35 to 1 and the house edge is only 5.26%.

Although the casinos run these games honestly, it is possible for a vigilant person to occasionally get the edge. With a table full of players, a distracted dealer may fall into a rhythmic pattern when spinning the wheel. With careful observation, it may be discovered that the spins have become predictable.

Just note the position of the wheel before it is spun and compare that to the winning position. If these positional pairs get repetitive, you may have found an advantageous circumstance. Pay particular attention to the Joker and Logo wheel positions—they are the moneymakers. If possible, do your observation from some distance away, and when you find a good situation, step up and start betting.

◆7◆
BLACKJACK

Blackjack is a very simple game to play. That is, it is an easy game to learn—all you have to do is try to get closer to a total card count of 21 than the dealer, without going over. The tough part is knowing how to do this in a manner that will maximize your chance of winning.

The primary emphasis of this chapter is on the multi-deck games that have become the mainstay of casino blackjack. Those casinos that still offer them, are slowly changing the rules for single-deck hand-dealt games, making them harder to beat. So much so that when you do find a good single- or double-deck game, it is almost impossible to get a seat at the table or else the minimum bet limit is at least $25. The recreational gambler, however, can do just fine at multi-deck games by playing according to the basic strategy recommendations given in the following pages.

The game begins when the dealer distributes two cards to each player. In a multi-deck game, the players' cards are always dealt face-up. She also gives herself two cards, one face-down and one face-up. Each player, in turn, is then given the opportunity to take additional cards, one at a time. Players may also exercise other options, such as splitting pairs and doubling down, all of which will be explained later.

The main goal for the player is to *beat the dealer*. This can be done in two ways. The first is to attain a total count higher than the dealer's hand without exceeding 21 (called busting). The second is to keep the hand alive by staying at 21 or under, in the hope that the dealer will bust and lose by default.

Since the dealer plays her hand last, the only clue players have for making their playing decisions is the dealer's upcard. In conjunction with the first two cards dealt to the player, the value of the dealer's upcard is the primary basis for good playing strategy.

Sometimes the players' cards are dealt face down, but this is only done in single- and double-deck hand-dealt games—and, today, such games are in the minority. Blackjack games in most casinos use four to eight decks of cards, all shuffled together and dealt from a shoe (see below). Although the advice and strategies given in this chapter are intended for multiple-deck blackjack games, it turns out that they work just fine for the single-deck games as well.

FUNDAMENTALS OF PLAY

THE EQUIPMENT

The implements used for playing blackjack in a casino are pretty basic. They include a half-moon table with stools for the players, several decks of cards, and a dealing shoe. These items are described below.

The playing table: Blackjack is played on a felt-covered table that is roughly semicircular in shape with six or seven player positions around the curved side (see illustration). The dealer stands at the flat side with a chip rack directly in front of her and a card-dealing shoe to her left. To the dealer's immediate right is a slot in the tabletop leading to a drop box. Whenever the dealer accepts cash from a player in exchange for casino chips, the cash is pushed into the drop box. Further to the dealer's right is a discard tray where the dealer deposits out-of-play cards that she has collected from the table.

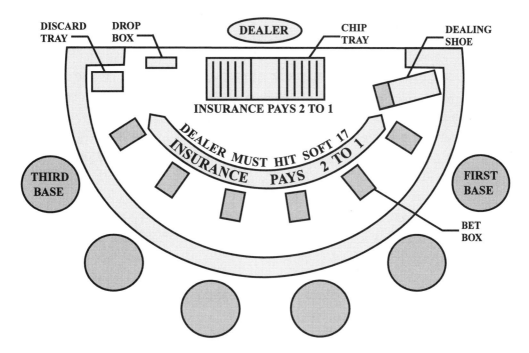

Typical Blackjack Table

At each player position is a betting spot in the shape of a rectangle or a circle. This is where the player's initial bet is placed before the first two cards are dealt. During a player's turn, additional bets may be placed alongside the original bet by splitting pairs or doubling down.

The first player seat to the left of the dealer is called **first base**. This spot is the first hand dealt in a round of play. The last seat to the dealer's right is called the **anchor position**, and is also referred to as **third base**. It is the last player hand dealt in a round.

The felt surface of the table has two or three basic game rules imprinted on it. The most common rule is: *Dealer must draw to 16 and stand on all 17s.* In some games (sometimes in the same casino), this rule is modified to read: *Dealer must hit soft 17.*

A second rule that appears on almost all tabletops is: *Insurance pays 2 to 1*. Some tables display a third rule: *Blackjack pays 3 to 2*. If a natural does not pay 3 to 2, there will almost always be a sign to that effect.

The dealing shoe: Most blackjack games use four, six, or eight decks of cards, which are dealt from a **dealing shoe**. The shoe, which was originally borrowed from the game of baccarat, is an elongated plastic box into which pre-shuffled cards are stacked. One end of the box has a slot and a finger notch so that the dealer may easily slide out the cards, one at a time.

The shuffling machine: To speed up the game, many blackjack tables are now equipped with an automatic shuffling machine or a continuous shuffling machine.

The cards: The game of blackjack uses one or more standard 52-card decks with the jokers removed. In most blackjack games, four, six, or eight standard decks are intermixed and dealt from a shoe.

Card values: In blackjack, the value of a hand is purely numeric; the card suits have no meaning and are completely disregarded. The numeric value of the cards 2 through 10 are their face value. That is, a 5 of spades counts as 5, and a 9 of hearts counts as 9.

The face cards, jack, queen, and king, are valued the same as a 10 card. Thus, any reference to ten-value or ten-count cards always includes the jack, queen, and king, as well as the 10 spot. Any statement that a hand contains a 10 means that it contains one of the ten-value cards. Since there are sixteen ten-value cards in a 52-card deck, they account for over 30% of the cards in each deck.

In blackjack, the ace possesses the trait of having a dual numeric value. It can be a one-count card or an eleven-count card, and automatically takes on the value that is most beneficial to the hand. Clearly, the ace is a very significant card in blackjack, especially since it is needed to complete a natural (see below).

THE PLAYERS' HANDS

A player's initial hand consists of two cards, which may be categorized in the following ways.

Hard hand: This is an initial hand that does not contain an ace and has a total count of more than 11. It is called **hard** because the total numeric value of the hand is fixed and an additional card can cause it to exceed a count of 21. For instance, if the two dealt cards are a 5 and a 9, the hand has a hard value of 14. A third card of 8 or higher will result in a total greater than 21.

Soft hand: This is an initial hand in which one of the cards is an ace. It is called **soft** because the value of the ace can be changed from 11 to 1, to prevent the total count of the hand from going over 21. Although, a hand consisting of a 4 and an ace may have a total value of either 5 or 15, it is called a soft 15. The main feature of a soft total is that it cannot be busted (see below), since the value of the ace can always be changed to 1. Whenever the value of the ace has to be changed from 11 to 1 to prevent busting, it becomes a hard hand.

An initial hand with two aces is a special case. Although it may have a value of 2 or 12, this is almost immaterial because in actual play the best strategy is to always split the aces into two separate hands.

Pat and stiff hands: A **pat hand** is one that cannot reasonably be improved. In blackjack, any hand with a hard count of 17 through 21 is considered pat. A **stiff hand** is one that is not pat and can be busted with the addition of a single card. Specifically, any hand with a hard total of 12 through 16 is considered stiff.

Blackjack (Natural): A **blackjack** is a two card initial hand consisting of an ace plus any ten-count card. Another name for a blackjack hand is a **natural**. In this chapter, the term natural is used to avoid confusion with the name of the game.

A natural is the best hand a player can get on the initial deal, and is an automatic winner if the dealer doesn't also have a natural. A winning natural pays 3 to 2 odds, that is, a $10 bet will win $15, and a $25 bet will win $37.50. The payoff should always be exactly 3 to 2, right down to the small change.

Since all other winning bets and hands in blackjack are paid even money, a natural is very good for the player. If the dealer also has a natural, however, the player's hand is tied and no money is won or lost. This is called a **push**. On average, a player will be dealt one natural about every 21 hands.

An ace plus a ten-count card constitutes a natural only on the initial two card deal. Any subsequent A 10 combination, such as might occur as a result of splitting a pair of aces, is not considered a natural.

Occasionally, the payoff for a natural will be something other than 3 to 2. In the past, some casinos have held promotions for limited periods during which naturals were paid at 8 to 5 or even 2 to 1. Some Las Vegas Strip casinos now offer single-deck games with only a 6 to 5 payoff for naturals. They claim that their playing rules are so enhanced that they have to shortchange the natural payoffs to balance the game. In fact, the rules are no better than in many other casinos that pay the standard 3 to 2. It is unlikely, however, that you will encounter a multi-deck game that pays less than 3 to 2 for a natural.

Busted hand: When, in the course of drawing additional cards, the total point count of the hand goes over 21, it is said to be **busted**. When that happens, the hand is an immediate loser; the dealer collects the bet and places the player's cards in the discard tray. The dealer's hand can be busted as well; however, since the dealer plays last, the busted player still loses if the dealer busts.

PLAYER OPTIONS

Once you've examined your initial two cards and determined if the hand is hard, soft, stiff, or pat, you are expected to take some action. A number of different player options are available, all of which are reviewed below. Some actions are communicated to the dealer with hand signals, while others are communicated by simply increasing the initial wager.

Hit: If you are not satisfied with the two card count, you may request additional cards, one by one. This is called taking a **hit**. Indicate your desire to take a hit by pointing at your cards with an index finger. Some players prefer to tap or scratch the felt directly behind the cards. Either way is acceptable. You may hit as many times as you want, so long as you don't go over 21. If the card count exceeds 21, you have busted and your bet is lost.

Stand: When you are satisfied with the card count and don't want any more hits, you may **stand**. Signal your intention to stand by waving your hand over the cards, palm down. You can stand at any time: after looking at your original hand, after taking one or more hits, or after splitting a pair. Standing is automatic if you double down (see below) because you are given just one card and are not allowed to take any hits.

Double down: You may **double down** on certain hands by placing another wager in the same amount as your original bet. Some casinos permit you to bet less than the amount of your original wager. Indicate your desire to double down by placing the new wager alongside your original bet.

You will then receive one additional card from the dealer and will not be permitted to take any further action on that hand. This is good strategy when your hand reaches a total of 10 or 11 and the dealer is showing a low card. You hope to get a 20 or 21 because of the prevalence of ten-value cards in the deck,

The rules for doubling vary quite a bit. Some casinos allow doubling only on the first two cards dealt, while others allow doubling after splitting a pair. Also, some casinos permit doubling on any two card count, while others restrict doubling to a total count of 10 or 11. The dealer will tell you whether or not you can double on a particular hand.

Split: Whenever you are dealt a pair, that is, two cards of equal rank, you have the option of **splitting** those cards into two separate hands. At almost all casinos, you may split mixed ten-value cards; that is, you could split a hand consisting of a jack and a king. However, splitting ten-value cards is not a recommended strategy and you should never do it.

Indicate your desire to split by placing a second wager alongside your original bet. It must be for the same amount as the original bet. Before acting on your signal, the dealer may ask if you intend to double or split. With a pair of fives, for instance, most dealers know that splitting is not good strategy, but doubling may be appropriate.

When it is clear that you are splitting, the dealer gives you two more cards, one on each of your original cards, so that you are now playing two hands of two cards each. You should then continue playing as if they are initial hands. The dealer will point to the first hand and wait for your signal. When you stand on that hand, she will point to the other one. You may play these hands the same as any other, except that some casinos do not permit doubling down or any further splitting.

A pair of aces is a special case. If you split aces (which is always recommended), you will be given one card on each ace and will not be allowed to take a hit or take any further action.

Resplit: If, when you split a pair, one or both of the cards you get from the dealer are the same rank as the original pair, you may split again. This is called **resplitting**. For instance, if you split a pair of eights and received another eight, you could resplit into three hands. Some casinos do not allow resplitting.

Again, aces are a special case. Most casinos that permit resplitting do not permit aces to be resplit.

Surrender: If you don't like what you see when you are dealt the first two cards, you may **surrender** (fold) your hand and forfeit half of your bet. If you decide to surrender, simply say that you are surrendering, and the dealer will take half of your bet and toss your cards into the discard tray. Once you take the first hit, you lose this option. You also lose it if the dealer has a natural, in which case you lose your entire bet. In a few specific instances, surrender is a useful option.

Surrender is not offered in Atlantic City. In other jurisdictions, the availability of surrender varies from casino to casino.

Insurance: If the dealer's upcard is an ace, the dealer will call out, "Insurance", and you are offered the opportunity to place an insurance side bet. You do this by putting up to half the amount of your original bet on the layout area marked: *Insurance pays 2 to 1*. If, after peeking at her hole card, the dealer turns up a natural, any insurance bets are paid off at 2 to 1 odds. If the dealer does not have a natural, the insurance side bet is lost. For a basic strategy player, this is not a good wager. Don't ever do it.

If you have a natural showing, the dealer may ask, "Even money?" This is the same as the insurance bet because if the dealer also has a natural, you will push on the natural and get paid 2 to 1 on your insurance half-bet. If the dealer does not have a natural, you will win 3 to 2 on your natural and lose the insurance half-bet. In either case, the result is an even money payout. Be sure to decline the even money offer because most of the time, you will win at 3 to 2.

DEALER FUNCTIONS

As a representative of the casino, the dealer manages and controls the blackjack game. She converts a player's money into chips, deals out the cards, collects from the losers, and pays the winners. She also enforces the table betting limits and makes sure that all the players follow the table rules.

Shuffling: Most multi-deck games use either six or eight decks of cards, all shuffled together. Shuffling of the cards is done in one of the following three ways:

- *Manual shuffling* – The dealer shuffles the cards by hand, which can be a tedious procedure with six or eight decks.

- *Automatic Shuffling Machine* (ASM) – The cards are shuffled by a machine, after which the dealer places the shuffled pack into a shoe.

- *Continuous Shuffling Machine* (CSM) – The cards are reshuffled by the machine each time the dealer inserts new discards. The machine feeds the dealer one card at a time. There is no conventional shoe and no shuffling delay.

More and more casinos are installing CSMs because they speed up play by about 20% and, thereby, increase the table income by the same amount. Since the discards are periodically shuffled back in with the unplayed cards, there is no way to keep track of the cards, which completely thwarts card counting.

Dealing: The cards are dealt out in a clockwise direction, starting from the dealer's left. Every player who has put out a bet is dealt two cards, usually face up. Whenever the player's cards are dealt face up, the player can look, but can't touch—all the card handling is done by the dealer. The dealer also gets two cards, one face up (called the **upcard**) and one face down (called the **downcard** or the **hole card**). A non-standard variation called *Double Exposure*, in which both of the dealer's cards are dealt face up, will be described later.

Checking for a natural: If the dealer's upcard is an ace or any ten-value card, she peeks at her downcard to see if she has a natural. If she does, the hand is terminated and everyone loses automatically except those players who also have naturals. Remember, when the dealer and a player both have naturals, it is considered a push and no money changes hands.

Since a dealer's natural is settled at the beginning of a round, the players never have an opportunity to increase their bets by doubling or splitting. Consequently, any player who doesn't also have a natural only loses his initial wager.

Advance knowledge of the dealer's downcard is of great benefit to a player, so when the dealer peeks, there is always the danger of cheating. A dishonest dealer may signal the value of the hole card to a confederate at the table, or a player may get a glimpse of it. To prevent these things from happening, some casinos have changed the peeking rules. Sometimes the dealer may only peek if the upcard is an ace, and sometimes she isn't supposed to peek at all.

When the dealer doesn't peek or only peeks under aces, a dealer's natural may not be apparent until everyone has finished playing out his hand. What about those players who increased their bets by doubling or splitting? In the United States, the extra bets are ignored and the players only lose their initial wagers.

In some parts of the World, mainly in Europe, the dealer's hole card is not even dealt out until all the players have acted on their hands. In this case, all players' bets made as a result of doubling and splitting are lost to a dealer's natural. This is referred to as the European no-hole-card rule. In the United States, you may occasionally run into a greedy casino that applies the no-hole-card rule, but this has never occurred in Nevada or New Jersey—not yet, anyway.

Dealer's playing rules: After all the players have acted on their hands, the dealer turns over her hole card for all to see and either stands or hits her hand. She can not double down or split—those are options reserved for the players. Assuming she doesn't have a natural, the dealer has to play her hand according to a fixed casino rule. In most casinos that rule is: Dealer must draw on all totals of 16 or less, and stand on all totals of 17 or more. The rule is always imprinted on the felt tabletop, and is usually stated as:

Dealer must draw to 16 and stand on all 17s

This rule is standard in most venues, including Atlantic City and Europe. However, many casinos have modified the above rule so that their dealers have to take a hit if they have a soft total of exactly 17. In that case, the rule imprinted on the felt is stated as:

Dealer must hit soft 17

That the dealer must draw to 16 and stand on hard 17 is understood. This rule modification is less favorable for the player and increases the casino's edge by 0.2%. It is mainly applied in downtown Las Vegas, some casinos on the Strip, and some casinos in Mississippi. At least it is easy to tell which rule applies by glancing at the tabletop, which is more than can be said for rule variations on player doubling and splitting.

Payoffs: When the dealer has finished playing her hand, she compares it to all players' hands that haven't busted. Any player who has a natural is an automatic winner if the dealer doesn't also have a natural, and is paid off at 3 to 2 odds. If the dealer peeked at her hole card at the start of the round, the naturals will already have been paid. If the dealer also has a natural, it is a push and no money is exchanged.

Of the rest of the players, those with a higher total than the dealer are paid even odds; that is, the dealer will pay them an amount equal to their total wager. Players with a total count less than the dealer lose their bets. Any hand that matches the dealer's is a push.

A NOTE ON PAYOFFS

A payoff described as *even odds* is the same as a payoff of 1 to 1. In other words, if you wager $10 and win, you will be paid an additional $10. If you are fortunate enough to get a natural, you will be paid odds of 3 to 2. The payoff odds are the ratio of the payoff vs. the amount of your bet. In other words, you will get paid three dollars for every two dollars that you bet, and you get to keep your original two-dollar bet.

For instance, if you had a $10 bet out (say, two $5 chips) and were dealt a natural, the dealer would leave your bet in place and give you another $15 (three $5 chips). In those games where a natural pays 6 to 5, your $10 bet would only win $12.

SUMMARY OF BLACKJACK FUNDAMENTALS
PLAYER HANDS

Hard hand — Does not contain an ace and has a total count of 12 or more.

Soft hand — Contains an ace that can be valued at 11 without busting.

Pat hand — A hard total of 17 through 21.

Stiff hand — A hard total of 12 through 16.

Natural — An initial hand consisting of an ace and any ten-count card

PLAYER OPTIONS

Hit — A request for an additional card.

Stand — A decision to not take further action.

Double down — Taking a hit of only one card in return for doubling the original bet.

Split — Converting a pair into two separate hands, with the same bet on each hand.

Resplit — Splitting a second time after getting a third card of the same rank.

Surrender — Folding the initial hand in return for giving up half of the original bet.

Insurance — A 2:1 side bet on whether or not the dealer has a natural.

BLACKJACK PLAYING RULES

When the only legal casinos in the United States were located in Nevada and New Jersey, the rules of casino blackjack were fairly well standardized. At that time, there were only a few minor rule variances between the two states. There were also some minor differences between the main venues in Nevada, namely: the Las Vegas Strip, downtown Las Vegas, and Northern Nevada.

Today, much of that has changed. With the proliferation of legal casinos in Mississippi, Louisiana, Illinois, and other states, along with the expansion of tribal casinos throughout the country, blackjack playing rules can no longer be easily defined by venue. The one exception is Atlantic City, where the rules are controlled by legal statute rather than by the individual casinos.

STANDARD RULES

Before getting into the rule variations, it would be useful to establish a set of *standard rules* as a baseline. The problem is that there is no single set of blackjack rules used by the majority of casinos. In fact, within some casinos the rules can change from one blackjack table to the next.

The only uniform venue in the United States is Atlantic City. Since the multi-deck rules used in Atlantic City are reasonably good for the player, they are a logical choice to use as a standard baseline.

> ### STANDARD BASELINE
> ### BLACKJACK RULES (AC)
> 1. Six- or eight- deck game.
> 2. Dealer must stand on all 17s
> 3. Resplitting of pairs allowed (except aces).
> 4. Double down on any two cards.
> 5. Double down after splitting allowed.
> 6. Surrender not an option.
> 7. All ties are pushes.
> 8. Natural pays 3 to 2.

SIX- OR EIGHT-DECK GAME

A multi-deck game dealt from a shoe increases the house edge by 0.55% for six decks or 0.57% for eight decks over a single-deck game. The multi-deck game is part of our standard baseline rules because that is the primary aim of this chapter. All games in Atlantic City are six- or eight-deck—mostly eight deck.

If you see a continuous shuffling machine (CSM), consider it the same as a multi-deck game. CSMs have been disparaged by blackjack players, believing that casinos would not have made the investment if they didn't derive some benefit—probably to the detriment of the players. The only detriment is to card counters, who are probably the biggest complainers. With a CSM, each new hand is effectively dealt from a freshly shuffled deck, making it impossible to maintain a count.

Use of a CSM does impart a financial benefit to the casinos. Since the delay caused by shuffling the cards and loading the shoe has been eliminated, about 20% more hands can be dealt every hour. Consequently, the net return from a table is increased by the same percentage.

For a non-counting basic strategy player (such as you), playing at a CSM-equipped table has no disadvantage. In fact, computer simulations have proved that a CSM reduces the house edge by 0.02% when compared to a hand-shuffled six-deck game. The mathematical reasoning for this gets a little complicated and has to do with something called the *cut card effect*. The insertion of a cut card (designed to make counting more difficult) instead of dealing out all the decks is also slightly detrimental to the non-counting player. Since there is no cut card in a CSM-dealt game, the house loses this mathematical advantage.

Dealer must stand on all 17s: As previously mentioned, this is the rule where the dealer must draw on all totals of 16 or less, and stand on all totals of 17 or more. It is easy to determine which games apply this rule because it is always imprinted on the felt tabletop. In Atlantic City, this rule is required by statute.

Resplitting of pairs allowed: When you split a pair and one or both of the cards you get from the dealer are the same rank as the original pair, you may split again. Most casinos do not allow resplitting of aces.

Double down on any two cards: This rule has to be specified in the baseline because some casinos only allow doubling on certain totals. Outside of Atlantic City, you will have to ask the dealer about any doubling restrictions.

Double down after splitting allowed: After splitting a pair into two hands, some casinos allow you to double down on one or both of the hands. This is a standard rule in Atlantic City. Elsewhere you will have to ask the dealer or a floor supervisor if doubling after splitting is permitted.

Surrender not an option: In some casinos, you may surrender (fold) your hand and forfeit half of your bet if you don't like your first two cards. Since it is not an option in Atlantic City, it is also not an option in the baseline.

All ties are pushes: If your hand ties the dealer's, you neither win nor lose and no money changes hands. This is a standard rule in casino blackjack, so you don't need to ask about it. If, on occasion, a casino gets greedy and changes this rule, you will know about it quickly enough.

Natural pays 3 to 2: Assuming the dealer also doesn't have a natural (which would be a push), your natural will pay off at 3 to 2 odds. This is often (but not always) imprinted on the felt. In any case, the rule is so standard that you don't need to ask. When a casino changes this rule, they almost always place a sign to that effect on the table.

BLACKJACK RULE VARIATIONS

The rule variations described in this section are commonly found in gambling jurisdictions outside of Atlantic City. Most of the variations are minor and have only a small effect on the house edge.

> ### BLACKJACK RULE VARIATIONS
> 1. Single-, double-, or four-deck game.
> 2. Dealer must hit soft 17.
> 3. Double down restrictions.
> 4. No double down after splitting.
> 5. Lose all to a natural.
> 6. Resplitting aces allowed.
> 7. Surrender is an option.
> 8. Natural payoff worse than 3 to 2.

Single-, double-, or four-deck game: One-, two-, or four-deck games are not as prevalent as six- or eight-deck games because they give the player a better advantage. However, in most cases, other rules are changed to compensate for this and bring the house edge back up again. A few one- or two-deck games can be found in most gambling venues except Atlantic City.

Dealer must hit soft 17: When the dealer hits a soft 17, the rule is always imprinted on the felt tabletop. This rule, which increases the house edge by 0.2%, used to be found only in Northern Nevada and downtown Las Vegas. Now it has spread to many Strip casinos, riverboat casinos, and tribal casinos. Atlantic City casinos still stand on a soft 17.

Double down restrictions: Most casinos allow doubling down on any two card total, but some casinos impose limitations. In Northern Nevada and downtown Las Vegas (except the Golden Nugget), for instance, you may double down only on a total of 10 or 11, giving the casino an added advantage of almost 0.2%. In Europe, doubling is restricted to 9, 10, or 11, which increases the house edge by 0.1%.

No doubling down after splitting: Many casinos do not allow you to double down after splitting, which increases the house edge by more than 0.1%. You will have to ask the dealer or a floor supervisor if doubling after splitting is permitted.

Lose all to a natural: In some casinos, where the dealer does not peek at the hole card (or it is not dealt) until all the players have acted on their hands, all increased bets made as a result of doubling and splitting are lost to a dealer's natural. Because this is prevalent in Europe, it is called the *European No-Hole-Card Rule.* This rule is also applied in Australia. If you use the correct strategy, the casino's gain is only about 0.1%.

Resplitting aces allowed: After splitting a pair of aces, some casinos permit resplitting a third ace. This is a minor benefit to the player, amounting to less than a 0.1% gain.

Surrender is an option: If you don't like your initial hand, some casinos allow you to fold your hand in return for half of your bet. This is a minor benefit to the player—less than 0.1%. When surrender is offered, it is usually at a multi-deck game. It is no longer an option in Atlantic City, but can be found at most Strip casinos as well as many riverboat and tribal casinos.

Natural payoff worse than 3 to 2: More and more often, you will find reduced payoffs of 6:5 or even 1:1. The 1:1 payoff is found in a copyrighted single-deck version called "Super Fun 21." Some casinos have gotten around the copyright by offering a similar game with a 6:5 payoff on naturals. A reduced payoff for a natural is usually indicated by a sign on the table. The good news is that reduced payoffs are not likely to be found in multi-deck games.

THE CASINO'S ADVANTAGE

Playing out your hand before the dealer plays hers, gives the casino a major advantage that is difficult to overcome. If, when you play your hand, you end up busting, you have automatically lost no matter what happens to the dealer's hand. For a more dramatic illustration, assume that all the players at a full blackjack table manage to bust their hands. If the dealer also busts, the house still wins all the wagers on the table.

There are two ways to diminish this major edge held by the house. The first is to play your hand according to the basic strategy rules. Doing this can reduce the house edge to where it approaches an even game.

The second is to track (count) cards in addition to applying the basic strategy. Doing this can reduce the house edge to zero and even swing it in favor of the player. Card counting techniques, however, are beyond the scope of this book.

So, what is the house edge when you play your hand exactly according to the basic strategy? That depends on several factors, including the number of decks used and the particular playing rules in use at a given table. The best of the commonly-found set of rules for multi-deck games, or games using a continuous shuffling machine (CSM), are the Standard Blackjack Rules that were previously established as a baseline. Depending on the number of decks used, these rules give the house an edge of 0.39% to 0.43%, as shown in the following chart.

STANDARD BASELINE RULES	
DECKS USED	**HOUSE EDGE**
Eight	0.43%
Six	0.41%
CSM	0.39%

These charts all use the convention that a positive percentage favors the house, and a negative percentage favors the player (because it reduces the house edge). As you can see in the above chart, the multi-deck house edge is well under half a percent, so it is still good for the player. Especially when compared to a game such as roulette with a 5.26% house edge. Other rules can make the standard baseline number a little better or a little worse, as shown in the following list.

PERCENT CHANGES FOR RULE VARIATIONS	
Resplitting aces allowed	-0.05%
Surrender option	-0.05%
Aces can be resplit	-0.08%
One deck (instead of 6 decks)	-0.55%
Two decks (instead of 6 decks)	-0.21%
Pair resplitting not allowed	+0.10%
No double after splitting	+0.14%
Dealer must hit soft 17	+0.22%
Double on 9, 10, or 11 only	+0.10%
Double on 10 or 11 only	+0.18%
Lose all to a natural	+0.10%
Natural payoff 6:5	+1.40%
Natural payoff 1:1	+2.30%

The above percentages assume that you are using the basic strategy outlined in the following sections. Working with the numbers is easier than it looks. Let's say you go to downtown Las Vegas and find a six-deck table where the dealer must hit soft 17, and they only permit you to double on 10 or 11. To calculate this, start with +0.41% for the six-deck game, add +0.22% for hitting soft 17, and add +0.25% for restricted doubling, as shown in the next page.

Six-deck game	+0.41%
Dealer must hit soft 17	+0.22%
Double on 10 or 11 only	+0.18%
Net casino edge =	**+0.81%**

Even with limited doubling and with the dealer hitting soft 17, the casino edge is less than 1%.

For a slightly more complicated example, you find a CSM game on the Strip with standard rules except that surrender is allowed and doubling after splitting is not allowed. Simply start with +0.39% for CSM, increase it by +0.14% for no doubling, and then reduce it by -0.05% for surrender, as shown below.

CSM game	+0.39%
No double after splitting	+0.14%
Surrender allowed	-0.05%
Net casino edge	**+0.48%**

That means the house edge is increased to just under half a percent, which is typical for CSM and multi-deck games.

A SIMPLE STRATEGY FOR THE NOVICE

Before employing any blackjack playing strategy, it is important that you first become familiar with the proper decision-making procedure. Knowledge of a playing strategy will be of limited value if you try to apply it haphazardly. There is a certain evaluation sequence that should be followed in order to make the best playing decisions.

PLAYING DECISIONS

Many novice blackjack players get flustered when it is their turn to make a decision on how to play their hand. Should they split? Should they double down? Should they hit? Should they stand? Suddenly there seem to be an unending number of decisions to make. Although they have carefully memorized the strategy rules, when their turn comes and the dealer is impatiently pointing at their hand, they draw a blank and end up taking the wrong action.

Experienced players, on the other hand, don't have this problem when it comes time to make a decision, because they already use such a methodical approach on a subconscious level. It is so automatic that most of them don't even realize they are doing it. Whether subconscious or not, if you follow the decision process outlined below while applying the basic strategy, you have the best chance of playing your hand correctly

Decide whether or not to surrender. Apply the basic strategy rules to determine if surrendering is the best action. If surrender is not offered by the casino or you are using a simplified strategy table, skip to pair splitting.

Decide whether or not to split a pair. Apply the basic strategy rules to determine if splitting is the best action. If your initial hand is not a pair, skip to doubling.

Decide whether or not to double down. Whether or not you have split a pair, apply the basic strategy rules to determine if doubling is the next best action.

Decide whether to hit or stand. If you did not double, apply the basic strategy rules to determine if you should hit or stand.

If you split a pair, repeat the above steps for each hand. These four fundamental playing decisions are summarized in the following simple, easy-to-remember chart:

DECISION SUMMARY
1. Surrender?
2. Split?
3. Double?
4. Hit or stand?

A SIMPLE STRATEGY

When you are a beginner, learning the entire Universal Basic Strategy table in the next section seems like a daunting task—especially when you are anxious to start playing. An easier approach is to first learn the simplified strategy presented in this section. Surprisingly, using the Simple Strategy costs the player less than 1% as compared to the Universal Basic Strategy. That is, the house advantage will still be only 1% or so—which is a lot better than the 3% to 5% advantage the house has over the average player.

The main differences between this strategy and the full-blown basic strategy are the lack of a surrender option and simplified splitting and doubling rules. When you apply the simplified rules, be sure to play non-split pairs like a hard hand, as the table indicates. If the strategy tells you to split a pair, then it is correct to resplit if you catch a third card of the same value. Before you ever step up to a blackjack table, be sure you have the following rules down pat, and have familiarized yourself with the above decision-making procedure, which you can reduce to three steps, since there is no surrender rule to consider.

Pair of aces: Always split a pair of aces. The value of the initial hand is either a 2 or a soft 12, neither of which is very good. By splitting, you get two chances of catching a 21. Remember that splitting aces is a special case. The dealer will give you just one card on each ace, and you cannot take any hits. If one of those cards is another ace, you should resplit to a third hand, if the casino permits you to do so.

Pair of 8s: Always split a pair of 8s. The value of the initial hand is 16, which is the worst hand you can have. Splitting the eights limits your losses because you are likely to develop better hands. The dealer will give you one card on each 8, and if one of those cards is another 8, you should resplit to a third hand. Now you can commence playing the hands, one at a time, according to the rules below.

Pair of 2s, 3s, 6s, or 7s: Split these pairs only if the dealer shows a 2 through 7. Statistically, the initial totals of 4, 6, 12, or 14 are worse hands when they are split. You should minimize losses by splitting if the dealer has a greater chance of busting.

Pair of 9s: Split the 9s only if the dealer shows a 2 through 7. Although a 9 is a pretty good starting card because it can turn into a 19, against a dealer 8 or higher, doubling the bet is too risky and you should stand on the hard 18.

Pair of 4s: Never split fours. The total of 8 is a much better hand than the individual 4s, so you should keep it. Catching a 10 will give you an 18, which is not a great hand, but is much better than 14.

Pair of 5s: Never, never split 5s. The total of 10 has a good chance of hitting to a 20 or 21. Play a pair of 5s as a hard hand, which means you should double down against a dealer's 2 through 9, just as you would for a hard 10.

Pair of 10s: Never split ten-value cards. A 20 is an excellent pat hand that you should never break up.

Soft A 2 to A 6: Never stand on these hands; they are poor hands that can't be busted, so you should try to improve them by hitting.

Soft A 7 to A 9: Always stand because these are strong hands that are not likely to be improved with a hit. In the Universal Basic Strategy, the A-7 hand is treated differently, but here it is simplified.

Soft A 10: This, of course, is a natural for which you are paid 3 to 2 if the dealer doesn't also have one.

Total of 9 or less: When your non-paired hand has a total count of 9 or less, it cannot be busted and should, therefore, always be hit.

Total of 10 or 11: These hands also cannot be busted and should always be hit, but only when the dealer shows a 10 or ace. When the dealer shows a 9 or less, the chances of getting 20 or 21 and beating the dealer are very good. You should, therefore, take advantage of this by doubling down, which doubles your wager.

Total of 12 to 16: This is a stiff hand that *can* be busted, so you should stand if the dealer shows a 6 or less, in the hope that the dealer will bust. A dealer upcard of 7 or higher indicates a possible pat hand. In this case, you probably have a losing hand, so you should take a hit and risk busting in an attempt to beat the dealer. Continue hitting until your total count exceeds 16.

Total of 17 to 21: This is called a pat hand, and you should always stand. Although you may not have the dealer beat, your risk of busting is too high to take a hit. The exception is an A 6 hand (see above), which should be hit. A 17 is not a good total—the best it can do against a dealer's pat hand is push. Since a soft 17 can't be busted, you have everything to gain and little to lose by hitting.

Insurance: Never take the insurance side bet because the odds always favor the house.

The above rules are summarized in the following chart.

SIMPLE STRATEGY

Player Hand	Player Action
Pairs	
8 or ace	Always SPLIT
2, 3, 6, 7, or 9	SPLIT if dealer shows 2 to 7, else play as hard hand
4, 5, or 10	Never SPLIT; always play as hard hand
Soft Hands	
A 2 to A 6	Always HIT
A 7 to A 10	Always STAND
Hard Hands	
5 to 9	Always HIT
10 or 11	DOUBLE if dealer shows 2 to 9; HIT on dealer 10 or Ace
12 to 16	STAND if dealer shows 2 to 6; HIT if dealer shows 7 to Ace
17 to 21	Always STAND

NEVER TAKE INSURANCE

THE UNIVERSAL BASIC STRATEGY

Early professional blackjack players learned that there was one right way and many wrong ways to play the game. By combining experience, sound reasoning, and their knowledge of odds, they developed winning playing strategies, which they applied very successfully. Only a select few people knew these strategies, however, and they intended to keep it that way.

During the early 1950s, Roger Baldwin, Wilbert Cantey, Herbert Maisel, and James McDermott, a group of sharp statistical analysts, published the first blackjack playing strategy in a mathematical journal. They applied their knowledge of statistical analysis to the game and after three years of plugging away on mechanical desk calculators, arrived at a surprisingly-accurate playing strategy. They called it the *basic strategy*, and the term has been with us ever since.

At that time, blackjack was only a moderately-popular game, so just a few people recognized the importance of their efforts. One of those people was Professor Edward O. Thorp of M.I.T. who, a few years later, refined the earlier work using an IBM 704 computer. Professor Thorp then published the first book describing a method for winning at blackjack by keeping track of the played cards. The basic strategy was the backbone of his innovative card-counting system.

In the following years, Julian Braun and others developed computer programs that simulated millions of blackjack hands. These simulations ultimately brought the original basic strategy to perfection. This perfect basic strategy is what is presented here.

THE UNIVERSAL BASIC STRATEGY

Now that you have memorized and practiced the Simple Strategy rules, you should be able to take on the full basic strategy. If you are not a card counter, basic strategy is the best way to play all blackjack hands. Therefore, to reduce the house advantage to the lowest possible percentage, it is necessary to slavishly follow every one of the prescribed instructions in the basic strategy.

This chapter covers the Universal Basic Strategy which, as the name implies, can be used with any multi-deck blackjack game that has normal game rules. It also works well for single- and double-deck hand dealt games. Specifically, it is an almost exact strategy for the set of baseline game rules that were previously defined. So that you won't have to thumb back in the book, these rules are repeated below

---

STANDARD BASELINE
BLACKJACK RULES (AC)

1. Six- or eight-deck game.
2. Dealer must stand on all 17s.
3. Resplitting of pairs allowed (except aces).
4. Double down on any two cards.
5. Double down after splitting allowed.
6. Surrender not an option.
7. All ties are pushes.
8. Natural pays 3 to 2.

The Universal Basic Strategy is also a close approximation for games with slightly different rules. It can be effectively used for any game with commonly-found rules, such as the following:

1. Dealer must hit soft 17.
2. Double down on 10 or 11 only.
3. No double down after splitting.
4. Resplitting aces allowed.

PAIRS

Some pairs are always split, some are never split, and some are split only for certain dealer upcards. If it is correct to split a pair, then it is correct to resplit if you catch a third card of the same rank. Whenever you don't split a pair, play it as a hard hand.

When double down is allowed after a split (and only then), the absolutely correct strategy is to split 4s against dealer upcards of 5 or 6. As a minor simplification, this split was deleted because the chart is also applicable when doubling after a split is not allowed, and the difference between splitting and not splitting is statistically miniscule. If you play exclusively in Atlantic City or where Atlantic City rules prevail, you may wish to white-out the "H" in the dealer 5 and 6 columns, and write in a "P."

SOFT HANDS

An initial hand in which one of the cards is an ace is called **soft** because it can be hit with no risk of busting. If, after taking one or more hits, the ace can continue to be counted as 11 without busting, then the hand is still soft. With the ace taking on the dual value of 1 or 11, a soft hand is much more versatile than a hard hand and must be played differently.

When you have a soft 17 (A 6) be sure that you take a hit when the dealer shows a 2, 7, 8, 9, 10, or ace. Where doubling is restricted, hit against all dealer upcards. Since standing on a hard 17 is correct, many players think they should stand on soft 17 as well. It should be made clear that 17 is not a good total—the best it can do against a dealer's pat hand is push. The only reason for standing on a hard 17 is to avoid the high risk of busting. But, a soft 17 can't be busted, so you have everything to gain and little to lose by hitting.

HARD HANDS

An initial hand that does not contain an ace and has a total count of 12 or more is called **hard** because the total numeric value of the hand is fixed and an additional card can cause it to exceed a count of 21. After taking one or more hits, any hand with an ace that has to be counted as 1 to keep from busting, is also a hard hand. Although, totals of 5 to

11 are not hard hands, they are included in this category for want of a better place.

When you have a hard 13 to 16 you should stand when the dealer shows a 6 or less, in the hope that the dealer will bust. A dealer upcard of 7 or higher often indicates a pat hand, so you probably have a loser. Consequently, you have to take a hit and risk busting in an attempt to beat the dealer's hand. Continue hitting until your total count exceeds 16.

THE COMPLETE UNIVERSAL BASIC STRATEGY CHART
On the following page is the complete Universal Basic Strategy chart. The chart is arranged in the same decision order that you use to evaluate your hand: pairs, soft hands, hard hands.

When you play in a multi-deck blackjack game, your best results will always come when you religiously abide by the Universal Basic Strategy. Any deviations are at your own risk. The chart will also serve you well if, at some time, you decide to play in a single- or double-deck game. It is so close an approximation that it doesn't pay to memorize a second set of strategy rules.

Key to chart abbreviations:
H = hit   **S** = stand   **P** = split pair
Dh = double down if allowed, else hit
Ds = double down if allowed, else stand
Fh = surrender (fold) if allowed, else hit

UNIVERSAL BASIC STRATEGY

Player's Hand				Dealer's Upcard						
	2	3	4	5	6	7	8	9	10	Ace
Pairs										
A A	P	P	P	P	P	P	P	P	P	P
10 10	S	S	S	S	S	S	S	S	S	S
9 9	P	P	P	P	P	S	P	P	S	S
8 8	P	P	P	P	P	P	P	P	P	P
7 7	P	P	P	P	P	P	H	H	H	H
6 6	P	P	P	P	P	H	H	H	H	H
5 5	Dh	Dh	Dh	Dh	Dh	Dh	Dh	Dh	H	H
4 4	H	H	H	H	H	H	H	H	H	H
3 3	P	P	P	P	P	P	H	H	H	H
2 2	P	P	P	P	P	P	H	H	H	H
Soft										
21 (A 10)	S	S	S	S	S	S	S	S	S	S
20 (A 9)	S	S	S	S	S	S	S	S	S	S
19 (A 8)	S	S	S	S	S	S	S	S	S	S
18 (A 7)	S	Ds	Ds	Ds	Ds	S	S	H	H	H
17 (A 6)	H	Dh	Dh	Dh	Dh	H	H	H	H	H
16 (A 5)	H	H	Dh	Dh	Dh	H	H	H	H	H
15 (A 4)	H	H	Dh	Dh	Dh	H	H	H	H	H
14 (A 3)	H	H	H	Dh	Dh	H	H	H	H	H
13 (A 2)	H	H	H	Dh	Dh	H	H	H	H	H
Hard										
17 - 21	S	S	S	S	S	S	S	S	S	S
16	S	S	S	S	S	H	H	Fh	Fh	Fh
15	S	S	S	S	S	H	H	H	Fh	H
14	S	S	S	S	S	H	H	H	H	H
13	S	S	S	S	S	H	H	H	H	H
12	H	H	S	S	S	H	H	H	H	H
11	Dh	Dh	Dh	Dh	Dh	Dh	Dh	Dh	Dh	Ace
10	Dh	Dh	Dh	Dh	Dh	Dh	Dh	Dh	H	H
9	H	Dh	Dh	Dh	Dh	H	H	H	H	H
5 - 8	H	H	H	H	H	H	H	H	H	H

DEALER MUST HIT SOFT 17

The rule that a dealer must hit soft 17 has become prevalent in many casinos. The casinos like the rule because it increases their edge by 0.2%. Using the exact strategy for this rule, however, provides a minimal gain over using the Universal Basic Strategy and it isn't really worth memorizing. The strategy adjustment requires only three changes for doubling and three changes for surrender, as shown in the following abbreviated chart.

Differences from Universal Basic Strategy when Dealer Must Hit Soft 17. Other Standard Blackjack Rules Are Unchanged										
Player's Hand	**Dealer's Upcard**									
	2	3	4	5	6	7	8	9	10	Ace
Pair										
8 8										Fspl
Soft										
18 (A 7)	Ds									
19 (A 8)					Ds					
Hard										
11										Dh
15										Fh
17										Fs

Key to chart abbreviations:
Dh = double down if allowed, else hit
Ds = double down if allowed, else stand
Fh = surrender if allowed, else hit
Fs = surrender if allowed, else stand
Fspl = surrender if allowed, else split

LOSE ALL TO A NATURAL

In the not too distant past, whenever the dealer dealt herself an ace or 10 upcard, she would immediately check her hole card to see if she had a natural. If she did, the hand was over and everyone automatically lost (except someone with another natural). Since the dealer's natural was settled at the beginning of the round, the players never had an opportunity to increase their bets by doubling or splitting. Consequently, any player who didn't also have a natural only lost his initial wager.

To eliminate another source of cheating, many casinos have changed the rule so that the dealer no longer checks for a natural at the start of a round. When the dealer doesn't peek at the hole card (or it is not dealt) until all the players have acted on their hands, a dealer's natural is not evident until all the hands have been played out. What about those players who increased their bets by doubling or splitting? In Atlantic City and other places in the United States where this procedure is used, the extra bets are ignored and the players only lose their initial wagers.

In Europe and Australia, however, all increased bets made as a result of doubling and splitting are lost to a dealer's natural. Because this is prevalent in Europe, it is called the European No-Hole-Card Rule.

By using the correct playing strategy, the casino's gain can be reduced to about 0.1%. The correct strategy is obvious: don't split or double down against a dealer upcard of ace or 10. There is one exception, however. You should still split a pair of aces against a dealer 10. To summarize:

> **Lose all to a natural**
> Never split or double when dealer shows an ace or 10.
> **EXCEPT**
> Split aces when dealer shows a 10.

BLACKJACK SIDE BETS

The casinos and casino suppliers have devised many different blackjack side bets for the purpose of increasing profits. A large sampling of these side bets is described below, mainly to show you that none of them are worth risking any money on. The house edge ranges from 3.8% to over 38%. If you encounter a blackjack side bet that is not listed below, you can assume the house edge falls within the same range.

FIELD BET
In a field bet, you are betting that your first two cards will be a total of 12 through 16. If you get an A A or an 8 8, the payout is double. The house edge for a field bet is 8.9%. 'Nuff said.

INSURANCE
Insurance is a side bet that is offered at just about every casino blackjack game. You are betting that the dealer has a natural, in which case all insurance bets are paid off at 2 to 1 odds. If the dealer does not have a natural, the insurance side bet is lost.

When the undealt cards are sufficiently ten-rich, a card counter will take the insurance bet. A basic strategy player, however, should never take the bet. In a six- or eight-deck game, the house edge on the insurance bet is more than 7%.

Suppose you have a natural—don't you want to protect it with insurance? No you don't! When you insure a natural, you are trading a 3: 2 payoff most of the time for a 1:1 payoff all the time. Even then the house still has the edge, although it is much less.

OVER/UNDER 13
You are betting that your first two cards will total either over 13 or under 13, with aces counting as 1. If you get exactly 13, you lose either

bet. The house edge on the "over" bet is 6.5%, and on the "under" bet is 10%. You decide which one to risk your money on, and I hope you decide that neither one is a good bet.

PAIR SQUARE

You are betting that your first two cards will be a pair. A pair pays 10 to 1 if it is unsuited and pays 15 to 1 if both cards are the same suit. Obviously, a same-suited pair can't happen in a single-deck game. In a six- or eight-deck game, the house edge is over 9%.

PROGRESSIVE BLACKJACK

Progressive Blackjack is a copyrighted game distributed by Mikohn Gaming. Other than the progressive side bet, it is a standard blackjack game. The $1 optional side bet gives you a chance of winning a bonus or the progressive jackpot when you are dealt one or more aces, in accordance with the following schedule.

PROGRESSIVE BLACKJACK	
HAND	PAYS
1 Ace	$3
2 Aces (mixed suits)	$15
2 Aces (same suit)	$50
3 Aces (mixed suits)	$200
3 Aces (same suit)	$1000
4 Aces	$2000
4 Aces (same color)	Jackpot

These aces have to be the first cards dealt to your hand with no intervening non-aces. In other words, to win the $3 bonus, the ace has to be the first card you are dealt. To win the $15 bonus, the first two cards dealt to your hand have to be aces; to win the $200 bonus, the first three cards dealt have to be aces, and so forth.

Whenever it is won, the progressive jackpot is reset to $25,000. The house advantage depends on the value of the progressive jackpot. At the reset level, the house edge is a ridiculous 38.9%. When the progressive meter reaches $100,000, the house edge drops to about 20%. For the house edge to finally get to zero, the progressive jackpot has to exceed $207,000!

RED/BLACK

In this side bet, you wager on the color of the dealer's upcard—either red or black. The casino's edge comes into play when the dealer shows a deuce of your color. In that case, your bet is a push. The house edge is 3.8%, which is better than most side bets.

ROYAL MATCH

When you make this side bet, you will win a bonus if your first two cards are the same suit, which is called an Easy Match. If the two cards are a king and queen of the same suit, you win a bigger bonus. This is called a Royal Match. The following chart shows the payoffs.

ROYAL MATCH	
HAND	PAYS
Easy Match	2.5 to 1
Royal Match	25 to 1

For a six- or eight-deck game, the house edge is about 6.5%. In some casinos there is an additional bonus of $1000 if both the dealer and player have a Royal Match, reducing the house edge to around 6%.

STREAK

In this optional side bet, you place a wager on how many consecutive hands you might win. You can bet on a winning streak of two, three, four, or five hands, and if you make it, you are paid according to the following schedule.

STREAK	
No. Of Wins	Pays
Two	3 to 1
Three	7 to 1
Four	17 to 1
Five	37 to 1

With a house edge ranging from 8% to 14%, you probably don't want to try this one.

SUPER SEVENS

When you make this optional side bet, you are hoping to get one or more 7s so that you are paid according to the following schedule.

SUPER SEVENS	
Hand	Pays
First card any 7	3 to 1
First two cards unsuited 7s	50 to 1
First two cards suited 7s	100 to 1
First three cards unsuited 7s	500 to 1
First three cards suited 7s	5000 to 1

Regardless of the seemingly-high payouts, the house edge is still over 11%, making it a bad bet.

UNCONVENTIONAL BLACKJACK GAMES

In an attempt to lure players away from standard blackjack to similar games that are more profitable, casinos have devised a number of modifications. One of the oldest is *Double Exposure*, in which the enticement is that both of the dealer's cards are exposed at the start of each hand. The most recent blackjack modification is *Super Fun 21*, which is covered in a separate chapter. Of course, since the casinos expect to make a profit, all of these games have ways of deceiving the player, some of which are not immediately obvious.

In general, the modified blackjack games have been moneymakers for the casinos, mainly because most players use incorrect strategy. With the proper playing strategy, however, the house edge is not unreasonable, usually staying under 1%. The only problem is that you have to learn another set of strategy rules.

In addition to a description of Double Exposure, the following sections also cover two interesting blackjack variations that don't have the disadvantage of requiring a new strategy. They are called *Multiple Action Blackjack* and *Twin Blackjack*.

MULTIPLE ACTION BLACKJACK

Multiple Action Blackjack, sometimes called Triple Action, is like playing three separate blackjack hands, except that you are dealt only one hand and play against three different dealer hands. At each player's position, there are three betting circles so that you can place one, two, or three bets. If you place only one bet, the game is identical to standard blackjack, and you play only against the first dealer hand. If you place two or three bets, you play your solitary hand against two or three different dealer hands.

Once the bets are down, the dealer gives each player two face-up cards and gives herself one upcard. After all the players are done acting on their hands, the dealer gives herself a second card and plays her hand just as in a standard blackjack game. At this point, the bet in the first circle is at risk and the dealer pays the winners and collects from the losers. If a player busts, however, all three bets are lost.

When the first round is finished, the dealer discards her draw cards, and retains her original upcard. Since the players based their playing strategies on that upcard, this keeps the game fair. All non-busted player hands remain in place. The dealer then draws new cards to complete a second dealer hand and compares it to the active player hands. Now, the bet in the second circle (if any) is at risk and the dealer again pays the winners and collects from the losers. This procedure is repeated a third time, after which all the cards are removed from the table and the players place their bets for a new game.

For example, let's say you put $10 in each betting circle. You are dealt a 9 and a king, and the dealer shows a 7. You happily stand on your 19. The dealer draws a 6 for a total of 13, and must draw again. The next card is an 8 for a total of 21, which beats your 19, so you lose your first bet.

After the dealer collects your $10 from the first betting circle, she discards her draw cards and retains the 7. For the second round, she draws a 10 for a total of 17, which loses to your 19. You win your second bet and the dealer pays you $10. She now discards the 10 draw card and, again, retains the 7. On the third round, her first draw is a 5 for a total of 12, so she has to draw another card. The second card is a queen, causing the dealer to bust. You win the third round and are paid $10.

Just like in standard blackjack, you may split a pair. If you do, however, you must double each of your original bets. When the dealer shows an ace, you may take insurance on any or all of your initial bets (which is never recommended).

When doubling down, you have the option of doubling any or all of your bets. If you are following basic strategy and doubling is the correct action, you should double all your bets. Should you be fortunate enough to get a natural, each of your bets will be paid off at 3 to 2, assuming the dealer doesn't also get a natural.

Many players like Multiple Action Blackjack because with three bets on the table, a streak of good hands will win more money than in standard blackjack. Of course, this also involves risking more money. Another positive feature is that when the casinos are crowded, the betting limits at Multiple Action tables are usually lower than at standard blackjack tables.

Strategy: Since Multiple Action Blackjack follows standard blackjack rules, you should play exactly according to the Universal Basic Strategy, or the simplified version. When you do this, the house edge is the same as for standard multi-deck blackjack.

Because of the risk of busting on all three bets, many players are reluctant to hit a 14, 15, or 16 when the dealer shows a 7 or higher. This is a serious mistake, which increases the casino's edge, and is one of the reasons the casinos like the game. Some players start with one or two bets and go to three bets if they are winning. Although this will reduce the volatility of the game, it will have no effect on the overall house edge.

TWIN BLACKJACK

As you might have guessed, in Twin Blackjack, there are two betting spots, and each player is dealt two hands. Except for the fact that there are special bonuses, and less favorable rules to compensate for the bonuses, it is very similar to playing two hands in a standard multi-deck blackjack game.

Although a player has the choice of betting one or two hands, the bonuses only work for two hands. Whenever a player gets simultaneous naturals in both hands, it is called "twin blackjacks" and each one pays 2 to 1. If the simultaneous naturals contain identical cards, it is called "identical twin blackjacks" and each one pays 4 to 1. Don't hold your breath, however, because the chance of getting a pair of identical naturals is about 40,000 to 1.

To compensate for the bonuses, you are only allowed to resplit one time and you cannot double down after splitting. Even so, with correct play, the house edge is similar to standard multi-deck games.

Strategy: Since Twin Blackjack pretty much follows standard blackjack rules, you should play exactly according to the Universal Basic Strategy, or the simplified version. When you correctly apply the Universal Basic Strategy, the house edge is about 0.44%. This is almost exactly the same edge as for an Atlantic City eight-deck game.

DOUBLE EXPOSURE

Double Exposure originated at Vegas World (the original name of the Stratosphere) in 1979, when Bob Stupak owned it. Since then, it has spread to several other casinos in Las Vegas, Atlantic City, and Mississippi. Although Double Exposure is the common name for this game, it is occasionally called Face Up 21 or Dealer Disclosure.

The distinguishing feature of this multi-deck game is that both of the dealer's initial cards are dealt face up. This gives the player a major strategic advantage, which is compensated by the following detrimental rules:

- Dealer wins all ties, except for a player natural
- Natural pays even money (instead of 3:2)
- Player may not resplit a pair
- Surrender is not allowed

Not being a copyrighted game, the other rules vary somewhat from casino to casino. For instance, the dealer may or may not hit a soft 17, or the player may or may not double down after splitting. In most casinos, when both the player and dealer have naturals, the player wins. Depending on which rules are in effect, the house edge can range from 0.7% to 1%. Avoid any game in which a simultaneous player/dealer natural is a push, as it will drive the house edge to over 1.5%

Because of the rule variations, the exact playing strategy that was developed by Stanford Wong takes as many as six charts to describe. Few people would consider memorizing these charts to effectively play a game that isn't all that worthwhile. If you do have a particular interest in Double Exposure and want to study the playing strategy, you should obtain a copy of my book *Beat Multiple Deck Blackjack*.

GENERAL PLAYING ADVICE

Some people, thinking they know more than the experts, have a tendency to do things in a half-cocked manner and then wonder why they keep losing money. In an attempt to discourage you from doing dumb things, this section is designed to help keep you on the straight and narrow. It begins with the most important advice I can give to the budding blackjack player: practice, practice, practice.

PRACTICE, PRACTICE, PRACTICE
The secret to learning the basic strategy well is to practice, and practice

some more—*before* you enter a casino and begin to risk real money. There are several ways to do this. You can gather together your family or a few friends and play for buttons or matchsticks. When you do this, always play by casino rules rather than home-game rules.

Actually, all you need is a deck of cards and you can play all by yourself. You first function as the dealer and dole out several players' hands. Then switch hats and act on each player's hand, in turn. When the player's hands are finished, you become the dealer again and play your hand according to the casino rules.

If you own a home computer, it gets even simpler. There is plenty of blackjack software available, although it is usually packaged with other casino games. The software will let you play many hands very rapidly with no significant delays for shuffling. Most programs have a tutorial mode that corrects you if you make a wrong play.

BAD PLAYING STRATEGIES
One good way to lose money while playing blackjack is to employ a bad strategy. This is especially inexcusable when you know the correct strategy, but as I said earlier, some people think they know better.

Two bad playing strategies that are often used by novice players do seem to have a certain logic. They are "mimic the dealer" and "never bust." Even some basic strategy players have reverted to one of these during an extended losing streak. Sometimes these strategies seem to work for a while, but in the long run, the house picks up a large advantage.

Mimic the dealer: Since the dealer wins most of the time by hitting 16 and standing on 17, it is obviously the best playing strategy. Shouldn't I do the same?

Absolutely not! When you mimic the dealer, you are not doing yourself any favors. The dealer doesn't win most of the time because she hits 16 and stands on 17; she wins because she plays her hand last. Consequently, when you bust, you always lose, and when the dealer busts, she only loses if you didn't bust first. This is such a large advantage for the dealer that if you try to mimic her, the house edge rises to almost 5.5%.

Never bust: Since I lose when I bust, even if the dealer busts, wouldn't I be better off never hitting a 12 or higher? Then I would win whenever the dealer busts.

Good try, but this is another way of rapidly thinning out your bankroll. On average, the dealer busts less than 29% of the time. That means you will be guaranteed a win on almost 29% of your hands. But what about the other 71%? When the dealer doesn't bust, it means she achieved a total count of 17 through 21—and she did that over 71% of the time. Every time you stand on a low count and the dealer doesn't bust, you lose. In fact, if you don't achieve an average count of 19 when the dealer shows a 7 or higher, you will lose most of the time. Using a no-bust strategy will increase the house edge to almost 4%.

TEN WORST PLAYING ERRORS

It is amazing how many players who are familiar with correct basic strategy are reluctant to make certain indicated plays. Whenever you don't follow the basic strategy playing rules, you will lose money in the long run. Yes, you may guess right occasionally, but if you follow your own imperfect intuition you will always end up losing more than you gain. The ten hands listed below seem to be the ones most often played incorrectly.

Hit an A A against a dealer 10. This hand should always be SPLIT. No matter how you look at it, a hand of 2 or 12 is not good. So, why are some players reluctant to split? Because they get only one card on each ace. What they don't understand is that the house allows only a single hit because it is such a strong play. It is exactly the same as getting one card when you double down on an 11, which is a good play—except that with split aces you have *two* good plays.

Stand on an A 6 against a dealer 7. Always HIT this hand. Unless the dealer busts, the best you can do is a push. However, with a 7 showing, the dealer will bust only 26% of the time. When you hit you cannot bust and you may improve the hand. Never stand.

Stand on an A 7 against a dealer 9. Always HIT this hand. Why hit a perfectly good 18? Because, contrary to popular belief, 18 is not a good hand, especially when the dealer shows a 9 or better. With a 9 upcard, the dealer will bust only 23% of the time and will beat your hand over 50% of the time. You must try to improve your holding. Never stand.

Stand on an A 7 against a dealer 10. Be sure to HIT this hand. Another perfectly good 18? Of course not! Not when the dealer will win over 56% of the time. Hit it!

Stand on a 9 9 against a dealer 9. Always SPLIT this hand. If you stand on this 18, it is no different than standing on an A 7: The dealer will beat you more than 50% of the time. Splitting gives you a better chance of winning.

Hit (or stand) on an 8 8 against a dealer 10. Always SPLIT this hand. No matter what you do, it is a loser. Normally, a 16 is the worst hand you can get. At least, when it comes as a pair of 8s, you have the opportunity to improve it slightly. Of the available options, splitting loses the least money—*even though you doubled the bet!*

Hit (or stand) on an 8 8 against a dealer ace. Always SPLIT this hand. This is essentially the same situation as above, and splitting is your best option.

Hit an 11 against a dealer 10. DOUBLE this hand. Getting a count of 11 in the first two cards is a winning situation. That's when you take advantage and double down, just as the basic strategy tells you to do.

Stand on a 12 against a dealer 3. HIT this hand. This is also a losing hand, but you will limit your losses when you hit, although not by much.

Stand on a 12 against a dealer 2. HIT this hand. Just like the above hand, you must take a hit to limit your losses.

CHEATING

Cheating is a controversial subject over which there is quite a bit of disagreement. There are, of course, two sides to the question: (1) Casinos cheating the players and (2) players cheating the casinos.

If you plan to cheat a casino, that is entirely your decision. Just be aware of the risks, and be aware of the severity of the consequences if you are caught.

As far as casinos cheating the players—it does happen, but very seldom in the major gambling venues. When it happens, it is usually the action of an individual dealer. Dealers cheat for any number of reasons, but one of the most common is that they are actually stealing from the casino. To avert suspicion, they then cheat the players to assure that the table drop on their shift is normal.

Cheating by card manipulation is almost entirely confined to hand-dealt games. Dealers rarely cheat individual players. Most cheating dealers simply give themselves good hands, thereby cheating all the players at the table.

Cheating with a dealing shoe is possible, but it requires the use of a specially-rigged shoe. It is so difficult and risky to get a rigged shoe into play without the help of management that it is rarely done in legal casinos. Furthermore, any casino caught using such a shoe would face a long license suspension. Thus, if you are playing at a multi-deck blackjack game, dealer cheating should be of no concern—so you needn't worry about it.

CARD COUNTING

Card counting is a specialized technique that requires a high level of study, practice, and concentration. Consequently, it is too extensive a subject to adequately cover in this book.

With diligent practice, however, you may eventually become an expert basic strategy player. You know you have arrived when the correct basic strategy play becomes second nature and you rarely make a mistake. Once you have reached that point, you may want to obtain a book on the subject and try your hand at counting cards.

◆8◆
CARIBBEAN STUD POKER

As the name implies, Caribbean Stud Poker originated in the Caribbean Islands and on the cruise ships that plied those waters. Because the original Caribbean Stud was not especially favorable for the player, when Las Vegas casinos adopted the game, they added a progressive jackpot sweetener. Although the jackpot doesn't benefit the player that much, it has helped to make the game popular enough to become a standard offering in Nevada and other gambling jurisdictions.

Caribbean Stud is played on a blackjack-like table. The game is similar to five card stud poker except that you play against the dealer's hand and not against the other players. You have two opportunities to place a bet on your hand, and you can also make an optional side bet to qualify for the progressive jackpot. If you know a little poker, Caribbean Stud is quite simple to learn because the winning hands are the same as those in standard poker. However, since you are not competing against the other players at the table, bluffing, and other playing strategies that are used in regular stud poker games, are of no value.

Just like poker, you start out by putting up an ante. At the same time, you have the option of investing an additional dollar in the progressive jackpot, which is entirely independent of the ante. Then the dealer distributes five cards to everyone, including herself. There are no draws, so what you are dealt is what you play. The only decision you have to make is whether or not your hand is likely to beat the dealer. If you think your cards are good enough to win, you may place an additional bet to stay in the running. If you think your hand is a loser, the best move is to fold and lose your ante.

Should your hand be a winner, and the dealer has a qualifying hand (more on that later), you will be paid in accordance with a basic bonus paytable; the better your hand, the higher the payoff. If you invested in the optional progressive side bet and are fortunate enough to get a royal flush, you will also win the progressive jackpot. A straight flush wins 10% of the amount on the progressive meter, while a lesser hand such as four-of-a-kind, a full house, or a flush is paid a fixed bonus, ranging from $50 to $500. As you can see, Caribbean Stud is a game based on bonus payouts. In fact, the two chances of collecting a bonus payment for each hand are the major attraction for most players.

FUNDAMENTALS OF PLAY

THE PLAYING TABLE

Caribbean Stud is played on a table that is very similar to a blackjack table and is usually located in or near the blackjack area. In most casinos it is easy to find because there is an elevated sign at the table identifying the game. The table has six or seven player positions around the curved side of the table (see illustration). The dealer stands at the flat side with a chip rack directly in front of her and a shuffling machine to her right. Most casinos use a Shuffle Master shuffling machine. It shuffles a single 52-card deck each time a new hand is dealt.

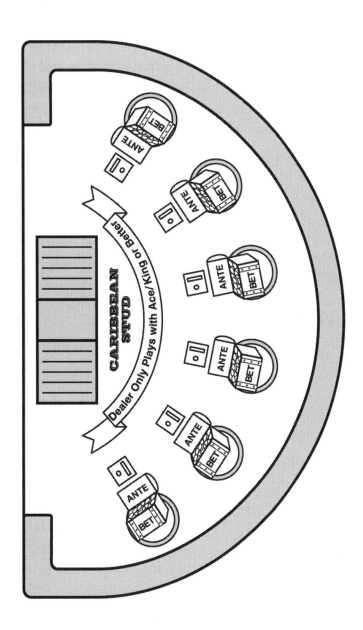

Caribbean Stud Table

There are two betting spots and a slot at each player position. The spot nearest the dealer, marked ANTE, is where the initial bets are placed. The other spot is marked BET. That is where you should put the second bet if, after viewing your dealt hand, you decide to continue playing. If you wish to participate in the progressive jackpot, you may place a $1 chip in the progressive slot located above the two betting spots.

HOW THE GAME IS PLAYED

The initial goal in Caribbean Stud is to get a better five card poker hand than the dealer. If that goal is met, and the dealer has a *qualifying* hand, the next goal is to get a strong enough hand to pay a basic bonus that is better than even odds. To be qualified, a dealer's hand must contain at least an ace and a king; this is explained more fully in the next section. If you invest a dollar in the progressive jackpot, the final goal is to get a flush or better hand, which will earn a progressive bonus payout. Or, better yet, to get a royal flush and win the entire progressive jackpot pool.

The game begins when everyone places their initial bets in the ANTE box. Most Caribbean Stud games have either a $5 or a $10 minimum bet requirement. At the same time, you may also place a dollar chip or coin in the progressive slot. This is entirely optional; however, if you do not invest the dollar, you will have no chance of winning a progressive bonus or the progressive jackpot. When all the bets have been placed, the dealer pushes a button causing the progressive bets to drop into a collection box. You'll then see a red light go on in front of those players who made the $1 bet and qualify for the progressive jackpot and bonuses. The ante bets stay in place on the table.

The dealer distributes five cards face down to each player. She also deals herself five cards face down and then turns one of her cards face up. The cards are usually dealt from a shuffling machine. Since you now have to make a strategy decision on the strength of your hand, the dealer's upcard is supposed to give you a clue as to how to proceed. Contrary to blackjack, this upcard only helps if you are willing to memorize very complex strategies.

You now have to decide if your hand is good enough to invest more money. This is the call or fold decision. If you believe your hand may beat the dealer, you can call (stay in the game) by placing an additional wager. This call bet is put in the BET box and must be exactly double the original ante. That is, if the ante was $5, then the additional bet must be $10, for a total investment of $15. After the call bet is placed, lay your cards face down to the left of the BET box. If you think your cards are not good enough to beat the dealer, you can avoid risking more money by folding your hand. This action forfeits the ante as well as the $1 progressive bet (if it was made).

After all the players have decided whether to call or fold, the dealer turns over her four downcards for everyone to see. If the dealer's hand is qualified, she turns over the active player's hands (those who didn't fold) one by one and pays off the winners. The amounts of the payoffs are based on the basic bonus paytable and depend on whether or not the dealer has a qualifying hand. In addition, those players who made the optional $1 progressive bet (and didn't fold), are paid in accordance with the progressive bonus paytable. The progressive payoff is not affected by the qualification status of the dealer's hand.

If the dealer's hand is not qualified and you made the call bet, you automatically win your ante bet at even odds, and your call bet is returned. No basic bonuses are paid; however, if you made the $1 progressive bet you will still be paid according to that paytable.

QUALIFYING THE DEALER
As was already mentioned, to be qualified the dealer's hand must

contain at least an ace and a king. Consequently, any pair or higher is also qualified, as well as straights, flushes, and straight flushes. The lowest qualified hand is A K 4 3 2, as shown below, which could be beat by a player holding A K 5 3 2 or better.

Lowest qualified dealer hand.

The highest *non*-qualifying hand is A Q J 10 9, as shown below. By the rules of poker, this is a lower hand than the minimum qualifying hand, because the second-highest card is a queen instead of a king.

Highest non-qualified dealer hand.

When the dealer has a qualifying hand, the game proceeds in a normal manner. That is, you have to beat the dealer's hand to win. When the dealer's hand is not qualified, the dealer folds and there is no competitive play. Regardless of how good a hand you hold, you only win the ante bet at even odds. In either case, if you made the $1 progressive bet *and didn't fold your hand,* you are paid according to the progressive jackpot and bonus paytable.

TABLE ETIQUETTE

As was said before, if you are new to a game just watch what the other players are doing and try to do the same. If you make a mistake in table protocol, the dealer will politely correct you.

The first thing you have to do is put out your ante wager. Place the bet directly on the ANTE box as soon as the dealer has collected all the cards from the previous round. Although it is not recommended, this is also the time to make the optional side bet by placing a $1 coin in the progressive slot.

After all the cards have been dealt, look at your five cards. Make your bet-or-fold decision quickly enough so as not to hold up the game. This is easy to do if you remember the strategy rules given in this chapter.

Since the players are supposed to hide their cards from each other until the dealer turns them over to determine the payoffs, you should make a reasonable attempt to shield them. This is simply an example of casino paranoia, because if you do get a glimpse of another player's hand, it won't be of much help in making the call-or-fold decision.

If you decide to fold, toss your cards (face down) toward the dealer. She will place them in the discard stack and remove your ante. If you decide to bet, place double the amount of your ante on the BET box and lay your cards face down next to the bet. Never touch your original ante wager. At this point you are done and the dealer takes over.

If the dealer's hand qualifies, the dealer will turn over each active player's cards, in turn, and make the appropriate payoffs. Should the dealer not qualify, she will simply collect the cards and pay the antes.

Important note: If you made the $1 progressive bet and your hand qualifies for a progressive bonus, you must be alert because some non-qualifying dealers may neglect to check your cards. To avoid being shortchanged, you must be ready to tell the dealer that you are a winner. Once your cards hit the discard stack, it is too late to prove that you won a bonus.

Tipping, of course, is a matter of personal preference. Instead of tipping a dealer directly, you may prefer to place a bet for the dealer. In Caribbean Stud, placing a bet for the dealer is discouraged because of the two-tier betting procedure. If you want to tip the dealer, it is easier to just toss her a chip.

THE PAYOFFS

THE BASIC BONUS

As mentioned earlier, how the payoffs in Caribbean Stud are handled depends on whether or not the dealer has a qualifying hand. When the dealer's hand is qualified, your hand is pitted against the dealer's and, if you win, you are paid in accordance with the basic bonus schedule. When the dealer's hand is not qualified, the dealer has effectively dropped out of the game and you are an automatic winner (if you didn't fold). However, you only win even odds on the ante bet, and the basic bonus paytable does not pay off.

Dealer's Hand Is Qualified: When the dealer's hand is qualified, your hand is compared against the dealer's. If the dealer's hand beats your hand, you lose both the ante and the call bet. If your hand beats the dealer's hand, you win both bets. The ante bet is paid even odds and the call bet is paid in accordance with the following paytable:

BASIC BONUS PAYTABLE	
Hand	Pays
Royal flush	100 to 1
Straight flush	50 to 1
Four of a find	20 to 1
Full house	7 to 1
Flush	5 to 1
Straight	4 to 1
Three-of-a-kind	3 to 1
Two pair	2 to 1
One pair or less	1 to 1

For example: Assume you start off with a $5 ante bet and are dealt three sevens plus two odd cards, as in the following hand:

Your hand

This looks like a good hand, so you stay in the game by placing a $10 call bet, which, according to the rules, is double the ante bet. The dealer turns over her cards and shows a pair of nines, which is a qualified hand.

Dealer's hand (qualified)

Since your three sevens beat the dealer's hand, you are paid $5 (even odds) for the ante and $30 (3 to 1 odds) for the call bet, winning a total of $35. You, of course, also get back your original investment of $15.

Tied Hands: When the player and the dealer have the same paying hand, such as a pair of sixes, the remaining cards are compared and the highest hand wins. If both hands have five identical cards (except for suit), the result is a push and no money changes hands.

Dealer's Hand Is Not Qualified: When the dealer's hand does not contain at least an ace-king, you automatically win the ante bet (at even odds), even if your hand is not as good as the dealer's. The call bet, however, becomes a push. That is, the call bet is returned to you with no additional payoff.

For example, assume, as before, that you start with a $5 ante bet and are dealt three sevens plus two odd cards, so you stay in the game by placing a $10 call bet. The dealer turns over her cards and shows an ace, a jack, and three small odd cards, which is not a qualified hand.

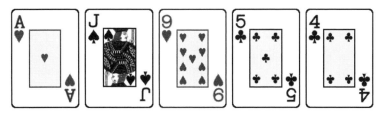

Dealer's hand (not qualified)

You are only paid $5 (even odds) for the ante and get nothing for the call bet of $10. So you win a total of $5 and also get back your original investment of $15.

This is the biggest disappointment in the game of Caribbean Stud, especially if you have a good hand. It basically means that if the dealer's hand is very weak, the casino gets off the hook by only paying off the ante bet—a very small penalty. This is the major failing of Caribbean Stud and has caused many players to gravitate to games that are more pleasant.

BASIC BONUS PAYOUT LIMIT

All casinos have a maximum dollar payout limit for the basic bonus. Depending on the casino, the limit can range from $5,000 to $50,000. This is actually a deceptive form of betting limit because, while they let you bet as much as you want (up to the table maximum, which can be quite high), they limit how much they will pay out if you win. The aggregate limit is usually stated on the same plaque that gives the table betting limits. If you don't see it, ask the dealer.

Suppose, that with a payout limit of $5,000, you make a $100 call bet and hit a royal flush. At 100 to 1 odds (per the basic bonus paytable), you should win $10,000; however, the casino will only pay you $5,000. What a bummer! To avoid being shortchanged on the payoff, never place a call bet that is more than one hundredth of the payout limit. For example, if the payout limit is $5,000, divide that number by 100 and keep your call bet to less than $50. Since the call bet is always twice the ante, the ante bet in this example should not exceed $25.

One bright note is that the payout limit only applies to the basic bonus. The progressive bonus (see below) does not have a limit because it pays predetermined dollar amounts.

THE PROGRESSIVE BONUS

The progressive bonus pays off whether or not the dealer's hand is qualified, so long as you placed $1 in the progressive slot at the start of the hand and you stayed in the hand by placing the call bet. Furthermore, you are paid *even if the dealer has a better hand*. This sounds marvelous, but it is only good for liberal payoff schedules and when the progressive meter gets quite high.

The Progressive Jackpot Meter that is located at the Caribbean Stud table is usually linked to all the Caribbean Stud games in that casino. Every time a player pays in a dollar, the meter goes a little bit higher. How fast it rises depends on how much of that dollar is added to the jackpot pool, and this depends on the particular casino. Some casinos put in as much as 75 cents, while the greedier ones may put in only about 50 cents out of every dollar collected.

In all casinos, a royal flush wins the entire progressive jackpot and a straight flush wins 10% of the amount on the progressive meter. A four-of-a-kind, a full house, or a flush will win a fixed dollar amount as defined on the progressive bonus paytable. The exact amount of these fixed bonuses varies from casino to casino, except in Atlantic City where the following paytable is prevalent.

PROGRESSIVE BONUS PAYTABLE FOR CARIBBEAN STUD (AC)	
Hand	**Pays**
Royal Flush	Full Jackpot
Straight Flush	10% of Jackpot
Four-of-a-kind	$500
Full House	$100
Flush	$50

If you want to invest in the progressive jackpot, you should search for the best payouts. Not only is the level of the progressive meter important, but the amount of the fixed payoffs can have a significant effect on the overall payback of the game. More specific information on these paytables is given in the section on playing strategy.

It should be noted that if two players got royal flushes on the same deal, the player nearest the dealer's left would get the full amount while the second player would get just the reset amount, which may be as low as $10,000 or $20,000. In some casinos, however, the progressive jackpot is split evenly between the winners. In the case of two straight flushes, the one nearest the dealer's left would get the full 10%, while the second winner would get 10% of what remained on the progressive meter after the first 10% was deducted. This should be of no great concern, however, since either event is highly unlikely. The other hands listed on the progressive paytable are always paid the full amount shown.

WINNING HANDS

The various card combinations that produce winning hands are the same as in regular poker. Caribbean Stud uses one 52-card deck with no wild cards. Suits have no relative value; they only come into play for a flush, a straight flush, or a royal flush. The importance of a hand depends on which of the following card combinations it contains, listed in order from the highest to the lowest:

Royal Flush: An ace-high straight flush is the highest-value hand in Caribbean Stud. The odds of being dealt a royal flush are 1 in 649,740 hands. Since suits do not have any relative value, two royal flushes of different suits constitute a tie. Since there is no record of this event ever having occurred, don't worry about it.

Straight Flush: Five consecutive cards, all of the same suit. The odds of being dealt a straight flush (excluding a royal flush) are 1 in 72,193 hands. Should the dealer and a player both have straight flushes, the hand containing the highest-ranking card is the winner. A king-high is the best straight flush. If both the dealer and player have identical straight flushes (except for the suit), then the dealer wins. The player will still win 10% of the progressive jackpot if the side bet was made. Should two players have straight flushes, and both made the side bet, the 10% jackpot is split.

Four-of-a-kind: Four cards of the same rank. The fifth card is unrelated to the others. The odds of being dealt four-of-a-kind are 1 in 4,165 hands. Should the dealer and a player both have four-of-a-kind, the one with the highest rank is the winner.

Full House: Three cards of the same rank and two cards of another rank, that is, three-of-a-kind and a pair. The odds of being dealt a full house are 1 in 694 hands. Should the dealer and a player both have a full house, the hand with the highest ranked three-of-a-kind is the winner. The ranks of the pairs are immaterial.

Flush: Five cards of the same suit, not in sequence. The odds of being dealt a flush are 1 in 509 hands. Should the dealer and a player both have flushes, the one containing the highest ranked card is the winner. If the highest ranked card in both hands is the same, then the second-highest ranked card is the tiebreaker. If that is also the same, then the third-, the fourth-, and the fifth-highest cards are compared. If all five cards in both hands are the same rank, the dealer wins.

Straight: Five consecutive cards of mixed suits. An ace may be either the lowest card as in A 2 3 4 5 or the highest card as in 10 J Q K A. The odds of being dealt a straight are 1 in 255 hands. Should the dealer and a player both have straights, the one containing the highest ranked card is the winner. If the highest ranked card in both hands is the same, the dealer wins.

Three-of-a-kind: Three cards of the same rank. The remaining two cards are unrelated. The odds of being dealt three-of-a-kind are about 1 in 47 hands. Should the dealer and a player both have three-of-a-kind, the one with the highest rank is the winner.

Two Pair: A pair of one rank and a pair of another rank. The fifth card is unrelated. The odds of being dealt two pair are about 1 in 21 hands. Should the dealer and a player both have two pair, the one with the highest-ranked pair is the winner. If the highest-ranked pair in both hands is the same, then the one having the highest-ranked second pair wins. If both pairs are the same rank, then the hand with the highest fifth card wins. If all cards are the same rank, the dealer wins.

One Pair: Two cards of the same rank. The three remaining cards are unrelated. The odds of being dealt a pair are about 1 in 2.4 hands. The highest-ranked pair wins. If two hands contain pairs of the same rank, then the one with the highest-ranked odd card wins. If that card is the same, then the fourth and fifth cards break the tie. If all cards are the same rank, the dealer wins.

Ace-King: A hand that contains none of the above poker hands, but does have one ace and one king, as shown below. The three remaining cards are unrelated. The odds of being dealt exactly one ace and one king (plus three mixed cards) is about 1 in 15 hands.

For the dealer, this is one of the lowest qualifying hands. If a player also has an ace-king hand, then the hand with the highest ranked of the remaining three cards wins. If all cards are the same rank, the dealer wins. The odds of being dealt an ace-king hand *or better* are about 1 in 1.8. The odds of being dealt an ace-king hand *or less* are 1 in 2. As you will see in the next section, these odds are important for determining the best playing strategy.

Low Cards: A hand that contains none of the above poker hands, but has mixed cards no higher than one ace and one queen. The odds of being dealt an ace-queen hand or lower are about 1 in 2.3 hands. This is a non-qualifying hand for the dealer. For the player, the hand has no value and should never be called.

PLAYING STRATEGY

From a statistical standpoint, Caribbean Stud is a negative expectation game. Unlike blackjack, there is no strategy that will overcome the house edge and make the game profitable for the player. Sure, you can simply wait until the progressive meter gets very, very high, but in most casinos the jackpot will have to exceed half a million dollars for the overall player expectation to become positive. So far this has never happened, but when and if it does, you will find it very difficult to get a seat at a Caribbean Stud table.

You must use some reasonable strategy when playing this game or you will deplete your bankroll very quickly. The Caribbean Stud player has three basic decisions to make: (1) How much money to ante, (2) whether or not to place the $1 progressive bet, and (3) whether to call (bet double the ante) or fold (lose the ante). Each of these three choices will have a major effect on how fast you will lose your money.

THE ANTE

The best approach in Caribbean Stud is to risk as little money as possible. Try to find a $5 table and only place the minimum bet. There is more than one reason for this strong recommendation. Being a negative expectation game, the heavier you bet, the more you will lose (barring a lucky streak). If this isn't enough to convince you, there is a second reason.

The big draw for most people who play Caribbean Stud is the progressive jackpot. And I agree that when the jackpot gets into the hundreds of thousands of dollars, it is a good time to invest in the $1 progressive bet. There is, however, an important point to keep in mind: *The progressive bonus and jackpot payoffs are exactly the same whether you placed a $5 ante or a $25 ante.* Why risk more money than you need to when the chance of making a good hand and the payoff for that hand have no bearing on the amount that you bet?

You also have to keep in mind when you ante, that you can't win anything unless you also place the call bet. That means a $5 ante turns into a $15 investment and a $25 ante turns into a $75 investment—*per hand*. You will fold your hand about half of the time, and each time you fold, you will lose your ante. It is better to lose $5 than to lose $25.

Finally, by placing a minimum ante bet, there is no chance that you will run up against the bonus payout limit. You wouldn't want to place a large bet, get a hot hand, and then be shortchanged on the payout. That would be a cruel blow.

THE PROGRESSIVE JACKPOT

One of the lures in Caribbean Stud is the possibility of getting a royal flush and winning the progressive jackpot, or winning lesser amounts for certain other hands. Entering the progressive jackpot pool is entirely optional; however, if you do not put up the dollar, you will have no chance of winning the progressive jackpot or one of the progressive bonuses.

The progressive bonuses and the progressive jackpot pay off whether or not the dealer's hand is qualified, so long as you placed $1 in the progressive slot at the start of the hand and you don't fold. If your hand is a flush, full house, or four-of-a-kind, you are paid a progressive bonus even if the dealer has a better hand. The same is true for a royal flush or a straight flush.

Investing in the progressive pool is only worthwhile when the progressive meter gets quite high. Following are examples of paytables showing the minimum jackpot needed for a positive expectation of winning. This positive expectation only applies to the progressive bonus or jackpot, not to the entire game. To overcome the house edge on the basic game, the progressive jackpot would have to reach levels that have never before been attained.

CARIBBEAN STUD PROGRESSIVE JACKPOT PAYTABLES			
Hand	No. 1	No. 2	No. 3	No. 4
Royal Flush	Full Jackpot	Full Jackpot	Full Jackpot	Full Jackpot
Straight Flush	10% Jackpot	10% Jackpot	10% Jackpot	10% Jackpot
Four-of-a-kind	$100	$150	$500	$500
Full House	$75	$100	$150	$100
Flush	$50	$50	$75	$50
Progressive Break even	$263,205	$246,784	$176,613	$218,047

Columns 1 to 3: Found in most Las Vegas casinos.

Column 4: Found in Atlantic City and Mississippi.

The calculations for the progressive break-even points were based on a $1 side bet. When you visit the casinos, you will see that the Caribbean Stud progressive meters don't get anywhere near the break-even points. The exact house edge for the progressive side bet (alone) depends on the amount of the jackpot, but it typically falls in the range of 25% to 30%.

TO CALL OR TO FOLD
The basic decision in playing Caribbean Stud is whether to call or to fold your hand. To begin with, all hands that contain at least one pair should always be called. In the fundamental strategy, the call/fold decision is boiled down to whether or not you have at least an A K J 8 3.

The Ace-King Hand: Since Caribbean Stud is a negative expectation game, limiting your losses is really the main strategy. To minimize your losses, the correct strategy advises that you should hold any hand that, in the long run, is likely to lose less than the amount of a forfeited ante.

Not taking the dealer's upcard into account, the poorest hand for which the expected long-term loss is less than the amount of the ante is an A K with a J 8 3, as shown below.

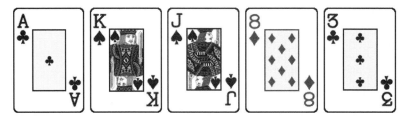

Lowest hand to continue playing.

This hand is the strategy breakpoint. You should call any hand that is an A K J 8 3 or better and fold any hand that is worse.

THE FUNDAMENTAL STRATEGY

Although there are several published strategies for Caribbean Stud, the one presented in this book is the easiest to learn. Other strategies take into account the dealer's upcard and can get quite complicated. Applying them only results in about a 0.1% improvement in the house edge. Furthermore, if you misapply a more complex strategy, you may be worse off. Following are the three easy-to-remember rules of the fundamental strategy.

Rule 1. Never ante more than the table minimum. The lowest table minimum you are likely to find is $5. Try to play at those tables.

Rule 2. Never bet on the progressive jackpot. Even disregarding the house edge, 99 percent of the time, investing $1 in the progressive jackpot is a negative expectation gamble. Avoid risking your money until the meter approaches the positive expectation breakpoint, which is a rare occurrence.

Rule 3. Call any hand containing an A K J 8 3 or better. Otherwise, fold. This means that you should also call when you have any pair or better. There is some benefit to playing other Ace-King hands, but you have to learn more complicated rules, and the advantage is very small. If you misapply the other rules, you may be worse off than if you just stick to the A K J 8 3 rule.

The fundamental playing strategy is summarized in the following chart:

THE FUNDAMENTAL PLAYING STRATEGY
FOR CARIBBEAN STUD POKER

Rule 1: Never ante more than the table minimum.

Rule 2: Never bet on the progressive jackpot.

Rule 3: Call any **A K J 8 3** hand or better. Otherwise, fold.

CONCLUSION

Caribbean Stud is an enigma. Although it has an excessive house edge of 5.3% and a progressive jackpot that seldom gets high enough to be worth playing, it somehow maintains its popularity. The most annoying aspect of the game is that the dealer may get off the hook by not qualifying when you finally get a good hand that should pay a nice bonus. Yet, many people do seem to enjoy playing it.

While watching the game, I have rarely seen a player who does not invest a dollar in the progressive, especially when the meter exceeds $100,000. Of course, most of them haven't a clue as to where the expectation breakpoint might be. For many people, risking one dollar on the chance of winning $100,000 or more is too much to resist, even if they know the positive expectation breakpoint is over $200,000. The state lotteries are played for the same reasons.

·9·
CASINO WAR

This is a silly little game offered by many of the larger casinos. It is similar to the one by the same name that you played as a small child on a rainy day when you couldn't find anything better to do.

Casino War is a simple card-matching game. One card is dealt to the player and one to the dealer. The cards are compared, and the higher card wins. The game gets slightly more exciting if a tie occurs. Then the player has the option of raising and two more cards are dealt. Again, the cards are compared and the higher card wins all.

FUNDAMENTALS OF PLAY

Casino War is played on a table that is very similar to a blackjack table. It is easy to find because there is an elevated sign at the table identifying the game.

One or more standard 52-card decks may be used, although most casinos use a six-deck shoe. Standard card rankings are applied, where the deuce is low and the ace is always high. Suits have no relative value.

The players must first make initial wagers. At this time, they may also make a side bet as to whether or not the hand will result in a tie. Most tables have a $5 minimum bet requirement.

Each player is dealt one card and the dealer also gets one card. When everyone has their cards, the player's cards are compared, in turn, with the dealer's. If you beat the dealer, you win even money. That is, if your initial wager was $5, you get back your initial bet plus $5. If the dealer's card is higher, you lose.

Whenever a tie occurs, if you made the tie side bet, you are paid 10 to 1. You also have two options as to how to play your hand. You can (1) fold your hand and forfeit half of your initial wager or (2) "go to war." If you decide to go to war, you must put up an additional wager equal to your initial wager, which the dealer matches.

The dealer then proceeds with an absurd procedure in which she burns three cards, deals one to you, burns three more cards, and deals one to herself. If you win on the second two cards, you get back both your bets, plus the dealer's matching bet. This amounts to a push on your first bet and an even-money payoff on your second bet. If you lose the hand, you lose all your bets.

If the second pair of cards is also a tie, you win the hand and get a bonus equal to your initial wager.

Let's say your first bet was $10 and the play resulted in a tie. If you fold, it will cost you $5 (half of your bet). If, instead, you decide to go to war, you have to put up a second bet of $10. The dealer will match it with $10 and deal two more cards. Should you lose this hand, you lose both bets ($20). If you win, you get back both of your bets ($20) plus the $10 put up by the dealer for the second bet. You also win if there is another tie, in which case you will be paid a bonus of $10.

WAR STRATEGY

The only strategy in this game is whether to go to war when a tie occurs, and whether to make the tie side bet. These decisions can be easily resolved by looking at the house edge for each option.

WAGER	HOUSE EDGE
Go to war on ties	2.9%
Forfeit half of bet on ties	3.7%
Make tie side bet	18.7%

The above chart makes it clear that you should never make the tie side bet and when a tie occurs, you should always go to war.

Understandably, this game is not very popular. Most Casino War tables just sit there with a bored dealer and no players. It is a dull little game that doesn't even have a big jackpot to keep you interested.

◆10◆
CRAPS

Of the many kinds of games available in casinos, craps is, without a doubt, the fastest and most exciting of them all. The game is favored by players who want fast action and the opportunity to make a variety of wagers whenever they want to. Not only that, but when the odds bet is properly utilized, the house advantage is the lowest to be found anywhere—less than half a percent.

So, how can the casino earn money on a game with such a low house edge? Just as in many other casino games, most players don't know how to take advantage of the odds and tend to make sucker bets on which the house earns a high percentage. Many people use a willy-nilly betting approach and don't have a rational, thought-out playing strategy. This is because they never learned how to play the game properly.

OBJECT OF THE GAME

Craps players have many betting options. They may bet with the dice, against the dice, or they may bet for or against particular numbers coming up. The most fundamental craps wager, however, is called the **pass-line wager**, which is a bet that the dice will **pass**.

The initial roll of the dice in a hand is called the **come-out**. The number that appears on that first roll produces one of the following three results.

1. If the number is a 7 or 11, which is called a **natural**, the pass-line bettor wins immediately, and the hand is over. The next roll is a new come-out.

2. If the number is a 2, 3, or 12, which is called **craps**, the pass-line bettor loses immediately and the hand is over. The next roll is a new come-out.

3. If the number is any one of the remaining numbers (4, 5, 6, 8, 9, or 10), it is called **the point**. There is, at this roll, no win/lose resolution for line bets, and the hand continues.

Now, the shooter's goal is to repeat the point number before rolling a 7. If the point appears first, it is called **making the point**, and the pass wager wins. If the 7 is rolled before the point is repeated, it is called **sevening-out**, and the pass wager loses. Although other bets can be made on any of the numbers, in terms of the pass wager, the point and the 7 are the only numbers that have any meaning and the hand proceeds until one or the other of those numbers appears on the dice.

While the shooter is rolling the dice, either during the come-out or while attempting to repeat the point, there are dozens of other wagers that can be made for or against specific numbers or groups of numbers. Some of these wagers are good and some are strictly sucker bets. All of them will be described in full detail.

FUNDAMENTALS OF PLAY

THE EQUIPMENT
The implements used for playing craps in a casino include a table with high sides and a layout showing the various craps wagers, a pair of dice, and a puck for identifying the established point. These items are described below.

The craps table: Unlike other table games, craps tables vary considerably in size. The typical craps table accommodates 16 to 20 standing players, and is manned by a crew of four: a stickman, two inside dealers, and a boxman. The largest tables, which can handle up to 24 players, often have two boxmen. Occasionally, you may find a very small table that is run by a single dealer and accommodates 8 or 9 seated players.

Regardless of size, all craps tables have high sides to contain the action of the dice. At both ends, the inside surfaces of the sides are covered with diamond-embossed rubber. This is where the thrown dice are supposed to bounce to assure a fair roll. The central portion of the long side opposite the boxman is mirrored so that he can easily see the opposite faces of the dice to ascertain that someone didn't switch in misspotted cubes.

The tops of the sides have rails with convenient grooves for holding the player's chips. Lower down on the outside is a ledge for holding drinks and ashtrays.

The layout: The felt surface of the craps table carries the imprinted betting layout, which has numerous boxes and spaces for placing wagers. To a newcomer, the layout may seem very complex, but as the nature and purpose of the various bets are explained, it will eventually become clear and logical. A typical double-ended craps layout is shown on the next page.

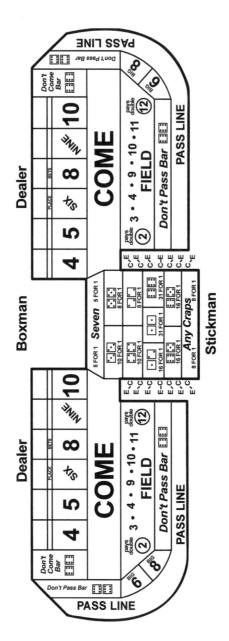

The Layout of a Craps Table

Almost all craps tables are double-ended, meaning that the layout is duplicated at both ends of the table to make the betting areas easier to reach by all the players. These end sections contain the most important and useful bets on the table. Between the two end sections is a large box containing the center bets, also known as the proposition bets, all of which are controlled by the stickman.

The dice: Modern casino dice are precision cubes made of cellulose acetate. Most dice have flush number spots. To maintain the correct weight and balance, each spot is slightly recessed and filled with a colored paint that is the same weight as the material that was removed. Casino dice have sharp edges rather than the rounded edges found on backgammon or home-game dice.

Standard casino dice in most of the world are 0.750-inch wide, but a few casinos may use slightly smaller dice. Each cube is usually embossed with the casino logo and a code number to make it difficult for cheats to switch in dishonest dice.

Each of the dice has six faces, and each one of the faces has one through six spots. The game of craps uses a pair of dice, so the possible numbers that can be rolled are 2 through 12.

The puck: A round plastic disk, black on one side and white on the other, is used to indicate when a point is established. This disk is called a **puck**, although in the past it has sometimes been called a buck. During a come-out roll the black side of the puck, which is marked with the word OFF, is lying face up. When a point number is rolled, the puck is turned over and placed at the appropriate numbered box to remind everyone which point was established. The white side of the puck (marked ON) is now facing up. The puck remains in this position until the point is made or the shooter sevens-out, whereupon it is removed from the number box and flipped to its black side.

The Two Sides of a Puck

THE PERSONNEL

The boxman: The fact that he wears a coat and tie instead of a dealer's uniform, makes it obvious that the boxman is the table supervisor. He sits at the center of the table with stacks of chips in front of him. To his immediate left and right are the inside dealers, and directly across the table from him is the stickman. When there is a big crowd at a large table, two boxmen often sit side-by-side, each one handling his end of the table.

The boxman oversees the entire game and settles any disputes that may arise. He controls the chips in the table bank and verifies that payouts by the dealers are made accurately. He also checks the dice and may disallow a bad roll.

The inside dealers: The double-ended craps layout requires a dealer to handle each end; thus, there are two inside dealers, one at each side of the boxman. While playing craps, the inside dealer at your end of the table is the employee with whom you will have most of your interactions. The inside dealer has a number of duties.

This dealer handles all your chip transactions. He will convert your cash into chips or change your chip denominations.

- He pays all winners and collects all losing bets, other than for the center bets.

- He properly positions come and don't come bets as well as the place bets, and returns wagers that are taken down by a player.
- He is responsible for positioning the puck on his half of the layout.
- He answers your questions about the various wagers.

The stickman: Standing directly across the table from the boxman is the stickman. He is easy to spot because he is always holding a long dice stick for handling the dice. Aside from returning the dice to the shooter, the only dealings he has with the players are the handling of the center bets.

The stickman's main duty is to control the dice. He uses his stick to push a selection of dice toward a new shooter so that the shooter can choose two of them for his come-out roll. After each throw, he slides the dice back to the center of the table and announces the number that was rolled, along with some appropriate comment about the result. He waits until everyone has placed their new wagers and then pushes the pair of dice over to the shooter.

A good stickman will maintain a continuous stream of patter to liven up the game. If a 7 is rolled on the come-out, he may say, "Seven, winner on the pass line, pass line bettors win." After announcing the result of a roll, he will often encourage players to place bets that are favorable for the house, such as the field or the hardways. When a point is established, he might say something like, "Point is eight, easy eight, make your come bets."

The floor supervisor: The person in the pit who is observing the overall action at the craps table is the floor supervisor. His job is to extend credit and to keep track of the betting levels of various players so he has a basis for giving out comps. He also keeps an eye out for cheating and other irregularities.

The pit boss: At the top of the pecking order in a craps pit is the pit boss. The pit boss watches the floor supervisor, who watches the box-man, who watches the dealers, who watch the players.

THE SHOOTER

The **shooter** is the player who throws the dice. Every player at the table wins or loses according to the number that appears on the dice, regardless of who threw them. The dice move around the table in a clockwise direction, so that everyone gets a turn to shoot. Whenever a player is offered the dice, he may either shoot them or give them up to the player on his left. There is no particular advantage or disadvantage to shooting the dice and there is no stigma attached to relinquishing them.

Before a shooter first rolls the dice, and before every succeeding come-out, he is required to make a line bet, which may be either a pass or don't pass wager.

It is rare for a shooter to make a don't pass wager because most people would rather not bet against themselves. Consequently, some confirmed don't pass bettors will give up their turn to shoot the dice.

A new shooter has to select a pair of dice from the several, usually five or six, that the stickman offers. The shooter, after placing his line bet, must then throw the dice so that they both bounce against the farthest wall of the table. Requiring the dice to bounce against the wall assures a random throw. If one or both dice don't bounce, the boxman has the option of declaring a bad roll by calling out, "No roll." In that case, all bets are off. A shooter who persistently underthrows the dice may lose his turn.

Should one of the dice land on a top rail or bounce clean off the table, it is automatically considered a bad roll and all bets are off. If one of the dice ends up leaning against a chip or against the table wall, the number counted is the one showing on the most horizontal surface. In most cases, the actual criterion used by the boxman is that he imagines how the dice would fall if the obstacle were removed.

If a point was established on the come-out roll, the shooter's turn continues until he sevens out. That is, he cannot lose his turn on the come-out and continues to shoot so long as he keeps making his points. However, he may give up the dice voluntarily any time that he has not established a new point, such as right before a new come-out. The only time a shooter *must* give up the dice is when he sevens out while trying to make his point. The dice then pass to the player on his left.

Other than the clockwise rotation of the dice, there is no further protocol for determining the next shooter. Thus, a new player may select any open spot and step up to a table, even if that makes him the next shooter.

THE COME-OUT ROLL

A craps hand consists of two phases: the come-out and the point phase. The start of every craps hand is the **come-out** roll. If a natural (7 or 11) or craps (2, 3, or 12) is rolled on the come-out, the hand is concluded and there is no point phase. Any other number appearing on the come-out establishes a point, and the hand continues into the point phase (see the following section).

When a natural (7 or 11) is rolled on the come-out, all players who bet that the dice will pass (made a pass-line bet) immediately win their bets, while players who bet against the shooter (made a don't-pass bet) lose. When craps (2, 3, or 12) is rolled on the come-out, the reverse is true: all pass-line bettors lose and all don't-pass bettors win (except that the 12 is a push, which will be explained later). The winning line wagers are paid even money.

If a shooter rolls craps during the come-out, he retains possession of the dice. To lose the dice, a shooter has to first enter the point phase of the hand by rolling a point number, and then has to seven-out while attempting to repeat the point.

A Note on Terminology: To a craps dealer, the term "natural" means any number that resolves the line bets on a come-out roll, that is, a 2, 3, 7, 11, or 12. To most players, the term means a pass on the come-out, that is, a 7 or 11, and most authors of craps books also define a natural as a 7 or 11, which is the definition that will be used in this chapter.

THE POINT PHASE

When any number other than a natural or craps is rolled on the come-out, that number becomes the point. The point number may be a 4, 5, 6, 8, 9, or 10. When one of these numbers is rolled on the come-out, the line bettors neither win nor lose; their bets are unresolved and remain in place on the layout.

For a pass-line bettor to win during the point phase, the established point number has to appear a second time before a 7 is rolled. Thus, it may take only one or two rolls, or it may take many, many rolls to resolve the line bets by repeating the point or tossing a 7. During this time, any other numbers that appear have no effect on the status of the line wagers. If a 7 appears before the point is repeated, the pass-line bettors lose. If the point is thrown before a 7 appears, the pass-line bettors win.

For example, if the first roll is a 3, the pass-line bettors lose, but the shooter retains the dice and throws another come-out. If the second come-out is a 6, that becomes the point. Should the third roll be another 3, the only winners would be a field bet or a bet on 3 (which will be explained later), but the 3 has no effect on the pass-line wagers. A fourth roll of 6 makes the point and the pass-line bettors win.

After winning the first point, the same shooter now rolls a 9 for a new come-out point. Then, after rolling a 2 and a 10, neither of which affect the line bets, the shooter rolls a 7. The pass-line bettors lose and the shooter loses possession of the dice.

BASIC CRAPS SUMMARY
- First roll by a new shooter is come-out
- If come-out is a 7 or 11, pass-line bettors win.
- If come-out is 2, 3, or 12, pass-line bettors lose.
- A come-out of 4, 5, 6, 8, 9, or 10 is the point.
- On subsequent rolls, if the point is repeated before a 7 appears, pass-line bettors win.
- If a 7 appears first, pass-line bettors lose.

PLAYING IN THE CASINO

SELECTING A TABLE

Just as with any other casino game, it is important that you select a table with reasonable care. Stepping up to a table and throwing out your money without first checking the limits and playing conditions may seem like a cool move, but it could prove expensive.

Table limits: Except for downtown Las Vegas where some casinos will still take a $1 bet, craps tables usually have a minimum limit of at least $5. Know ahead of time how much you intend to wager and find a table with appropriate limits. If you can't find a table with a low enough limit to fit your playing budget, go to another casino. Playing at a limit higher than you intended can be financially disastrous.

Table ambience: Before putting your chips or money down at any craps table, stand back and watch the action for a few minutes. The table should feel comfortable to you and not so crowded that you would have to squeeze into a small space. Unless you are only there to watch, avoid a table populated with overbearing and obnoxious characters.

OBTAINING CHIPS

Although you can place a bet with cash, the casino prefers the use of chips. To get chips, put your money on the table in front of a dealer and tell him what denominations you want. Don't drop a $100 bill on the table and ask for $50 in chips and $50 change. A casino craps table does not deal in cash—all cash is shoved into a slot in front of the boxman and drops into a strongbox that is mounted under the table. If you have a $100 bill and want only $50 in chips, go to the cashier's cage where they will accommodate you.

If you need to change the denomination of the chips you already have, put them near the dealer and ask for a color change. You should never hand money or chips directly to a dealer, and he will never hand chips directly to you. By first placing the money or chips on the table, the surveillance camera can properly monitor the transaction. Be careful, however, not to toss your chips onto the table, getting them mixed-in with the chips already there.

The craps table has grooves on the top rail where you can store your chips. It is your responsibility to protect your own chips. Just as there are occasional pickpockets, there are people around who watch for inattentive players and will swipe unmonitored chips. Be sure to guard your chips just as if they were real money, which they are. When you are finished playing, you can convert your chips back to currency at the cashier's cage.

THE WAGERS

There are over three dozen different wagers that can be made in a casino craps game. Some of these bets are good, some are not very good, and some are terrible. An overview of the various craps wagers is given below. Later, these wagers are described in considerable detail so that you can tell the good from the bad.

Pass bet: This is not only the most fundamental wager on the craps table, but with a house edge of 1.41%, most players consider it the best bet. The pass bet, which is made immediately before a come-out roll, is a bet that the dice will pass (win). It is called a **contract bet** because it cannot be removed until it is either won or lost. A 7 or 11 rolled on the come-out is a pass bet winner, while the 2, 3, and 12 are losers. Any other number is the point, which has to be repeated before a 7 appears for the pass bet to win. After the come-out roll, an additional odds bet can be taken, the details of which are described later.

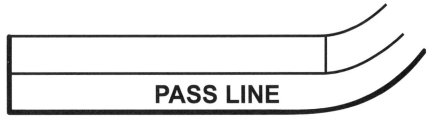

The Pass Line

Come bet: Except for the timing, a come bet is similar to a pass wager, with the same house edge. It is also a contract bet and can be made at any time except before a come-out. This results in a different point (than for the pass bet) being established, which has to be repeated before a 7 appears in order to win. Like the pass bet, the first roll of a come bet is won if a 7 or 11 appears, and is lost if a 2, 3, or 12 appears. Any other number is the point for that come bet. Odds can also be taken on a come bet.

Don't pass bet. This is essentially the opposite of a pass bet; it is a bet against the dice. It loses when the pass bet wins and it wins when the pass bet loses, except that the 12 is a push. That is what is meant on the layout where it says "Bar 12." The reason for this is explained later. An odds bet is also allowed on a don't pass wager.

The Don't Pass Line

Don't come bet: The don't come bet loses when a come bet made at the same time wins, and it wins when the come bet loses, except that the 12 is a push. An odds bet can be added to a don't come wager.

Place bet: This wager is very similar to a pass bet, except that there is no come-out and the point is chosen by the bettor. When you make this wager, you are betting that the place number you bet on will be rolled before a 7. The choice of numbers are the ones in the six place number boxes on the layout, namely, 4, 5, 6, 8, 9, and 10. **Buy bets** and **lay bets** are versions of place bets that are explained later.

		PLACE	BETS		
4	**5**	*SIX*	**8**	*NINE*	**10**

Place Number Boxes

Field bet: This wager, which is displayed prominently across the layout, covers the numbers 2, 3, 4, 9, 10, 11, and 12 in a single bet. The field bet is a **one-roll bet** that one of these numbers will appear at the next roll of the dice. If one of the four missing numbers, 5, 6, 7, or 8, is rolled, you lose the bet. This is not a good bet because the losing numbers are much more likely to appear.

The Field Wager Box

Big 6 and big 8 bets: Most craps layouts have two boxes at each end marked BIG 6 and BIG 8. A wager in one of these boxes means you are betting that a 6 (or 8) will appear before 7. If you win, the bet pays even money, which isn't enough to make it a fair bet.

The Big 6 and Big 8 Boxes

Proposition bets: These are mainly long-shot bets with high payoffs, which is why many players make them. The prop bets are all located in the center section of the layout and are controlled by the stickman. You simply toss him your chips and tell him which bet to put them on, and if you're a winner, he pays you. The house edge for these bets ranges from 9.1% to 16.7%, which makes them the worst bets on the craps layout.

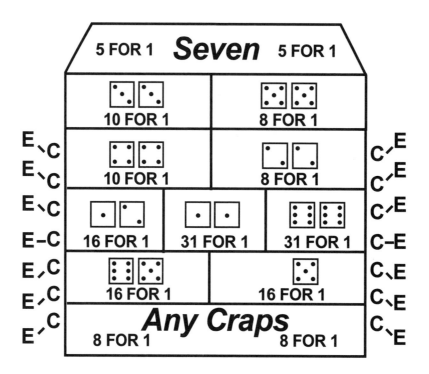

The Center Bets

MAKING WAGERS

There are three ways to place a wager. Choose which method to use depending on the bet. Some bets are positioned by the player, some by the inside dealer, and some by the stickman, and you should know which is which.

Bets placed by player: The player positions all wagers from the COME box down to the PASS LINE. These bets include pass, don't pass, come, don't come, field, big 6, and big 8. They are the only bets on the layout that can be set up by a player without the assistance of a dealer or stickman.

Bets placed by dealer: The inside dealer sets up all wagers above the COME box, which are primarily the place bets. Once come bets and don't come bets have been moved to a number box by the dealer, the player may not touch them. These boxes are controlled by the dealer so he can position the chips in such a way that he knows who made the bet.

Bets placed by stickman: The stickman controls and pays off all the wagers in the center section. These bets include the hardways and one-roll proposition bets.

Call bets: A call bet is when you tell a dealer what you want to bet, but, for one reason or another, there are no chips on the table. On some layouts there is a printed rule that says *No Call Bets*, which means that oral bets are not allowed—the chips have to be on the table. This rule, however, is not strictly enforced. You might, for example, throw down a $100 bill, telling the dealer you want to put $10 on the pass line. If the dealer doesn't have enough time to obtain the chips from the boxman and verify the count before the come-out roll, he will say, "You're covered." After the dice are rolled, he will give you your chips plus any winnings, or subtract $10 from your change if the bet lost.

Taking down bets: Should you change your mind about a bet that has not yet been resolved (has not yet won or lost), and would like to remove it, simply ask the dealer to "take down my bet." You are allowed to take down any bets on the layout except the pass or the come bets, which have to remain in effect until they are resolved. There are no restrictions, however, on removing any odds bets that you may have added to your pass or come wagers.

Turning bets OFF and ON: If you want to temporarily call off a bet, instead of taking it down, you may ask the dealer to turn it off, and at a later time ask him to turn it on again. When you ask for a bet to be turned off, be sure the dealer heard your request by checking that he placed an OFF button on top of your bet. Then, when you want it to be active again, tell the dealer and he will remove the OFF button. Most wagers on the layout can be turned off. The only exceptions are the pass line and come bets.

Pressing bets: If you have just won a bet and you want the winnings to ride, tell the dealer to "press my bet." He will interpret this to mean that you want to double your bet, so he will add an equal amount of your winnings to your original bet and return the difference to you. For instance, if you won a $10 place bet on the 9, the payoff is $14. The dealer will add $10 to your original bet and return $4 to you.

ROLLING THE DICE

As explained earlier, every player has the right to throw the dice when it is their turn. Possession of the dice rotates around the table in a clockwise direction, and if a player declines to roll, the dice are passed to the next player in the rotation. All players at the table win or lose their bets according to the numbers that appear on the dice, regardless of who the shooter was.

After the shooter makes the required line wager, the stickman will offer him five or six dice, from which he has to select two. Both dice must then be thrown together so that they strike the far wall of the table. The stickman announces the number that was rolled and slides the dice to the center of the table. After the bets are settled and new bets are made, the stickman slides the two dice back over to the shooter, so that the shooter can roll again. The hand continues in this manner until the shooter sevens out. The dice are then offered to a new shooter.

Tossing the dice is not difficult. Simply pick them up *with one hand* and lob them in a shallow arc toward the far wall of the table. Do not use two hands or you may be suspected of switching dice. For the same reason, do not rub the dice against any part of your body or your clothing. Always keep the dice in plain view. These handling rules are for the protection of all the players.

The casino wants the dice to strike the far wall of the table to assure a random throw. If they don't reach the wall, the shooter will be gently admonished, but the roll will usually stand. If it happens a second time, the roll will probably be disallowed by the boxman. You'll know this when he says, "No roll—all bets off."

Often, a new player who was previously admonished for a short roll, will now throw the dice too hard so that one or both may bounce off the table. When this happens, the stickman will offer up the remaining dice so that the shooter can select two new ones. At this point, one or more players may call out, "Same dice." These superstitious players are asking you to request the same dice as the ones you had been rolling. Unless you are also superstitious, I recommend you don't do it because it will only hold up the game. Before the two original dice can be returned to you, the boxman has to first verify the logo and the serial numbers, and then has to check them very carefully for balance and other characteristics to be sure that misspotted or loaded dice weren't switched in. This process may take several minutes, during which time the game is stopped.

A good way to toss the dice is to visualize a coffee mug or a small cereal dish sitting on the table about a foot in front of the far wall. You try to lob (not too high) the dice into the dish without bouncing them out. By doing this, the toss will be easy enough not to leave the table, but will still have enough forward momentum to hit the wall.

TABLE ETIQUETTE

In the game of craps, there are several things to consider when it comes to table etiquette. The main thing is to avoid any action that might interfere with the shooter or slow down the flow of the game. It is also very important not to do or say anything that could upset other players. Craps players tend to be superstitious, especially the old-timers, and there are certain protocols that you need to be aware of. To keep from being reproved by a dealer or getting nasty stares from other players, be sure you remember the following rules.

Don't rely on the dealer. Before you step up to a table, know what you are doing. Although dealers can be very helpful, don't depend on or expect help, especially at a crowded table.

Try to be reasonably neat. Don't put your drink on the table or drop cigarette ashes on the felt. There is a shelf under the chip rack for those items.

Keep your opinions to yourself. Be friendly and enthusiastic, but avoid interacting with players you do not know. Do not give advice or criticize someone's bets or betting style.

Buy in at the appropriate time. The best time to buy in or change color is right after the bets from the last roll are paid and before the stickman slides the dice over to the shooter. At any other time, you will probably be ignored because you are interfering with the game. The *worst* time to buy in is the moment the stickman asks if you wish to shoot. Fumbling through your wallet, you pull out some bills, and wait until the boxman counts your money. This stalls the game.

Make your bets promptly. The time to bet is when the dice are sitting in front of the boxman and the stickman calls out, "Place your bets." If you wait until the stickman gives the dice to the shooter, your bet may be disallowed. You'll know this when you hear, "No bet." When there is money involved, there can be no ambiguity on a bet—every wager has to be clear and understandable.

Don't interfere with the shooter. When the stickman slides the dice over to the shooter, get your hands out of the table. Have your bets down before the shooter is given the dice. If the dice hit your hand and the result is a seven-out, guess who gets blamed? YOU! You can argue that all you did was randomize the throw a little more, but all the hostility will still be directed at you.

Don't interact with the shooter. The other players will always perceive anything you do to distract the shooter, such as touching or talking, in a negative way. They believe anything that breaks the shooter's concentration can result in a bad roll. This includes any form of encouragement or a request for a particular number.

Never say seven. Never utter the word "seven," especially after the come-out. It is considered bad form and bad luck. Since most players will lose if a seven is rolled after the come-out, it is an unmentionable number. The dealers, however, are exempt from this rule.

Don't hold up the game. Throw the dice as soon as you get them. Don't waste time fiddling with them. Don't turn around and announce to your friends what number you are going to roll. This is not about you—there are other players at the table who are invested in this hand. If the stickman urges, "Please pick up the dice and shoot them," he's acting for everyone at the table.

Hit the far wall. You may get away with a short roll once, but you will be requested to hit the wall the next time you throw. The casino wants to assure everyone that the roll is random and that they are running an honest game. Throw hard enough to reach the wall, but don't throw so hard that the dice knock down stacks of chips or bounce off the table.

Keep a low profile when making don't bets. Above all, keep your mouth shut. Remember, you are (seemingly) betting against most of the players at the table, even though you are really betting against the house.

THE DICE COMBINATIONS

Craps is played with a pair of standard six-sided dice. Each of the six sides has one or more spots representing the numbers 1 through 6. Thus, each of the dice can be rolled in six different ways, the lowest number being 1 and the highest being 6. When two dice are rolled, the spots on the uppermost surfaces are added together to obtain the final number; the lowest is 2, and the highest is 12. The total number of combinations that can be produced by two dice is 36.

Although one pair of dice can produce the numbers 2 through 12, the probability of rolling each of these numbers is not the same. The diagram on the next page gives the different possible ways each number can be rolled, which is the basis for figuring the probabilities in craps.

CRAPS

NUMBER	WAYS	COMBINATIONS
2	ONE	
3	TWO	
4	THREE	
5	FOUR	
6	FIVE	
7	SIX	
8	FIVE	
9	FOUR	
10	THREE	
11	TWO	
12	ONE	

Possible Dice Combinations

Of the many combinations that can be made by the two dice, some numbers are more likely to appear than others. For instance, a 2 can be made only when both dice show a single spot, and a 12 can only be made with a 6+6. On the other hand, a seven can be made with 1+6, 2+5, 3+4, 4+3, 5+2, and 6+1, a total of six different ways.

Some people have the mistaken belief that a 7 can only be made three ways: 1+6, 2+5, and 3+4. They don't take into account that the numbers on the two dice can be reversed, and that produces three additional ways. To make this clearer in the above diagram, each pair of dice is shown as one black and one white. In this way, it is more obvious that a 1+6, for example, can also be rolled as a 6+1.

REMEMBERING THE COMBINATIONS

When you examine the chart of dice combinations, note the symmetry on either side of the 7. The number of ways to roll a 6 is the same as an 8, a 5 is the same as a 9, and a 4 is the same as a 10. Furthermore, if you look at the numbers 7 and below, the ways to roll are exactly one less than the number itself. That is, a 2 can be rolled one way, a 3 can be rolled two ways, a 4 can be rolled three ways, on up to a 7, which can be rolled six different ways. The numbers higher than 7 are simply the complements of the lower numbers. For instance, the 4 and 10 can each be rolled three different ways: 1+3, 2+2, and 3+1 for a 4, and 4+6, 5+5, and 6+4 for a 10.

Now, if you memorize the five symmetrical pairs: 2-12, 3-11, 4-10, 5-9, and 6-8, you can easily remember the ways to roll any number. It is always one less than the lower of the complementary pair.

FIGURING THE ODDS

With a pair of dice, there are a total of 36 possible combinations, so the ways of making and not making a particular number on a single roll have to add up to 36. Since there are four ways to make a 5, there are 32 ways of not making a 5 (36 minus 4). That means the odds of rolling a 5 are 4 in 36, and the odds against rolling a 5 are 32 to 4, or 8 to 1. The odds against making any other number is figured in the same way, and the results are shown on the following chart.

ODDS ON THE NEXT ROLL			
Number	Ways to Roll	Odds	Odds Against
2	1	1 in 36	35 to 1
3	2	1 in 18	17 to 1
4	3	1 in 12	11 to 1
5	4	1 in 9	8 to 1
6	5	5 in 36	6.2 to 1
7	6	1 in 6	5 to 1
8	5	5 in 36	6.2 to 1
9	4	1 in 9	8 to 1
10	3	1 in 12	11 to 1
11	2	1 in 18	17 to 1
12	1	1 in 36	35 to 1

To figure the odds of rolling any one of a group of numbers, add together the ways all of the desired numbers can be rolled to determine the number of ways to win. For instance, to win on the come-out, you have to roll a 7 or 11. Since a 7 can be made six ways and an 11 can be made two ways, there are eight ways to win and 28 ways (36 minus 8) to roll craps or a point. Thus, the odds of winning on the come-out are 8 in 36, which can be reduced to 1 in 4. The odds against winning on the come-out are 28 to 8, or 7 to 2, or 3.5 to 1.

The above numbers are **correct odds**, which are different than the numbers on a craps layout. When a casino pays off a winning bet, they don't pay correct odds because they expect to make a profit. Instead, they pay **house odds**, which are slightly poorer than the correct odds. See Chapter 4 for a more complete explanation of house odds and house edge.

THE PASS LINE AND COME WAGERS

The line bets are those based on the fundamental premise of the game of craps, in which the shooter establishes a point and then tries to repeat it before rolling a 7. The two line bets are called the pass and the don't pass wagers. These wagers are the best bets on the table in terms of low house advantage.

THE PASS LINE WAGER

The **pass line** wager is the most basic bet on any craps table. A person making a pass wager is betting that the shooter makes his point. He would also win if the shooter rolled a 7 or 11 on the come-out, and lose if he rolled a 2, 3, or 12. A winning pass bet pays even money, meaning that for a $10 bet, the winner gets to keep his $10 bet and is paid an additional $10.

A pass bet should be made just before a come-out roll, that is, when the black side of the puck is facing up. To make the bet, put your chip or chips on the pass line, which runs the full length of both the left and right betting sections on the layout. You *can* make a pass bet after the come-out, but then it is no longer a good bet because the best odds of winning occur on the come-out roll.

WHAT IS A PUT BET?

A late pass bet (one made after the come-out) actually has a name: it is called a **put bet**. Although most dealers will warn you against this, some casinos love put bettors because the house edge is 9.1% on a point of 6 or 8, 20% on a point of 5 or 9, or a whopping 33% on a point of 4 or 10. On a point of 4 or 10, you would have to take at least 20x odds to reduce the house edge to anywhere close to a pass bet *with no odds*. This is undoubtedly the worst bet in craps.

Since there are six ways to make a 7, and two ways to make an 11, the chances of winning on the come-out are 8 out of 36. There are 4 chances out of 36 that craps will be rolled. Thus, on the come-out, the likelihood of winning is twice as good as losing. The rest of the time, 24 chances out of 36, a point will be established and the hand will continue.

Once the point is established, the chance of winning a pass bet drops considerably. This is because a 7 can be made six different ways while any of the point numbers are less likely, as the following chart shows.

ODDS OF REPEATING THE POINT BEFORE ROLLING A SEVEN			
Point	Ways to Roll the Point	Ways to Roll a Seven	Odds
4	3	6	1 to 2
5	4	6	2 to 3
6	5	6	5 to 6
8	5	6	5 to 6
9	4	6	2 to 3
10	3	6	1 to 2

Thus, it would seem logical to remove your pass bet after the come-out, but the casino will not allow you to do that.

THE COME WAGER

Some craps players find the **come** wager confusing. The come bet is very easy to understand because, except for the timing, it is identical to the pass wager. The come bet can be made at any time *except* before a come-out roll, that is, a come bet can be made any time a pass bet is not normally made. When a come bet is made, the very next roll acts as a come-out for that come bet, independent of what is happening with the pass bets.

In other words, by placing a come bet, any roll can become a come-out for that bet, and the same rules apply as for a pass bet. You can make as many or as few come bets as you wish. In this way, you can make bets on additional points while the pass line shooter is trying to repeat his original point. Thus, depending on how many come bets you make, you can have two or more points working at the same time.

To make a come bet, place your chip or chips in the big COME box, which you should do only when the white side of the puck is facing up. If the next roll is not a natural (which you would win) or craps (which you would lose), then it is your come point and the dealer will move your bet to the appropriate numbered box. This is so both you and the dealer know which number has to be repeated for you to win the come bet. Now the only numbers that have meaning on the succeeding rolls are a 7 (you lose) or your come point (you win). As you can see, this is the same as making a pass bet, except that the point is a different number.

When you win your come point, the dealer will move your original bet back into the COME box and stack the winnings alongside. It is then your responsibility to retrieve the chips, or they will be considered a new come wager. Once made, you cannot take down or turn off a come bet.

As an aid in understanding come wagers, the following example shows how the pass bets and come bets are handled during a typical sequence of rolls:

Action: The player makes a bet on the pass line.

The come-out roll is a 9. A point of 9 is established and the dealer moves the puck to the 9 box with the white ON side facing up.

Action: The player now places a bet in the come box.

The first point roll is a 4. A point of 4 is established for the come bet and the dealer moves the bet to the 4 box. The pass bet is unaffected.

The second point roll is another 4. *The come bet wins* and the player is paid for the come bet. The pass bet is unaffected.

Action: The player makes a new come bet.

The third point roll is a 5. A point of 5 is established for the come bet and the dealer moves the bet to the 5 box. The pass bet is unaffected.

The fourth point roll is a 9. *The pass bet wins* and the player is paid for the pass bet. The dealer moves the puck out of the 9 box and turns the black OFF side up. This ends the hand and the next roll is a come-out. The come bet is unaffected by the 9. It is still waiting for either a 5 or a 7, which are now the only two numbers that have any effect on the come bet.

Action: The player makes a new pass bet.

The come-out roll is an 8. A point of 8 is established and the dealer moves the puck to the 8 box with the white ON side facing up. The come bet is unaffected.

The first point roll is a 7. *This is a seven-out and both the pass and the come bets lose.* The dealer moves the puck out of the 8 box and turns the black OFF side up. This ends the hand and the shooter loses the dice.

Action: The player makes a new pass bet.

The come-out roll is a 6. A new shooter establishes a point of 6 and the dealer moves the puck to the 6 box with the white ON side facing up.

Action: The player makes a new come bet.

The first point roll is a 7. *This is a seven-out for the pass bet and a win for the come bet. The player loses the pass bet and wins the come bet.* The dealer moves the puck out of the 6 box and turns the black OFF side up. This ends the hand and the shooter loses the dice. The next roll is a new come-out.

In the last roll of this example, the come bet won on the 7 because it was the initial roll for that come bet and a point was not yet established. Had that roll been a 2, 3, or 12, the come bet would have lost.

TAKING ODDS

The small table-limit sign on the inside wall of the craps table is the only clue to the existence of the odds bet. Beneath the table limits is a line that may say, *"Full Double Odds"* or *"3X - 4X - 5X Odds"* or some other statement that defines the maximum odds permitted at that table. There is no clue anywhere on the craps layout itself that this bet exists. When the odds bet wins, it is paid at correct odds (rather than house odds), which means that the payoff for winning is exactly the same as the risk of making the bet, leaving the house with a zero advantage. It is the best bet in the game of craps and (unless you are a blackjack card counter) is also the best bet in the casino. Accordingly, it is a very important and worthwhile wager that is necessary for every craps player to completely understand.

The odds bet is not an independent wager. It has to be made as an add-on to an existing pass-line or come wager, and is called **taking odds** on the point. The only time odds can be taken for a pass bet is after a point is established, and the bet is made by stacking additional chips behind your pass bet, as shown below. You can take odds at any time so long as you have a pass bet working, but it is best to do so right after the come-out.

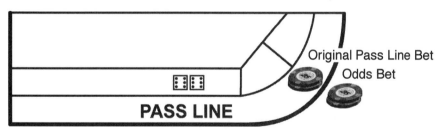

Odds Bet: Pass Line

For a come bet, odds can only be taken after a point is established for that come bet. Thus, the odds bet can be made after the dealer moves the come bet to a point number. In this case, instead of putting the chips behind the come bet, they should be given to the dealer while saying, "Odds on the come." The dealer will then place them on top of your come bet with an offset, so he can tell which portion of the bet is the come and which is the odds.

The payouts for the different point numbers are shown in the following chart, which is an expansion of the previous chart on pass bets.

ODDS PAID FOR EACH POINT			
Point	Ways to Roll	Odd Against	Odds Paid
4	3	2 to 1	2 to 1
5	4	3 to 2	3 to 2
6	5	6 to 5	6 to 5
8	5	6 to 5	6 to 5
9	4	3 to 2	3 to 2
10	3	2 to 1	2 to 1

As the chart shows, the mathematical odds against making a point are exactly the same as the payoff odds, giving the casino a zero advantage. Of course, the casino still has an edge on the original pass-line or come wager.

Should you have a come bet working during a new come-out, the odds portion of the bet will automatically be turned off. That means if the come bet wins (by repeating its point) or loses (by a roll of 7) during the come-out, the odds portion is unaffected and would be returned to you. This rule is designed to eliminate the conflict you would experience if you also had a pass bet working. Otherwise, if the shooter rolled a 7, you would win the pass bet, but lose the come bet with its large odds bet. If this doesn't bother you, or you didn't make a pass bet, you can ask the dealer to "Keep my odds bet working," and he will place a small ON button on top of your chips.

Because the casino has no edge on the odds portion of the bet, taking odds effectively reduces the overall edge. The amount of the reduction depends on the size of the odds bet. Originally, an odds bet was restricted to the size of the pass or come bet, and this was called **single odds**. Today, almost all casinos in the United States allow double odds, and many offer triple odds. As a result of stiff competition, some casinos in Las Vegas offer 10x odds, and a few offer as much as 100x odds. Even in Atlantic City, some casinos are now offering 5x and 10x odds on their $25 limit tables.

The odds bet can be made for any amount up to the maximum allowed by the casino. Thus, if you made a $10 pass bet and the casino allows 3x odds, you can take any amount of odds up to a maximum of $30.

The effect of the odds bet on the combined house edge for the pass line or come bet is as follows.

HOUSE EDGE FOR PASS OR COME WAGERS	
Pass Line or Come Bet	**House Edge**
With no odds	1.41%
With 1x odds	0.85%
With 2x odds	0.61%
With full double odds*	0.57%
With 3x odds	0.47%
With 3-4-5x odds*	0.37%
With 5x odds	0.33%
With 10x odds	0.18%
With 100x odds	0.02%

*WHAT ARE FULL DOUBLE ODDS OR 3-4-5X ODDS?

Some casinos use the term **Full Double Odds**, which means that a player can take 2.5x odds on a point of 6 or 8, and 2x odds on all other points. This is done to facilitate the 6:5 payoff for a point of 6 or 8 when the amount of the bet isn't a multiple of 5. Double odds on a $12 pass bet, for instance, would be $24, which can't be paid correctly in whole dollars for a point of 6 or 8. Not wanting to deal in small change, most casinos would pay the winner $28 instead of the correct amount of $28.80. To avoid shorting the payoff, the player can bet $30 (2.5 x $12), which will then pay the winner the correct amount of $36.

When a casino uses the term **3-4-5x Odds**, it means that a maximum of 3x odds is allowable on a point of 4 or 10, 4x odds on a 5 or 9, and 5x on a 6 or 8. This is done to simplify the payouts for players who take the maximum odds. Regardless of the point, when a 3-4-5x bettor wins, the total payout (pass bet plus odds bet) will always be 7 times the amount of the pass bet. Many casinos in Las Vegas are now offering 3-4-5x odds.

Most casinos don't deal in small change and pay off only in whole dollars. To assure that you get the correct payoff when taking odds on a point of 5 or 9, the amount of the bet should be an even number. For instance, if the point is 9 and your odds bet is $15, you will be paid only $22 instead of the correct amount of $22.50. To avoid being shortchanged, your odds bet should have been either $14 or $16. The payoff odds of 3:2 can always be correctly made with whole dollars if the bet is an even number.

In the above example, you were likely playing at a table with triple odds and made a $5 pass bet. Now the shooter rolls a 9, so what do you do? You would like to take maximum odds, but the maximum odds bet is $15, leaving you with the potential of being shorted on the payoff. To avoid this, it is customary to just add another dollar to your bet to make it $16, which will pay off at an even $24.

The other problem is with the points 6 or 8, where the payoff is 6:5. The only way that payoff can be made correctly in whole dollars is if the bet is divisible by five. Say you are at a double odds table, the point is 8, and you want to take maximum odds on a $6 pass bet, which would be $12. You have two choices. You can either put out $10 or you can ask the dealer if you can bet $15 instead of $12. At a "full double odds" table, this is accepted procedure, but most double odds tables will allow it as well.

With odds of 2:1, the points 4 and 10 do not present a payoff problem. The payoff is simply double the amount of the bet.

THE DON'T PASS AND DON'T COME WAGERS

An interesting aspect of craps is that you can bet either with the shooter or against him. A player who bets that the dice will pass is sometimes called a **right bettor**, and a player who bets that the dice will not pass is sometimes called a **wrong bettor**. This is because those players who make pass-line or come bets are betting against the house, while those who make don't pass or don't come bets *seem to be* betting with the house. Because of the negative implication, however, casino employees use the terms **don't bettor** and **don't bet**. To the casino, everyone who places a bet is a right bettor.

Since the house has a built-in edge, it would appear to be smarter to bet with the house, however, as will be explained later, the house has a slick way of compensating so that it has the edge either way. In other words, no matter how you bet, you are betting against the house.

THE DON'T PASS WAGER

The **don't pass** bettor is hoping that the shooter does not make his point. This is the exact opposite of the pass bettor. In fact, a don't pass bet wins if the shooter rolls a 7 before repeating his point. The don't pass win pays even money, just like the pass bet.

Since everything appears to be opposite on this bet, you would expect the payouts at the come-out to be opposite. That is, the don't pass bettor should win on a 2, 3, or 12, and lose on a 7 or 11. This isn't quite the case; if it were, the don't pass bettor would have a mathematical advantage over the house.

Since we know the casino doesn't give anything away, how does it get its edge on don't bets? Very simply: by not paying for a 12 on the come-out. This is what is meant by the notation *"BAR 12"* on the don't pass line. In other words, when a 12 is rolled at the come-out, for don't pass bettors the 12 is a push rather than a win. This simple rule gives the house a 1.40% edge, which is almost identical to the edge on a pass bet.

Some casinos bar the 2 instead of the 12. It doesn't matter which of these numbers is barred because each one can be rolled only one way. If you find a casino that bars the 3, avoid making a don't bet or, better yet, leave the casino. A 3 can be made in two ways, so barring it substantially raises the house advantage on don't bets.

Just as for a pass bet, a don't pass bet must be made just before a come-out roll, that is, when the black side of the puck is facing up. To make the bet, put your chip or chips on the don't pass line, which is smaller than the pass line because there are far fewer don't bettors than pass bettors.

The casino does not allow you to make a don't pass bet after the come-out because the best odds of winning occur after the come-out roll. For the same reason, the casino will not allow you to increase your don't pass bet after the come-out. You can, however, lay odds, which will be explained later.

Since there are six ways to make a 7, plus two ways to make an 11, the chances of losing on the come-out are 8 out of 36. By the same reasoning, there are 3 chances out of 36 that a 2 or 3 will be rolled, while the 12 is a standoff. Thus, on the come-out, your chance of losing is over twice as high as winning. The rest of the time, 24 chances out of 36, a point will be established, and the hand enters the point phase.

Once the point is established, your chance of winning increases considerably. This is because a 7, which is a winner for the don't bettor, can be made six different ways. The chance of repeating any of the point numbers is less than the possibility of rolling a 7, as the following chart shows.

	ODDS OF ROLLING A 7 BEFORE REPEATING THE POINT		
Point	Ways to Roll the Point	Ways to Roll a Seven	Odds
4	3	6	2 to 1
5	4	6	3 to 2
6	5	6	6 to 5
8	5	6	6 to 5
9	4	6	3 to 2
10	3	6	2 to 1

Although the casino will allow you to remove your don't pass bet after the come-out, you would be foolish to do so. The chart clearly shows that, although your chances of winning on any point (by rolling a 7) are significantly better than even, the casino will pay you even money.

THE DON'T COME WAGER

As you have probably figured out by now, the don't come wager is the opposite of the come bet. The relationship between the don't come wager and the don't pass bet is the same as the relationship between the come wager and the pass bet. As with the come bet, the don't come bet can be made at any time *except* before a come-out roll, that is, a don't come bet can be made any time a don't pass bet is not normally made. When a don't come bet is made, the very next roll acts as a come-out for that don't come bet, independent of what is happening with the pass and don't pass bets.

By placing a don't come bet, any roll (except the come-out) can establish a point for that bet, and the same rules apply as for a don't pass bet. You can make as many or as few don't come bets as you wish. In this way, you can make bets against additional points while the pass line shooter is trying to repeat his original point. Thus, depending on how many don't come bets you make, you can have two or more points working at the same time.

To make a don't come bet, place your chip or chips in the small don't come box—you should do this only when the white side of the puck is facing up. If the next roll is neither a 7 or 11 (which you would lose) nor a 2 or 3 (which you would win), then it is your point and the dealer will move your bet to a small box above the appropriate place-number box. Now the only numbers that have meaning on the succeeding rolls are a 7 (you win) or your don't come point (you lose). As you can see, this is the same as making a don't pass bet, except that the point is a different number.

LAYING ODDS

Just like the pass bettor, the don't bettor can add an odds bet to his don't pass or don't come wager. The only difference is that the pass bettor *takes* odds, meaning that if he wins, he gets paid more than the amount of his bet, whereas the don't bettor has to **lay odds** because he gets paid less than even money on the odds portion of the bet.

Like pass bettors, when don't bettors win, they are paid at true odds for the odds portion of their bet. They are paid less than even money, however, because they have a better than even chance of winning the bet as the previous chart indicated.

Just as for pass bettors, the odds bet has to be made as an add-on to an existing don't pass or don't come wager. The only time a player can lay odds for a don't pass bet is after a point has been established.

The bet is made by stacking additional chips alongside the don't pass bet. The dealer will reposition the chips, but you don't have to worry about that.

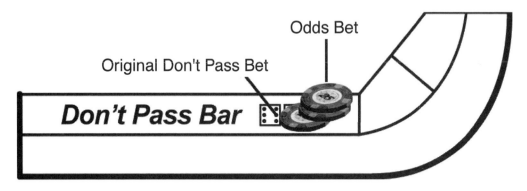

Odds Bet: Don't Pass

For a don't come bet, you can lay odds only after a point is established for that don't come bet. The odds bet can be made after the dealer relocates the don't come bet behind the appropriate point number. Instead of putting the chips next to the don't come bet, put them in the don't come box and tell the dealer that you want to lay odds. The dealer will then place them alongside your don't come bet and **heel** the stack, so he can tell which portion of the bet is for the odds. When a stack is heeled, the bottom chip lays flat and the rest of the stack is tilted so that it is half on and half off the bottom chip.

The payouts for the different point numbers are shown in the following chart, which is an expansion of the previous chart on don't pass bets.

ODDS PAID FOR EACH POINT			
Point	Ways to Roll	Odds Against	Odds Paid
4	3	1 to 2	1 to 2
5	4	2 to 3	2 to 3
6	5	5 to 6	5 to 6
8	5	5 to 6	5 to 6
9	4	2 to 3	2 to 3
10	3	1 to 2	1 to 2

The mathematical odds against rolling a 7 before repeating the point are the same as the payoff odds, giving the casino a zero advantage. Of course, the casino still has an edge on the original don't pass or don't come wager.

In most casinos the odds portion of the bet will be off if you have an active come bet working during a new come-out. This is not true for a don't come bet—the entire bet is working all the time. It can keep working because there is no conflict. Both the pass-line bettors and the don't come bettors hope for a 7 on the next come-out.

When laying odds, the amount you are allowed to bet depends on how much you may win, and that depends on the point. For instance, if you made a $10 don't pass or don't come bet at a full double odds table, you can lay $30 in order to win $25 for a point of 6 or 8. The rule used by the casino is that the most you can lay is the amount you would win if you took the limit on a pass bet. If you have trouble with this, the dealer will be glad to help you figure it out.

Consequently, for the same odds multiple, the amount a don't bettor is allowed to lay is always larger than the amount a pass bettor is allowed to take. This results in a stronger reduction of the combined house edge when a don't bettor lays odds, as the following chart shows.

HOUSE EDGE FOR DON'T WAGERS

Don't Pass or Don't Come Bet	House Edge
With no odds	1.36%
With 1x odds	0.68%
With 2x odds	0.45%
With full double odds	0.43%
With 3x odds	0.34%
With 3-4-5x odds	0.27%
With 5x odds	0.23%
With 10x odds	0.12%

The house edge calculation, of course, is based on the actual amount of money risked, not on the odds multiplier.

SPECIAL NOTE ON THE HOUSE EDGE

Granted, knowing the exact house edge down to the second decimal is not that important to the player, but you may have noticed in the above chart that the house edge percentages for don't wagers are different than those published in most other gambling books. The inconsistency in the house edge for don't bets has two aspects to it. The first concerns the basic don't wager without odds, which can be calculated in two ways. One way does not count ties (the push on the 12) and gives a value of 1.40%. The second way counts ties as a money bet (since money *is* at risk) and gives a result of 1.36%, which is the value used here. See the chart on next page.

HOUSE EDGE FOR DON'T WAGERS		
Don't Wager	**This Book**	**Other Books**
With no odds	1.36%	1.40%
With 1x odds	0.68%	0.83%
With 2x odds	0.45%	0.59%

The second aspect involves the house edge calculation for the combined don't wager and laying odds. The explanation and mathematical proof is beyond the scope of this chapter, however, if you are really interested, you can find it in my book, *Beat the Craps Table*.

THE PLACE NUMBER WAGERS

The place number wagers consist of a variety of bets for which you can choose your own point number. They are very similar to pass-line bets, except that there is no come-out and the point has already been selected by the bettor. On the layout, the place number wagers are the six numbered boxes directly above the large COME box (see illustration). The amount of the payoff for a win depends on the point number and whether the wager was for a regular place bet, a buy bet, or a lay bet.

		PLACE	BETS		
4	**5**	**SIX**	**8**	**NINE**	**10**

Place Number Boxes

THE PLACE BET

The basic place number wager is the **place bet**. When you make this wager, you are betting that the number you bet on will be rolled before a 7. The choices of numbers are the ones in the six place number boxes on the layout, namely, 4, 5, 6, 8, 9, and 10. Although a place bet can be made at any time, it is usually made right after a come-out roll because all place bets are turned off (not working) during a come-out.

Winning place bets are paid off at less than true odds, giving the house a hefty percentage on most of the numbers. The payoff and house edge for each number is shown on the following chart.

PLACE BET PAYOFFS			
Place Number	True Odds	Payoff Odds	House Edge
4	2 to 1	9 to 5	6.7%
5	3 to 2	7 to 5	4.0%
6	6 to 5	7 to 6	1.5%
8	6 to 5	7 to 6	1.5%
9	3 to 2	7 to 5	4.0%
10	2 to 1	9 to 5	6.7%

To make a place bet, put your chips in the Come box and tell the dealer which number or numbers you want to bet on. The dealer will then move your chips to the appropriate place number box, positioning them so that he knows which player made the bet. You should never put your chips in any of the point number boxes—only the dealer is permitted to do that.

To be assured of getting the full payoff, your bet should be in multiples of $5 for the place numbers 4, 5, 9, or 10, and should be in multiples of $6 for the 6 or 8. Otherwise, an exact payoff would involve small change. If, for example, you made a $5 bet on 8, at 7:6 odds the exact payoff would be $5.83. You will likely be shorted on this payoff because most craps tables do not deal in increments of less than a dollar.

When you win a place bet, the dealer will return your winnings, but leave the original wager on the layout so that you still have a bet working on that number. You can, of course, ask that your original bet be returned. Just say to the dealer, "Please take down the 8," or whatever number you are betting on.

Just as you can make a place bet at any time, you can also remove or **take down** the bet at any time. Alternately, instead of taking it down, you can ask the dealer to **turn off** your bet for one or more rolls. He will then put an OFF button on top of your chips. You can also reduce or increase your bet whenever you want to.

Place bets are popular because you don't have to wait for a number to appear twice in order to win, as you do with a pass or come bet. For instance, a $5 come bet on the 5, with $10 odds ($15 total action) will win $20 the second time the 5 appears. A $15 place bet on the 5 will win $21—and it will win the *first time* the 5 appears. The second time the 5 appears the place bettor will be ahead $42. Of course, the place bettor loses the odds advantage of the come-out roll.

To get the most action, many of these players do not bet just one number at a time, but spread their bets over several place numbers at once. For example, if you bet "$32 across," you will be betting all the place numbers, and the dealer will put $5 each on the numbers 4, 5, 9, and 10, and put $6 on the 6 and the 8 ($5 + $5 + $5 + $5 + $6 + $6 = $32). If you bet "$22 inside," you will be betting all four inside numbers: 5, 6, 8, and 9. If you bet "$20 outside," you will be betting all four outside numbers: 4, 5, 9, and 10. The dealer will determine from the amount of money you give him whether or not you want a duplicate bet on an established point.

THE BUY BET

A **buy bet** is simply a place bet that is paid off at the correct odds. In return for being so generous on the payoff, the casino charges a 5% commission when you win. This results in a house edge that is generally less than regular place bets, as shown in the following chart.

ODDS PAID FOR EACH BUY NUMBER			
Number	Ways to Roll	Odds Paid	House Edge
4	3	2 to 1	1.7%
5	4	3 to 2	2.0%
6	5	6 to 5	2.3%
8	5	6 to 5	2.3%
9	4	3 to 2	2.0%
10	3	2 to 1	1.7%

To make a buy bet, give the dealer your chips and say, "I'm buying the 4," (or whatever number you are buying). The dealer will stack your bet in the 4 box and put a BUY button on top to show that it isn't a place bet. If the 4 is rolled before a 7 appears, you will be paid 2:1 odds (less 5% commission) on your bet. This is significantly better than the 9:5 odds that would have been paid if it was a place bet.

Since the minimum commission at most tables is $1, you should never bet less than $20 on a single buy bet. If you make a bet larger than $20 that is not divisible by 20, most casinos will round the commission up to the nearest dollar. Some casinos, however, will round down, so that you can make a larger bet and still only pay a $1 commission. Whenever you want to make a buy bet, ask the dealer how they round the commission for odd-amount bets.

Buy bets are automatically off (not working) during a come-out, unless you request otherwise. You can remove your buy bet at any time by asking the dealer to, "take down my buy bet." No matter how you juggle the buy bets, however, you still face a higher house edge than if you make pass and come bets or make place bets on the 6 or 8.

THE LAY BET

The **lay bet** is the opposite of a buy bet and is used by don't bettors. That means the lay bet wins if a seven is rolled before the selected number appears. As with the buy bet, there is a 5% commission, except that the 5% is figured on the potential win rather than the amount of the wager. For instance, a $40 bet on the 4 would be charged a $1 commission because the payoff would be $20. As shown in the chart below, a 4 is paid off at 1:2 odds.

ODDS PAID FOR EACH LAY NUMBER			
Number	Ways to Roll	Odds Paid	House Edge
4	3	1 to 2	2.4%
5	4	2 to 3	3.2%
6	5	5 to 6	4.0%
8	5	5 to 6	4.0%
9	4	2 to 3	3.2%
10	3	1 to 2	2.4%

Like all don't bets, the payoff for a lay bet is always less than the amount of the bet. This is because a 7 can be rolled six ways, which is more than any other number. Since the chance of winning is better than even, a fair payoff would have to be less than even.

As the chart shows, the house edge for lay bets is always more than for buy bets. Making bets in odd amounts, however, can drive the house edge higher because most casinos round the commission up to the next dollar. To avoid paying excess commission, use a multiple of $40 for lay bets on the 4 or 10, a multiple of $30 on the 5 or 9, and a multiple of $24 on the 6 or 8.

Unlike buy bets, which are always off during a come-out, lay bets are always working. Like buy bets, you can remove your lay bet at any time. Just be sure the dealer returns the commission along with the bet, if it was charged up front. Since the bet was not resolved, it was as though the bet was never placed.

Lay bets are not a good way to go for most craps players. They are mainly used by don't bettors who have already made don't pass and don't come bets. Some aren't satisfied until they have covered the rest of the numbers. Even for don't bettors, this is not good craps strategy.

THE REMAINING BETS

The rest of the wagers on the craps layout are bets that an astute craps player rarely makes. With a house edge that ranges from 5.6% to 16.7%, saying they are bad bets is an understatement.

THE FIELD BET

As the name implies, a **field bet** covers a large group of numbers in a single bet. The numbers are 2, 3, 4, 9, 10, 11, and 12. This is a one-roll bet that one of the these numbers will appear at the next roll of the dice. If one of the field numbers does appear, then you win even money except for the 2 or 12, which pay 2:1 odds. If one of the four missing numbers, 5, 6, 7, or 8, is rolled, then you lose the bet.

To make the bet, put your chips in the large box marked FIELD, which is just below the COME box. The FIELD box with its long string of numbers is prominent at both ends of the layout because the casino loves field bettors.

To a novice craps player, the field bet appears to be a good wager, since seven numbers can win and only four lose. This misinterpretation of the bet is what the casino depends on. Inexperienced craps players often make a field bet without first figuring their true chances of winning. Referring back to the dice combinations chart, if you add up the ways to make all the numbers in the field, the result is 16. If you add up the ways to roll the missing four numbers, you might be surprised to find that there are 20 different ways to roll them. Even paying double on the 2 and 12 doesn't make this a very good wager, with a house edge of 5.7%.

Casinos in downtown Las Vegas pay 3:1 instead of 2:1 on the 12. To meet the competition, more and more casinos on the Las Vegas Strip have also changed to a 3:1 payoff. This reduces the house edge to 2.8%, which makes it a more reasonable bet. It should be noted that on some field layouts there is a 5 in place of the 9, which doesn't change the odds, since either number can be rolled four ways.

THE BIG 6 AND BIG 8 BETS

A wager on the big 6 (or 8) means you are betting that the shooter will roll a 6 (or 8) before rolling a 7. If you win, the bet pays even money. If this wager looks exactly like a place bet on the 6 or 8, you are correct. There is just one significant difference: the house edge on the place bet is 1.5%, while the house edge on the big 6 or big 8 is a whopping 9.1%. This is because the place bet pays 7:6, while the big 6 or big 8 bet pays even odds for essentially the same bet. In fact, there are three ways to make a similar bet on the 6 or 8, as shown in the following chart.

POSSIBLE BETS ON 6 OR 8	
Wager	House Edge
Big 6 or 8	9.1%
Buy 6 or 8	4.7%
Place 6 or 8	1.5%

The only gambling jurisdiction where the big 6 and big 8 wagers are no longer offered is Atlantic City. More and more casinos in Las Vegas have also decided to do away with the big 6 and big 8 wagers. Hopefully, this trend will spread to other jurisdictions.

THE PROPOSITION BETS

The proposition bets, **prop bets** for short, are mainly long-shot bets with high payoffs, which is why many players make them. Because the house edge ranges from a low of 9.1% to an astronomical 16.7%, prop bets are the worst bets on the craps layout. There is no reason to ever give the casino that kind of edge on a single wager.

The prop bets are all located in the center section of the layout, and are controlled by the stickman. You simply toss him your chips and tell him which bet to put them on. If you're a winner, he pays you. Since prop bets tend to invite math errors, to avoid being shorted, don't make a prop bet unless you know what it should pay.

There are two basic kinds of prop bets in the center section: the *hardway* bets and the *one-roll* bets. Except in Nevada, hardway bets are usually off during the come-out. In Nevada, you will hear the stickman call, "Hardways work unless you call them off on the come-out roll!" One-roll bets are working all of the time.

HARDWAY WAGERS

When a point number comes up as a pair, it is referred to as the **hardway** because there is only one way it can be done. Since the sum of two identical numbers cannot be odd, there are just four such bets. A hardway 4 occurs when the dice show a 2+2, a hardway 6 is a 3+3, a hardway 8 is a 4+4, and a hardway 10 is a 5+5.

To win a hardway bet, the number has to be rolled as a pair before that number shows any other way or before a 7 appears. For instance, if you bet a hardway 6, you can only win if a 3+3 is rolled before a 5+1, 1+5, 4+2, 2+4, or a 7 (which can be made six ways). Because there are ten ways to lose this bet and only one way to win it, the odds against making it are 10 to 1. The casino, however, only pays 9 to 1 odds, which gives it an edge of 9.1%. The odds and the house edge for each of the four hardway wagers is shown in the following chart.

SUMMARY OF HARDWAY WAGERS					
Hardway Bet	Ways to Win	Ways to Lose	True Odds	Payoff Odds	House Edge
2+2	1	8	8 to 1	7 to 1	11.1%
3+3	1	10	10 to 1	9 to 1	9.1%
4+4	1	10	10 to 1	9 to 1	9.1%
5+5	1	8	8 to 1	7 to 1	11.1%

Remember that 8 *for* 1 is the same as 7 *to* 1, and 10 *for* 1 is the same as 9 *to* 1.

ONE-ROLL WAGERS

The remaining proposition bets are called one-roll wagers because you either win or lose the bet on the very next roll of the dice. All one-roll wagers are bad bets with a house edge of 11.1% or higher.

CRAPS

Any seven: This wager is won if the next roll is a 7, and lost if any other number appears. Since there are six ways to make a 7, there are six ways to win and thirty ways to lose. Thus, the odds against winning are 5 to 1. The casino, however, only pays a winner 4 to1 odds, which makes it the worst bet on the layout with a house edge of 16.7%

Any craps: This wager is won if the next roll is a 2, 3, or 12, and is lost for any other number. There is one way to make a 2, one way to make a 12, and two ways to make a 3. Since there are four ways to win and 32 ways to lose, the odds against winning are 8 to 1. The casino, however, pays only 7 to 1, giving it an edge of 11.1%.

The 2, 3, 11, or 12: Each of these one-roll wagers is in the lower half of the center section. A 2 or a 12 can be made one way each, which means the odds against either one are 35 to 1. When the payoff is 30 to 1, the house edge is 13.9%. A few greedy casinos, however, only pay 29 to 1 (30 for 1 on the layout), which kicks the house edge up to 16.7%.

Since a 3 or an 11 can be made two ways each, the odds against winning either of these bets is 17 to 1. When paid off at 15 to 1, the house edge is 11.1%. Those same greedy casinos, however, only pay 14 to 1 (15 for 1 on the layout) for a house edge of 16.7%.

Horn bet: This is an ingenious wager thought up by the casinos that lets you make four sucker bets at one stroke. It is a simultaneous one-roll bet on the 2, 3, 11, and 12, and you have to toss out a multiple of four chips as though you made these bets individually. If you are fortunate enough to hit one of the numbers, you are paid accordingly, but the casino keeps the other three losing bets. Most of the time, the casino gets to keep all four of your bets. The house edge for the less greedy casinos is 12.5%. A variation of the horn bet is called the *horn high* bet, in which you double your bet on one of the numbers, so that you can lose even more.

Hop bet: This bet is as absurd as the horn bet. Here you bet that a particular dice combination will come up on the next roll. For instance, you might wager that a 9 is rolled with a 3+6 showing on the dice. To do this, you tell the stickman that you want to bet the 3-6 on the hop. Since there are two ways to win (3+6 and 6+3), the odds against winning are 17 to 1. The casino, however, pays 15 to 1 for an edge of 11.1%.

It is called a **hardway hop** when your two chosen numbers are identical, such as a 3+3. Then there is only one way to win, and the odds against winning are 35 to 1. The casino pays this off at 30 to 1 for an edge of 13.9%.

Craps-Eleven: Known as a C&E wager, this is actually a combination of two separate wagers. The C portion is the same as the Any Craps bet, and the E portion is the same as a one-roll bet on 11, as described above. The payoffs are the same as for the individual bets. When you make this bet, the stickman puts your chips on the C and E circles at either side of the center section.

CRAPS BETTING STRATEGY

Since craps is a negative expectation game, there is no betting strategy that will guarantee winning over the long-term. There are intelligent strategies, however, that can minimize losses and take advantage of winning streaks.

With one exception, the casino will allow you to make any craps wager at any time. The single exception is the don't pass bet, which may only be made before a come-out roll, that is, before a point is established. Just because you are allowed to make all other bets at any time, it doesn't mean you should.

A common example of a badly-timed wager is placing a chip on the pass line after a point has already been established. This is usually done by a person who just stepped up to the table, saw that the point was a number he liked, and decided to bet on it. This is legal, but dumb.

Why is it dumb? Because if the person won his pass line bet, the payoff would be even money, regardless of the number. That is, if he bet $10 on a point of 9, he would win $10. If, instead, he put his $10 on a place bet of the same number, his winnings would be $14.

A SIMPLE STRATEGY

Many beginning craps players make serious betting mistakes, and get disgusted with the game because they keep losing money. Often, they will bet the field or the big 6 and big 8. Many are lured by the seemingly high payback odds of the proposition bets, and then wonder why they seldom pay off.

New craps players should start by only placing simple pass-line bets that have the greatest chance of winning. Once they have become comfortable with the game and have acquired a good working knowledge of the various wagers, they can graduate to more complex betting schemes. Until then, however, it is important that they stick with a good elementary strategy, such as the one described here.

The most basic wager on the craps table is the pass-line bet, and is the best bet for a novice to make—especially if the extra odds are taken. To do this, determine the appropriate size of your bet from the guidelines in the chapter on Money Management, and bet this amount on the pass line just before the next come-out (when the black side of the puck is up). If the shooter passes or craps on the come-out, you should repeat the bet regardless of whether you won or lost. Continue repeating the bet as long as the shooter keeps passing or rolling craps.

Eventually, the shooter will roll a point. When this happens, put an odds bet next to your original pass bet. Remember that if the point is 6 or 8, the odds bet should be a multiple of five, and if the point is 5 or 9, it should be an even number of dollars. In this simple strategy, you should take single odds, which means the odds bet should be an amount as close to the original bet as possible. Taking the odds is important because it reduces the house edge to well under 1%.

Continue betting in this way until it feels natural to you. Whatever you do, don't listen to the stickman and make any of the high-odds bets that he might suggest. If the shooter is hot and you have won an amount at least twice your original wager (pass plus odds), start taking double odds.

Anytime you begin losing, go back to taking only single odds. If you lose twice in a row, quit betting until the dice pass to a new shooter. If you lose twice in a row with the new shooter, quit betting and leave the table.

Keep using the same strategy until you are very comfortable with it. The Simple Strategy may seem slow and boring, but it gives you as good a chance at winning as any other bets on the table, so you should stick with it until you feel competent enough to branch out.

EXAMPLE OF SIMPLE STRATEGY
Action: Make a $15 pass-line wager just before a new come-out.
Come-out roll is a 3. This is craps, so the hand is over and all pass bets lose. You lose $15.
Action: Make another $15 pass-line wager.
Come-out roll is a 9. A point of 9 is established.
Action: Take $16 odds on your pass bet. (Because the point is 9, your single odds bet should be an even number.)
First point phase roll is a 5. The pass bets are unaffected.

Second point roll is a 3. Although this is craps, the pass bets are unaffected.

Third point roll is a 9. The shooter made her point, the hand is over, and the pass bets win. You win $15 on your pass bet plus $24 on the odds portion (which paid 3 to 2), for a total of $39. Your net gain is now $39 - $15 = $24.

Action: Make a $15 pass-line wager.

Come-out roll is a 7. This is a pass, so the hand is over, and all pass bets win. You win $15 on your pass bet and your net gain is $39.

Action: Make another $15 pass-line wager.

Come-out roll is a 4. A point of 4 is established.

Action: Take single odds of $15 on your pass bet.

First point roll is a 10. The pass bets are unaffected.

Second point roll is a 4. The shooter made her point, the hand is over, and the pass bets win. You win $15 on your pass bet plus $30 on the odds portion (which paid 2 to 1), for a total of $45. Your net gain is $84.

Action: Make a $15 pass-line wager.

Come-out roll is a 6. A point of 6 is established.

Action: You are $84 ahead, so you take double odds of $30 on your pass bet.

First point roll is a 7. This is a seven-out, so all pass bets lose, and the shooter loses possession of the dice. You lose $45 on your pass bet and odds.

Action: You are down to a net gain of $39. Continue making pass bets, but cut back to single odds. If the new shooter is also a loser, quit betting and leave the table. Had you continued to win, however, you would have incrementally increased your odds bet (1x at a time) whenever your net gain doubled, to as much as the craps table allowed.

CONSERVATIVE STRATEGY

Once a new player has gotten used to the game and no longer has trouble following the sequence of play, it is time for him to graduate from the Simple Strategy described above and start making additional wagers. The next best step is to follow the pass bet with a come bet, both with odds. This is a popular betting combination that is used by many conservative, but skillful and successful players.

You start by making a wager on the pass line just before a new come-out. Once a point is established, you have to make two additional bets: (1) take single odds on your pass line bet and (2) make a come bet. The come bet should be for the same amount as your pass wager.

Now the shooter is in the point phase, and if he doesn't seven-out on the next roll (in which case, you lose your pass bet and win your come bet), you should take single odds on the come bet. You now have two bets working on two different points, each one with odds. If the shooter makes his point on that first point-phase roll, however, you win your pass bet and your come bet is still working. In that case, you should make a new pass-line wager. The idea is to always have a pass-line wager plus one come wager working at all times.

Until you are money ahead, stay with the single odds wagers. If you begin to win steadily, to where your net gain is twice your total bet amount (pass bet with odds plus come bet with odds), start taking double odds. If you keep on winning, increase the odds incrementally to as much as the craps table allows.

Whenever you begin losing, however, go back to taking only single odds. *Never chase your losses!* Any time the shooter craps out, make another minimum pass-line wager.

The Conservative Strategy is a fine betting system that is used by many smart and experienced players. If this strategy is comfortable for you, you should stick with it rather than advance to more complex and riskier strategies. Should you want to advance, be sure that you have developed enough experience at the tables that keeping track of your bets has become second nature.

EXAMPLE OF CONSERVATIVE STRATEGY

Action: Make a $15 pass-line wager just before a new come-out.

Come-out roll is a 7. This is a pass, so the hand is over, and all pass bets win. You win $15.

Action: Make another $15 pass-line wager.

Come-out roll is a 10. A point of 10 is established.

Action: (1) Take single odds of $15 on your pass bet and (2) make a $15 come wager.

First point phase roll is a 5. A point of 5 is established for the come bet. Your pass bet is unaffected.

Action: Take single odds of $16 on your come bet. (Because the point is 5, the odds bet should be an even number.)

Second point roll is a 3. Although this is craps, your pass and come bets are unaffected.

Third point roll is a 10. The shooter makes her point, the hand is over, and all pass bets win. You win $15 on your pass bet and $30 on your odds bet (which paid 2 to 1), for a total of $45. Your net gain is $60. Your come bet is unaffected and is still working.

Action: Make a new $15 pass-line wager

Come-out roll is a 7. This is a win for your pass bet and a seven-out for your come bet. The hand is over. You win $15 on your pass bet and lose $15 on your come bet. The odds portion of your come bet is returned to you because it was automatically turned off during the come-out. Since this roll was a wash, your net gain remains at $60.

Action: Make another $15 pass-line wager.

Come-out roll is a 4. A point of 4 is established.

Action: (1) Take single odds of $15 on your pass bet and (2) make a $15 come wager.

First point roll is a 10. A point of 10 is established for your come bet. Your pass bet is unaffected.

Action: Take single odds of $15 on your come bet.

Second point roll is a 10. The point is made for your come bet, and your pass bet is unaffected. You win $15 on your come bet plus $30 on the odds portion (which paid 2 to 1), for a total of $45. Your net gain is $105.

Action: Make a new $15 come bet.

Third point roll is a 7. This is a seven-out for the pass bet and a win for your come bet. The hand is ended and the shooter loses possession of the dice. You lose your $15 pass bet as well as the $15 odds portion, and you win your $15 come bet, for a net loss of $15. Your net gain dropped to $90.

Action: Make a $15 pass-line wager.

Come-out roll is an 8. A point of 8 is established.

Action: (1) Take single odds of $15 on your pass bet and (2) make a $15 come wager.

First point roll is a 6. A point of 6 is established for your come bet. Your pass bet is unaffected.

Action: Take single odds of $15 on your come bet.

Third point roll is an 8. The shooter makes her point, the hand is over, and all pass bets win. You win $15 on your pass bet plus $18 on the odds portion (which paid 6 to 5), for a total of $33. Your net gain is now $123. Your come bet is unaffected and is still working.

Action: Make a new $15 pass-line wager

Come-out roll is a 9. A point of 9 is established.

Action: You are $123 ahead, so you take double odds of $30 on your pass bet.

First point roll is a 7. This is a seven-out for both your pass bet and your come bet. You lose your $15 pass bet as well as the $30 odds portion, and you lose your $15 come bet, along with the $15 odds portion. Your net gain dropped to $48.

Action: Make a $15 pass-line wager. Although you are still $48 ahead, you just lost so you cut back to single odds. If you start winning again, you may incrementally increase your odds bets (1x at a time) to as much as the craps table allows. Should you continue losing, however, you should quit betting on this shooter. If you lose twice on the next shooter, stop betting and leave the table.

CONVENTIONAL STRATEGY

This strategy consists of a pass wager and two come wagers, so that there are as many as three points working at one time. It is a somewhat higher-risk betting system, but it pays off handsomely when a shooter makes a lot of sequential rolls without sevening out.

Two versions of the Conventional Strategy are presented below. Other than the amount of odds taken, both versions are essentially identical. The double odds version is a little riskier than the single odds version, but can also result in greater returns.

Single Odds Version: As before, you start by making a wager on the pass line just before a new come-out. Once the shooter establishes a point, you have to make two additional bets: (1) take single odds on your pass line bet and (2) make a come bet. The come bet should be for the same amount as your pass wager.

Now the shooter is in the point phase, and assuming he doesn't seven-out on the second roll, you should then take single odds on the come bet and make a second come bet. You now have two bets working on two different points, each one with odds, plus a new come bet for which a point has not yet been established. If, on the third roll, the shooter neither makes his point nor sevens out, take single odds on the second come bet. Assuming he didn't make his pass line point or your first come point, you now have all three of your bets working with odds.

This is the stage at which your wagers are at their greatest risk. If the fourth roll is a 7, all your bets are lost. However, by this time in the hand, there are many other possibilities that could have occurred. For example, the shooter might have made his point at roll two, three, or four, in which case you would have made a new pass wager. He might also have made one of your come points, in which case you would have made a new come bet. The idea is to try to have a pass-line wager plus two come wagers working at all times.

As in the previous strategies, until you are sufficiently ahead, stay with the single odds wagers. Once you begin winning steadily, start taking double odds. If you keep on winning, increase the odds incrementally to as much as the table allows. Anytime you begin losing, however, go back to taking only single odds. *Never chase your losses!*

Double Odds Version: The betting sequence of the double odds version is the same as for the single odds version. The only difference is that you start by taking double odds on the pass and come wagers. Then, if you are winning consistently, start taking triple odds, and whenever you start losing, go back to double odds.

AGGRESSIVE STRATEGY

For those players who want to cover more than three points, the Aggressive Strategy extends the Conventional Strategy out to a fourth point. Since working more than two come bets at a time can sometimes result in a concentration of outside numbers (4, 5, 9, 10) which are harder to make, in the Aggressive Strategy the fourth point is covered by a single place bet on the 6 or the 8. You now have to keep track of four separate wagers, so this strategy should not be applied until you have accumulated considerable experience and feel very comfortable at the craps table.

Start the Aggressive Strategy by making a pass-line wager with double odds, followed on successive rolls by two come wagers, each with double odds, until three points are covered, exactly as previously explained in the Conventional Strategy. Then, assuming the dice are still favorable, make a place bet on the 6 or 8. The amount of the bet should be similar to your pass wager plus odds, but should be a multiple of six (see below). Select whichever of the two numbers is not already covered by your pass bet or your two come bets. If both the 6 and 8 are already covered, make a third come bet, instead. In this case, a third come bet is less risky, since the inside numbers are covered.

GETTING THE FULL PAYOUT ON A PLACE BET

Getting the correct payoff for a place bet was covered in the section on place bets, but is worth repeating here. A place bet on the 6 or 8 pays 7 to 6. To assure getting the full amount for a win, the place bet must be a multiple of $6. That is, a $12 wager will win $14, an $18 wager will win $21, etc. If you make the mistake of betting $10, for example, the correct payoff is $10 x 7/6, which is equal to $11.67. Most casinos don't deal in small change, so you will be paid only $11.

Try to keep four points working by replacing bets as they are won or lost. Maintain the ratio of one pass bet, two come bets, and one place bet. The place bet should always be your fourth bet and should never be made on any numbers other than the 6 or 8, or the house edge gets too high. Remember, the place bet and the odds on the come bets are turned off whenever there is a new come-out roll. Do not turn them on.

As in the other strategies, if things are going well and you are consistently winning most of your wagers, start taking triple odds on new bets. If the dice continue to perform well, keep increasing the odds incrementally (only on the new bets) to as much as the craps table allows. Eventually, however, the dice will turn cold. When this happens, immediately cut back to double odds, and if the dice continue to perform badly, stop betting.

COMMON STRATEGY ERRORS

If I keep making center bets, sooner or later I'll get a 30 to 1 payoff and win big.

Yes, you will get a big payoff, but most of the time, you will have lost much more than you won. The 2 and the 12 may pay 30:1, but each of these numbers will appear an average of once in every 36 rolls. The payoff doesn't begin to compensate for the risk, which gives the house a 13.9% edge.

If I haven't seen a 7 in over ten rolls, wouldn't the 7 be due and wouldn't that be a good time to make a bet on Any Seven?

The dice don't have a brain and don't contain a memory chip, so there is no way they can know that a 7 hasn't appeared for a while. The long-term probability of a 7 being thrown is 6 times in 36 rolls, and this probability does not change from roll to roll. If the law of averages was absolute, a 7 would regularly appear once in every six rolls. The fact that this does not happen shows that the dice are actually quite random, and that each roll is an independent event. Consequently, the Any Seven wager has the same chance of winning or losing no matter how often a 7 has appeared or not appeared.

But, doesn't the law of averages mean that eventually a 7 has to appear more often for the mathematical odds to be correct?
Not really, but even if that were true, the correction might not occur until next week or next year.

Isn't the Field Bet a good deal because you win on seven numbers and only lose on four?
At first glance, the field bet might appear to be a smart wager, but if you figure the dice combinations, you'll change your mind. The 2 or 12 can be made one way, the 3 or 11 can be made two ways, the 4 or 10 can be made three ways, and the 9 can be made four ways. This adds up to 16 ways to win. The losing numbers are 5, 6, 7, and 8, which can be made four, five, six, and five ways, respectively, giving you twenty ways to lose. Even with a double payout on the 2 and a double or triple payout on the 12, this is still a poor bet.

If the come-out establishes a number I like, shouldn't I make a pass bet at that time?
No. You would be much better off making a place bet on that number. If the shooter made his point, the payoff on the late pass bet would be even money, whereas the payoff on an equivalent place bet would be 9:5 on the 4 or 10, 7:5 on the 5 or 9, and 7:6 on the 6 or 8, all of which are better payoffs than even money.

I like to hedge my bets. Why don't you ever discuss the various hedge bets?
Because the space in this chapter can be used more constructively in other ways. There are dozens of different hedge bets, and almost all of them will increase the combined house edge. There is no combination of craps bets that will give you a lower house edge than a pass bet with odds.

If I'm losing, I like to increase my bets so that I can recoup faster when I start winning.

This is a very bad idea. Since there is no way to know ahead of time when your luck will turn, bigger bets will only cause you to lose faster. Risking more money will not change your luck or change the inherent odds of the game you are playing.

If, I double my wager every time I lose, won't I eventually recoup all my losses?

This is called a Martingale system and has been around for at least 300 years. It seems to work until you encounter a long losing streak. Then, in an attempt to retrieve your losses, you will run up against the table limit if you don't run out of money first. Even when starting as low as $5, a doubling system multiplies the amount of the bet very quickly, i.e., $5, $10, $20, $40, $80, $160, $320, $640.

I don't like to memorize odds. Why can't I just bet on certain numbers by intuition?

There are more bad bets than good bets on a craps layout. If you bet by intuition, you will end up making more bad bets than good ones, and you would be better off playing roulette.

BETTING AGAINST THE DICE

Don't betting is not for beginners and is not for the timid. It is a useful technique for those experienced craps players who can read a craps table and who never chase their losses. Properly applied, it can be very profitable for the perceptive player.

The strategy of don't betting is beyond the scope of this chapter. If you are an experienced craps player and want to try your hand at don't betting, you should get a copy of a specialty book such as *Beat the Craps Table*

CRAPLESS CRAPS

Crapless Craps, also known as *Never Ever Craps*, is an old sucker version of casino craps that dates back to antiquity and periodically gets revived. One of the more recent revivals was by Bob Stupak in the early 1980s when he offered the game at his Vegas World casino (now the Stratosphere). It was then dormant until the mid-1990s, when it reappeared in Mississippi.

The lure in Crapless Craps is that there are no craps numbers, that is, there is no way to lose on the come-out. It seems like a good deal until you learn that the only way to win on the come-out is to roll a 7; the 11 is not a winner. In fact, if you roll an 11, it becomes the point. The former craps numbers of 2, 3, and 12 also become point numbers if they appear on the come-out.

Thus, all numbers except the 7 are potential points. This seems to be reasonable until you figure out that since there is only one way to roll a 2 or 12 and six ways to roll a losing 7, the odds of repeating those points are 1 in 7. Since there are two ways to get a 3 or 11, the odds of repeating those points are 1 in 4. In other words, if one of those former craps numbers becomes the point, you have an excellent chance of losing. On top of that, the 11, which was an automatic win on the come-out, could now become a hard-to-make losing point.

ODDS OF REPEATING THE POINT BEFORE ROLLING A SEVEN IN CRAPLESS CRAPS			
Point	Ways to Roll the Point	Ways to Roll a Seven	Odds
2 or 12	1	6	1 to 6
3 or 11	2	6	1 to 3
4 or 10	3	6	1 to 2
5 or 9	4	6	2 to 3
6 or 8	5	6	5 to 6

An odds bet is offered on all the point numbers, including the additional points of 2, 3, 11, and 12. On the 2 and 12, the odds are 6:1, and on the 3 and 11, the odds are 3:1. Crapless craps has a high house advantage, mainly caused by the loss of the 11 winner. The following chart shows a comparison of the house edge for crapless and traditional craps.

HOUSE EDGE FOR CRAPLESS AND TRADITIONAL CRAPS		
Pass or Come Bet	Crapless	Traditional
With no odds	5.38%	1.41%
With 1x odds	2.94%	0.85%
With 2x odds	2.02%	0.61%
With 3x odds	1.54%	0.47%
With 5x odds	1.04%	0.33%
With 10x odds	0.58%	0.18%

It should be no surprise that the house percentage for crapless craps is almost four times higher than that of the traditional game. Because of this heavy edge, there are no don't bets available on a crapless table. The don't bettor's advantage would be so strong that adjusting the don't payoffs downward to compensate would be impossible without it looking ridiculously obvious.

You can make a place bet on any number except the 7. As can be seen in the following chart, place betting the 6 or 8 is one of the best wagers in crapless craps. Of course, when you make place bets, you are not concerned with getting craps on the come-out, so you might as well be playing the traditional game.

CRAPLESS CRAPS PLACE BETS			
Place Number	True Odds	Payoff Odds	House Edge
2 or 12	6 to 1	11 to 2	7.1%
3 or 11	3 to 1	11 to 4	6.3%
4 or 10	2 to 1	9 to 5	6.7%
5 or 9	3 to 2	7 to 5	4.0%
6 or 8	6 to 5	7 to 6	1.5%

If you are paranoid about losing to craps on the come-out, then, maybe crapless craps is the game for you. Just be aware that eliminating the losing craps numbers will end up costing you more in the long run.

◆11◆
DEUCES WILD HOLD'EM FOLD'EM POKER

Deuces Wild Hold'em Fold'em Poker is a new table game that seems to be catching on in Las Vegas as well as in Mississippi. The game is distributed by T & P Gaming and is often called "Wild Hold'em Fold'em" or "Hold'em Fold'em where all the Deuces are Wild." The game is similar to Let It Ride, in that you are neither playing against the dealer nor the other players. Instead, the value of your final hand is based on a fixed payout schedule.

Deuces Wild Hold'em Fold'em Poker is loosely based on stud poker and is played on a blackjack-type table. A standard deck of 52 cards is used and all the deuces are wild. That is, any deuce appearing in a hand becomes whatever card rank and suit gives the hand its maximum value.

The game is easy to learn, especially if you already know the relative values of poker hands. When the game begins, you have to put up an ante wager. You are then dealt three cards. If you think the hand has potential, you can place an additional bet equal to your ante. You are then dealt a fourth card. If your hand still looks good, you can place a third wager equal to double the ante. When the fifth card is dealt out, your hand is evaluated by the dealer and, if you have a pair of aces or better, you are paid according to the paytable.

If this game interests you, it should not be hard to find; at least a dozen casinos in Nevada and at least another dozen in Mississippi now offer it. At the time of this writing, it is not yet offered in Atlantic City.

FUNDAMENTALS OF PLAY

THE PLAYING TABLE

Deuces Wild Hold'em Fold'em Poker is played on a table that is very similar to a blackjack table and is usually located in or near the blackjack area. The table has six player positions around the curved side of the table (see illustration). The dealer stands at the flat side with a chip rack directly in front of her and, sometimes, a card-shuffling machine to her right.

There are three betting boxes at each player position that are labeled, from left to right, RAISE, BET, and ANTE. A complete payout schedule is imprinted on the felt just below each set of betting boxes.

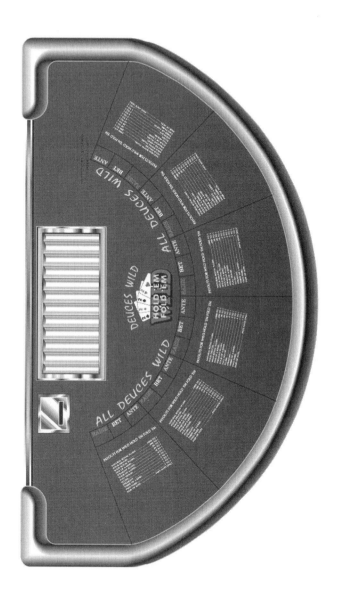

Deuces Wild Hold'em Fold'em Table

HOW THE GAME IS PLAYED

Before the cards are dealt, each player has to put a wager in the ANTE box. Each player is then dealt an initial hand of three face-down cards. The players examine their cards and decide if they are worth risking more money. They are not allowed to show their hands to other players. If the hand is already a winner (pair of aces or better) or looks like it might win with one or two additional cards, the player can "hold'em" (stay in the game) by putting a second wager in the BET box. This additional wager must be equal to the amount of the ante.

Any player who does not want to risk more money on this hand must "fold'em" and drop out of the game, losing the ante wager. When this is done, the player should place the cards face-down on the dealer side of the wager.

For those players still in the game, each receives a fourth face-down card. Again, the players have to evaluate their hands and decide whether to "hold'em" or "fold'em." To stay in the game, a player must put a wager in the RAISE box equal to double the ante bet. Dropping out at this point forfeits both the ante and the bet wagers.

Finally, the dealer gives each of the remaining players a fifth card. This card is placed face-up on the dealer side of the wager. The dealer then examines the hands one by one and pays all winning hands according to the paytable. Players with losing hands, lose all three bets.

Winning hands are based on standard poker hands, with all four deuces wild. The best payoff of 1000 to 1 is for a royal flush made without any wild cards. The lowest paying hand is a pair of aces, which pays even money on only the ante wager; the other two wagers are a push. This is equivalent to an overall payoff of 1 to 4.

Many other table games have pointless idiosyncrasies and this one is no exception. Even though the players are not competing against the dealer, as she deals cards to the players, she also deals herself a hand. The dealer's cards are dealt face down and are never exposed, thus the dealer's hand is meaningless.

THE PAYOFFS

T & P Gaming offers casinos four different payout schedules that have house edges ranging from 3.96% to 6.86%. So far, however, the casinos have opted to use only the schedule with the highest house return, which is the following:

PAYTABLE FOR WILD HOLD'EM FOLD'EM POKER	
Hand	**Payoff**
Natural Royal Flush	1000 to 1
Four Deuces	200 to 1
Wild Royal Flush	30 to 1
Five-of-a-kind	20 to 1
Straight Flush	10 to 1
Four-of-a-kind	4 to 1
Full House	4 to 1
Flush	4 to 1
Straight	3 to 1
Three-of-a-kind	1 to 1
Two Pair	1 to 1
Pair of Aces	Pays ante only

Except for a pair of aces, a winning payoff applies to the total amount wagered by the player. For instance, a player who antes $10 and stays in to the end, will have a total of $40 invested in the hand. For a full house, such as K K 2 5 5, he will be paid 4:1. Thus, he will get his $40 back plus an additional $160.

If he had just a pair of aces, he would be paid even money on his ante only. Thus, he would get his $40 back plus an additional $10.

In the future, when more casinos install this game, competition may cause some of the better payout schedules to emerge.

WINNING HANDS

The various card combinations that produce winning hands are the same as in regular poker. Deuces Wild Hold'em Fold'em uses one standard 52-card deck with the four deuces wild. The value of a hand depends on which of the following card combinations it contains, listed in order from the highest to the lowest:

Natural Royal Flush: Five consecutive cards, ten through ace, all of the same suit, and containing no deuces. Simply stated, it is an ace-high straight flush.

Four Deuces: A hand containing four deuces (four-of-a-kind). The fifth card is immaterial.

Wild Royal Flush: A royal flush containing one, two, or three deuces as wild cards. (If there were four deuces, it would be a four-deuce hand.)

Five-of-a-kind: Five cards of the same rank. Since there are only four cards in each rank, this hand necessarily contains one, two, or three deuces. (If there were four deuces, it would be a four-deuce hand.)

Straight Flush: Five consecutive cards, all of the same suit. One, two or three deuces may be included. (If there were four deuces, it would be a four-deuce hand.)

Four-of-a-kind: Four cards of the same rank, which may include one or more deuces. The fifth card is unrelated to the others.

Full House: Three cards of the same rank and two cards of another rank, that is, three-of-a-kind and a pair. One deuce may be included. (If the hand includes two deuces, it would be at least four-of-a-kind.)

Flush: Five cards of the same suit, not in sequence. One or two deuces may be included. (If the hand includes three deuces, it would be four-of-a-kind.)

Straight: Five consecutive cards of mixed suits. An ace may be either the lowest card as in A 2 3 4 5 or the highest card as in 10 J Q K A. One or two deuces may be included. (If the hand includes three deuces, it would be four-of-a-kind.)

Three-of-a-kind: Three cards of the same rank, which may include one or two deuces. The remaining two cards are unrelated.

Two Pair: A pair of one rank and a pair of another rank, which may include one deuce. (If the hand includes two deuces, it would be at least three-of-a-kind.) The fifth card is unrelated.

Pair of Aces: Two aces, one of which may be a deuce. (If the hand includes two deuces, it would be at least three-of-a-kind.) The three remaining cards are unrelated.

PLAYING STRATEGY

With a house edge of almost 6.9%, Deuces Wild Hold'em Fold'em is clearly a negative expectation game. There is no strategy that can overcome the house edge and make the game profitable for the player. You must, however, use some reasonable strategy when playing this game or you can deplete your bankroll very quickly. The strategy advice given below was developed by Michael Shackleford (known as The Wizard of Odds), and is the best available.

When you play Deuces Wild Hold'em Fold'em there are three basic decisions you have to make: (1) How much money to ante, (2) whether to hold or to fold after looking at the first three cards, (3) whether to hold or to fold after looking at the fourth card.

THE ANTE

The total amount you wager in this game can be more than you anticipated, especially if you are an optimistic person and don't follow the recommended strategy. You can make up to three bets: the ante, the bet, which is equal to the ante, and the raise, which is *double* the ante. If you don't fold and play your hand all the way to the end, your total monetary risk is four times the ante.

Thus, a $10 ante quickly becomes a $40 bet, and a $25 ante becomes a $100 bet. This escalation of wagers, combined with the high house edge, makes it prudent to minimize the ante.

THREE CARD HAND

At the three card level, the recommendation is to fold unless you have the following:

- Any hand with a deuce

- Any pair or three-of-a-kind.
- Three cards to a flush, if it includes an ace.
- Three cards to a straight flush.

FOUR CARD HAND

With four cards, the recommendation is to fold unless you have the following:

- Any hand with a deuce.
- Any pair, two pair, or three-of-a-kind.
- Four cards to a straight, flush, or straight flush.

The complete playing strategy is summarized in the following chart:

PLAYING STRATEGY
FOR DEUCES WILD HOLD'EM FOLD'EM

Three card Strategy — Fold unless you have the following:
- Any hand with a deuce.
- Any pair or three-of-a-kind.
- Three cards to a flush, if it includes an ace.
- Three cards to a straight flush.

Four card Strategy — Fold unless you have the following:
- Any hand with a deuce.
- Any pair, two pair, or three-of-a-kind.
- Four cards to a straight, flush, or straight flush.

CONCLUSION

As most people know, casinos don't bank the poker games in their poker rooms. They only supply the table, the cards, and the dealer, for which they take a commission out of each pot. Deuces Wild Hold'em Fold'em is an example of the casinos trying to get yet another chunk of the potential poker business by catering to players who would rather not go head-to-head with poker experts or dealers.

Thus, in this game the dealer is not an adversary player, but only distributes the cards and makes the payoffs. Playing against a fixed payout schedule rather than trying to beat unknown hands seems to attract wannabe poker players, but these players eventually pay the price by bucking a rather high house edge. On the other hand, playing against a paytable is more relaxing and predictable than when the dealer is the opponent.

◆12◆
KENO

The game of Keno originated in China over 800 years ago and was used as a means of financing the construction of the Great Wall. It was brought to the United States by the Chinese railroad workers in the mid-1800s. The modern version using ping-pong-like balls to determine the winning numbers was developed in Nevada.

Keno is a game of pure luck. Except for knowing how to mark the tickets correctly, it requires no skill. Its appeal is similar to the state lotteries: for a small investment, you have a chance of winning a very big payoff. Although most players are aware of the high house edge, they are usually not aware of the astronomical odds against winning the top jackpots.

In each game of keno, twenty out of a total of eighty numbers are randomly selected, and the winning numbers are posted on keno flashboards throughout the casino. When you play the game, your goal is to correctly guess as many of those twenty numbers as possible. The more numbers you get right, the bigger the payoff.

Keno payoffs vary from casino to casino, as does the house edge. In fact, within a single casino, the house edge varies with the type of game and with the total amount of numbers selected. Thus, the only useful strategy is to find the lowest house edge and the best return for your money. That is the goal of this chapter.

FUNDAMENTALS OF PLAY

A keno wager is made by marking numbers on a keno ticket. This is a slip of paper about 5-1/2 inches square that contains a grid of numbers from 1 to 80. With a black crayon, you X out any or all numbers that you hope will be drawn during the next game and the more numbers you hit, the more you win.

After marking the numbers, bring the ticket to the keno counter or give it to a keno runner. The runner will bring back a receipt, called an outside ticket, which is the only proof that you made a bet. Check the outside ticket to be sure it accurately reflects what you marked on your ticket.

When a game starts, twenty ping-pong-like balls, each with an imprinted number, are randomly drawn from a total of eighty balls that are blown about in a clear plastic globe, sometimes called a goose. As each number is recorded, it blinks on all the keno flashboards in the casino, continuing until 20 numbers are shown.

Check your numbers, and if you win, let the keno runner know right away. If she isn't around, hurry to the keno counter to collect your winnings. If you don't get there before the next game starts, you may lose out. In most casinos, a new game starts every five to eight minutes.

In the keno lounge, as well as in all the restaurants and bar areas, are holders containing keno booklets, blank tickets, and crayons. Examine the folders or booklets to see what kinds of games can be played and what the payoffs are. There are numerous versions of keno, the most popular of which are described below.

TYPES OF KENO

Regular keno is usually called a straight ticket. Some other varieties of keno that are found in most casinos include the 20-spot ticket, top/bottom keno, way ticket, and multi-game keno.

Straight ticket: This is the standard keno game and the one that most people play. It is the simplest and often the best game to play. In most casinos, you can select 1 to 15 numbers. The more numbers you mark, the higher the payoff for catching them all, and the lower the payoff for catching fewer numbers.

20-spot ticket: This is a special version of a straight ticket in which you mark 20 numbers. The top payoffs are for catching 17, 18, 19, or 20 numbers, but the odds against winning any of them are huge.

Top/bottom keno: You choose the top or bottom half of the ticket and if your half catches 11or more numbers, you win. In some casinos, you can bet either the right or left half of the ticket instead. If you pick the winning half, the payoff is usually 2 to 1. In some games, the payoff for 11 numbers is a push, while 12 or more numbers pay an increasing amount as you hit more numbers. A second version pays off if you hit fewer than 8 or more than 12 numbers on either half.

Way ticket: This is a method for combining several straight ticket wagers into a single ticket. Instead of writing two separate 4-spot tickets, you can mark all 8 numbers on a single ticket and then circle the two groups of 4 numbers that you would have marked on the individual tickets. The payoffs are the same either way. With two 4-spot groups marked, you can also combine them to play one 8-spot group in addition to the two 4-spots.

Multi-game (or multi-race) keno: This is a method for playing the same ticket several games in succession. In almost all casinos, you can play two to twenty games, and in some, you can play as many as 1000 games. The only constraint is that it must be for the same set of numbers and for the same wager. Your winnings are paid at the conclusion of the succession of games.

PLAYING A STRAIGHT TICKET

Using a blank keno ticket, X out each of your chosen numbers with a crayon. You can usually select up to 15 numbers. Check the pamphlet to see the payoffs and verify how many numbers you can pick. The minimum bet is usually $1 or $2 and you can wager any multiple of those amounts.

After you marked your numbers, write the amount of your bet in the upper right corner and write the number of picks in the right margin as shown in the illustration below. Give the completed ticket to a keno writer at the keno counter or to a keno runner and you will get back a computer-printed receipt (outside ticket) showing the details of your wager. Check it to be sure it is correct.

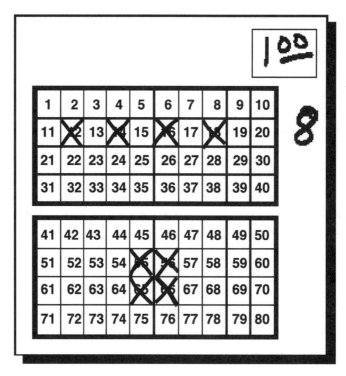

8-Spot Straight Keno Ticket

If you are indecisive about which numbers to select, just tell the keno writer how many numbers you want and say, "Quick-pick." The computer will randomly choose your numbers and print the ticket.

PLAYING A 20-SPOT TICKET
A 20-spot ticket is played just like a straight ticket except that you mark 20 numbers. You then follow the same procedure for playing a straight ticket. As mentioned above, the chances of hitting a big payoff are infinitely small. For example, the odds of catching 17 numbers are over 1 in 90 million, and the odds of catching 18 are over 1 in 10 trillion. The odds of catching 19 or 20 spots are in the quadrillions and quintillions, numbers that are hard to visualize. Furthermore, you have almost a 63% chance of catching 4, 5, or 6 spots, which are the losers.

PLAYING TOP/BOTTOM KENO
In top-or-bottom keno, which can often be played side-by-side, you don't mark any numbers. Instead, you wager on which half of the keno ticket catches more numbers. Draw a horizontal line across the middle of a blank ticket and mark a large T on the top half or a B on the bottom half, depending on which half you think will win. In most casinos, you can also draw a vertical line down the middle and mark an L on the left half or an R on the right half. Check the keno pamphlet or ask the keno writer if you can do this.

A second version is called top-*and*-bottom keno, although some casinos still call it top-or-bottom. In this case, you are betting that either half will catch fewer than 8 numbers, or more than 12. If either half catches 8, 9, 10, 11, or 12 numbers, you lose your wager. This version can also be played left-and-right in most casinos. The following illustration shows how to mark the tickets.

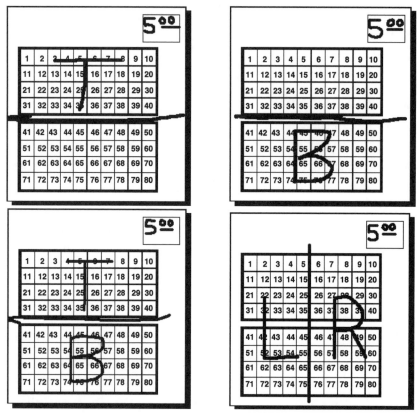

Clockwise from top left: Top-or-Bottom ticket (top numbers), Top-or-Bottom ticket (bottom numbers), Top-and-Bottom ticket, Left-and-Right ticket

PLAYING A WAY TICKET

Instead of filling out several straight tickets, you can often combine those bets into a single way ticket. This works best if the picks for each wager are grouped relatively close together on the ticket.

For example, if you write a way ticket with three groups of four picks each, you can make seven different wagers. The three groups of 4-spots can be combined into three different 8-spots and one 12-spot for a total of seven combinations. The correct way to write this ticket is shown in Example A, below.

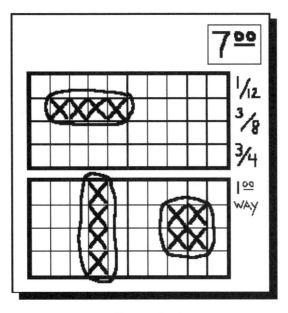

Example A

In the right margin, under the total price of the ticket, write "1/12" to indicate one 12-spot, "3/8" to indicate three 8-spots, and "3/4" to indicate three 4-spots. Then write "1.00 per way" or "$1.00 ea," or however much you want to bet. The total wager is then entered in the box at the upper right corner, which should be the amount of your bet times the number of ways.

If you don't want to bet on all of the possible ways, indicate only the ones you want in the margin. Example B, below, shows the same ticket without the 12-spot, and Example C shows a ticket with only the three 8-spots.

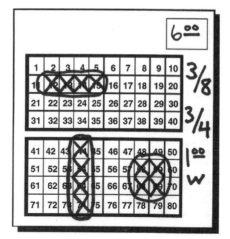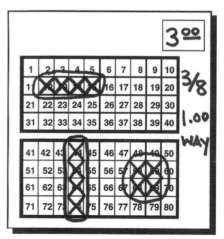

Examples B and C

When you only bet the 4-spot groups, it is called a way ticket. If you combine the 4-spots to make 8-spot and/or 12-spot wagers, it is called a combination ticket. If you mark and then circle a single number, it is called a king or king number, and a ticket containing a king is called a king ticket. The king number never plays by itself, but is automatically combined with each of the other number groups on the ticket.

Since the combinations in which a way ticket can be written are almost unlimited, some players get very creative. This, however, is not necessarily a good way to gamble, as is explained in the Strategy section.

PLAYING A MULTI-GAME TICKET

Some keno people like to bet the same number combination repeatedly, thinking that it will eventually win. To accommodate this line of thinking, the casinos allow them make the same wager in successive games without submitting a new ticket each time.

All you have to do is mark the number of games you wish to play in the appropriate box at the top of the ticket. You can always play two to twenty games in succession. Those casinos that have newer computers with larger memories and better tracking capabilities will allow up to 1000 games in succession. When you play successive games, your bet must be for the same amount and for the same set of numbers.

If you play up to twenty games, you must remain in the casino and collect your winnings after the last game on your ticket and before the draw for the next game. Be sure you get to the keno counter on time or you may lose out. If you play more than twenty games, you have up to a year to collect your winnings.

KENO STRATEGY

In playing keno intelligently, the best playing strategy is to pay attention to the following three points:

1. Keep your wagers small. In keno, it usually takes many attempts to win a big jackpot. Betting big reduces the number of games you can play before you deplete your bankroll, and also risks running up against the aggregate payoff limit. Betting small gives you far more chances to win.

2. Try to find a game with the lowest house percentage. The house edge varies from game to game and from casino to casino. In Las Vegas alone, the house edge for *exactly the same game* can range from a high of 35% to a low of 20%. In New Jersey, the highest keno house percentage is limited to 30% by law. Nevada does not have a legal restriction, and the house edge has been known to be as high as 90% in some casinos and, in others, as low as 5%.

3. Don't play a game where the odds of winning are astronomical. Some jackpots are so elusive that you are not likely to win during a lifetime of continuous play. Betting that kind of ticket is a total waste of money.

STRAIGHT TICKET

Overall, the straight ticket is the simplest and best way to play keno. Just don't get carried away and make too many picks. Most experienced keno players don't pick more than 7 or 8. The following chart shows the odds of catching all the numbers.

ODDS OF CATCHING ALL THE NUMBERS	
Spots	**Odds**
1	1 in 4
2	1 in 17
3	1 in 72
4	1 in 326
5	1 in 1551
6	1 in 7753
7	1 in 40,979
8	1 in 230,115
9	1 in 1,380,688
10	1 in 8,911,711
11	1 in 62,381,978
12	1 in 478,261,833

Clearly, the chances of catching all the numbers gets tougher as you pick more numbers. By the time you get to 7 spots, the odds are about the same as hitting a natural royal flush in video poker. Catching 10 out of 10 is an extremely rare event, and catching 12 out of 12 is practically unheard of.

20-SPOT TICKET

This is not a good game to play because you can do better playing a straight ticket. As mentioned earlier, the chances of hitting the top jackpot are almost zero. Furthermore, the payoff for an intermediate win is substantially better with a straight ticket. Besides, a 20-spot ticket will cost you $5 or $10, which will buy you five or ten straight tickets.

TOP/BOTTOM KENO

Like the 20-spot, a top and/or bottom ticket will cost you at least $5. The house percentage for most payout schedules is high and the odds of hitting the top payout are more than 1 in 25 million. Not a good game to play.

WAY TICKET

Way tickets do have a reason for being. It allows the player to make several different wagers on a single ticket, which is a convenience for everyone. At most casinos, way tickets can be played at a reduced rate. Often, three or more ways reduces a $1 minimum bet to 50 cents, 10 or more reduces it to 25 cents, and 100 or more reduces it to 10 cents.

The disadvantage of way tickets is that you are more apt to win $1500 or more on a single ticket. When that happens, the casino must report the win to the IRS on a W2-G form. Had this win been split between two separate straight tickets, and one or both of them was for less than $1500, you could have avoided the dreaded W2-G form by having your wife or friend cash in the second ticket.

When playing way tickets, follow the same advice given above for straight tickets and don't pick too many spots for each way. Finally, if you get too creative, you can easily lose sight of the three basic strategy rules given at the beginning of this section.

MULTI-GAME TICKET

Since it takes the same amount of time and effort to write a multi-game ticket as a single ticket, some casinos give you a bargain rate. How this is handled depends on the casino. In some cases, the payoff is increased and in others, you might get twelve games for the price of ten. However it is done, it can reduce the house percentage to a very low value, sometimes to less than 5%. If possible, play multi-race games only at those casinos.

Multi-game tickets, however, have the same disadvantage as way tickets in that your winnings are more likely to exceed the IRS limit for submitting a W2-G form. Take that into consideration when you make your wagers.

FIGURING THE HOUSE PERCENTAGE

The main strategy in keno is to find games with the lowest house edge. The casino, of course, does not give you this information, so you have to figure it out for yourself. If you are fairly adept with a pocket calculator, this is not too hard to do.

The simplest example is a 1-spot ticket. Since twenty numbers are selected out of a total of eighty, the odds of hitting your solitary number are 1 in 4. If this bet is paid at correct odds, you would win $4 for a $1 wager. However, the casino will pay you only $3, giving the casino a 25% edge. Calculating the house percentage for other tickets gets a little more complicated, but can easily be done with the information provided below.

In his outstanding book *Complete Guide to Winning Keno*, David W. Cowles includes tables of probabilities for the different straight tickets. An abbreviated version of these tables is given below along with his method of figuring the house edge.

KENO

SPOTS CAUGHT	PROBABILITY IN PERCENT
1 NUMBER MARKED	
0	75.00
1	25.00
2 NUMBERS MARKED	
0	56.013
1	37.975
2	6.0127
3 NUMBERS MARKED	
0	41.650
1	43.087
2	13.875
3	1.3875
4 NUMBERS MARKED	
0	30.832
1	43.273
2	21.264
3	4.3248
4	0.30634
5 NUMBERS MARKED	
0	22.718
1	40.569
2	27.046
3	8.3935
4	1.2092
5	0.064492

SPOTS CAUGHT	PROBABILITY IN PERCENT
6 NUMBERS MARKED	
0	16.660
1	36.349
2	30.832
3	12.982
4	2.8538
5	0.30956
6	0.012898
7 NUMBERS MARKED	
0	12.157
1	31.519
2	32.665
3	17.499
4	5.2191
5	0.86385
6	0.073208
7	0.0024403
8 NUMBERS MARKED	
0	8.8266
1	26.646
2	32.815
3	21.479
4	8.1504
5	1.8303
6	0.23667
7	0.016046
8	0.00043457

The probabilities in the above tables have been rounded to eight digits or less, since that is the maximum capability of most pocket calculators. To arrive at the house percentage, make a chart as shown in the example below and then perform the indicated arithmetical operations. Add up the right-hand column to get the player payback, and subtract this number from 100 to get the house edge. If the player payback is more than 100%, either you made an error or there is an error in the casino payout schedule.

HOUSE PERCENTAGE FOR 6-SPOT KENO TICKET							
Spots Caught	**Pays**		**Ticket Price**		**Probability In Percent**		**Player Payback**
0	0	÷	2.00	×	16.660	=	0
1	0	÷	2.00	×	36.349	=	0
2	0	÷	2.00	×	30.832	=	0
3	2.00	÷	2.00	×	12.982	=	12.982%
4	10.00	÷	2.00	×	2.8538	=	14.269%
5	150.00	÷	2.00	×	0.30956	=	23.217%
6	4,000.00	÷	2.00	×	0.012898	=	25.796%

TOTAL PLAYER PAYBACK = 76.264%

HOUSE PERCENTAGE = 100 − 76.264 = 23.736%

The house edge for most keno games typically ranges from 20% to more than 30%. A game that calculates out to less than 25% is generally considered good (for keno). The printing of pay schedules is not an error-free process, and by regularly checking the house percentages, you may occasionally find a misprint giving a particular game an unusually low or high house edge. This can be a winner for you, especially if the edge favors the player, which has been known to happen.

PROGRESSIVE KENO

The basic appeal of keno, that you might win big for a relatively small investment, is exemplified in progressive keno. If you want to take that idea to its extreme, find a casino that offers progressive keno. The only difficulty is that your chances of winning the big prize are almost illusory.

In most progressive keno games, you have to catch 9 out of 9 or 10 out of 10 numbers to win the progressive jackpot. In order to catch 9 out of 9, you have to buck odds of 1 in 1.38 million, and 10 out of 10 is even worse at odds of 1 in 8.9 million. If you do manage to beat those odds, the payoff for a $5 wager may only be $300,000 or $400,000, and sometimes a lot less. Of course, there are also smaller payoffs for catching fewer numbers, but you get those in regular keno as well.

The house edge in a progressive game is a function of the size of the jackpot. If you really want to play the progressive game, at least make the house percentage calculations as described above, and only play when the progressive jackpot gets very high and the house edge gets very low.

PLAYING STRATEGY FOR KENO

Rule 1: Keep your wagers small.

Rule 2: Try to find a game with the lowest house edge.

Rule 3: Don't play a game where the chances of winning are almost nil.

VIDEO KENO

Video keno machines offer an alternative to regular keno. They have screens that are formatted very similarly to paper keno tickets and operate just like standard slot machines. Although there are nickel and dollar keno machines, most machines take one to four quarters.

When you start to play, be sure that you first press the ERASE or WIPE CARD button to clear the screen. You can then select the numbers you want by touching the screen with the light pen that is attached to the machine. For each selection you make, the number will shift color. You can change your mind at any time by pressing the ERASE button and starting over. In some cases, the machine has a keyboard instead of a light pen.

When you are satisfied with your picks, press the PLAY or START button and twenty random numbers begin to appear on the screen one by one as they are selected by the internal random number generator. Any of your numbers that hit change color, and the amount of your winnings are displayed and added to the credit meter.

Whenever you are ready to cash out, press the COLLECT or CASH OUT button and your winnings will clatter into the tray. Larger amounts are hand paid by an attendant.

HOUSE PERCENTAGE

The house edge for video keno is much lower than for regular keno, typically ranging from about 8% to 18%, although there are some greedy casinos that take as much as 30%. As with standard slot machines, the nickel machines have the highest house edge and the dollar machines usually have the lowest, however, it does vary from casino to casino. To figure the exact house edge for any paytable, you will have to perform the calculations described in the previous section.

PLAYING STRATEGY

Be aware that video keno is a much faster game than regular keno. In the time it takes to play one regular keno game, you can easily play 30 or 40 video keno games. Thus, even with a lower house edge, you will lose money at a faster rate.

Whenever possible, calculate the house percentage for any game of interest to you. If you always play one type of game, such as a 6 spot straight ticket, after a while you will get to know a good pay schedule when you see it.

Finally, when you examine the paytables, be sure the top payout is 10,000 coins or credits, or the machine isn't worth playing.

♦13♦
LET IT RIDE

Most table games have a history. They have either been around for a long time or they are a modification of another game that has been around for a long time. Let It Ride is different. It was invented by Shuffle Master to help market its single-deck shuffling machines. Let It Ride was introduced to Nevada casinos in 1993 and quickly became a hit with many table-game players.

Let It Ride is played on a blackjack-like table with, of course, a shuffling machine. It is an unusual type of poker game where you put up all your bets before the first cards are dealt and then you can pull your bets back one-by-one if you don't like the way your hand develops. If you *do* like the cards, you just let your bets ride, as indicated by the name of the game. You can also make an optional side bet to qualify for an additional bonus payout.

The game is easy to learn. Winning hands are based on the standard poker hands, and there are no wild cards. However, unlike blackjack and regular poker, you don't play against the dealer or the other players at the table. Instead, the value of your final hand is determined by a fixed payout schedule. Consequently, the bluffing and normal playing strategies that are used in traditional poker games do not apply.

When the game begins, you put up three equal bets. You can also place an optional $1 side bet which qualifies you for a separate bonus payout. Three cards are then dealt to each player and two additional community cards are placed in the center of the table. The community cards are exposed one-by-one, becoming a part of each player's hand

225

to eventually form a five card poker hand. Before the first community card is turned over, you have to decide if your three card hand is a potential winner or loser. Accordingly, you may either let your first bet ride or pull it back.

The dealer then exposes the first of the two community cards. You now go through the same decision process again and either pull back the second bet or let it ride. Finally, the second community card is turned over so you now have a five card poker hand. You cannot pull back the third bet—it is kind of a late ante. Also, there are no draws, so the three cards you are dealt plus the two community cards are all you have to work with.

The dealer now evaluates your hand and makes the appropriate pay-offs in accordance with the two paytables. To qualify for any kind of a payout, your hand must be at least a pair of tens. If your bets were $5 apiece and you let all of them ride, you could win as much as $15,000 for a royal flush. If you placed the optional side bet, you could win an additional $20,000.

So, isn't Let It Ride simply another version of poker games that use community cards? In a way, but who ever heard of a game in which you put up all your bets before getting a single card and then pull them back one by one? It sounds silly, but the popularity of the game indicates that it works for many people.

FUNDAMENTALS OF PLAY

THE PLAYING TABLE
Let It Ride is played on a table that is very similar to a blackjack table and is usually located in or near the blackjack area. In most casinos, it is easy to find because there is an elevated sign at the table identify-

ing the game. The table has six or seven player positions around the curved side of the table (see illustration). The dealer stands at the flat side with a chip rack directly in front of her and a card-shuffling machine to her right.

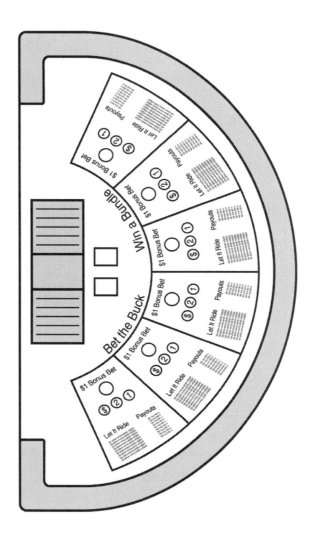

Let It Ride Table

At each player position are three betting circles. In most casinos they are marked, from left to right: "$", "2," and "1" (some casinos reverse the order). These circles are where the three mandatory bets are placed prior to dealing a hand. There is also a red-lighted spot above the three betting circles where an optional $1 bonus side bet may be placed. The spot will light up to indicate which players are qualified for the bonus.

Directly in front of the chip rack are two rectangular boxes, sometimes marked with the numbers "1" and "2." This is where the dealer places the two community cards (initially face down).

HOW THE GAME IS PLAYED

The most important goal in Let It Ride is to end up with a five card poker hand that is at least as good as a pair of tens. For players who invested an extra dollar to qualify for the bonus payout, the secondary goal is to get a hand that is equal or better than the minimum bonus payout. Depending on the particular paytable, this may be a pair of tens, two pair, or three-of-a-kind.

At the start of each game, you have to place equal bets in each of the three betting circles. Most Let It Ride tables have either a $5 or a $10 minimum bet requirement. This is a little misleading because a $5 minimum means you must bet at least $15 ($5 in each circle). However, if you are unhappy with how your hand develops, you can pull back as much as $10 of your initial $15 bet. When you place your three bets, you may also put a dollar on the red bonus spot. This is entirely optional; however, if you do not invest the dollar, you will have no chance of winning the extra bonus, regardless of how good a hand you might have.

Once all the bets are placed, the dealer distributes three face-down cards to each player from a shuffling machine. The dealer also places two face-down cards on the two rectangular boxes at the center of the table. These are the two community cards that will ultimately be a part of each player's hand. In some casinos, the community cards are not dealt out until each player has made the first betting decision. You may now look at your three cards, but you aren't supposed to show them to anyone else.

If your hand is a sure winner (has a pair of tens or better), or if you believe the addition of the two community cards will make your hand a winner, you should let the first bet ride. Do this by squaring up the cards and laying them face down directly behind the center bet.

If the hand appears to be a loser, you should lightly scratch the cards on the table (similar to asking for a hit in blackjack). The dealer will then push the first bet out of the circle so that you may retrieve it. Note that pulling back your bet is not the same as folding your hand. You continue to play—you just have less money riding on the hand.

After all the players at the table have made their betting decisions, the dealer turns over the first of the two community cards, and the entire process is repeated. You re-evaluate your hand just as before except that you now have four cards on which to base your judgment. At this time, you can pull back your second bet if the hand does not look good, or "let it ride" if it does. *Keep in mind that you may pull back your second bet even if you let the first bet ride.*

Finally, the dealer turns over the second community card, giving each player the equivalent of five cards. She then proceeds to turn over each player's hand, one by one, and pays off the winners. The actual payout schedules will be described in the section on payoffs.

Until the dealer turns them over, players are supposed to hide their cards from each other. If you do get a glimpse of another player's hand, it can occasionally help your decision making process. How to take advantage of such added information will be covered in the section on playing strategy.

TABLE ETIQUETTE

The first thing you have to do is to put out three equal bets. Place these bets directly on the three circles in front of you as soon as the dealer has collected all the cards from the previous round. Although it is not recommended, this is also the time to place a $1 bet on the red bonus spot.

After all the cards have been dealt, look at your three cards. Since it is against casino rules to show your cards to anyone else, you should make a reasonable attempt to shield them. Make your betting decision quickly enough so as not to hold up the game. This should be easy to do if you remember the strategy rules given in this chapter.

If you decide to "let it ride," square up your cards and place them face down directly behind the center bet. To get your bet back, wait for your turn and then scratch the cards on the felt (like getting a hit in blackjack). Wait for the dealer to push the bet toward you so that you can retrieve it. Once the cards are dealt, you are not allowed to touch any chips that are on the betting circles.

When the first community card is turned up, the betting decision is repeated. After the second community card is turned up, place your cards face down in front of you. The dealer will then turn over every player's cards, in turn, and make the appropriate payoffs. Do not toss your cards; let the dealer turn them over even if you do not have a winning hand.

Tipping, of course, is a matter of personal preference. Instead of tipping a dealer directly, you may prefer to place a bet for the dealer. In this game, placing a bet for the dealer is discouraged because of the multi-tier betting procedure. Most casinos do let you place a dealer bet at the "$" circle. Because the return on this bet is unfavorable, do yourself and the dealer a favor by just tossing her a chip.

THE PAYOFFS

The primary payoffs in Let It Ride are based on a standard paytable that is used by most casinos. Also shown is an alternate paytable that may be used in some jurisdictions. There are, however, many different bonus paytables for the optional $1 side bet, none of which pay as well as they should. These schedules are all described in this section.

STANDARD PAYTABLES

After the second community card is exposed, the dealer pays off all the winning hands in accordance with the following paytable.

LET IT RIDE NEVADA PAYTABLE	
Hand	**Pays**
Royal Flush	1000 to 1
Straight Flush	200 to 1
Four-of-a-kind	50 to 1
Full House	11 to 1
Flush	8 to 1
Straight	5 to 1
Three-of-a-kind	3 to 1
Two Pair	2 to 1
Pair of Tens or Better	1 to 1

You don't have to beat anyone to win, neither the dealer nor the other players. If, for example, your final holding is three-of-a-kind and you let all three $5 bets ride, you will be paid $45 ($15 x 3) and get to keep your original bets. If, during the game, you pulled one of your $5 bets back, you will get $30 ($10 x 3) plus your original $10. Should you be fortunate enough to get a royal flush and let all three of your $5 bets ride, you would win $15,000 ($15 x 1000). The payoffs in this game can be very nice.

In some gambling jurisdictions outside of Nevada, the paytable can vary somewhat. Following is an example of such an alternate schedule.

LET IT RIDE ALTERNATE PAYTABLE	
Hand	Pays
Royal Flush	500 to 1
Straight Flush	100 to 1
Four-of-a-kind	25 to 1
Full House	15 to 1
Flush	10 to 1
Straight	5 to 1
Three-of-a-kind	3 to 1
Two Pair	2 to 1
Pair of Tens or Better	1 to 1

Note that the payoff odds for a full house and flush are higher than in the Nevada paytable. Although this partially compensates for the lower royal flush, straight flush, and four-of-a-kind payoffs, the house edge for this schedule is still about 0.3% higher than for the Nevada paytable.

AGGREGATE PAYOUT LIMIT

Many casinos have a maximum aggregate dollar payout limit on winning hands. This limit is typically $25,000 but, depending on the casino, can range from $10,000 to $100,000. It is actually a deceptive form of betting limit because, while they let you bet as much as you want (up to the table maximum, which can be pretty high), they limit how much they will pay out if you win. The aggregate limit is usually stated on the same little plaque that gives the table betting limits. Or it may be printed on the layout. If you don't see it, ask the dealer.

Ignoring the aggregate limit could cost you a lot of money. Suppose, you are playing at a table with a payout limit of $25,000 and you place three $10 bets as well as a $1 bonus bet. You then let all your bets ride and hit a royal flush. At 1000 to 1 odds (per the standard paytable), you should win $30,000 plus a $20,000 bonus for a total of $50,000; however, the casino will only pay you $25,000. This is very deceptive, but the casinos make the rules and all you can do is avoid falling into the trap. To keep from being shortchanged on the payoff, never place more than the minimum bet, and don't give them the extra dollar for the bonus bet.

BONUS PAYOUT SCHEDULES

If you opt to invest an extra dollar on the bonus bet, you will also be qualified for a bonus payoff on certain winning hands. Although almost all casinos offer the bonuses, the paytables are not as standardized as the regular payout schedules. At the present time, there are at least two dozen paytables used in the various gambling jurisdictions around the United States.

Unlike the standard paytables, the payoff odds for the various bonus paytables vary all over the place and the house edge can range from a low of about 14% to higher than 35%. Consequently, the $1 bonus is not a recommended bet. The most prevalent paytables are shown below, along with the house percentage for each one.

LET IT RIDE BONUS PAYTABLES FOR $1.00 SIDE BET					
Hand	Chart 1	Chart 2	Chart 3	Chart 4	Chart 5
Royal Flush	$20,000	$20,000	$20,000	$25,000	$20,000
Straight Flush	$2,000	$1,000	$2,000	$2,500	$2,000
Four-of-a-kind	$400	$100	$300	$400	$100
Full House	$200	$75	$150	$200	$75
Flush	$50	$50	$50	$50	$50
Straight	$25	$25	$25	$25	$25
Three-of-a-kind	$5	$4	$5	$5	$9
Two Pair	$0	$3	$0	$0	$6
Pair Tens or Better	$0	$1	$0	$0	$0
House Edge	25.5%	23.7%	35.1%	24.1%	13.8%

Chart 1 – Most Las Vegas Strip casinos.
Chart 2 – Most Las Vegas downtown casinos and some Strip casinos.
Chart 3 – Some Las Vegas casinos.
Chart 4 – Atlantic City.
Chart 5 – Many Nevada locals casinos. Although the house edge is significantly lower, the dollar investment still can't be recommended.

WINNING HANDS

The various card combinations that produce winning hands are the same as in regular poker. Let It Ride uses one standard 52-card deck with no wild cards. The value of a hand depends on which of the following card combinations it contains, listed in order from the highest to the lowest:

Royal Flush: Five consecutive cards, ten through ace, all of the same suit. Simply stated, it is an ace-high straight flush. This is the highest-value hand in Let It Ride. The odds of getting a royal flush are 1 in 649,740 hands.

Straight Flush: Five consecutive cards, all of the same suit. The odds of getting a straight flush (excluding a royal flush) are 1 in 72,193 hands.

Four-of-a-kind: Four cards of the same rank. The fifth card is unrelated to the others. The odds of being dealt four-of-a-kind are 1 in 4,165 hands.

Full House: Three cards of the same rank and two cards of another rank, that is, three-of-a-kind and a pair. The odds of getting a full house are 1 in 694 hands.

Flush: Five cards of the same suit, not in sequence. The odds of getting a flush are 1 in 509 hands.

Straight: Five consecutive cards of mixed suits. An ace may be either the lowest card as in A 2 3 4 5 or the highest card as in 10 J Q K A. The odds of getting a straight are 1 in 255 hands.

Three-of-a-kind: Three cards of the same rank. The remaining two cards are unrelated. The odds of getting three-of-a-kind are about 1 in 47 hands.

Two Pair: A pair of one rank and a pair of another rank. The fifth card is unrelated. The odds of getting two pair are about 1 in 21 hands.

One Pair: Two cards of the same rank. The three remaining cards are unrelated. The odds of getting any pair are about 1 in 2.4 hands. The lowest winning hand in Let It Ride is a pair of tens. The odds of getting a pair of tens or any better hand is 1 in 1.63.

PLAYING STRATEGY

Statistically, Let It Ride is a negative expectation game. There is no strategy that will overcome the house edge and make the game profitable for the player. You must, however, use some reasonable strategy when playing this game or you can deplete your bankroll very quickly.

When you play Let It Ride there are four basic decisions you have to make: (1) How much money to wager on the three betting circles, (2) whether or not to place the $1 bonus bet, (3) whether or not to let the first bet ride, and (4) whether or not to let the second bet ride. Each of these four choices will have a major effect on how much you win.

THE PLAYING STRATEGY

There is only one reasonable approach to Let It Ride playing strategy, and it is described in this section. The four rules given for the playing strategy work very well for most serious and recreational players. It squeezes the last little bit out of the house advantage and may keep you from losing your shirt too quickly.

Rule 1. Never bet more than the table minimum. Since Let It Ride is a negative expectation game, the more you bet, the faster you will drain your resources. The lowest table minimum you are likely to find is $5. Try to play at those tables. If, for instance, you decide to raise your bet to $10, you will actually have to place $30 worth of bets. Also, by placing minimum bets, there is no chance that you will run up against the aggregate payout limit. You wouldn't want to place large bets, get a hot hand, and then be shortchanged on the payout.

Rule 2. Never place a $1 bonus bet. Investing $1 in the bonus bet is a much greater negative expectation gamble than the basic game. In most casinos, the house edge on the bonus payout ranges from 25% to 35%, or more. Yes, there are schedules that pay the house only 13% or less, but they are very hard to find. Since the house edge on the basic game (with perfect strategy) is as little as 3.5%, why hurt yourself by betting the bonus.

Rule 3. Three card strategy.

Let the first bet ride if your initial three card hand contains any paying hand. With three cards the only possible paying hands are three-of-a-kind or a pair of tens or better. If you have one of these winning hands, you don't have to think any further. Just let both bets ride and collect your winnings!

Let the first bet ride if your initial three card hand contains a possible royal flush. A possible royal consists of any three cards from a ten to an ace, all of the same suit. Since the payoff for a royal is 1000 to 1, the reason for this rule is obvious.

Let the first bet ride if your initial three card hand contains a possible outside straight flush with no card lower than a three. The term "outside" means three sequential cards with no gaps. This hand is worth going after because of the high 200-to-1 payoff; and if you miss it, you may still get a flush, a straight, three-of-a-kind, or two pair.

Let the first bet ride if your initial three card hand contains a possible straight flush with a spread of four cards and one or more high cards. A spread of four cards means that there is one gap in the sequence. High card means a ten, jack, queen, king, or ace. If you miss the payoff for a straight flush, you still have a chance of getting a flush, a straight, three-of-a-kind, two pair, or a high pair.

Let the first bet ride if your initial three card hand contains a possible straight flush with a spread of five cards and two or more high cards. A spread of five cards means that there are two gaps in the sequence. High card means a ten, jack, queen, king, or ace. With two gaps in the sequence, your chance of getting a straight flush is much less, but you still have a good chance of getting a flush, a straight, three-of-a-kind, two pair, or a high pair.

Three card hands that should not be played: In Let It Ride, there seems to be a tendency for some people to ride out hands for which the bet should be pulled back. Many of them will hopefully play a three card straight with the odds against completing it being much higher (24 to 1) than the meager payoff odds of 5 to 1. Also, never play a pair lower than tens. The chance of picking up a third card of the same rank or making two pair is worse than the payoff odds of 3 to 1.

Rule 4. Four card strategy.

Let the second bet ride if your four card hand contains any paying hand. In addition to three-of-a-kind and a pair of tens or better, a pat four card hand can also be two pair or four-of-a-kind. If you have any of these, you know what to do!

Let the second bet ride if your four card hand contains all cards of the same suit. In addition to a possible flush, this would include possible straight flushes.

Let the second bet ride if your four card hand contains an open-ended straight. This is a four card sequence with no gaps and open at both ends. Thus, the lowest card should not be lower than a deuce and the highest card should not be higher than a king.

Four card hands that should not be played. Some people have a tendency to play inside straights. This is never a good idea unless all four are high cards, which gives you a decent chance of getting a high pair. So you started off with a three card straight flush and the first community card was out-of-suit and turned it into an inside straight. Cut your losses and pull that bet. Or, you were hoping to convert that low pair into a trip. It didn't happen with the first community card, and it probably won't happen with the second one.

PLAYING STRATEGY FOR LET IT RIDE

Rule 1: Never bet more than the table minimum.

Rule 2: Never place a $1 bonus bet.

Rule 3: Three Card Strategy — Let the first bet ride if your initial three card hand contains any of the following:
- Any paying hand (pair of tens or better)
- A possible royal flush
- A possible outside straight flush (3 or higher)
- A possible four spread straight flush (one high card)
- A possible five spread straight flush (two high cards)

Rule 4: Four Card Strategy — Let the second bet ride if your four card hand (including the first community card) contains any of the following:
- Any paying hand (pair of tens or better)
- All cards of the same suit
- An open-ended straight

PEEKING AT OTHER CARDS

As mentioned earlier, the rule is that you are not supposed to show your cards to any other players. Some people, however, are sloppy card handlers and it is sometimes easy to get glimpses of other cards. How helpful is this? Sorry to say, but most of the time it is not very worthwhile, and sometimes can even lead you into making incorrect strategy decisions.

This happens because, although you know the playing strategy, you may not know the statistical basis for it. For instance, you hold a four card straight flush and see one of the cards you need in another player's hand. As a result, you decide to pull your second bet. This is a wrong decision because your hand still has a positive expectation of winning. If you don't make the straight flush, you still have a good chance of getting a flush.

On the other hand, if you are holding a four card outside straight and see one of the cards you need, the situation is so marginal that how you play it depends on the strength of your straight. If the straight contains a ten or higher, let it ride; if it doesn't, pull the bet. This is because you also have a chance of hitting a high pair if your straight contains one or more high cards.

 A hundred card combinations could be enumerated along with the practical effect of seeing additional cards, but the list would be almost impossible to memorize. The bottom line is that, unless you do memorize such a list, your judgement call is as likely to be wrong as it is to be right. In the long run, you are better off to just ignore the other player's cards.

CONCLUSION

Let It Ride has two interesting characteristics that sets it apart from other table games. The first is that the players have to put up three equal wagers before the first card is dealt. This intimidates many beginning players until they get used to the idea. Of course, they can always get back two of those three bets if their hand doesn't develop well.

The second is that the dealer is not an adversary player, but only distributes the cards and makes the payoffs. This seems to have a positive effect on the table atmosphere. Furthermore, playing against a fixed payout schedule rather than an unknown quantity (the dealer's hand) seems to reduce overall tensions. Consequently, the game is usually pretty relaxed and more sociable than most other table games. Even with a house edge of 3.5%, I find the game restful and rather enjoyable. Of course, I never make the bonus bet.

◆14◆
PAI GOW POKER

Pai Gow Poker is an American version of the old Chinese game of Pai Gow. Actually, it is a blending of Pai Gow and poker that, in its earliest form, probably dates back to the mid-1800s. In 1986, a modern version of Pai Gow Poker got its start in California card rooms and, in 1987, the casino version (in which the house may act as banker) was introduced in Las Vegas. A few years later, the New Jersey Casino Control Commission approved Pai Gow Poker. Since then, it has become one of the fastest-growing games in American casinos.

The original game of Pai Gow, which uses special dominos, is symbolic, enigmatic, and difficult to learn. Pai Gow Poker, on the other hand, uses a regular deck of cards and is based on standard poker hands. It is comparatively easy to learn and play—our casinos wouldn't have it any other way.

Pai Gow Poker is played on a blackjack-like table with six player positions. It uses a standard 52-card deck plus one joker. With a couple of exceptions, winning hands are almost the same as standard poker hands. That is where the similarity to poker ends. You only play against the banker's hand, and you have only one opportunity to place a bet. Consequently, the bluffing and normal playing strategies that are used in regular poker games are of no value.

The game begins after the banker is selected and each player puts up an initial bet. The selection procedure for the banker, who may be the dealer or one of the players, will be explained later. Seven cards are then dealt to everyone at the table, including the dealer. You now have to split your seven cards into two separate hands: a two card hand and a five card hand.

You win if both hands *beat* both of the banker's hands. If one hand beats the banker and the other doesn't, it is considered a push and no money changes hands. Hands that are exactly alike are called copy hands and are won by the banker. Although the house already has the edge (unless a player is the banker), to be certain it can never lose money, it assesses a 5% commission on all winning bets.

Pai Gow Poker moves at a leisurely pace. Originally, the dealing process was somewhat involved and convoluted, and many players were very slow and deliberate in deciding how to split their hands. Today, however, most casinos have figured out ways to speed up the game and most players are experienced enough to arrange their hands quickly. Your bankroll will fluctuate less than in other games because all the bets are even money, and almost half the hands are pushes.

FUNDAMENTALS OF PLAY

THE PLAYING TABLE
Pai Gow Poker is played on a table that is similar to a blackjack table and is usually located in or near the blackjack area. In many casinos, it is easy to find because there is an elevated sign at the table identifying the game. There are six player positions around the curved side of the table (see illustration). The dealer stands at the flat side with a chip rack directly in front of her and a shuffling machine to her right.

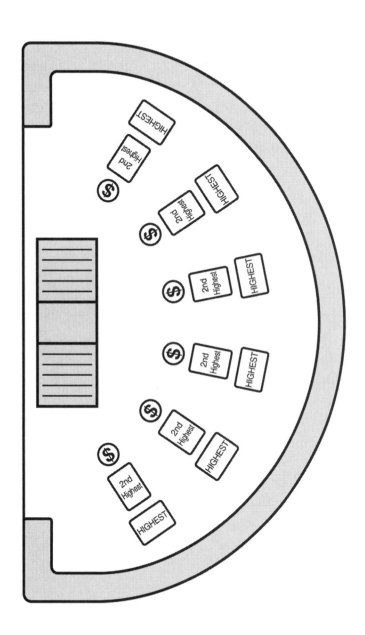

Pai Gow Poker Table

The older tables have a row of marked spaces where the dealt hands are first placed. To either side of the spaces are commission boxes marked 1,2,3 and 4,5,6. You won't, however, see such markings on the newer tables. To speed up the game, most casinos have dispensed with the intermediate dealing and commission collection steps. Originally, three dice were rolled before each deal to determine which player received the first hand. (The player positions are marked 1 through 6.) Now most casinos use a random number generator that reveals a new number at the start of every deal. This number is usually displayed in a window on the surface of the table.

At each player position is a betting circle where your bet is placed. Below the betting circle are two boxes where your two hands should be laid face down after splitting them. The lower box, which is marked HIGH, is for your five card hand, and the upper box, marked 2nd HIGHEST, is for your two card hand.

HOW THE GAME IS PLAYED

The game begins after all the players have placed their wagers. The minimum bet requirement in most casinos can range anywhere from $10 to $100, although you may find a $5 minimum in some smaller places. The dealer then shuffles the cards (usually with the aid of a shuffling machine) and deals out seven hands of seven cards each. All hands are dealt regardless of the number of players at the table. The first hand is given to the player designated by the number-generator display. The remaining hands are dealt counter-clockwise from that position. (Some casinos deal in a clockwise direction.) After all the hands are dealt out, the dealer removes the cards from the vacant player positions.

The **bank** rotates from player to player, and may be accepted or declined. If a player declines the bank, the dealer will always take the player's turn and act as banker for that hand. The dealer is included in the rotation of the bank, so that it is offered to each player on every seventh hand. A white plastic marker identifies the current banker.

After the cards are dealt and the banker selection formalities are concluded, it is time to examine your hand. The object is to arrange your seven cards to make the best combination of five card (high) and two card (2nd highest) poker hands that you can. This is called **setting the hand**.

The only rule is that your five card hand *must* have a poker value higher than your two card hand. If it does not, your bet is forfeited. Your bet is also forfeited if you do not lay out your two hands properly. The two card hand must be positioned above the five card hand (from the player's viewpoint). After all the players have set their hands, the dealer turns over her cards and sets her hand according to specific house rules.

All players bet against the bank, therefore, the goal of the game is for both of your hands to beat both of the banker's hands. To win, your two card hand must have a higher poker value than the banker's two card hand, and your five card hand must have a higher value than the banker's five card hand. Should one of your hands exactly match the banker's hand, it is called a *copy*, and the banker wins all copies. If you win one hand, but lose the other, it is considered a push and no money changes hands.

To illustrate the effect of a copy, suppose you beat the banker's five card hand and you both have a two card ace-queen. This is a push because the two card hand, being a copy, is won by the banker. On the other hand, if the banker's five- card hand was better than yours, you lose because both of your hands were beat.

The dealer's hand is the first one to be compared against the banker's (unless the dealer is the banker). Then the remaining hands are compared against the banker's hand, and the dealer settles the bets. The dealer makes all the payouts and collections, whether or not the dealer is the banker. Winning hands are paid even money, less a 5% commission. Losing hands lose the amount wagered. A commission is not charged against losing or tie hands.

Although the dealer represents the casino and handles the cards and the payoffs, from the playing standpoint she is just another player at the table. Her hand is on an equal footing with the other players' hands. The casino earns its profit from the 5% commission. The hand you have to beat is the banker's, who may or may not be the dealer.

Finally, don't be put off by the ritualistic procedures and seeming complexity of the game. This stuff is all handled by the dealer. All you have to do is put up your wager and set your hand. In most ways, it is simpler to play than blackjack.

THE BANKER

Each time a hand is dealt, the position of the bank rotates one step counter-clockwise (clockwise in some casinos). As was mentioned earlier, the dealer is included in the rotation, so each player gets the opportunity to be banker on every seventh hand. The dealer substitutes as banker for any player who passes and for all vacant player positions. A white plastic marker indicates the current position of the bank.

A few casinos have different procedures for determining how often a player gets to be banker. When no other players want the bank, some casinos will allow you to bank as often as every other hand. If you accept the bank, you must be able and willing to cover all wagers on the table. If you cannot cover all the bets, many casinos will agree to co-bank with you on a 50-50 basis. When co-banking, the banker's cards have to be set according to the casino rules.

When you accept the bank, you are betting against all the other players *and* the house. The dealer will place a bet for the house equal to your previous bet. You may request to have this bet reduced to the table minimum. In some casinos, you may decline to bet against the house. There is no good reason for doing this, however, since you have the same advantage (you win all copies) over the house that you have over the other players.

Whenever you assume the bank, the dealer continues to handle all the chips and makes the necessary payouts and collections. At the end of each hand, you are charged a 5% commission against your net aggregate winnings; that is, the total wins minus the losses.

Getting a poor hand while acting as banker could be very costly. So, why would anyone assume such a risk? Because, in the long run, being banker gives you an edge over the other players—just like the casino's edge. That is, you win all copy hands. For this reason, professionals and expert players try to bank as often as possible.

SETTING THE HAND

Although the basic method for setting a Pai Gow Poker hand has already been explained, this section will include more detail to give you a deeper understanding of the procedure. Pai Gow Poker uses a standard 52-card deck plus one joker. The joker may only be used as an ace or to complete a straight, a flush, or a straight flush. When used in a straight or straight flush, the joker becomes the rank and suit of the card needed to complete the hand. When used in a flush, it becomes the highest ranking missing card of the flush suit. It can never be used as part of a pair, three-of-a-kind, four-of-a-kind, or five-of-a-kind for any card other than an ace. If it is used alone, the joker becomes an ace. In poker parlance, such a joker is known as a *bug*.

To reiterate, you are dealt seven cards, which you arrange to make two hands: a two card hand and a five card hand. The poker value of the five card hand must be higher than the two card hand. Since this can be done in more than one way, the object is to set the two hands so that they have the best chance of beating the banker's two hands. The highest possible five card hand is five aces, which consists of the four aces and the joker. The highest two card hand is a pair of aces. The two card hand cannot be a straight or a flush.

When you first receive your cards, the best procedure is to arrange them in order, from the highest rank to the lowest rank. Then look for the possibility of a flush or a straight. If you were dealt the joker, check to see if it can complete a flush or straight, or make a pair of aces. Finally, look for pairs and triplets. Once you have reviewed the hand and are aware of all the possible combinations, set it according to the strategy rules shown in the Playing Strategy section, below.

When you have decided how to set your hand, place the cards face down in two stacks with the two card hand above the five card hand. At every player position, there are two boxes. The one marked HIGH is where the five card hand goes, and the one marked 2nd HIGHEST is where the two card hand goes. The five- card hand is sometimes referred to as the back hand, and the two card hand is sometimes called the low hand or the front hand.

You should be very careful and deliberate when setting your hand. This is especially true when it contains the joker. The basic idea is to make the two card hand as high as possible without exceeding the value of the five card hand. If you don't have good enough cards to make two winning hands, you should try for a push by forming one hand that will not lose. For example, if you are dealt the following cards:

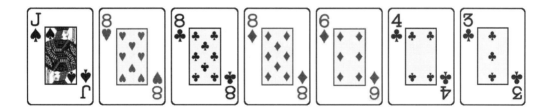

It is pretty obvious that you should five card the three eight's and two card the highest odd cards, as follows:

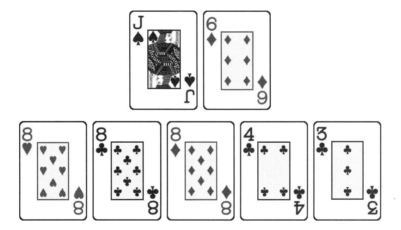

Although the J 6 is a losing hand, you don't have any other options. Since the five card hand has an 85% chance of winning, you will at least push.

If you are dealt two pair (and nothing else worthwhile), you should sometimes split the pairs, depending on the ranks of the odd cards. In the following hand...

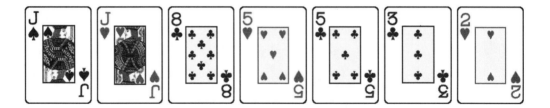

you should split the pairs by putting the fives in the two card hand.

This is necessary because keeping the pairs together in the five card hand would result in an unacceptably weak two card hand of 8-3, which is almost certainly a loser. On the other hand, if the odd cards are strong enough as in the following hand:

the two pairs should be kept together, as follows:

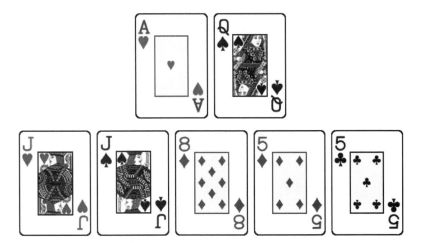

The A Q is a reasonably strong two card hand and the J J 5 5 is a very strong five card hand with an 81% chance of winning.

The following is an example of how easy it is to misplay a hand that contains a joker:

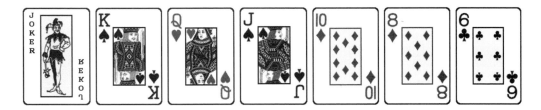

In this hand, don't make the mistake of misplaying the joker by five carding an ace-high straight. As you will see later, you should make the two card hand as high as possible without compromising the five card hand. Thus, the best way to set this hand is as follows:

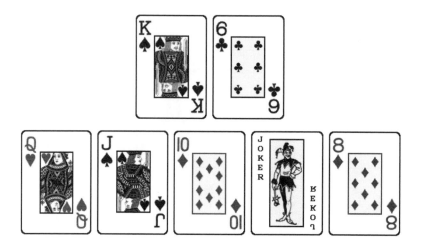

Although it will probably lose, a K 6 is still a lot better than 8 6. Whether the straight is ace-high or queen-high doesn't really matter because either one has more than a 90% chance of winning.

These are only a few examples to give you a taste of how the cards should be set. In the section on Playing Strategy, you will be shown the best setting rules for players. You will also be shown the house rules that the dealers use to set their cards.

DEALER ASSISTANCE

If you can't figure out the best way to set your cards, you may ask the dealer for assistance. The dealer will suggest how to set them according to the house rules, but will not take responsibility for winning or losing hands. If one of the other players is the banker, you should avoid doing this because seeing your cards will give that person a distinct advantage in setting his own hand (he knows what he has to beat), especially if there are few players at the table.

PLAYING TWO HANDS

In some table games, you are permitted to play multiple hands. In Pai Gow Poker, however, most casinos allow you to play only one hand at a time. A few casinos circulate a *Dragon* marker when there are one or more vacant player positions. When you are offered the Dragon marker, you may play a second hand if you wish. If you accept, you may wager any amount on the second hand so long as it is at least half of your original bet.

You must set your original hand first, and then set the second hand. Any benefit comes from the fact that you get to see a total of 14 cards (over 26% of the deck), which may be an advantage for setting the second hand. Since the opportunity for playing a second hand is small, I am only making you aware that it exists without providing any specific strategy information.

ADDITIONAL BETTORS

In Pai Gow Poker, it is permissible for another person to place a side bet on your hand, if you agree. This person may be a bystander or another player at your table. Whenever you give such permission (and it is customary to do so), you still maintain full control on how your hand is set. In some casinos, the floor supervisor must also give permission. When extra betting occurs, the total amount wagered on your betting circle cannot exceed the table limit.

TABLE ETIQUETTE

Before sitting down at any new table game for the first time, it is always a good idea to stand nearby and watch several rounds of play. This is especially true for Pai Gow Poker. When you do sit down, just watch what the other players are doing and try to do the same. If you make a mistake in table protocol, the dealer will politely correct you.

The first thing you should do (after you get chips from the dealer) is place your bet. Put the bet directly on the bet circle any time after the dealer has collected all the cards from the previous round. If the bank is offered to you, decline it unless you are a very experienced player.

After all the cards have been dealt, look at your seven cards. It is against casino rules to show your cards to anyone else, and it is also against your best interest to do so. Set your cards carefully, but try not to hold up the game. You usually have plenty of time because some players are unhurried and may even ask the dealer for help.

When you set your cards be sure that the five card hand is the better hand and that you place it below the two card hand. If you fail to do these things correctly, you will automatically lose your bet. In fact, you will also lose your bet if you miscount the cards when you split the hand, such as 3-4 instead of 2-5. The player is penalized for making mistakes, while the dealer and the banker are not.

You cannot touch your cards once the banker's or the dealer's cards are exposed. From this point on, the dealer handles all of the cards.

WINNING HANDS

The various card combinations that produce winning hands in Pai Gow Poker are similar to regular poker. The main exception involves straights and straight flushes (see below). Pai Gow Poker uses one standard 52-card deck with one joker. The joker can only be used as an ace, or to complete a flush, straight, straight flush, or royal flush. Suits have no relative value; they only come into play for a flush, a straight flush, or a royal flush.

FIVE CARD HAND

The value of a five card hand depends on which of the following card combinations it contains, listed in order from the highest to the lowest:

Five Aces: Four aces and the joker, as shown below, is the highest value hand in Pai Gow Poker. Insomuch as the joker can only be used as an ace or to complete a straight, flush, or straight flush, there are no other possible five-of-a-kinds. Since there is only one way to make this hand, it is very rare.

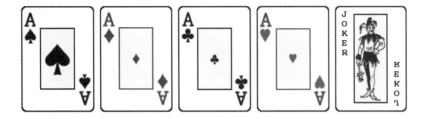

Royal Flush: An ace-high straight flush is the second-highest hand in Pai Gow Poker. The joker may be used to complete a royal flush. Since suits do not have any relative value, two royal flushes of different suits constitute a copy. The banker wins copies.

Straight Flush: Five consecutive cards, all of the same suit. The joker may be used to complete a straight flush. Should the banker and a player both have straight flushes, the higher-valued one is the winner. In Pai Gow Poker, an A 2 3 4 5 is the best straight flush and a king-high is the second best straight flush. If both the banker and player have identical straight flushes (except for the suit), then the banker wins.

NOTE: Some casinos use standard poker rankings so that the best straight flush is king-high, and the lowest is A 2 3 4 5.

Four-of-a-kind: Four cards of the same rank. The fifth card is unrelated to the others. Except for aces, the joker cannot be used to convert three-of-a-kind to four-of-a-kind. Should the banker and a player both have four-of-a-kind, the hand with the highest rank is the winner.

Full House: Three cards of the same rank and two cards of another rank, that is, three-of-a-kind and a pair. Except for aces, the joker cannot be used to complete a full house. Should the banker and a player both have a full house, the hand with the highest ranked Three-of-a-kind is the winner. The ranks of the pairs are immaterial.

Flush: Five cards of the same suit, not in sequence. The joker may be used to complete a flush. For the purpose of breaking a tie, the joker is considered to be an ace. Should the banker and a player both have flushes, the one containing the highest ranked card is the winner. If the highest ranked card in both hands is the same, then the second-highest ranked card is the tiebreaker. If that is also the same, then the third-, the fourth-, and the fifth-highest cards are compared. If all five cards in both hands are the same rank, that is considered a copy and the banker wins.

Straight: Five consecutive cards of mixed suits. The joker may be used to complete a straight. Should the banker and a player both have straights, the higher-valued one is the winner. In Pai Gow Poker, an A K Q J 10 is the best straight, an A 2 3 4 5 is the second-best straight, and a king-high is the third-best straight. If both hands have identical straights, the banker wins.

NOTE: Some casinos use standard poker rankings so that the second-best straight is king-high, and the lowest is A 2 3 4 5.

Three-of-a-kind: Three cards of the same rank. The remaining two cards are unrelated. Except for aces, the joker cannot be used to convert a pair to three-of-a-kind. Should the banker and a player both have three-of-a-kind, the one with the highest rank is the winner.

Two Pair: A pair of one rank and a pair of another rank. The fifth card is unrelated. Again, except for aces, the joker cannot be used to make a pair. Should the banker and a player both have two pair, the one with the highest-ranked pair is the winner. If the highest-ranked pair in both hands is the same, then the one having the highest-ranked second pair wins. If both pairs are the same rank, then the hand with the highest fifth card wins. If all cards are the same rank, the banker wins.

One Pair: Two cards of the same rank. The three remaining cards are unrelated. The highest-ranked pair wins. If the banker's and player's five card hands contain pairs of the same rank, then the one with the highest-ranked odd card wins. If that card is the same, then the fourth and fifth cards break the tie. If all cards are the same rank, the banker wins.

High Card: A hand that contains none of the above poker hands. The highest-ranked card in the hand determines its relative value. If the banker and a player have the same high card, then the second, third, fourth, and fifth cards break the tie. Of course, if all cards are the same rank, the banker wins.

TWO CARD HAND

As you would guess, flushes, straights, and straight flushes are not valid in two card hands. Multiples of a particular rank greater than one pair, such as three- or four-of-a-kind, are not possible. The value of a two card hand depends on which of the following card combinations it contains, listed in order from the highest to the lowest:

One Pair: Two cards of the same rank. The best two card hand is a pair of aces. If the banker's and player's hands contain pairs of the same rank, the banker wins.

High Card: A two card hand that does not contain a pair. The highest-ranked card in the hand determines its relative value. If the banker and a player have the same high card, then the second card breaks the tie. If both cards are the same rank, the banker wins.

PLAYING STRATEGY

The primary strategy in playing Pai Gow Poker is how to set your hand. A mathematically-perfect strategy is far too complicated for anyone to memorize. In fact, such a strategy has never been published. One reason for this is that its exactness depends on the particular house setting rules that are used, and these vary somewhat from casino to casino.

A choice of two playing strategies is presented. The first is a simplified version for casual players called a *short strategy* and the second is a more complex version for serious players called a *long strategy*. In addition, for reference purposes, an example of typical house rules for setting the dealer's hand is shown at the end of the chapter.

To simplify the wording of the strategy rules, the verbs *two card* and *five card* are used extensively. For example, in a hand containing two pair, "two card the smaller pair" means to put the smaller of the two pair into the two card hand. It is assumed that the remaining five cards are put into the five card hand.

A *singleton* is an odd card that is not a part of a poker combination such as a pair, a triplet, a straight, or a flush. For instance, a hand containing two pair and no other combinations will have three singletons. Finally, when describing specific card sequences in the text, the joker is abbreviated "Jok."

A SHORT STRATEGY

At first, you may wonder what is so short about the following strategy. After you see the long strategy, you may think it is *too* short. The short strategy only covers the most common hands. This works because 85% of the hands dealt contain no pair, one pair, two pair, or a triplet. The more infrequent hands such as three pairs or two triplets are so strong that you will likely win even if you don't set them exactly right.

GENERAL RULES
Rule 1: Set the two card hand as high as possible without compromising the five card hand. This rule will set your hand correctly 60% of the time. Just remember that that the five card hand *must* be a higher poker value than the two card hand. Also, remember that the joker is the same as an ace, unless it is completing a flush, straight, or straight flush.

Rule 2: Break-even for two cards is A 8. Break-even for five cards is J J. Try to exceed break-even on both hands. It is important to remember these break-even hands. Break-even means that you have a 50% chance of winning the hand. If both hands are above break-even, you have a good chance of winning money. Knowing the break-even points will keep you out of trouble, especially for the more complex hands.

SPECIFIC COMMON HANDS
High card: Two card the 2nd- and 3rd-highest cards. For instance, if you have K J 10 7 5 4 3, two card the J 10 and five card the K 7 5 4 3.

One pair: Two card the two highest singletons. This means that the pair goes in the five card hand along with the three lowest singletons. For instance, if you have K J J 9 7 5 4, two card the K 9 and five card the J J 7 5 4.

Two pair: A two-pair hand is the one involving the most complex strategy. A glance at the long strategy in the next section makes this very apparent. Although, this is the area of greatest simplification, the following two rules should serve the casual and recreational player well.

> **Without singleton Ace: Always split pairs.** For instance, if you have Q Q J 9 4 4 2, two card the 4 4 and five card the Q Q J 9 2.

> **With singleton Ace: Split J J, 7 7 or better.** For instance, if you have A Q Q J 9 9 4, two card the 9 9 and five card the A Q Q J 4. If you have A Q Q J 9 4 4, two card the A J and five card the Q Q 9 4 4.

Three-of-a-kind: Split A A A. Do not split other triplets. For instance, if you have Jok A A Q 9 8 4, two card the Jok Q or A Q (it makes no difference) and five card a pair of aces. If you have K J J J 9 8 4, two card the K 9 and five card the J J J 8 4.

Straight: Five card the lowest five cards in straight. For instance, if you have K Q J 10 9 8 5, two card the K 5 and five card the Q J 10 9 8.

Flush: Five card the lowest five cards in flush. Split, as necessary, to meet Rule 2. For instance, if you have Jok A♦ Q♣ 10♥ 9♥ 7♥ 5♥, two card the A♦ Q♣ and five card the Jok 10♥ 9♥ 7♥ 5♥. Although you broke up the pair of aces, both hands are above break-even. If you have A♥ Q♣ Q♥ J♦ 7♥ 5♥ 4♥, split the flush and two card the A♥ J♦. Both hands are above break-even. If, instead, you saved the flush, the resulting Q♣ J♦ hand would be below break-even.

These strategy rules are greatly simplified, but General Rules 1 and 2 will carry you a long way, especially if you have read the other material and developed a general understanding on how best to set hands. Following is a summary of the Short Playing Strategy.

SHORT PLAYING STRATEGY
FOR PAI GOW POKER

General Rules

Rule 1: Set the two card hand as high as possible without compromising the five card hand.

Rule 2: Break-even for two cards is **A 8**. Break-even for five cards is **J J**. Try to exceed break-even on both hands.

Strategy for Specific Common Hands

High card: Two card the 2nd- and 3rd-highest cards.

One pair: Two card the two highest singletons.

Two pair: Without singleton ace: Always split pairs.
         With singleton ace: Split J J, 7 7 or better.

Three-of-a-kind: Split A A A. Do not split other triplets.

Straight: Five card the lowest five cards in straight.

Flush: Five card the lowest five cards in flush. Split flush, as necessary, to meet Rule 2.

THE LONG STRATEGY

The following rules do not represent perfect playing strategy, which is far too complicated for the average player to memorize, but they do represent an accurate approximation. These are the rules you really need to know if you want to become a serious Pai Gow Poker player.

High card: A hand consisting of seven unrelated cards (singletons), with no flush, no straight, and no pairs.

- Two card the second- and third-highest cards.

- If the two highest cards are A K or A Q, two card the second- and fourth-highest cards

One pair: Five singletons with no flush and no straight. This is the most common hand in Pai Gow Poker.

- Two card the two highest singletons.

Two pair: Three singletons with no flush and no straight. To split means: two card the smaller pair and five card the remaining cards.

- High pair is A A: Split.
- High pair is K K: Split.
  Except if low pair is 5 5 through 2 2 with A J or higher: Two card the highest singletons.
- High pair is Q Q: Split.
  Except if low pair is 9 9 through 2 2 with A J or higher: Two card the highest singletons.
- High pair is J J: Split.
  Except with A J or higher: Two card the highest singletons.
- High pair is 9 9 or 10 10: Split.
  Except with singleton ace: Two card the highest singletons.
- High pair is 6 6 to 8 8: Split.
  Except with singleton king or better: Two card the highest singletons.
- High pair is 3 3 to 5 5: Split.
  Except with singleton queen or better: Two card the highest singletons.

Three pairs: Plus one singleton.

- Two card the highest pair.

Three-of-a-kind: Four singletons with no flush and no straight. To split means: break the triplet and five card the resulting pair.

- A A A: Split and two card one ace plus the highest singleton.
- K K K with J 10 or higher: Two card the highest singletons.

- K K K with J 9 or lower: Split and two card one king plus the highest singleton.
- Q Q Q: Two card the highest singletons.

Straight: Two singletons with no flush and no pair. May include the joker.
- Five card the straight
- For a six or seven card straight, five card the lowest-value straight.

Flush: Two singletons with no straight and no pair. May include the joker.
- Five card the flush
- For a six or seven card flush, five card the lowest-value flush.

Straight or flush, with external pair: The pair is external to the straight or flush.
- Two card the pair, five card the straight or flush.

Straight and included pair, no joker: One of the pair is shared by the straight.
- Six or seven card straight: Five card the lowest five cards of the straight.
- Hand contains no Ace: Five card the straight.
- Ace-high straight with Q Q, J J, or 10 10: Five card the pair and two card the A K.
- Ace-high straight with A A or K K: Five card the straight.

Straight and included pair, with joker: One of the pair is shared by the straight.
- Ace or joker not needed to complete straight: Five card the straight.

- A Jok pair needed to complete ace-high straight: Five card the ace and joker plus three lowest singletons.
- A Jok pair needed to complete ace-low straight: Five card the straight.
- Jack-high (or higher) joker straight: Five card the pair.
- Ten-high (or lower) joker straight: Five card the straight.

Flush and included pair: One or two of the pair are shared by the flush.

- Six or seven card flush: Five card the lowest five cards of the flush.
- Ace and/or joker not needed to complete flush: Five card the flush.
- Ace and/or joker needed to complete flush: Five card the pair if second-highest card is 10 or better and pair is 10 10 or better. Otherwise, five card the flush.

Straight and flush or straight flush: No pairs.

- Five card the straight or the flush, whichever leaves the highest two card hand.
- The rule is the same for a straight flush or royal.

Straight and flush and one pair: Or straight flush.

- If possible, two card the pair and five card the straight or flush or straight flush.
- If pair is included, use above rules for straight or flush with included pair.

Straight or flush and two pair: Or straight flush.

- If possible, two card one of the pairs and five card the straight or flush.

- If both pairs are included, split the straight or flush and use above rules for two pair.

Full house: Plus two singletons. May include the joker.

- Split the full house and two card the pair.

Three-of-a-kind plus Three-of-a-kind: Plus one singleton.

- Two card a pair from the higher triplet and five card the lower triplet.

Four-of-a-kind: Plus three singletons.

- A A A A or K K K K: Split the quad and two card a pair.
- Q Q Q Q or J J J J: With a singleton ace, five card the quad. Otherwise, split.
- 10 10 10 10 or 9 9 9 9: With a king or higher, five card the quad. Otherwise, split.
- 8 8 8 8 or 7 7 7 7: With queen or higher, five card the quad. Otherwise, split.
- 6 6 6 6 or lower: Five card the quad.

Four-of-a-kind plus one pair: Plus one singleton.

- Five card the quad and two card the pair.
- Exception: If quad is Q Q Q Q or higher *and* pair is 4 4 or lower, two card two of the quad and five card two pairs.

Four-of-a-kind plus three-of-a-kind: No singletons.

- Two card the highest pair and five card either a quad or a full house.

Five aces: Plus two singletons.

- Two card a pair of aces.

HOUSE RULES FOR SETTING CARDS

In casino parlance, the house setting rules are called the **house way**. The house way falls somewhere between the Short Strategy and the Long Strategy in complexity, and it is perfectly reasonable for you to apply the house rules for setting your own cards. The house way varies somewhat from casino to casino, but the rules shown below are typical.

No pair: Two card the second- and third-highest cards.

One pair: Two card the two highest singletons.

Two pair: When splitting, always two card the lowest pair.
- If high pair is A A: Split.
- Without singleton ace: Split if low pair is 7 7 or better.
- With singleton ace: Split if high pair is J J or better and low pair is 6 6 or better.

Three pairs: Two card the highest pair.

Three-of-a-kind:
- A A A: Split and two card one ace plus the highest singleton.
- Other triplets: Two card the highest singletons.

Three-of-a-kind plus three-of-a-kind: Two card a pair from the highest triplet.

Straights, flushes, and straight flushes: With a choice to play either a flush, straight, or straight flush, five card the category that will allow two carding the highest two cards while preserving the flush, straight, or straight flush.
- With one pair: Two card the pair if a straight, flush, or straight flush can be preserved.

- With two pair: If pairs are 10 10 or better, use two pair rule. Otherwise, preserve the straight, flush, or straight flush.
- With three pairs: Use three pairs rule.
- With three-of-a-kind: Two card a pair of the triplet.
- With full house: Use full house rule.

Full house: Two card the pair.

Three-of-a-kind and two pair: Two card the highest pair.

Four-of-a-kind:

- Jacks or better: Split and two card a pair of the quad.
- 7s through 10s: Two card A K, A Q, A J, or extra pair. Otherwise, split.
- 2s through 6s: Never split. Two card highest singletons.

Five aces: Split and two card a pair of aces. If hand contains a pair of kings, then two card the kings.

SEEING OTHER CARDS

The casino rule is that you are not supposed to show your cards to any other players. Is there any advantage to seeing other players' cards? Only for the banker, and especially if the banker is another player. Theoretically, there is no advantage to the dealer because she has to set her hand strictly according to unvarying house rules. However, there is no assurance to the player that this always happens. It would, without a doubt, be a tremendous advantage for a player to see the banker's cards, but this is unlikely to ever happen.

Of course, the rule is broken whenever a player asks the dealer for help in setting his hand. This gives the banker/player a look at what he has to beat. It doesn't matter as much at a full table, because if the banker/player breaks strategy rules to beat the exposed hand, he might end up losing against more of the other hands. With only two or three players, however, there is a clear advantage.

OVERCOMING THE HOUSE EDGE

Aside from blackjack, Pai Gow Poker is the only casino game in which it is theoretically possible to overcome the house edge. The modifier *theoretical* is used because from a practical standpoint, beating the house is not easy to do. However, because it *is* possible, this is a subject that needs to be addressed.

The theoretical possibility of beating the house is due to the fact that a banker/player in Pai Gow Poker can have as much as a 0.4% edge over the house under optimum conditions. Most of the time the advantage probably comes closer to 0.2%, but it is still an advantage. Besides winning all copy hands, the other benefit is that the 5% rake is applied to the net aggregate win (wins minus losses) instead of each individual win. Since a player usually gets the opportunity to bank on every seventh hand, how is it possible to overcome the player's negative expectation of 2.5 to 2.8%? It ain't easy!

Obviously, the only way to overcome the house edge in Pai Gow Poker is by trying to bank as often as possible. And that alone is not enough. The following conditions are necessary to have any chance of overcoming the house edge:

- A table in which the other players are betting heavily—considerably above the table minimum.
- A table in which the players are all declining the bank and the dealer is willing to let you bank every second or third hand. This situation is no longer easy to find.

- When not banking, you should wager no more than the table minimum.

When the above conditions are optimal, the long-term expectation can actually become positive. To succeed, however, you must fully understand the best playing strategy and your bankroll must be large enough to sustain potential losses when banking the game.

CONCLUSION

Having gotten its start in the cardrooms of California, Pai Gow Poker is really a gambler's game. Nevada upped the rake to 5% so it is more difficult to beat the edge, even for a player who banks a lot. Yet, if you never take the bank, the house edge is only 2.85%, assuming you play correctly. Because all the betting is at even money and there are so many pushes, your bankroll will not fluctuate excessively. All in all, the game is a fun and leisurely experience that will not drain your bankroll at an excessive rate. Although the strategy can get somewhat complicated, Pai Gow Poker is basically a very easy game to play.

◆15◆
RED DOG

This is an old American game that dates back to the gambling halls of the early West and was also played extensively as a private game, especially by newspaper reporters. Because the game became such an easy mark for cheaters, it eventually fell out of popularity.

Some casinos revived the old Red Dog a number of years ago, but changed the game so that it is significantly different from the original. This version is sometimes called *Casino Red Dog*. It didn't become very popular, and is now rather hard to find in the newer casinos

In Casino Red Dog, after the players make their bets, one community hand of two face-up cards is dealt out in front of the dealer. Players may raise their bets if they think the rank of a third card will fall between the ranks of the first two cards. If it does, the players win and are paid as much as 5 to 1 or as little as even money, depending on the spread of the first two cards.

FUNDAMENTALS OF PLAY

The casino version is quite simple. One or more standard 52-card decks are used, and the cards are ranked the same as in poker. The suits don't matter. The cards are valued 2 through 14, with jack = 11, queen = 12, king = 13, and ace = 14. That is, deuce is low and ace is high.

After an initial ante, the dealer places two cards face-up on the table. Unless the cards are the same or consecutive, the dealer announces the spread, which is the number of ranks between the two dealt cards. For instance, if the two cards are 5 and 9, the spread is 3.

The players may then raise their bets up to the amount of their ante if they think the rank of a third card will fall between the ranks of the first two cards. All the players are in the same boat. They all win if the third card dealt falls *between* the first two cards, otherwise they lose.

A consecutive hand, such as 8 and 9 is considered a tie, and the dealer does not draw a third card. This is a push and the players neither win nor lose.

For a pair hand, such as 8 and 8, the dealer automatically draws a third card, and the players do not get an opportunity to raise. If the third card is the same rank as the first two, the players are paid 11 to 1 on their ante bets. If the third card is different, it is a push.

PAYOUTS

If the third card falls within the spread, payouts are made according to the following schedule:

CASINO RED DOG PAYTABLE	
Spread of 1	Pays 5 to 1
Spread of 2	Pays 4 to 1
Spread of 3	Pays 2 to 1
Spread of 4 through 11	Pays 1 to 1

RED DOG STRATEGY

In Casino Red Dog you don't get to handle any cards and the only decision is whether or not to raise your bet. If you can find the game, the best strategy is to raise only when the two card spread is seven or greater. With the correct playing strategy, the overall house edge is about 2.8% to 3.2%, depending on the number of decks used—the more decks, the lower the edge.

Whatever you do, don't raise on spreads of 1, 2, or 3, even though the payoff is better. The house edge on each of these bets is well over 20%.

PLAYING STRATEGY FOR RED DOG

Raise the initial ante only if
the two card spread is at least 7.

·16·
ROULETTE

Roulette is the oldest of all the casino games being played today, and the modern roulette wheel has been the dominant symbol of casino gambling for more than 200 years. Whether it is a scene in a movie or TV show, or simply a photograph of a casino gaming room, the roulette wheel is usually visible and is frequently the center of attention. In many European casinos, roulette accounts for more than half the legal gaming revenue, and is so popular that getting a seat at a roulette table is often a challenge. However, in the United States, roulette is not the game of choice for most gamblers, and accounts for less than 5% of total casino revenues.

In Europe, there are few casinos in which roulette wheels are not the main focus of interest. The chief reason for this is the prevalence of the single-zero French roulette wheel, which has more favorable odds than the double-zero American wheel.

It has been said that roulette, in one form or other, is as old as the wheel itself. In fact, its origins have been lost in history. However, most historians agree that the modern roulette wheel configuration and game rules were developed in France more than 200 years ago, where it has been popular ever since.

One of the earliest descriptions of the present form of roulette can be found in the French novel *La Roulette ou le Jouer* by Jacques Lablee, which was published in 1801. In the novel, the wheel is described as having ball pockets with the numbers 1 through 36 plus two extra pockets marked with a zero and a double zero. The zero and double-zero pockets were reserved for the bank and represented the casino's mathematical advantage. The novel also describes the French betting layout very much as it appears today.

In 1843, when the twin brothers, François and Louis Blanc, opened their casino in Homburg, Germany, they introduced the first single-zero roulette wheel in a successful ploy to take business away from other European casinos. As will be explained later, the single-zero wheel is more advantageous to the player and pays off better than the double-zero wheel.

Twenty years later, François Blanc purchased the failing casino in Monte Carlo. He rebuilt it and installed single-zero roulette wheels to insure the casino's popularity. Monte Carlo became so successful that it set the gaming standards for the rest of Europe. Ultimately, any European casino that expected to stay in business had little choice but to install single-zero wheels.

During the mid-nineteenth century, some surplus double-zero French wheels found their way from Europe to New Orleans. At that time, the standard wheel in the United States had 28 numbered pockets plus three house pockets marked with a zero, a double zero, and an eagle. Typically, the house paid single-number odds at only 26 to 1, giving it an enormous 12.9% advantage. Because of this, it was not a very popular game.

When single-number odds were paid at 35 to 1, the double-zero French wheel had a house advantage of only 5.26%. This was much better than the 12.9% edge that American gamblers had been playing against. Consequently, the new wheel was greatly favored by knowledgeable players. The French terminology on the betting layout was soon replaced with English, and, before long, the 38-pocket double-zero wheel became the standard roulette wheel in the United States.

Compared to other table games such as craps and blackjack, roulette is a quiet and relaxing experience. Although it may not seem so at first glance, it is a very simple game to play and there is plenty of time between spins of the ball to consider what bets to place. You just put one or more chips on a number, the dealer spins the ball, and if the ball lands in a pocket with your number on it, you are paid.

There are a variety of other bets that can be made, such as betting on adjacent numbers or on all the odd numbers or on all the red numbers. With one exception, the house percentage on every bet is the same, which eliminates the concern that some bets may be a better deal than others.

FUNDAMENTALS OF PLAY

Different kinds of roulette wheels are used in different parts of the world. To avoid any confusion at the outset, the main types of wheels are briefly defined and described below. The main purpose for these descriptions is to establish the terminology used throughout the chapter.

THE AMERICAN WHEEL

The roulette wheel that is prevalent in the United States is generally called the **American wheel**. Its **wheelhead** (the rotating center piece) contains 38 numbered ball pockets that are alternately colored red and black (see illustration). In addition to the numbers 1 through 36, there is a zero and a double zero. This is why the American wheel is often called a double-zero wheel.

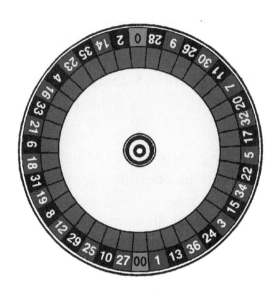

American Roulette Wheel

The ordering of the numbers around the wheelhead is called the American number sequence, distinguishing it from the French number sequence, which is entirely different. Also, the layout terminology is in English and non-value colored roulette chips are used to differentiate bets placed by the various players.

For all bets and bet combinations except one, the house advantage for the American wheel is 5.26%. In Atlantic City only, the Surrender rule is in effect and this reduces the house edge to 2.63% for even-money outside bets. The surrender rule is essentially the same as the *Le Partage* rule used in the United Kingdom. These special rules are explained later.

THE FRENCH WHEEL

The roulette wheel that is prevalent in continental Europe is called the **French wheel**. Its wheelhead contains 37 numbered ball pockets that are alternately colored red and black (see illustration). In addition to the numbers from 1 through 36, there is a zero, but no double zero, thus the French wheel is often called a single-zero wheel.

French Roulette Wheel

The ordering of numbers around the wheelhead is unique to French wheels and is called the French number sequence. As expected, the betting layout uses French terminology. Regular casino value chips are used for placing bets on the layout. Since everyone uses the same types of chips, arguments frequently arise as to which player placed a winning chip.

The lack of a double zero is the main distinguishing factor from the American wheel, and this reduces the house advantage for the French wheel to 2.7% for all inside bets. Moreover, the *En Prison* rule reduces the house edge to 1.35% for even-money outside bets.

THE ENGLISH WHEEL

A third type of wheel that is becoming more common is best described as an American-style wheel with only a single zero. This is the only kind of wheel that is legal in the United Kingdom; hence, it is called the **English** wheel. It is the result of the British Gaming Act of 1968. Since this roulette wheel uses both French (single-zero) and American (English-language layout) characteristics, it is a kind of hybrid wheel.

Because the English wheel has 37 pockets and no double zero, the house advantage for inside bets is the same as for the French wheel: 2.7%. The *Le Partage* rule, which is used in England and is very similar to the *En Prison* rule, reduces the house edge to 1.35% for even-money outside bets.

In those instances where a single-zero roulette wheel is used in an open casino in the United States, it is almost always an English wheel. But the Surrender or *Le Partage* rule is not commonly applied to single-zero wheels, even in Atlantic City.

BOULE AND VINGT-TROIS

These are roulette-like games that are mainly popular in France, Switzerland, Macau, and Malaysia. In both games, a rubber ball is spun around in a wooden bowl, eventually coming to rest in a numbered cup or cavity. There are several versions of boule, differing mainly in the number of cups (18, 25, or 36) and whether or not the bowl rotates. Vingt-trois has 27 cups and is very similar to boule.

In all countries except Switzerland, the house enjoys an 11.11% edge on most bets in either boule or vingt-trois, so they can only be described as sucker games. In Switzerland, the payoff odds for boule are even less favorable, resulting in an astonishing house edge of 22.22%. The fact that Swiss casinos attract any customers at all says something about the desperation of Swiss gamblers. Since there is no apparent way for a player to prevail over the house advantage in either of these games, further discussion of boule and vingt-trois is of little value.

HOW THE GAME IS PLAYED

Before you start playing, you should buy one or more stacks of **special roulette chips** from the dealer. Each player at the table is assigned chips of a different color to avoid confusion as to who placed what bet. The value of each chip is the table minimum (usually fifty cents to five dollars) unless you ask the dealer to set a higher value. More on this later.

The roulette table consists of a betting layout with the wheel situated at one end of the table as shown in the illustrations of an American roulette table and a French roulette table. More often in Europe, but sometimes in the United States, a double-ended layout is used with the roulette wheel located in the center. One dealer (called a *croupier* in France) operates each layout. When the crowd gets very heavy, a second dealer, called a **checkracker** or **mucker**, helps by stacking the roulette chips. Some casinos in the United States now use automatic checkracking machines, which speeds up the game.

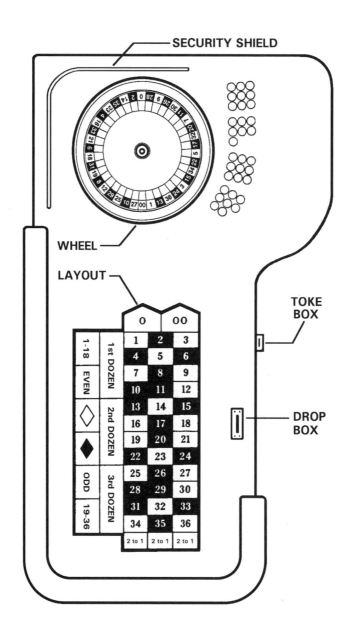

American Roulette Table

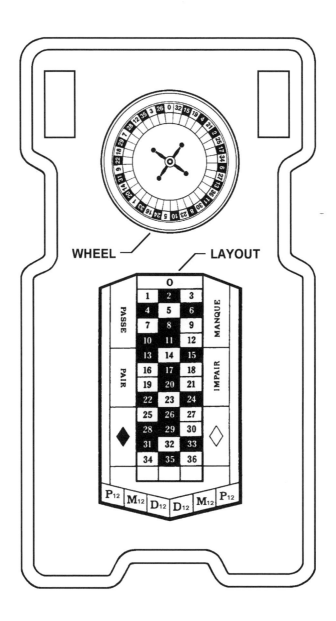

French Roulette Table

A roulette wheel consists of two major parts. The outer section is called the **bowl** and contains the circular track on which the ball spins. The rotating inner section is called the **wheelhead** and contains the numbered pockets where the ball lands and comes to rest. In an American wheel, the wheelhead has 38 separate pockets numbered from 1 to 36 (not consecutively), plus 0 and 00. The pockets are alternately colored red and black except for the 0 and 00 pockets, which are colored green.

In the United States, the ball is usually spun in a clockwise direction while the wheelhead is rotating counterclockwise. In many European casinos, where the game moves at a more leisurely pace, the rotating wheelhead is stopped while the winning bets are being paid off, and is then started in the opposite direction for the next spin of the ball. In all cases, the ball is spun in the direction opposite to the wheelhead rotation.

As the game begins, the players select their bets by placing chips on the betting layout. After most of the bets are down, the dealer picks the ball out of the wheelhead and launches it on the track around the bowl. The placing of bets may continue while the ball is spinning.

When the ball slows down to where it has about two or three revolutions to go, the dealer calls out, "No more bets," sometimes with an accompanying pass of the hand over the layout. Any bets placed after that announcement may be disallowed by the dealer. Whether or not the dealer verbally cuts off the betting, bets put down after the ball lands in a numbered pocket are always disallowed. The placing of bets after the ball falls off the track is called **past posting** and doing this more than once will surely attract the attention of a floor supervisor.

After the ball settles into one of the pockets, the dealer places a **win marker** on the winning number, sweeps off the losing chips and begins to pay the winners. When the payoff is complete, the dealer removes the marker and the players start placing their bets for the next spin of the ball.

GETTING STARTED

Playing roulette is simplicity itself. First, find yourself a comfortable seat at the roulette table. The best seats for reaching the entire betting layout are at the center of the front of the table and the last seat around the back side, next to the dealer. If the table is crowded, the first seat that opens up will have to do.

Once seated, you need to buy one or more stacks of twenty roulette chips from the dealer. Since all the players at the table intermingle their bets on the same betting layout, each person is issued roulette chips of a different color to avoid mix-ups.

The value of each roulette chip depends on what you paid for the stack. In Nevada, the minimum price for a twenty-chip stack will be between $10 (50 cents per chip) and $100 ($5 per chip), depending on the casino and the time of day. If you pay more than the minimum, the dealer will place a special marker, called a **lammer**, on the rim of the wheel to remind her of what your particular chips are worth.

Roulette chips may be bought with cash or with regular casino chips that were obtained from the cashier or brought from another table game. When you are finished playing, the dealer will exchange your remaining roulette chips back to regular casino chips. You are not allowed to remove the colored roulette chips from the roulette table—they cannot be used anywhere else and only the dealer you bought them from knows how much they are worth.

Occasionally, a person will step up to the table and play cash or regular casino chips. This is usually acceptable unless a second person does the same thing, in which case the dealer might ask one of them to buy the colored roulette chips to avoid confusion.

PLACING BETS

Bets may be made by placing one or more chips on individual numbers, on combinations of numbers, or on one of the betting areas around the outside of the main number field. If a particular bet consists of more than one chip, the chips should be arranged in a single stack. If someone has already placed chips on a number you wish to bet, it is okay to stack your chips directly on top of the others.

Wagers for the next spin should not be placed until the dealer removes the win marker from the layout. If you forget this rule, the dealer will remind you.

Betting may continue after the dealer spins the ball, but bets should not be placed after the dealer announces, "No more bets." Bets should never be placed after the ball falls into the wheelhead, whether or not the dealer made the announcement. If you forget this rule, your bet will be disallowed. If you think that the floor supervisor is an attractive person, forgetting this rule more than once would be a way of getting acquainted.

INSIDE BETS

There are two main categories of bets: inside bets and outside bets. All bets on the field of numbers in the center portion of the layout are called **inside bets**. These are either single-number (straight-up) bets, where the chips are placed on an individual number, or combination bets, where the chips are placed on a line between the numbers. In a combination bet, a single chip or a stack of chips can cover two through six numbers. These bets are described below.

Straight-Up Bet (One Number)

A bet on a single number is called a **straight-up bet**. To place this bet properly, put the chip, or stack of chips, directly on the desired number without touching any of the borders around the number. If the bet wins, the payoff is 35 to 1. That is, for every chip that was bet on the winning number, the dealer pays out 35 chips, and you get to keep your original bet. This bet can be placed on any of the 36 numbers in the field, as well as the 0 and 00. Chip position "A" in the layout illustration below shows the correct place for a straight-up bet on number 4.

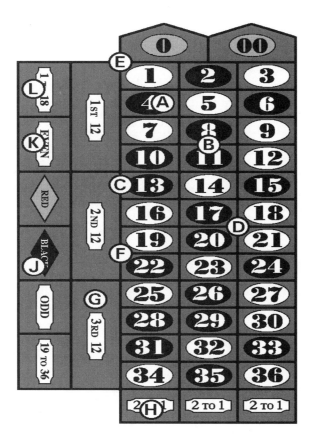

American Betting Layout

Split Bet (Two Numbers)

A combination bet that is placed on the line between any two adjacent numbers is called a **split bet**. Chip position "B" in the layout illustration shows the correct place for a split bet on numbers 8 and 11. If either of the two numbers wins, the payoff is 17 to 1. That is, for every chip that was placed on the line between the numbers, the dealer pays out 17 additional chips. In this bet, you are effectively splitting the value of the chip between the two numbers. If you were betting more than one chip, you could place half of the chips as a straight-up bet on each of the two adjacent numbers to get exactly the same result.

For instance, if a two-chip split bet wins, you would get 17 chips apiece for each of the two chips in your bet for a total payout of 34 chips. Since you get to keep the original bet of two chips, your total return would be 36 chips. If instead, you placed a straight-up bet on two different numbers with each of those two chips and one of the numbers won, you would get back 35 chips. One of the two chips you bet would have been on a losing number, but the other one is a winner so you get to keep that chip. Therefore, your return on the straight-up bets would also be 36 chips. This logic applies to all the other inside combination bets as well.

Street Bet (Three Numbers)
A **street bet** is a three-number combination bet on any of the three-number rows on the layout. To place this bet, put the chip, or stack of chips, on the outside border next to the first number in the row. Chip position "C" in the layout illustration shows the correct place for a street bet on numbers 13-14-15. If one of those three numbers wins, the payoff is 11 to 1.

Corner Bet (Four Numbers)
A **corner bet** is a four-number combination bet on any square block of four numbers. This is also called a **square bet**. To place this bet, put the chip, or stack of chips, on the intersection of the horizontal and vertical lines in the center of a block of four numbers. Chip position "D" in the layout illustration shows the correct place for a corner bet on numbers 17-18-20-21. If one of the four numbers wins, the payoff is 8 to 1.

ROULETTE

Sucker Bet (Five Numbers)
There is only one five-number bet on the layout, and it is made by placing the chip on the left line intersection between the 1 and the 0, as shown by position "E" in the layout illustration. This bet covers the numbers 0-00-1-2-3. It is called a sucker bet because the payoff is only 6 to 1. To be mathematically equivalent to the other roulette bets, the payoff should really be 6.2 to 1. As a result, the house advantage for this bet is 7.90% instead of 5.26%. Because there is no 00, the five-number bet does not exist on French or English roulette wheels.

Line Bet (Six Numbers)
A **line bet** is a six-number combination bet on two adjacent rows; thus, it is also called a **double street bet**. Chips are placed like a street bet except that they are placed at the intersection between two rows. Chip position "F" in the layout illustration shows the correct place for a line bet on numbers 19-20-21-22-23-24. If one of the six numbers wins, the payoff is 5 to 1. Although the line bet covers six sequential numbers on the betting layout, it should be noted that these numbers do not appear sequentially on the wheelhead.

OUTSIDE BETS
All bets outside of the main field of numbers are called **outside bets**. These are a variety of bets that include the columns, the dozens, black, red, odd, even, low (1-18) and high (19-36). Each of these bets is described below.

Dozens
The betting layout is divided into three groups of twelve numbers each, which are called the **dozens**. They are usually designated as "1st 12" (numbers 1 through 12), "2nd 12" (numbers 13 through 24), and "3rd 12" (numbers 25 through 36). Some layouts show them as "1st DOZEN," "2nd DOZEN," and "3rd DOZEN." Note that the 0 and 00

are not included in any of the three groups of dozens, so that if the winning number is 0 or 00, all dozens bets lose. Chip position "G" in the layout illustration shows the correct place for a dozens bet on numbers 25 through 36. If one of the twelve numbers in your group wins, the payoff is 2 to 1.

Columns

The betting layout is divided into three columns of twelve numbers each. At the bottom of each column of numbers is a box marked "2 to 1", which is the place to make a **column bet**. Note that the 0 and 00 are not a part of any column, so that if the winning number is 0 or 00, all column bets lose. Chip position "H" is an example of a column bet. As the notation in the box indicates, the payoff is 2 to 1, the same as for the dozens.

Color

At the center of the outside betting area, below the "2nd 12" box, are two diamonds, one is red and the other is black. Sometimes the words "RED" and "BLACK" appear in these boxes. This is where you can bet on either the eighteen red or the eighteen black numbers. The 0 and 00 are neither black nor red—they are green, and represent the house edge. If the winning number is 0 or 00, all color bets lose. Chip position "J" shows the correct place for a bet on the black numbers. The payoff for a winner is even money (1 to 1).

Even or Odd

On either side of the color diamonds are boxes marked "EVEN" and "ODD." These are areas where a bet can be placed on the eighteen even or eighteen odd numbers. Although, in mathematics, zero is considered to be an even number, this is not true in roulette. The numbers 0 and 00 are losers for wagers on even or odd. Chip position "K" shows the correct place for a bet on the even numbers. The payoff for a winner is even money (1 to 1). That is, for every chip in the winning stack, the dealer pays out 1 additional chip.

Low or High

At the corners of the outside betting layout, are boxes marked "1-18" and "19-36", which is where you can place a bet on the eighteen low numbers (1 through 18) or the eighteen high numbers (19 through 36). Note that 0 and 00 are not included in the low or high number groups, so that these numbers are losers for any bets on low or high. Chip position "L" shows the correct place for a bet on the low numbers. The payoff for a winner is even money (1 to 1).

BETTING LIMITS

At each roulette table there is a small plaque, called a table limit sign, explaining the betting limits. The wording on this sign seems to change from casino to casino, and in some cases can get rather confusing, but they are all trying to say the same thing. The following is an example of one of the less ambiguous signs:

> **MINIMUM INSIDE OR OUTSIDE BET: $10**
> **MAXIMUM OUTSIDE BET: $2000**
> **MAXIMUM INSIDE BET: $100**
> **Any Way to the Number**

When placing your wagers, you have to stay within the minimum and maximum bet requirements stated on the sign, if you can understand what it means. The first time I saw one of them, I had to ask a pit boss to explain it to me, especially the part about any way to the number! It seems that understanding the table limits is the most complicated aspect of playing roulette.

Table Minimum

Although the table minimum is often the same for inside and outside bets, they are treated differently. Minimums are typically $5 to $25 in Nevada and $10 to $50 in New Jersey. The following explanation assumes that the table minimum is $10 and the chips are worth $2 apiece.

For **outside bets**, a stack of at least five chips must be played on each bet to meet the minimum requirement. The chips cannot be spread around. That is, if you place a bet on red, it must be at least five chips. If you also want to bet the first dozen, it must be another five chips.

For **inside bets**, at least five chips must be played, even if you placed an outside bet (and vice-versa). In this case, however, the five chips may be spread around on different numbers. Note that you are free to place either inside or outside bets, or you can bet on both. If you play both, however, you must meet both minimums.

Table Maximum

The maximum limit for **outside bets** typically ranges from $1000 to $10,000, depending on the casino. The limit applies to each individual bet; that is, you can place a maximum bet on red and place another maximum bet on the 1st dozen.

The maximum limit for **inside bets** typically ranges from $25 to $1000, depending on the casino. The limit is usually stated as: "Maximum inside bet: $100 any way to a number." This means that you can make multiple $100 bets on a number in as many different ways as you can find. For instance, you can place a straight-up bet for $100, a split bet for $200 ($100 per number), a corner bet for $400 ($100 per number), etc., and all these bets can include the same number. If you actually placed those three bets and the number won, the payoff would be $100 x 35 plus $200 x 17 plus $400 x 8 for a total of $10,100. Obviously, this is only of interest to high rollers.

Maximum Payout

Some of the smaller casinos post maximum payouts on the inside numbers. This is shown on the table limit sign in place of a maximum inside bet limit. The maximum payout is an aggregate limit and may be set as low as $1750 in the more paranoid casinos. Although they will allow you to bet as much as you want, with a $1750 payout limit, you would be shortchanged if you won any straight-up bet of more than $50. Unless you are a heavy bettor, you needn't be especially concerned, but you should be aware of the existence of payout limits.

THE PAYOFFS

Now comes the best part. If you placed a single-number (straight-up) bet on the number that won, the dealer will place the win marker on your chips and pay you 35 to 1 odds. That is, you get to keep your original bet and are paid 35 additional chips for every chip you had on the winning number. If you only placed an outside bet such as odd or even or black or red, the payoff is merely even money. If you prefer a happy medium, you can bet on the various combinations. The following list shows all of the bet payoff odds for roulette. The letters are keyed to the layout illustration on page **287**.

Many casinos have information cards stacked next to the wheel showing the roulette layout and listing the bet payoffs (so you do not have to cut up this book). The following list was taken from one of those little cards. Experienced dealers in the major casinos rarely make payoff errors, but in some smaller places, it would be prudent to watch carefully. Except for the five-number bet, all bets have the same house advantage. The five number bet, which consists of the numbers 0, 00, 1, 2, and 3, only exists on the American wheel. It gives the house a 7.90% advantage and, under normal circumstances, is never recommended.

ROULETTE PAYOFF ODDS

A.	Straight up bet (1 number)	Pays 35 to 1
B.	Split bet (2 numbers)	Pays 17 to 1
C.	Street bet (3 numbers)	Pays 11 to 1
D.	Corner bet (4 numbers)	Pays 8 to 1
E.	Five number bet	Pays 6 to 1
F.	Line bet (6 numbers)	Pays 5 to 1
G.	Dozen bet (12 numbers)	Pays 2 to 1
H.	Column bet (12 numbers)	Pays 2 to 1
I.	Red or black bet (18 numbers)	Pays even
J.	Odd or even bet (18 numbers)	Pays even
K.	High or low bet (18 numbers)	Pays even

NEIGHBORS

The term **neighbors** refers to adjacent numbers on the wheelhead. In most casinos outside the United States, a player may call out a number and ask the dealer to place a neighbor's bet. This would be a straight-up bet on each of three or five numbers that are next to each other on the wheelhead. The player does not need to know the wheelhead number sequence, but only has to specify the central number for the group. The dealer keeps track of the bet by using a special marker. Since each of the numbers is a straight-up bet, if any one of them wins, the payoff is 35 to 1.

SPECIAL RULES

In some casinos, a special rule gives players a second chance to win an outside bet if the winning number is 0 or 00. The special rule applies only to those outside bets that pay even money, namely, Red, Black, Even, Odd, Low (1-18), and High (19-36). The three variations of this rule are explained below.

En Prison

This rule is applied only to the French single-zero wheel and is in effect at most European casinos and other casinos using French wheels. Whenever the winning number is 0, a player who has placed an even-money outside bet has the option of losing half the bet or allowing the entire bet to be held over (imprisoned) for the next spin. This reduces the house advantage on a French wheel from 2.70% to 1.35% for even-money outside bets.

In some European casinos, imprisonment is the only option and the player does not have the choice of giving up half the bet. Depending on how the imprisoned bet is handled when there are two or more winning zeros in succession, the house edge can range from 1.35% to 1.39%.

Le Partage

This rule, which is applied throughout the United Kingdom, is similar to the *En Prison* rule, except that the player loses half the bet and does not have the option of letting it ride. The monetary result is the same, in that the house advantage is reduced from 2.70% to 1.35% for even money outside bets.

In the United States, this rule is occasionally found on single-zero wheels in high-limit areas. The Bellagio and the Mirage in Las Vegas, for instance, have been known to apply the rule to their single-zero high-limit wheels. Since the roulette wheels in high-limit rooms of the classier casinos are often sitting idle, if you have a large bankroll (and the casino knows it) they will likely apply the rule on request just to get your business.

Surrender

This rule is in effect in Atlantic City and is applied only to American double-zero wheels. It is identical to the *Le Partage* rule except that it is applied when the winning number is either 0 or 00. The rule reduces the house advantage on an American wheel from 5.26% to 2.63% for even-money outside bets. Although the Surrender rule is not applied to the few single-zero wheels you might find in Atlantic City—they might have a change of mind if you are a high roller.

TABLE ETIQUETTE

When you first sit down at a roulette table, the best time to buy in is right after the dealer has finished making payoffs and has removed the win marker from the layout. The same applies to buying additional stacks of chips. You may buy in with cash or with regular casino chips.

You should not place any new bets while the dealer is still making payoffs. Wait until she has removed the win marker from the layout.

Place your bets with reasonable care. If you win a straight-up bet, but your chip was (unintentionally) touching one of the lines around the number, it may be interpreted as a split bet, which pays only 17 to 1.

If another bettor has already placed chips on the number you want to bet, just put your chips directly on top of the others. If the number wins, the dealer will sort out the different colored chips and make the appropriate payoffs. If the number loses, it doesn't matter because the chips will just get swept off the layout.

Be careful not to place any bets after the ball has dropped into the wheelhead. (This rule, of course, does not apply if you are a professional past poster.)

Do not walk off with any colored roulette chips; the chips stay with the table. If, for example, you have to go to the rest room, you have no choice but to cash in your chips and give up your seat.

THE QUIRKS OF ROULETTE

Roulette probably has more casino-originated quirks and eccentricities than any other table game. The modern form of roulette has been around for two centuries and, during that time, ingenious gamblers have devised many techniques, strategies, and devices for overcoming the house advantage. The more paranoid pit bosses and floor supervisors use little ploys that they believe will impede anyone trying to predict where the ball might land, or that will break a streak of luck. Being aware of these gimmicks is helpful in determining whether or not they have a significant effect on the particular playing technique being applied.

BIASED ROULETTE WHEELS

Although a roulette wheel is supposed to be a random device, the notion of a perfectly-random roulette wheel is a myth. The high-quality wheels used in most casinos are made to tight tolerances and are precisely balanced. However, small irregularities in the construction of new wheels are unavoidable and may spawn non-random traits after a few years of heavy use. If these non-random traits become sufficiently pronounced, they can be of great advantage to the player.

Because of the counter-rotation of the ball and the wheelhead, many people think that randomness is guaranteed. Not so. Almost all roulette wheels are biased. The problem for the player is to find those wheels with a strong enough bias to overcome the house edge. Although most biases occur accidentally, a wheel can be deliberately set up to favor particular numbers or colors. The many ways in which a roulette wheel can become biased are described in the sections on biased wheels.

It is fortunate for the biased-wheel player, that most of the little gimmicks and ploys used by casinos to break a streak of luck are not effective against a truly-biased wheel. The only way a casino can counteract a biased wheel is either to fix it or take it out of service. In actual fact, if a wheel continues to generate good revenue, the casino is not likely to remove it from the floor.

BALL BOUNCE

Like piano keys, roulette balls at one time were made of ivory. Today most of them are molded out of materials such as acetal, nylon, or phenolic. Although the material a ball is made out of is not easy to determine without close examination, it is an important factor because it directly affects its liveliness. A lively, bouncing ball does make visual and computer number prediction more difficult. On a biased wheel, however, a lively ball is desirable because it will cross more pockets before it finally stays put. This gives it a better chance of getting trapped in the biased section of the wheel.

WHEELHEAD SPEED

In the larger and more elite casinos, where the roulette wheels are carefully maintained, the dealer usually keeps the wheelhead turning at a moderately slow speed—typically three to four seconds per revolution. This is how it should be. The winning number is always easy to see and there is practically no chance that the ball will ever be kicked out of the wheelhead.

In smaller casinos, however, the wheels may not be maintained as well and sometimes slow down quickly due to worn or dry bearings. To compensate for this, the dealer will often keep the wheelhead rotating faster. Furthermore, pit bosses in the smaller casinos are less experienced and more paranoid, and a faster-turning wheelhead raises their comfort level. They think if the wheelhead rotates faster, it will be harder to beat.

BALL SWITCHING

In many casinos, the dealer has two or three spare balls at the roulette table so that she can switch balls at will. Ball switching is often done when a player is winning consistently. It is akin to changing the dice at a craps table or opening a new deck of cards at a blackjack table. Most of the time, the dealer does not know what physical effect it has, but it is a standard casino ploy used to break a player's lucky streak.

DEALER'S SIGNATURE

Every dealer puts a different spin on the ball when she launches it. The force of the initial launch, the amount and direction of english (lateral spin), or lack of english, is collectively known as the dealer's signature. Added to that should be consistency. Unless the dealer launches the ball in a consistent manner, spin after spin, the signature would be too variable for the other characteristics to have any meaning.

When a new dealer takes over a table, the dealer's signature changes. Floor supervisors believe that changing the dealer's signature by rotating dealers can effectively thwart a player who may be beating the game using unsavory means. This is another one of those ploys that falls in the category of `it might not help, but it won't hurt.'

BALL SPEED

American casinos have learned that many roulette players like to place their bets while the ball is spinning around the track. For some compulsive players there seems to be an urgency to place bets just before the ball drops or the dealer cuts off the betting. As long as there is plenty of betting activity at the table, most casinos like their dealers to do long spins—at least twenty or twenty-five revolutions—to give the players more time to lay down their bets.

When only two or three players are at the table and there is not much betting activity, the dealers are taught to do short spins in order to speed up the game. A short spin can be as little as four or five revolutions, which is not enough to dissipate the dealer's signature. If the dealer does a short spin at a busy table with a slowly-turning wheelhead, she is probably trying to aim the ball.

BALL AIMING

Sometimes a dealer will attempt to aim the ball at, or away from, a particular number. According to a seasoned veteran who has worked the pits in Las Vegas and was a roulette dealer for many years, aiming the ball accurately is impossible to do. Although, the opposite opinion has been given by reputable sources, these sources probably did not realize that they were observing a gaffed wheel.

If you suspect a dealer is trying to aim the ball, there are three clues to look for. First, the ball will be launched with less force so that it travels fewer than ten revolutions before it drops. Second, the wheelhead is kept rotating at a very slow, steady speed.

The third clue is that the dealer must be watching the wheelhead for a few moments until the numbers rotate to a predetermined position. Because they are easier to recognize than the other numbers, the dealer usually selects the green 0 or 00 as her reference and waits until the chosen number is passing under her hand before she launches the ball. You can spot this by observing the dealer's eyes when she releases the ball. If the dealer is not watching the wheelhead at the time the ball is launched, you can be certain it is not being aimed.

FOREIGN CASINOS

To a person who has mastered certain aspects of the game and developed winning playing techniques, the idea of playing roulette in foreign casinos can be fascinating. The table limits are higher, the payoff odds are better and, compared to the hustle and bustle of Las Vegas or Atlantic City, it can be an exotic experience.

Since most foreign casinos have single-zero wheels, the house advantage is only 2.7%, and can be as low as 1.35% for even-money outside bets. Furthermore, in the classier European casinos, the permissible maximum bet is usually much higher than in most U.S. casinos.

If you are going abroad and intend to visit any casinos, obtain information ahead of time about the local gambling rules. If you wait until arriving at your destination, you may be disappointed because of a lack of advanced preparation. For example, while most European casinos have no dress requirements for women, they require a man to wear a coat and tie. A few casinos have an even stricter dress code, requiring semi-formal evening wear.

In London, all casinos are private clubs and admission is restricted to members and their guests. If you don't know a club member, you will have to submit a membership application form and wait twenty-four hours before you will be admitted. Consequently, the best procedure is to apply at the casino or casinos of interest as soon as possible after you arrive. You can then enter the casino on the following day. In other parts of the United Kingdom the casino admission rules are more lenient.

In Latin America you have to be flexible, because in many countries the gambling situation is unstable and major changes can occur with little warning. If you manage to come out ahead, your winnings will be in the local currency and, often, will not be easy to get out of the country—so plan to spend the money during your stay.

THE CLASSICAL SYSTEMS

Apart from some nefarious roulette prediction techniques, which are beyond the scope of this chapter, a non-biased roulette wheel can be played in only two ways. The first way is the "hunch" method, which may be the digits in your daughter's birthday, the latest winning lotto numbers, or just your personal "lucky" numbers. Whatever the justification, there is no scientific or analytical reason for selecting these numbers—they are just based on a hunch. Most Americans use the "hunch" method when playing roulette.

The second way is the "system" method. In Europe, most roulette players use a mathematically-based system and consider hunch players to be fools who will soon be parted with their money. The system player believes that roulette should be approached methodically, using some sort of numerical or logical basis. European casinos act nonchalant and cater to this mentality by providing note pads and pencils at the roulette table. Of course, when a system player starts winning consistently, the casino managers tend to lose their composure.

Betting systems have received a bad rap because of the large number of people who have lost money trying to play them. Of course, the main reason they lose is that they have not learned or practiced the fine points of system play, which is the difference between winning and losing. Although the casinos perpetuate the myth that a mathematical system cannot win consistently and try to act unconcerned, most of them dread an intelligent and knowledgeable systems player.

If there is even a single system that consistently works, why isn't everyone playing roulette and beating the house? Some are. However, most people do not take the time and effort to learn how to do things properly and wonder why they always lose. Just look at what happened to the game of blackjack after Dr. Thorp published his method for beating it in 1962. The popularity of blackjack soared and the casinos, after some initial concerns, installed more tables and earned more money than they ever did before. Yes, there are people who beat blackjack regularly, just as there are people who beat roulette. Those few consistent winners, however, are so heavily swamped out by the hordes of losers that they have little effect on the overall casino profits.

This section will describe in some detail how the major classical roulette betting systems are intended to work. At first glance, they all appear to be quite foolproof, but each of them has limitations and pitfalls that need to be fully understood and compensated for. Consequently, playing the systems exactly as they are depicted is not recommended. The adjustments and fine points that most people never seem to learn, but which are required to make the systems perform profitably are described in a later section. Before jumping to that section, however, it is recommended that you first acquire an understanding of the basic systems.

Most roulette betting systems are designed around the even-money bets, which are the six bets along the outside of the roulette betting layout. They are: red, black, even, odd, low (1-18), and high (19-36). On an unbiased wheel, all of these bets are monetarily and statistically equivalent, so keep in mind that, from a system standpoint, it makes no difference which one of the six is played.

THE MARTINGALES

The Martingale and its variations are the most popular and best-known betting systems in the world. Also known as doubling-up or progression systems, they are praised by those who have won big and damned by those who have lost their shirts. There is no question that they can produce either result. The basic Martingale principle, which can be applied to any repetitive even-money wager, was devised at least 300 years ago and its popularity has never waned.

As with almost all roulette betting systems, this one is applied to the even-money outside bets, as defined above. In its most fundamental form, the amount of the initial bet is doubled after each successive loss. After each win, the bet is reduced to its initial value and remains there until the next loss occurs. In this way, all losses are eventually recovered with a net gain in the amount of the initial bet.

For instance, if an initial bet of 5 units is lost, the next bet would be doubled to 10 units. If the second bet also lost, the third bet would be 20 units; if the third bet lost, the fourth bet would be 40 units, and so forth. If the 40-unit bet won, the amount of the first three bets (5 + 10 + 20 = 35) would be recovered with a net gain of 5 units. Whenever any bet is won, the next bet is reduced to the initial value of 5 units.

The danger in this system is that eventually a long string of successive losses will keep increasing the amount of the bet until it reaches the table limit. At many roulette wheels, the table limit for outside bets is set to 200 times the minimum bet. This ratio will allow seven consecutive bet doublings before the table limit is encountered. At a table with a 1000 unit limit, starting with 5 units, a continuous string of losses will look like this:

1	2	3	4	5	6	7	8
5	10	20	40	80	160	320	640

After the eighth loss, the next doubling will reach the table limit.

Eight losses in a row for an even-money bet is not as rare an occurrence as one might think. Statistically, it will happen an average of once for every 170 spins of the ball. In most U.S. casinos, a roulette ball is typically spun sixty to eighty times every hour. Consequently, for a particular even-money bet one can expect such a losing streak to occur on an average of about once every two hours on any given wheel. Even more worrisome is the fact that it could happen in the next ten minutes.

The classical Martingale is obviously not for everyone, especially if you think in terms of dollars instead of the innocuous "units." After seven straight losses, the idea of risking an additional 640 dollars in an attempt to recoup the 635 dollars already lost, and ending up with a five-dollar profit seems ludicrous to most people.

SYSTEM TABLE LIMITS

For many years, gambling industry experts and consultants such as John Scarne have advised casinos to "protect" themselves from systems players by maintaining tight table limits. As a result, most casinos have kept the minimum-to-maximum bet ratio at their roulette tables to no greater than 100 to 1, or, at most, 200 to 1, thus limiting the number of bet doublings to six or seven.

Detractors of progressive betting systems such as the Martingale usually cite the casino table limits as the main obstacle to preventing these systems from being successful. This is really not so. The main obstacle is the ineptness of the average system player. The accomplished system player has always known of methods that compensate for low table limits, methods that will be presented later.

Recently, more and more casinos have dramatically increased the maximum bet limits, probably because they finally figured out that they can't really get hurt. After a long string of losses, most Martingale players run out of money or get cold feet before they encounter the table limit. Raising the limit has a minimal effect on the proficient player and simply allows the inept players to lose more.

Today, some of the most profitable Las Vegas strip casinos have posted minimum bet limits of $3 to $5 and maximum limits of $10,000 to

$20,000 for outside bets. This amounts to eleven or twelve bet doublings. Obviously, they are not worried.

THE GRAND MARTINGALE

The Grand Martingale, sometimes called the Great Martingale, is probably the most popular variation on the basic Martingale system. After every loss, in addition to doubling the bet, one more unit is added. If a bet of 5 units is lost, the next bet is 11 instead of 10 units, and after the next consecutive loss the bet is increased to 23 (22 plus 1). Starting with a bet of 5 units, this results in the following loss sequence:

1	2	3	4	5	6	7	8
5	11	23	47	95	191	383	767

The advantage to this variation is that whenever a series of losses is broken by a win, the net gain is greater than just the initial bet. Using the above sequence, a win after a string of four losses would result in a net gain of 9 units instead of 5 units for the standard Martingale system. This is calculated by subtracting the four losses (5 + 11 + 23 + 47 = 86) from the 95-unit win for a net gain of 9 units.

Certain gamblers concluded that by doubling their bet and adding two units instead of one after each loss, they could still sustain eight losses before running into the table limit. For those who have plenty of disposable funds, this line of thinking does have merit. If someone is going to take big risks, they may as well try to make it more worthwhile.

REVERSE MARTINGALE

Some gamblers feel confident enough not to chase their losses, as is done in the standard Martingale, but would rather take advantage of winning streaks. Instead of doubling the bet after every loss, in the reverse Martingale the bet is doubled after every win and reverts to the initial bet after every loss. As one can imagine, this system gets kind of tricky.

As with most "reverse" systems, good judgement has to be used in determining how far to carry a winning streak. One cannot just let it run to the table limit because a streak of eight consecutive wins occurs only about every 395 spins. Since the first loss will wipe out all potential gains from the streak, it has to be cut short (reverting to the initial bet) to preserve any profits. Since each spin of the ball is an independent event, how does one determine when a winning streak should be deliberately abandoned? That is the tricky part.

THE D'ALEMBERT SYSTEM

The D'Alembert system, also called *montant et demontant* (upwards and downwards), is often called a *pyramid* system. It was named after a French mathematician because it was based on a mathematical equilibrium theory he published more than 200 years ago. Since winning or losing large amounts using the D'Alembert system is less likely, it is favored by players who want to keep the amount of their bets and losses to a minimum.

Like the Martingale, this system is applied to the even-money outside bets. The betting progression is very simple: After each loss, one unit is added to the next bet, and after each win, one unit is deducted from the next bet. Although exceeding the table limit is rarely a problem, with a low initial bet, a string of wins runs the risk of bumping into the table minimum, thereby breaking the sequence. This can be avoided by starting with an initial bet somewhat higher than the table minimum. Starting with an initial bet of 10 units, a typical series would be as follows:

	TYPICAL D'ALEMBERT SEQUENCE		
Bet #	Units Bet	Result	Net Gain
1	10	lose	-10
2	11	lose	-21
3	12	win	-9
4	11	win	+2
5	10	win	+12
6	9	lose	+3
7	10	win	+13
8	9	win	+22
9	8	lose	+14
10	9	lose	+5
11	10	lose	-5
12	11	win	+6

In the above example, the player won six times and lost six times, resulting in a net gain of six units. The three sixes in the previous sentence are not a coincidence: *Whenever the number of wins equals the number of losses, the net gain is equal to the number of wins.* This is the beauty and elegance of the D'Alembert system that makes it a classic.

The fly in the ointment is that, over time, the number of wins is usually less than the number of losses for even-money bets. In fact, because of the zero and double-zero on an American wheel, an average of 18 wins and 20 losses will occur for every 38 spins of the ball. However, the system works fairly well on a single-zero wheel with the *Le Partage* or *En Prison* rule, and this accounts for the popularity of the D'Alembert system in Europe.

REVERSE D'ALEMBERT

The reverse version of the D'Alembert system is sometimes called contra-Alembert. Like all "reverse" versions, it was probably devised by players who couldn't consistently win with the regular version. Using somewhat faulty logic, they decided that reversing the system rules would put them in the position of the casino, instead of the player. One of the earliest references to the reverse D'Alembert was by a Lord Beresford in a pamphlet he published in 1926. It is doubtful, however, that he was the actual originator of the system.

The playing rules for the reverse version should be fairly evident: Decrease the bet by one unit after every loss and increase the bet by one unit after every win. As in the reverse Martingale, instead of chasing losses, this method builds on winning streaks and has the same problem of how to determine when a winning streak should be abandoned.

A common way of dealing with winning streaks is to revert to the initial bet after a predetermined number of consecutive wins. A typical number is four wins. The reverse D'Alembert system is surprisingly popular, an indication that it must be working for some people.

THE LABOUCHERE SYSTEM

Another popular system is the Labouchere, also known as a cancellation system. Like the Martingale, it is a progressive method of betting, but is less likely to run up against the table limit. Although it has a French name, a connection has been made to a finance minister in the service of Queen Victoria, whose name was Labouchere and who had a taste for gambling. Whether or not he had anything to do with inventing the system is not certain.

The Labouchere system is more complicated than most, requires the use of a pencil and paper, and is applied only to the even-money outside bets. It starts with an arbitrary line of numbers such as 1-1-2-3.

The initial bet is the sum of the first and last numbers in the line, in this case: 4 (1 + 3). If the initial bet wins, the first and last numbers in the line are canceled, leaving: 1-2. The second bet would then be 3, the sum of the first and last numbers in the remaining line. If the second bet also wins, then the line is cleared and a new 1-1-2-3 line is started. Whenever the line is cleared, the net gain is the sum of the digits in the original line, in this case: 7.

Starting over with the original line, if the initial bet of 4 units loses, the amount of the bet is added to the end of the line. The new line is then: 1-1-2-3-4, and the next bet would be 5 (1 + 4). If the second bet also lost, it would again be added to the end and the line would become: 1-1-2-3-4-5. The following is a typical sequence:

TYPICAL LABOUCHERE SEQUENCE			
Bet Line	Units Bet	Result	Net Gain
1-1-2-3	4	lost	-4
1-1-2-3-4	5	lost	-9
1-1-2-3-4-5	6	lost	-15
1-1-2-3-4-5-6	7	won	-8
X-1-2-3-4-5-6	6	won	-2
X-X-2-3-4-5-6	6	lost	-8
X-X-2-3-4-5-6-6	8	lost	-16
X-X-2-3-4-5-6-6-8	10	won	-6
X-X-2-3-4-5-6-6-8	9	won	+3
X-X-2-3-4-5-6-6-8	4	lost	-1
X-X-2-3-4-5-6-6-8-4	8	won	+7

The last win cleared the line with a net gain of 7 units, which is the sum of the numbers in the original line. The important point here is that a net gain was obtained with six losses and only five wins—a distinct advantage over the D'Alembert system.

It should also be noted in the above series that when the line got down to a single 4, the next bet was also 4. The rule is: *When the line is reduced to a single number, that number is considered the total of the first and last numbers.*

The starting line can be any length and contain numbers of any values or can be as simple as 1. The larger the numbers and the longer the line, the more aggressive the play. Other than the higher net gain, long lines do not seem to carry any special advantage; they just take more time to play out. A short line with high numbers will increase the net gain but will also increase the betting levels and the capital required. Typical starting lines, from mild to aggressive, are:

Typical Labouchere Starting Lines	
Mild	1-1
	1-2
	1-1-1
	1-2-3
Aggressive	1-2-3-4-5

Although a betting line can be abandoned at any time, the potential net gain can only be assured if the line is played out. Since a loss adds one number and a win cancels two numbers, this will happen eventually. Of course, long strings of losses can drive the betting levels higher and higher, but the risk of running into the table limit is fairly low except with the more aggressive starting lines.

REVERSE LABOUCHERE

Although there is a tendency to belittle reverse versions of roulette betting systems, in 1966, an Englishman and his team of twelve players broke the bank at one of the French casinos in Nice with the reverse Labouchere system. The Englishman's name is Norman Leigh and some people have called him a con artist and accused him of exaggeration. That may or may not be true, but he did write a very interesting book about the experience.

As in the regular Labouchere system, a line of numbers is written down, and the first bet is the sum of the first and last numbers in the line. At this point the rules are reversed: Whenever a win occurs, the amount of the bet is added to the end of the line, and whenever a loss occurs, the first and last numbers in the line are canceled. When the line ultimately clears, there is a net loss instead of a net gain.

When Mr. Leigh and his team were playing, they used the aggressive starting line of 1-2-3-4, and every time the line played out it cost them ten units. Winning streaks were allowed to run to the table limit, if possible. The theory was that the small losses are eventually paid back when a long winning streak occurs. In the case of Norman Leigh and his companions it worked out as planned, but that does not mean it always will.

INSIDE BETTING SYSTEMS

Inside bets are any bets placed directly on the main field of numbers. This includes single-number bets that pay 35:1 through six-number bets that pay 5:1, and everything in-between. It does not include dozens, column bets, or any even-money bets.

Most inside bet systems are based on the notion that a **sleeper** will eventually have to awaken. Although the term sleeper is the common vernacular, a more descriptive term is **overdue number**. It is commonly believed that if a particular number has not won in a long time, it is "due" or "overdue."

On the surface, the idea seems to have some merit. Since the probability of a given number winning is 1/38, or 1 chance out of 38, the expectation is that each number on the wheel will win an average of once every thirty-eight spins of the ball. If a particular number has not appeared in, say, seventy or eighty spins, it is overdue and should show up very soon, if only to comply with the law of averages. What isn't always understood is that the so-called "law of averages" can only be relied on over the very long term. In roulette, the *long term* could mean thousands or tens of thousands of spins.

Actually, if a particular number comes up very seldom or not at all, it is probably because the wheel is not random. It is not at all difficult to cause a wheel, either accidentally or deliberately, to favor or disfavor certain numbers. If, for instance, the number 29 has not won in a long time, it may be because the pad at the bottom of the pocket had at one time been replaced during routine maintenance. If the replacement material had a different resilience, the ball may now bounce out of that pocket more readily than the other pockets. This would be enough to cause a substantial reduction in the probability of occurrence for number 29. Thus, any bet placed on that number is a losing proposition, even though the number always seems overdue.

Another point to remember is that a roulette wheel has no memory. Every spin of the ball is an independent event that has no bearing on what happened in the past. If the wheel is truly random, then the probability of a given number coming up continues to be 1 out of 38, no matter how long it has been since the last time that number won. Let us say the number 29 came up five times in the last 38 spins—five times the expectation. What is the probability of 29 winning on the 39th spin? If the wheel is unbiased: Exactly one chance out of thirty-eight.

Well, what happened to the law of averages? Was it repealed? Of course not. Three weeks later, on that same hypothetical wheel, number 29 may not show up for 200 spins of the ball. After the first 100 spins, some players will notice the "sleeper" and start betting on 29. One-hundred spins later, after they all lost their bankrolls, 29 finally appears. They do not believe it, but the law of averages is intact.

A word to the wise: Any inside bet system that is based on the notion of sleepers or overdue numbers should be avoided.

PLAYING THE SYSTEMS

The successful systems player rarely executes a classical roulette system in the manner in which it is described in the books. All systems have limitations and potential pitfalls that have to be mitigated. To consistently win one must adjust the playing technique to overcome these weaknesses. These adjustments, which are described in the following sections, constitute the fine points of system play.

A PLAYABLE MARTINGALE

As previously explained, the Martingale is a mathematically sound system, but the classical version has two problems that make it dangerous to play. The first is the limited number of loss doublings, sometimes only seven or eight, before the required bet gets so large that it runs into the table limit. The second, is the sizable bankroll that is at risk every time a sequential string of losses occurs.

Both problems can be mitigated with the proper application of **null bets**. What in the world is a null bet? It is a zero-value bet; a bet that is never actually placed and is called a null bet because no money is at risk.

When sitting at a table to play a Martingale, assuming a 5-unit minimum and 1000-unit maximum, the following loss string can be anticipated:

1	2	3	4	5	6	7	8
5	10	20	40	80	160	320	640

before reaching the table limit. If the eighth bet loses, we are in trouble and, as was pointed out earlier, that can occur an average of every 170 spins of the ball. There is, however, a way to deal with this problem.

When first seated at the table, there are six even-money bets to choose from, and at least three of them just lost at the previous spin. If a bet is placed on one of the previous losers, that would effectively be the second bet in a potential loss string. The first bet was, therefore, a null bet because no money was at risk. This null bet had the effect of extending the theoretical loss string to nine bets, one longer than before, as shown below:

1	2	3	4	5	6	7	8	9
0	5	10	20	40	80	160	320	640

A string of nine successive losses will occur an average of every 323 spins, which is a big improvement.

This idea can be taken further by not placing the first wager until one of the even-money bets experiences two or three straight losses. To see the effect, assume that the first money wager is not placed until after three consecutive losses have occurred. The theoretical loss string will now start with three null bets and look like the following sequence:

1	2	3	4	5	6	7	8	9	10	11
0	0	0	5	10	20	40	80	160	320	640

The table limit will not be encountered until the eleventh loss and this will occur on the average of every 1165 spins, the equivalent of fifteen to nineteen hours of play.

A dilemma with trying to apply null bets while taking up a seat at a roulette table, is that a seated player is expected to place real bets for every spin of the ball. Ways to overcome this problem will be explained later.

In recent years, many casinos have dramatically increased the maximum outside bet limits to $10,000 and higher. Starting with three null bets followed by a $5 initial wager, this would allow as many as 14 losses in the sequence. That many straight losses have a probability of occurrence of $1/7990$, or once every 7990 spins of the ball. This is a comfortable margin for most players. Of course, it could happen on the very next 14 spins, but it is more likely that your bankroll will run out long before.

GRAND AND REVERSE MARTINGALES

The grand and reverse versions of the Martingale are not recommended for ordinary players. The bankroll requirements can get very steep and there is no certain way to mitigate the high risk levels for either version.

THE D'ALEMBERT SYSTEM

The attractiveness of the D'Alembert system is that the bankroll requirement usually stays within reason. Unlike the Martingale, the risk of bumping into the table limit is relatively low. The problem is that it takes the same number of wins as losses to clear the betting line. As said earlier, for every 38 spins of the ball there will be an average of 20 losses and only 18 wins.

The only way to overcome this obstacle is to start each sequence with null bets, such as described for the Martingale, above. The D'Alembert does not fare well when played on a double-zero wheel and is, therefore, not recommended for play in the United States. On a French wheel with the *en prison* rule, however, it gives good results for players who apply null bets and use sound judgement as to when to abandon a betting sequence and start over.

REVERSE D'ALEMBERT

Although, compared to the reverse Martingale, losses are likely to remain reasonable, there is no sure way to overcome the inherent risks or insure good judgement in deciding when to abandon a winning streak. Therefore, this system is not recommended for ordinary players.

THE LABOUCHERE SYSTEM

It seems surprising that the Labouchere system is not as popular as either the Martingale or the D'Alembert. It is based on the solid principle of canceling two losses with every win. Furthermore, running into the table limit is not very likely. If losses exceed wins by more than 2:1, however, the player is in trouble, but this would be true no matter what system was being used.

Where most Labouchere players get into difficulty, is using too long and aggressive a starting line. This can lead to the kind of problem that depletes a bankroll rather quickly. A long starting line of, for example, 1-2-3-4-2-1 is tempting because clearing it results in a net gain of 13 units. Following is a short sequence showing what can happen:

	EXAMPLE OF LABOUCHERE SEQUENCE WITH LONG STARTING LINE		
Bet Line	Units Bet	Result	Net Gain
1-2-3-4-2-1	2	won	+2
X̶-2-3-4-2-X̶	4	won	+6
X̶-2̶-3-4-2̶-X̶	7	lost	-1
X̶-2̶-3-4-2̶-X̶-7	10	lost	-11
X̶-2̶-3-4-2̶-X̶-7-10	13	won	+2
X̶-2̶-3̶-4-2̶-X̶-7-1̶0̶	11	lost	-9
X̶-2̶-3̶-4-2̶-X̶-7-1̶0̶-11	15	lost	-24
X̶-2̶-3̶-4-2̶-X̶-7-1̶0̶-11-15	19	won	-5

After only eight spins, the bets are rapidly escalating and we are losing money even though, so far, we have the same number of wins as losses. Isn't one win supposed to cancel two losses? Yes, but it takes three wins just to cancel that long original starting line, even if no losses have occurred. That is the part of the Labouchere theory that is rarely mentioned and that most unsuccessful Labouchere players do not understand. In the above example, two of the wins canceled all four losses and the other two wins reduced the length of the bet line, but it will take one more win to completely clear the line.

Although this is only one example, it should be apparent that a long starting line is not at all advantageous because of the additional wins needed to clear it. This is especially true since the full profit potential cannot be achieved until the line is completely cleared.

Consequently, Labouchere starting lines should be kept reasonably short to reduce the number of extra wins needed to clear the line. Recommended starting lines are: 1-1 or 1-2. Two-number starting lines need only one extra win to clear. The sequence 1-2-3-4 is a popular starting line whenever a minimum bet of 5 units is required. Actually, a line of 2-3 would be much better. The fact that 1-2-3-4 is popular, shows that most players do not fully understand the underlying principles of the Labouchere method.

Even when everything is done right, there will still be situations that get a little uneasy. If, for instance, the line starts getting long or the bets start to escalate, there is nothing wrong with abandoning the line altogether. Using a little judgement, a point can usually be chosen where the loss is minimized. In the above example, a good place to abandon would have been after the third win, resulting in a profit of two units.

Although, when played properly, the Labouchere holds up quite well on its own, starting a new betting line only after observing the occurrence of at least one loss is prudent. Since any one of the six even-money bets can be chosen, this is just a matter of paying attention. Every system has its weaknesses, and the Labouchere is no exception. The ever-present danger is a series of short losing streaks (not uncommon) interspersed with only single wins.

REVERSE LABOUCHERE
Despite the fact that Mr. Norman Leigh broke the bank at a French casino in 1966 using the reverse La0Bouchere system, this method is not recommended for ordinary players. The bankroll requirements can get very steep and there is no certain way to mitigate the high risk levels.

MAKING NULL BETS
Anyone taking up a seat at a roulette table is expected to place minimum bets for every spin of the ball. This can be a problem when trying to use the null-bet gambit recommended for the even-money betting

systems. One way to get around this is to play the system on two or three different even-money bets at the same time. When a line clears on one of the sequences, the others will still be going and, thereby, continue to meet the minimum bet requirement. Another way to deal with the minimum bet requirement is by placing a small bet on an inside number.

Keep in mind that whenever a betting line is cleared, a different outside bet must be selected when starting the new line. At least switch to the opposite side. If, for instance, a line was just cleared on black, then red must have sustained at least one loss.

Remember that six different even-money bets are available on the roulette betting layout. If the wheel is unbiased, it does not matter which one is played—statistically they are all identical. Always watch all six to keep track of what null bets (losses) have already occurred. Then, when the current bet line is cleared, the best outside bet on which to start the new line has already been scoped.

A FINAL WORD ABOUT SYSTEM PLAY

System play is a more cerebral and methodical form of gambling that many seat-of-the-pants gamblers do not appreciate. Maybe they tried a system once and lost money because they did not know how to compensate for its weaknesses. As a result, many of them tend to denigrate all mathematical betting systems.

A similar situation exists in books on statistics. Yes, a case can be made to show that, in the end, every mathematical system will eventually lose money. None of these books, however, take into account any of the adjustments and modifications for mitigating system weaknesses. They also don't take into account that by paying close attention, an intelligent player will know when to take the money and run.

In Europe, where roulette players have the advantage of playing against a 1.35% house edge for outside bets, system betting is very popular. Undoubtedly, some of these players have figured out how to mitigate the system limitations, and may even be using techniques that we don't know about. These are the players who grind out a small but steady return, while the flashy big-money players give the casinos their profits.

In the United States, where the house advantage is much larger, making a consistent profit with system play is not as simple. However, if the above techniques are applied intelligently and methodically, it should be easy enough to break-even most of the time and occasionally make a small profit at minimal risk.

BIASED WHEELS:
How They Get That Way

Biased roulette wheels are a fact of life. Casino management, however, would rather not discuss the subject and would lead you to believe that wheel bias is an extreme rarity. This section describes the various types of roulette wheel biases and the actual physical anomalies that cause a wheel to be non-random. These biases can be introduced accidentally or deliberately, or may simply be the result of long-term wear and tear.

A SUFFICIENTLY-RANDOM WHEEL

For a roulette wheel to be random, it must be perfectly symmetrical, accurately dimensioned, and precisely balanced. In particular, the width and depth of every ball pocket must be identical, the pocket separators must all be exactly the same height and have the same stiffness, and the pocket pads must all have the same resilience. Furthermore, the ball track must be absolutely flat (unwarped) and circular, and must be smooth and uniform over its entire circumference. In the real world, such a wheel does not exist.

Even the finest quality roulette wheels have built-in manufacturing tolerances and variances. The best that can be done is to manufacture a wheel that is "sufficiently random." This means that any bias unavoidably built into the wheel is not easily discernable and, in particular, is not strong enough to overcome the house advantage.

Not only should a wheel be sufficiently random when it is new, but it should be rugged enough to maintain that condition after years of continuous service. These are goals that are not always met, and when they are not met, it is often not obvious. One reason for this is that randomness is not an easy characteristic to observe accurately or to test for.

Even if a wheel is sufficiently random when it is new, as it ages it may develop irregularities causing it to exhibit non-random characteristics. Such irregularities may be the result of ordinary wear and tear, accidental damage, or deliberate tampering. Even small construction anomalies that are insignificant when the wheel is new, may eventually spawn certain non-random traits.

After a few years of heavy use, many wheels develop wear patterns that result in exploitable biases, especially if they have not been carefully maintained. These biases can usually be discovered by methodical and patient observation of the wheels while they are being played. When a wheel becomes biased, for whatever reason, it takes on special interest to the resourceful player.

NUMBER BIASES

Because of the counter-rotation of the ball and the wheelhead, many people think it is impossible for a roulette wheel to exhibit a preference for particular numbers. Although it usually happens accidentally, deliberately setting up a wheel to favor one or more contiguous groups of numbers is quite simple to do. A wheel can also be set up to favor black or red or odd or even.

Today, most wheel biases do occur accidentally, but sometimes a wheel is intentionally altered. If the bias is obvious, the casino will soon observe this and try to correct the problem. If it is subtle enough, casino personnel might never notice, and someone has probably been working the wheel a long time for a small, but steady profit. Following are descriptions of some of the most common causes of bias.

POCKET SEPARATORS

Occasionally a wheel may have one or more slightly-loose pocket separators (frets) between the ball pockets in the wheelhead. This may be the result of mishandling during wheel relocation or maintenance, or the wheel may have been deliberately rigged.

A wheel with loosened frets will almost always favor certain numbers. When a lively ball strikes a loose fret, energy in the ball is absorbed by the movement of the fret, causing the ball to stop bouncing and land in a nearby pocket. The effect can get very strong if several adjacent frets are loose, but if the result is too strong, casino personnel will eventually notice and have the wheel repaired. Loose frets are most potent with lively balls that skip around the wheelhead a lot, contacting a greater number of frets before finally coming to rest.

Pocket separators are usually made of brass, chrome-plated brass, or aluminum alloy. In most wheels, each individual fret is held in place with one or two small screws, which are accessible from the underside of the wheelhead. This type of fret can become loose when a mechanic's wrench is accidentally dropped into the wheelhead. It could also be caused deliberately by wiggling a fret with a tool or striking it with a small hammer. If done correctly, the loosened frets are not noticeable and can be hard to find, the amount of loosening being so slight that it can't be easily seen or felt.

The best method for finding loose frets is to move the wheel to a quiet location and then tap each of the thirty-eight frets with a hardwood implement, while listening for a difference in the tone. This procedure takes time and patience, and is probably done very infrequently.

Occasionally, a fret may get damaged and have to be replaced. Finding an exact replacement is sometimes difficult, especially for an older wheel. If the replacement fret is not exactly the same height, the random characteristics of the wheel will be corrupted. A slightly-high fret will catch the ball and favor the nearby pockets, whereas the ball will skip over a lower fret. If the replacement fret is a little thinner, the pockets on either side will be slightly wider, causing them to be favored.

In some newer wheels, the entire circle of ball pockets is made from a single casting called a pocket ring. Although it is touted as eliminating loose frets, this construction probably has more to do with cost savings. Since it is a single-piece design, it eliminates thirty-eight separate frets and associated mounting hardware, and greatly simplifies wheel assembly.

Some pocket rings are independently adjustable, that is, they can be rotated relative to the circle of numbers. By rotating the pocket ring, any biases caused by particular pockets will be shifted to different numbers. For example, if a wheel has a bias that favors the 8-12-29 number group, rotating the pocket ring clockwise by five numbers will change the number bias to 21-6-18. This could totally foul up anyone who has been clocking this wheel. The moveable ring could be a powerful countermeasure for wheel clockers if it were reset on a daily basis. However, since a wheel mechanic must perform the adjustment, it probably is not done more often than once a week, if that.

If you see a wheel that may have a moveable pocket ring, go ahead and clock it. Just be aware that if too much time passes between clocking and playing, the bias may have moved. Since resetting the pocket ring requires the wheel to be shut down for a short time, it is usually done early in the morning when the wheels are inactive. A good procedure, therefore, is to clock the wheel during the day shift and play the bias during the swing shift.

POCKET PADS

The pocket pads, that is, the material at the bottoms of the ball pockets in the wheelhead can be quite a range of substances. In the older wheels, it is usually a vinyl material that is cemented in place. Except for the zero and double-zero, the vinyl is colored red and black in alternating pockets. In some wheels the pads are a green or blue felt material. Many of the newer wheel designs have pocket bottoms with a hard plastic surface, which imparts a greater bounce to the ball.

When pads have to be replaced because they have become worn or damaged, it needs to be done with diligent care. Often the replacement pad material does not match the thickness and resiliency of the original and sometimes the mechanic is not meticulous enough in applying an even layer of cement. This can create air pockets under the pad that can modify the resiliency characteristics.

If the resilience of the pads is not identical in all the pockets, the wheel will lose its random characteristics. A softer, non-resilient pad will absorb energy from the ball and tend to retain it in the pocket. A harder, highly-resilient pad will tend to kick the ball out of that pocket.

Casinos and their wheel mechanics do not usually pay too much attention to the pocket pads, not realizing that an easy way to rig a wheel is to manipulate the pads. A wheel can be made to favor or disfavor certain numbers or colors by changing some pads to a material with different resilience.

WHEEL LEVELING

Often a roulette wheel and/or the table on which it is resting is not exactly level. When the wheel is off level by as little as 1/8 inch, any non-randomness in the wheel can be magnified.

Every time a roulette wheel is repositioned on a table or moved to another table, it should be re-leveled. This is not always done. Although leveling is one of the easiest things to check on a roulette wheel, many casinos are rather unconcerned about it, probably because they do not really understand what difference it makes. This is good for the players and bad for the casinos.

BIASED WHEELS:
How to Find Them

As previously explained, a roulette wheel can become biased in many ways. For a wheel that is in service for two shifts a day, in one month the ball will have circled the track more than 300,000 times and the wheelhead will have turned well over 500,000 revolutions. After a few months of this kind of wear and tear, any wheel that does not start to lose its random characteristics would be very unusual. No matter how well it is constructed, after a few years of service, with tens of millions of ball spins and tens of millions of wheelhead revolutions, a wheel would have to be made out of Kryptonite to retain its original random characteristics.

There are, and will continue to be, plenty of biased roulette wheels available. There are more than 4,000 roulette wheels in legal casinos around the world, over 800 of them in the United States, so if you can't find a biased wheel, you aren't really looking. Following are some ideas on the best ways to go about locating them.

CLOCKING A WHEEL

Clocking is the term used for collecting and recording the winning numbers as they occur on a roulette wheel. It is the basic technique used for determining if the wheel is biased. How is this accomplished? Usually with a pencil and paper and lots of patience. Will the casino ask you to cease and desist? Not likely.

For example, if you are writing down numbers while seated at a roulette table, they should not care so long as you also keep laying down your bets. If you start winning big, they will wonder what kind of system you are using. If you continue winning, they *may* ask you to stop writing down numbers. They would be reluctant to do this, however, because there is always the fear that such a request might cause you to cash in your chips and leave. The only people that casinos worry about more than big winners are big winners who quit while they are ahead.

If you are not playing, you can write down numbers all night long and they will probably ignore you. Whatever you do, do not get so apprehensive that you devise some kind of hidden device for recording the numbers surreptitiously. This can get you into serious trouble. Just use a pen or pencil and a small pocket notebook. Keep in mind that there is no law against wheel clocking, but do not get arrogant; always try to maintain a low profile.

Many of the larger casinos have a routine where each roulette wheel is rotated a small amount, typically, 1/8 turn every week. They do this primarily to redistribute the wear on the ball track and to avoid developing a groove on the side where the dealer releases the ball. To confuse wheel clockers, some casinos also move wheels from table to table, usually on a monthly basis.

Therefore, when you start clocking a wheel, try to identify it and its position on the table as explicitly as possible. To do this, you should inspect the wheel meticulously for any individualistic characteristics and record them in your notebook. This is not so easy in a casino where all the wheels are the same make and model, so you have to look carefully for flaws such as scratches in the finish, wear patterns, or discolorations. Then, if you return to that table more than one shift later, be sure that the wheel characteristics match.

When you start to record the winning numbers, write them down in order of occurrence and try not to miss any. Professional clockers typically collect at least 400 numbers before making a preliminary decision as to whether or not the wheel has possibilities. If it appears to be biased, they will collect another 800 to 1000 numbers for verification. These people, however, have to be conservative because when they sit down to play a biased wheel, large sums of money are at risk.

For amateur work, 200 winning numbers should be adequate for the initial evaluation. If the data looks good, go back and collect 300 to 400 more. This is not as tedious as it sounds. Typically, a roulette wheel in the United States is spun 60 to 80 times per hour, thus, it should take around three hours to collect the initial data and not much more than five hours to verify it. Eight hours of your time is a small price to pay to be able to play a wheel that will make you a sure winner.

Actually, it's not quite that simple. In order to find a potentially-biased wheel, you may have to collect initial data on many, many wheels. But then, nobody said getting rich is easy.

CLOCKING MULTIPLE WHEELS

There is a major shortcut that can make clocking less tedious. In some places it is possible to clock more than one wheel at the same time. If you find a casino that has two or three wheels in the same pit, or grouped closely together, there is no reason that you cannot stroll around and clock all of them simultaneously. Just be careful that you do not mix them up in your notebook.

All of the new casinos and most of the old casinos are installing electronic number displays. These displays show the most recent sixteen or twenty (depending on the model) winning numbers. Each time a new number wins, it appears at the top of the display and the oldest number scrolls off the bottom. Number displays are made to order for wheel clockers. Not only can you clock more wheels simultaneously, but I even noticed one situation where you could see the numbers on three different displays while seated at a bar stool. How good can it get?

One caution on number displays: Although they are generally quite dependable, an occasional one will malfunction. This is usually in the form of showing a spurious repeat number, which is probably caused by a misaligned sensor unit. If you see a display with repeat numbers, watch the wheel for a while and verify that the numbers are actually repeating. An excellent practice is to monitor any wheel you are clocking for fifteen or twenty spins before depending entirely on the number display.

Clocking can get very boring, especially if you are in a casino with only one or two wheels. To while away the time, you could collect the numbers while you are playing your favorite betting system on the wheel. Sometimes, this may be the best procedure and your system play could result in a profit whether or not the wheel is biased.

IDENTIFYING A BIASED WHEEL

Once a sufficient amount of data is collected for a particular wheel, it has to be evaluated to establish whether it reveals any biases. Start by determining which numbers in the data set have the highest frequency of occurrence. The probability of a particular number winning is 1 chance out of 38 (on an American wheel), or once every thirty-eight spins, over the long-term. Since the most dominant number in the data would be occurring more often than the average, the next question is: What frequency of occurrence is outside the normal range for a random wheel?

The answer to that question gets into statistical areas such as significance tests and confidence levels. Let's avoid that if possible, but we still need some guideline as a basis for deciding whether or not the initial data for a wheel suggests that it is worth pursuing further.

The recommended empirical rule is: If a number wins ten or more times in 200 spins *and* both adjacent numbers also exceed the average (for an American wheel) of 5.3 wins per 200 spins, you should get really interested in that wheel. For instance, if in 200 spins, the number 17 wins eleven times, this would not be significant unless the numbers 5 and 32 won at least seven times each. There is a good reason for this.

Since the probability of winning is 1/38, then the winning number would be expected to occur 2.63% of the time. A number that wins 10 times out of 200 spins is occurring 5% of the time (10 divide by 200 = 0.05), or almost twice the expected rate. That alone is nothing to rave about. In fact, if the number won twice that often, it still could be a random characteristic. However, if the adjacent numbers on both sides were also winning more often than the expected probability, we *might* be looking at a crude normal curve.

The **normal curve** was devised in 1733 by Abraham de Moivre, a French mathematician, in the course of supplementing his income by analyzing games of chance for wealthy gamblers. It is a bell-shaped curve that can mathematically represent many different kinds of data and is particularly applicable to numerous gambling situations.

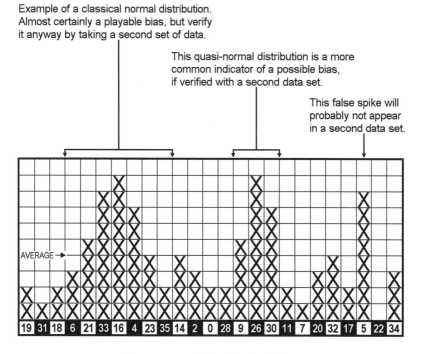

Frequency Distribution Plot

An example of a frequency distribution plot is shown above. This example (which spans about two-thirds of an American wheel) illustrates the difference between a normal curve, a quasi-normal curve, and a random spike. Random spikes are not likely to be caused by wheel bias and will probably not be replicated in the verification data. Any plot that looks similar to the bell shape of a normal curve, however, has serious possibilities. To determine this, the data should always be plotted on a frequency distribution chart.

On the following two pages are blank frequency distribution charts for American and French wheels. Although the entire contents of this book are copyrighted, you are hereby given permission to make copies of these charts for your personal use.

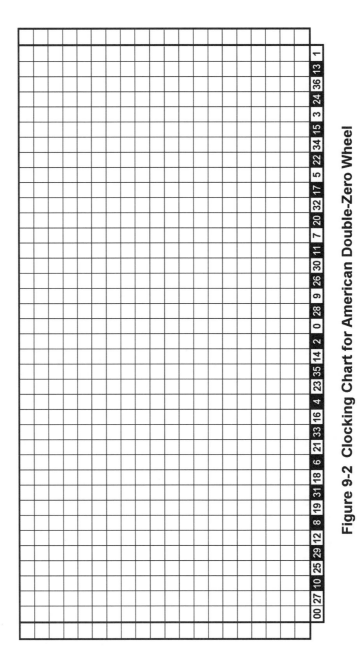

Figure 9-2 Clocking Chart for American Double-Zero Wheel

Clocking Chart for American Double-Zero Wheel

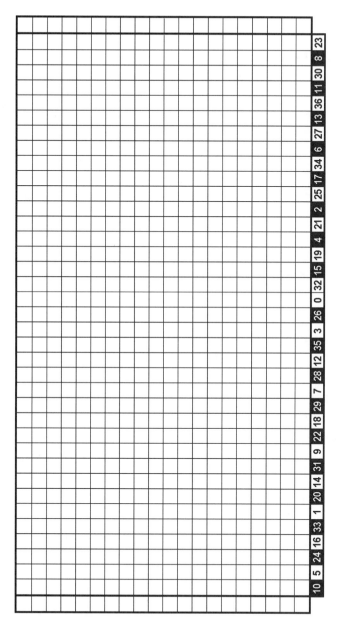

Figure 9-3 Clocking Chart for French Single-Zero Wheel

Clocking Chart for French Single-Zero Wheel

The best way to apply the charts is to first collect a set of data in a small notebook. Then find a quiet corner and transfer each set of data to a chart. Keep in mind that the chart is a linear representation of a circular wheel and that the right end connects to the left end.

To determine the average wins for any wheel number in a given data set, divide the number of data points by 38 (37 for a French wheel). For instance, if you have 230 data points, the average will be about 6 wins per number. In this case, draw a line or make a mark on the chart six boxes from the bottom. By doing this, you can easily tell which wheel numbers are exceeding the average, and by how much.

Next, analyze the frequency distribution plot and look for a pattern that resembles a normal or a quasi-normal curve. If the central number is at least double the average and the numbers on either side of the central number both exceed the average, get another set of data on that wheel—it has distinct possibilities. If the second data set exhibits a similar normal curve, you have almost certainly hit pay dirt.

A truly-random wheel (if there is such a thing) can easily come up with winning number sequences that will absolutely convince you that it is biased. However, it will rarely duplicate the same phony bias in two separate data-collecting sessions. This is why the verification process is so important. If the second set of data shows a similar bias, then the wheel is probably worth playing. Once you have determined that a particular wheel is biased, it is always worthwhile to triple check by collecting and evaluating a third set of data, before risking your money.

CONCLUSION

Because of the seemingly-high house edge of 5.26% on American roulette wheels, the game gets a bad rap from many gambling writers. The fact that seems to be ignored by them is that you will lose less money per hour at roulette than at most table games. Fast moving games such as craps or three card poker have a lower house edge, but the speed of the game effectively multiplies that edge several times as compared to roulette. In other words, the faster the game, the faster you lose your stake.

Roulette is a very pleasant and relaxing game to play, and if you are an intelligent systems player, you may even come out ahead. Furthermore, if you manage to locate a biased wheel, you will almost certainly end up a winner.

◆17◆
SIC-BO

This is Asian game that is a fixture in the casinos of southeast Asia, Macao, and South Korea, and has taken up residence in Las Vegas and Atlantic City. Sic-Bo, which literally means "dice pairs," is also called Tai-Sai (big-small) and Cu Sic (guessing dice).

Sic-Bo is played on a rectangular table with a layout consisting of numbers and dice faces that represent most of the combinations that can be made with three dice. There are more than fifty wagers to choose from with payouts that range from even money to 150 to 1 (180 to 1 in Atlantic City).

FUNDAMENTALS OF PLAY

The Sic-Bo table consists of a large rectangular betting surface with spaces for all the betting combinations, on which the players place their chips (see illustration). The table surface is translucent and, after every game, all the winning dice combinations are illuminated. The idea of the game is to try to predict the numbers that will appear on three dice by placing wagers on appropriate places on the layout.

339

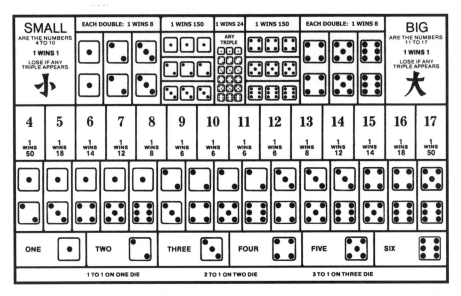

Sic-Bo betting layout

After the players have finished placing their wagers, the dealer, using a special dice box (called a *shaker*) that contains three dice, shakes the box. When the numbers on the dice are revealed, the dealer presses certain buttons, causing the winning numbers and combinations to automatically light up on the surface of the table. Losing bets are raked in and the winning bets are paid off. The players then place their bets for the next shake of the dice.

PAYOUTS

The amount paid to a winner depends on the wager and can range from even money to as much as 150 to 1 or 180 to 1, as shown in the following charts. The house edge varies all over the map, with some bets being reasonable and others being outrageous.

Although the betting layout may look complicated, there are just seven different types of wagers. Starting across the top of the layout, they are:

1. SMALL or BIG: These wagers would probably be better understood if they were labeled LOW or HIGH. A bet on SMALL wins if the number of pips on the three dice add up to a total of 4 through 10. A bet on BIG wins with a total of 11 through 18. Winning either bet pays even money.

2. Pair: A winning bet on any specific pair from 1 1 to 6 6 pays 8 to 1, except in Atlantic City where it pays 10 to 1.

3. Triplet: A winning bet on any specific triplet from 1 1 1 to 6 6 6 pays 150 to 1, except in Atlantic City where it pays 180 to 1.

4. Any triplet: If all three dice have the same number, a bet on any triplet pays 24 to 1, or 30 to 1 in Atlantic City.

5. Total of the three dice: The numbers across the center of the table indicate the total number of pips on the three dice. You can bet on any total from 4 to 17. The house edge jumps all around, and in most cases, the payoff odds don't make much sense.

6. Two-number combination: The row of 15 two-dice combinations across the width of the table allows you to wager on any combination from 1-2 to 5-6. A winning bet pays 5 to 1.

7. Single number: A bet on a single number has three ways to win. If it appears on one die, it pays even money. If the selected number appears on two dice, it pays 2 to 1, and if it appears on three dice, it pays 3 to 1.

SIC-BO PAYOUTS — MOST CASINOS

Wager	Description	Pays	House Edge
SMALL	Pays on total of 4-10	1 to 1	2.8%
BIG	Pays on total of 11-18	1 to 1	2.8%
Total of 4	Pays on total of 4	50 to 1	29.2%
Total of 5	Pays on total of 5	18 to 1	47.2%
Total of 6	Pays on total of 6	14 to 1	30.6%
Total of 7	Pays on total of 7	12 to 1	9.7%
Total of 8	Pays on total of 8	8 to 1	12.5%
Total of 9	Pays on total of 9	6 to 1	19.0%
Total of 10	Pays on total of 10	6 to 1	12.5%
Total of 11	Pays on total of 11	6 to 1	12.5%
Total of 12	Pays on total of 12	6 to 1	19.0%
Total of 13	Pays on total of 13	8 to 1	12.5%
Total of 14	Pays on total of 14	12 to 1	9.7%
Total of 15	Pays on total of 15	14 to 1	30.6%
Total of 16	Pays on total of 16	18 to 1	47.2%
Total of 17	Pays on total of 17	50 to 1	29.2%
Specific two-number combination	Pays on any one of 15 two-number combinations	5 to 1	16.7%
Specific pair	Pays on any specific pair	8 to 1	33.3%
Specific triple	Pays on any specific triplet	150 to 1	30.1%
Any triple	Pays if any triplet appears	24 to 1	30.6%
Single number	Pays if number appears on one, –	1 to 1	7.9%
	two, –	2 to 1	
	or three dice –	3 to 1	

SIC-BO PAYOUTS — ATLANTIC CITY

Wager	Description	Pays	House Edge
SMALL	Pays on total of 4-10	1 to 1	2.8%
BIG	Pays on total of 11-18	1 to 1	2.8%
Total of 4	Pays on total of 4	60 to 1	15.3%
Total of 5	Pays on total of 5	30 to 1	13.9%
Total of 6	Pays on total of 6	17 to 1	16.7%
Total of 7	Pays on total of 7	12 to 1	9.7%
Total of 8	Pays on total of 8	8 to 1	12.5%
Total of 9	Pays on total of 9	6 to 1	19.0%
Total of 10	Pays on total of 10	6 to 1	12.5%
Total of 11	Pays on total of 11	6 to 1	12.5%
Total of 12	Pays on total of 12	6 to 1	19.0%
Total of 13	Pays on total of 13	8 to 1	12.5%
Total of 14	Pays on total of 14	12 to 1	9.7%
Total of 15	Pays on total of 15	17 to 1	16.7%
Total of 16	Pays on total of 16	30 to 1	13.9%
Total of 17	Pays on total of 17	60 to 1	15.3%
Specific two-number combination	Pays on any one of 15 two-number combinations	5 to 1	16.7%
Specific pair	Pays on any specific pair	10 to 1	18.5%
Specific triple	Pays on any specific triplet	180 to 1	16.2%
Any triple	Pays if any triplet appears	30 to 1	13.9%
Single number	Pays if number appears on one, –	1 to 1	7.9%
	two, –	2 to 1	
	or three dice –	3 to 1	

SIC-BO STRATEGY

This is a pure luck game with no strategy except to choose bets with a reasonable house edge—and there aren't many of those. Most of the bet combinations give the house an advantage of 10% to 30%, and two bets carry an outrageous 47% edge. To top it off, you don't even get to roll the dice!

If you *must* lay down a bet, look for the squares marked SMALL and BIG, which have a house edge of only 2.8%—the lowest on the table. When you bet on SMALL, you win even odds if the three dice add up to a total of 4 through 10. You win on BIG when the dice add up to a total of 11 through 17. So, bet either SMALL or BIG, or just stand around and watch the table light up. Any other course of action (other than walking away) would be a foolish risk of money.

Actually, with a return of 180 to 1 and a house edge of 16.2%, a wager on a specific triple in Atlantic City is better than many keno bets. For the long-shot bettor, this might not be a bad choice.

PLAYING STRATEGY FOR SIC-BO

Place wagers only on SMALL or BIG.

◆18◆
SLOT MACHINES

Over the past ten to fifteen years, slot machine technology has undergone a major revolution. Many machines have become a form of computer game, which has little resemblance to the old mechanical contraptions of twenty or more years ago. Yet, other than pushing a button instead of pulling a lever, most slot players have not changed their playing style.

Typically, slot players enter the casino with a few hundred dollars in their pockets, plop down at an unoccupied machine, and begin to spin the reels. When they eventually run out of gambling money, they go see a show or just go home. If they do get lucky and win a jackpot, they keep on playing until they have given all their winnings back to the casino. They never expected to come out ahead, anyway. That is the sum total of their casino experience.

Most people think that, unlike video poker players, slot players don't have to make any decisions—they just drop in coins and hit the SPIN button. WRONG!!! Slot players have plenty of decisions to make, and if they make wrong decisions, or arbitrary ones, they will rarely come out ahead. So what are these important decisions?

The first, and most important one, is the selection of the right machine. But, aren't they all basically the same? Absolutely not! There is such a variety of slot machines in the casinos, made by numerous competing manufacturers, that some of them are bound to be better than others. The trick is to know how to tell the good from the bad. This chapter will provide useful guidance in that regard.

Once a suitable game is selected, the second decision is to determine how many coins or credits to wager on each spin. Today, there are no single-coin slot machines; all modern machines take multiple coins. The misguided advice to always bet the maximum coins or credits can cause serious damage to your wallet. Although this advice is valid for video poker, for other kinds of slots it is not necessarily the best way to play. You need to know which specific types of games are best played with a minimum wager and which always require the maximum. Do it incorrectly and you will substantially reduce your chances of winning.

But, things get even more complicated. How do you play a game designed to accept as many as ninety or 100 credits at a time? Do you really want to play a nickel machine and invest as much as $5.00 on a single spin?

Slot machine manufacturers are always trying to invent new ways to encourage people to keep on paying and playing. In their enthusiasm, they have devised a class of machines called banking games, in which points or some type of assets are accumulated and finally paid out as a big bonus. Knowledgeable players have discovered that these games often reach a point of being profitable to play. Yes, some slot machines in the casinos are actually beatable. Later in this chapter, you will find out how to locate these machines and how to win the bonus.

A LITTLE HISTORY

The spinning reel slot machine was invented over 100 years ago by August Fey, a German machinist who had immigrated to San Francisco. His invention was called the Liberty Bell, which was a three-reel device in a metal box that contained symbols such as bells, stars, and horseshoes. The top prize was paid when three bells appeared in the window, and it was popularly called a Bell machine. That name stuck for a long time, being generically applied to any slot machine.

SLOT MACHINES

Fey's machines soon became very popular, and in 1907, an enterprising fellow in Chicago by the name of Herbert Mills copied Fey's mechanism and started manufacturing slot machines on a large-scale basis. Mills modified Fey's design, however, in that his machine had twenty symbols per reel instead of ten. He also widened the window so the player could now see three rows of symbols, but only the row under the centerline paid anything. Being able to see winning symbols that just missed the payline, encouraged many people to keep playing with the thought that they might hit it big on the next pull. This teaser window design soon became a standard feature in all slot machines.

Before long, Mills' slot machines were being distributed throughout the country and were installed mostly in saloons and pool halls. In 1912, Nevada legalized slot machines as a form of vending machine, so long as they did not pay out cash awards. This started a period during which slot machines paid winners with chewing gum and other products. The reels carried pictures of various fruits that represented the different flavors of gum, and some of these symbols remain in use today.

The Mills Novelty Company was very successful and by the late 1920s had more than 1000 employees. During the prohibition period, slot machines evolved into full-fledged gambling devices and rows of them could be found in every speakeasy. By that time, slot machine manufacturing had become a big business, drawing in other competitors, but Mills remained the leader.

The popular Mills Blue Bell, circa 1949

By the early 1930s, most slot machine installations were controlled by the mob. When Mayor Fiorello LaGuardia ran the slots out of New York City, the mob took them to New Orleans by invitation of Governor Huey Long, who made millions in kickbacks. Machines controlled by the mob had such a poor payback (typically about 50%) that they became known as "one-armed bandits."

Meanwhile, after Nevada legalized gambling in 1931, the first legal casinos installed slot machines for the purpose of distracting and entertaining wives and girlfriends, while the serious gamblers played at the gaming tables. By the time the Flamingo Hotel opened in 1947, many casinos began to view slots as a profit center and improved the payouts to attract more business. This enticed some of the serious gamblers to the slots and began a long-term escalation in the popularity of slot machines in gambling casinos.

All the early slot machines were purely mechanical devices, the internal mechanism consisting of wheels, gears, levers, springs, and cams. In 1931, the Jennings Company developed the first electromechanical slot machine with motor-driven reels. It was not very successful because, at that time, many gamblers were wary of such new-fangled technology.

Further improvements were minimal until the 1960s when Bally Manufacturing Company (now named Bally Gaming Systems), a major supplier of pinball machines, entered the market with newly-designed electromechanical slots. Soon Bally was introducing machines with multiple coin acceptors and motor-driven coin hoppers that were capable of making much larger and faster payouts. These machines were so successful that, by the 1970s, Bally controlled 90% of the slot machine market.

In 1975, the development of the first all-electronic video slot machine by the Fortune Coin Company constituted a major departure from the traditional electromechanical machine. In 1978, the Sircoma Company, later renamed International Game Technology (IGT), bought out Fortune Coin, and the product line was soon expanded to include four-reel video slot machines. Although slot machines with video screens were not that much different than their mechanical cousins, they ultimately led to the introduction of video blackjack machines, quickly followed by video poker machines.

IGT had bet its future on the video concept and soon became the leader in video games of all kinds. The versatility and proliferation of video poker and video slot machines ultimately resulted in IGT supplanting

Bally as the market leader. Today, IGT is the industry powerhouse, although Bally is working hard to make a comeback.

SLOT MACHINE FAMILIES

For a long time, a slot machine consisted of three side-by-side **reels** that displayed pictures of bells, bars, sevens, and various fruits such as cherries, lemons, and plums. The action was entirely mechanical and, after inserting a coin, the reels were set in motion by pulling down a long handle at the right side. The machine paid off by dropping coins into a tray when certain **symbols** lined up in the window behind the horizontal **payline**.

Those old mechanical slot machines are now considered to be antiques. Although modern slot machines still use the basic principle of spinning reels with symbols on them, they have become very sophisticated computer-controlled devices. Instead of pulling a handle (which is still an option on some machines), most players activate the reels by pushing a button.

Today, almost all slots take multiple coins and have built-in paper currency validators that accept any denomination from $1 to $100. In some of the newest machines, there are as many as six simulated spinning reels displayed on a video screen, using a large variety of symbols.

Since the 1980s, when the first video and computer-controlled slot machines appeared in casinos, the number of different types and styles of machines has virtually exploded. By organizing them into the following families, you will get a better understanding of the seemingly endless variety of slots on the casino floors today.

SPINNING REEL SLOTS

These are machines with actual mechanical spinning reels, although the reels are completely computer controlled. The major kinds are as follows:

Multiplier Game: The payout is multiplied by the number of coins or credits wagered.

Multi-Line Game: Additional paylines can be activated by wagering more coins or credits.

Option-Buy Game: Additional winning symbol combinations are activated by betting the maximum number of coins or credits.

Banking Game: Points or some form of assets are accumulated in a "bank" and eventually paid out as credits.

VIDEO SLOTS

These are the newest generation of machines where the spinning reels are simulated on a video screen. The major kinds are:

Bonus Game: Certain symbol combinations cause a bonus mode to appear on a secondary screen.

Banking Game: Points or some form of assets are accumulated in a "bank" and eventually paid out as credits.

Multi-Game: The player has a choice of several different games on a single machine.

PROGRESSIVE SLOTS

These slots have a dynamic top jackpot that grows larger by pooling a fraction of each wager as the games are played. Groups of machines are usually linked together, all contributing to the same progressive jackpot. The major kinds of progressive machines are:

Stand-Alone Progressive: A solitary progressive slot machine that is not linked to any other machine.

Local Progressive: One of a bank or carousel of similar progressive machines that are linked together within a single casino.

Wide Area Progressive Slots (WAPS): One of a large number of similar progressive machines that are linked together over a wide geographic area such as a city or a state.

SLOT MACHINE ELEMENTS

To fully understand how a slot machine works, it is helpful to know the functions of its various components. Although, in times past, slot machines consisted of little more than a coin slot and an actuating handle at the right side, today they are far more complex with many buttons, displays, and symbols.

THE PAYTABLE

Every spinning reel machine has the payouts for the winning symbol combinations shown on a posted paytable (also known as the **glass**). The table is usually located on a panel above the reels and, in some cases, is so extensive that a portion of it is below the reels. It is very important to study the table carefully before starting to play. Among other things, it will tell you if the machine is a multiplier or an option-buy—very important information to know. The paytable also provides the information you need to decide if you should play maximum coins or if you can reasonably play one coin at a time.

Some video machines also have posted paytables, but on most of them you have to press a button to bring the paytable to the screen. This button may be marked PAYTABLE or SEE PAYS. With their bonus and banking features, video paytables can be quite extensive, but it is always worthwhile to study them.

REELS, SYMBOLS, AND PAYLINES

As the name implies, spinning reel slot machines contain spinning **reels**. These are side-by-side rotating wheels with pictures of various **symbols** on the outside rims. A small section of the reels may be viewed through a window, which usually displays about three rows of symbols. Originally, the symbols were pictures of bells, bars, sevens, and various fruits such as cherries, lemons, and plums. In modern slots, there are hundreds of different symbols—just about anything the machine designers can dream up.

Across the center of the window is a horizontal line called a **payline** (see illustration). If a winning symbol combination falls directly under the payline, a payoff occurs. The position of a reel when it comes to rest is called a **stop**. A reel may stop when a symbol is under the payline or when the blank space between two symbols falls under the payline. A blank space is equivalent to a symbol, and some games actually provide a minor payout for three blank spaces. The symbols just below or just above the payline do not count, unless otherwise stated on the payout display.

Slot window with a single payline

In video machines, spinning reels are simulated on a video screen. Some video machines mimic the popular three-reel spinners, while many others display five simulated reels and three rows of symbols. Such machines always have multiple paylines, and the blank spaces have been eliminated.

No matter if the reels are mechanical or simulated on a video screen, almost all of today's machines are under the full control of built-in microprocessors and random number generators. More on that, later.

SPECIAL SYMBOLS

Considering the proliferation of new symbols in modern slot machines, it is nothing short of amazing that many of the symbols used 50 to 100 years ago can still be found on some of the most popular machines. In any casino, a quick look around at the various slot paytables will disclose plenty of bells, 7s, and cherries, all of which are historic symbols dating back to the early days of the twentieth century. Lately, however, slot manufacturers have come up with some new twists, which are described below.

Substitute (wild) symbols: Many machines now contain symbols that substitute for any other symbol on the reels, thus they are called **substitute symbols**. These wild symbols can combine with other symbols to produce a winning combination. For example, 7, 7, Wild will give the same payout as 7, 7, 7, and Bar, Wild, Bar will result in the same payout as Bar, Bar, Bar.

Multiplier symbols: As you are examining the payout schedules, searching for that perfect machine, you might enjoy playing one that pays double or triple for certain payline combinations. Such machines have a doubling or tripling substitute (wild) symbol that will multiply the payout for any winning combination. Two doubling symbols on the same payline will quadruple the payout, and two tripling symbols on the same payline will multiply the payout by nine. In addition to multiplying the payout, these symbols act as wild cards. Most of these are IGT machines and the most popular ones are called Double Diamond and Triple Diamond.

Machines with 5x and 10x multipliers are becoming more prevalent. These multipliers operate on the same principle as doubling symbols. If, for example, two 10x symbols appear on the same payline, the amount of the payout is multiplied by 100. IGT has a couple of these called Five Times Pay and Ten Times Pay.

Nudge symbols: How many times have you been rankled because a payoff symbol appeared just above or below the payline? You probably can't count the times when the reels came to rest with two bars on the payline and the third bar just one stop above or below the payline. Exasperating, isn't it?

Not missing a bet, IGT designed some machines with certain symbols that are nudged to the payline after the reels stop spinning. The best example is Double Diamond Deluxe, which is a three-reel machine with Diamond Bar **nudge symbols**. When the reels stop and a Diamond Bar appears just above or below the payline, that reel will move one stop up or down, depending on which way the point of the diamond is facing. Since the diamond is superimposed over one, two, or three bars, this nudge symbol will complete a row of bars. Another example is the Balloon Bars game, in which a hot air balloon will float up to the payline if it landed one stop below.

Keep in mind, however, that nudge symbols are just a psychological gimmick. You may think you are getting a second chance, but the internal microprocessor had already determined the final position of the reels before they even started spinning.

Scatter symbols: When certain symbols appear anywhere on the screen of a video game, a payout can occur. These **scatter symbols** do not have to be lined up on any payline, but there usually needs to be at least three of them showing.

Spin till win symbols: When this symbol appears on a payline, the reels will respin by themselves and keep respinning until they stop on a winning combination. Which winning combination you end up with is an entirely random process.

Repeat the win: Although there is no particular symbol involved, some machines will sometimes **respin** the reels after a win to repeat that win. Whether or not this occurs is supposed to be randomly determined.

Any Bar (on paytable): Many machines have single-, double-, and triple-bar symbols with separate payouts for each type. The Any Bar designation on the paytable means that, on a three-reel machine, you get a payoff for any mix of one, two, or three bars.

Any Symbol (on paytable): This is similar to the Any Bar designation on the paytable, except that you will win with any mix of symbols, so long as there is no blank under the payline.

PLAY BUTTONS

Electrical pushbutton switches that are pressed by a player, activate nearly all of the operating functions of a slot machine. In most video games, the functions also appear on the video screen and may be activated by touching the screen. The most common buttons on reel-spinners and video games are as follows:

Play buttons on a nine-payline game

BET ONE: Pressing this button will register in the machine as a one-credit bet. It is exactly the same as if you put one coin into the slot, which is an alternative. If you press the button a second time, it will register as a two-credit wager. If you press it a third time, you bet three credits, and so forth. On some machines, this button is marked BET 1 CREDIT.

PLAY 1 LINE, PLAY 3 LINES, (etc.): This row of buttons is found on 5-reel video games, and typically gives you a choice of 1 line, 3 lines, 5 lines, 7 lines, or 9 lines. If you don't press any button, some machines default to the maximum number of paylines.

BET 1 PER LINE, BET 2 PER LINE, (etc.): After selecting the number of paylines on a video game, you have to decide how many credits per line you want to bet. The usual choice is 1 through 5, although on some games you can bet as many as 10 credits per line. This type of machine ordinarily does not have a SPIN button, so pressing the BET PER LINE button activates the reels.

BET MAX: Pressing this button causes two actions to occur. First, it registers a maximum credit bet, whatever it might be for that machine. If it is a two-coin machine, it will register two coins; if it is a three-coin machine, it will register three coins and so forth. Second, it automatically spins the reels; you don't have to press the SPIN button. On some machines, this button is marked PLAY MAX CREDITS.

REBET: Pressing this button spins the reels, repeating the exact wager you made on the previous spin.

SPIN: After indicating the number of credits you wish to bet or after inserting one or more coins, pressing this button starts the game by causing the reels to spin. If you did not wager any coins or credits, the button will do nothing. On some machines, this button is marked SPIN REELS.

A few machines still have a pull-handle at the right side. Pulling this handle does exactly the same as pressing the SPIN button; in fact, it simply activates an electrical switch that is wired in parallel with the switch under the SPIN button. In times past, when machines had only a pull-handle and no SPIN button, the average rate of play was 200 to 250 spins per hour. Today, with almost everyone using the buttons, the average rate of play has gone up to over 400 spins per hour. You can bet that the casinos will completely phase out the pull-handles as quickly as they can.

HELP: Most video games have a HELP button that brings up a screen with information for novice players, such as the purpose of the various buttons, the configuration of the paylines, and what to do if something malfunctions.

PAYTABLE: Pressing this button on a video game brings the paytable to the screen. Often, it is several pages in length. Sometimes this button is marked SEE PAYS.

CASH OUT: Pressing this button converts any credits accumulated in the machine to coins that are noisily dumped into the metal coin tray. You would normally do this whenever you are ready to leave that machine or any time you want to convert your credits into coins. In casinos that use cash tickets, you will receive a ticket instead of coins. The ticket can be converted to currency by any cashier at that casino. This button is sometimes marked CASH/CREDIT or COLLECT.

Before pressing the button, always note how much credit you have, and then, after the coins have stopped dumping, check the credit meter again to be sure it registers zero. If it doesn't, call an attendant by pressing the CHANGE button (see below). If a large number of credits is involved, pressing the CASH OUT button may result in the appearance of an attendant who will pay you by hand.

CHANGE: Pressing this button illuminates the service light on top of the machine, summoning the change person. Besides calling for change, you should also press the button any time something seems to go wrong with the machine. This button is often marked SERVICE.

DISPLAYS

There are several displays to help the player keep track of bets, credits, and amounts won. There may be some location and terminology variations between different types of machines, but they all perform the same basic functions.

COIN IN: This indicator shows how many coins or credits you have committed on the next spin. On some machines, it may be labeled BET or COINS PLAYED. Somewhere on most machines is a sign that states:

Pays Only on Coins Accepted. So, before you hit the SPIN button, be sure the machine accepted as many coins as you intended to bet.

LINES BET: This indicator shows how many paylines are currently activated, based on which PLAY LINES button you pressed.

BET PER LINE: This indicator shows how many credits you intend to wager on each payline, depending on which BET PER LINE button you pressed.

TOTAL BET: This is the total amount of your intended wager, which is the number of activated paylines *times* the number of credits per payline.

CREDITS: This keeps track of the amount of credits you have accumulated in the machine. The denomination of each credit is the same as the game denomination; that is, if you are playing a quarter machine, each credit is worth a quarter. The total number of credits goes up whenever you slide a bill into the currency acceptor. On a quarter machine, for example, a ten-dollar bill will add forty credits. The number of credits also goes up when the machine pays off a winning combination. On the other hand, when you press the BET ONE or MAX BET button, the appropriate number of credits are deducted from the total.

WIN PAID: Whenever you win, the amount of the payout is shown by this indicator. This amount is also added to the total in the CREDITS indicator. On some machines, this display is labeled PAID or WINNER PAID.

INSERT COIN: This message is illuminated whenever the machine is idle with no bets registered. It turns off when a coin is dropped in or a credit is bet.

COIN ACCEPTED: When you drop in a coin, this message lights up to tell you that the machine is ready for a spin. Of course, the message will not illuminate if the coin is rejected and drops through to the coin tray.

MONEY MATTERS

As we all know, slot machines are driven by money—money that you risk and money that the casino hopes to keep. Not very long ago, the only money needed to activate any gaming device consisted solely of coins. Today the money takes on several different forms, including paper currency, credits, and cash tickets. Coins, in fact, are becoming one of the least important kinds of money used in modern slot machines.

DENOMINATIONS

The denomination of a slot machine is defined as the smallest amount of money needed to spin the reels. The casinos and the slot manufacturers have taken this about as far as possible, in that there are machines in all logical denominations from 1¢ to $500.

Yes, there are still penny slot machines out there. The new ones accept paper money and allow you to bet up to 250 coins, so they are quite profitable for the casinos. The advice, however, is to not play them because they tend to be very tight. At the other end of the spectrum are the $100 and $500 machines. If you haven't seen one of these, just step into the high-limit slot area of the classiest casinos. The majority of the machines, however, accept nickels, quarters, or dollars—quarters being the most popular in most venues.

As you search through the casino aisles looking for games in your favorite denomination, pay attention to the lights on top of the machines, known as candles or service lights. They are color-coded according to denomination, which can be a help in locating your favorite games. If you forget the following code, you can easily remind yourself just by looking at the different machines when you get to the casino.

> RED = nickel
> GREEN = dime
> YELLOW = quarter
> ORANGE or GOLD = half dollar
> BLUE = one dollar
> PURPLE = five dollar

When most slot machines began accepting paper money and registering credits, it was inevitable that multi-denominational machines would be the next step. And, sure enough, they have arrived. Some of the first ones offer a choice of 5¢, 10¢, or 25¢, while others offer a choice of 25¢, 50¢, or $1. All the player has to do is insert a bill and then push a button indicating the denomination choice. After that, the machine plays like any other.

COINS, BILLS, AND CREDITS

Not very long ago, almost all slot machines accepted only coins and paid out jackpots by dumping coins into the metal coin tray with a loud clatter. Then came the credit machines that converted coins to credits and paid out winnings by running up more credits on the credit meter. The only time you would hear the clatter of coins was when someone pushed a CASH OUT button. Today, almost all machines accept bills and register the amount on the credit meter. As the casinos hoped, most players now find that playing credits keeps their hands cleaner and is generally more convenient than inserting coins into a slot. The advantage to the casinos, of course, is that by speeding up play, it increases the casino take.

CASH TICKETS

Another solution to the coin-handling problem is the use of cash tickets. When you cash out, instead of dumping a bunch of coins into the tray, the machine spits out a printed ticket. You may then bring the ticket to a cashier and convert it into real money. This is more convenient than toting around a bucket of coins. For the casinos, the advantages are even greater. They no longer have to employ all the people who spent much of their time filling and emptying coin hoppers and spent the rest of their time keeping records on where the coins went. The lines at cashier cages move faster because buckets of coins don't have to be counted, and there aren't any jammed coin counters holding everybody up.

Typical cash ticket

The newest generation of cash tickets can be inserted into other slot machines as if they were real currency. These tickets have a printed bar code (see illustration) that the machine reads to register the appropriate number of credits. Although the tickets look as if they are easily reproducible with a copy machine, don't try it. Each one contains a unique numeric security code. Any attempt to use or cash a second ticket with the same code will set off alarms.

This completely coinless system has become prevalent in Tribal casinos, and several Las Vegas casinos are trying it out as well. When one of the newest casinos in Las Vegas, The Palms, opened its doors in 2001, all of its slot machines had cash ticket capability. Clearly, the use of cash tickets is rapidly spreading.

If you play in a casino that uses cash tickets, handle the tickets you receive as if they were cash. Actually, you should handle them more carefully because they are printed on thin paper and are more fragile than greenbacks. Not only are they fragile, but they usually expire in thirty days, so be sure to cash them in before leaving the casino.

Of course, this evolution toward cashless gambling will eventually lead to the use of smart cards that will credit and debit your account as you play. Such cards are currently under development and are expected to be similar to slot club cards. As you can well imagine, these coinless and cashless systems only benefit the casinos and are especially detrimental to compulsive gamblers.

CASHOUT AND HANDPAY

At some point in your slots play, you will want to cash out your credits. You must do this by pressing the CASH OUT button. Before pressing the button, however, note how much the machine owes you. After it has finished dumping coins, check the credit meter again to be sure it registers zero. If it doesn't, either the coin mechanism has jammed or the hopper ran out of coins. This is the time to call an attendant by pressing the CHANGE or SERVICE button.

When cashing out, a machine will only dispense a certain maximum number of coins because of limitations in the coin hopper capacity. Depending on the denomination of the particular game, this number may be anywhere between 500 and 1000 credits, as indicated by a sign on the cabinet. If the credit meter exceeds that number, pressing the

CASH OUT button will bring an attendant instead of the expected clatter of coins. The attendant will first check the machine and then **handpay** you with paper currency.

All jackpots of $1200 or more must be hand paid by an attendant to meet the IRS requirement of submitting a W-2G form. Many smaller jackpots are also hand paid to keep from depleting the machine's coin hopper. For instance, on a nickel machine, a win of over $50 amounts to more than 1000 coins and will certainly be paid by hand. Whenever you receive a handpay jackpot, don't leave the machine without checking the credit meter for credits you may have previously accumulated. Press the CASH OUT button to get what it owes you.

Finally, whenever you play the slots, be sure to carry some form of legitimate photo identification, such as a driver's license. For a payout of $1200 or more, the IRS requires the casino to verify your identity for the W-2G form. If you do not have a photo ID in your possession (a slot club card will not do), you'll have to jump through a number of hoops to get your money.

GENERAL PLAYING ADVICE

The casinos make sure that playing a slot machine is a relatively simple procedure: You insert a coin or a bill, press a button or two to make the reels spin, and if the right symbols line up behind the payline, you win some money (or credits). If the winning symbols don't line up, you lose your investment and (the casino hopes) you try again. However, in the real world there is a little more to it than that, as explained below.

When you are looking for a suitable slot machine to play, do not crowd the other slot players. Slot machine play tends to be a solitary activity, so many patrons do not like a stranger looking over their shoulder while they are spinning the reels.

Before you sit down at a machine, be certain that it is not in use. Check that the person sitting one or two seats away is not playing more than one machine. Ask, if necessary. A cup on the handle, a purse or sweater on the chair, an inserted slot club card, or a burning cigarette, are all signs that someone stepped away from the machine for a moment. Yes, it is foolish to leave personal belongs at a machine to reserve it, but that's what some people do.

If you want to reserve a machine while you go to the restroom, ask an attendant and he/she will usually accommodate you by placing a RESERVED sign on the machine. If the casino is not crowded the attendant may even agree to reserve the machine while you go to dinner. However, the casino will not be happy if you reserve one machine and then go off to play another.

Although most casinos have an overabundance of security people, don't let that lull you into doing foolish things like placing your purse in the space between two machines. Always keep it on your shoulder or on your lap. Laying down rolls of quarters is also not a good idea; keep them in your pocket or purse. Always assume that there are opportunists hanging around in every casino waiting for you to let down your guard.

Better yet, don't bring a purse when you go gambling. A fanny pack is more secure, but only if you keep it strapped securely to your body. As soon as you remove it, it is no safer than a purse. The best approach is to carry everything in your pockets.

Finally, successful players are aware that alcoholic intake dulls a person's judgment. Consequently, most of them never drink alcoholic beverages during a playing session. They reserve this activity for celebrating a big wins or bemoaning their losses.

SLOT CLUBS

Most people believe there is no such thing as a free lunch. If you believe this, you haven't spent much time in Las Vegas. Slot clubs actually give you more than a free lunch. You can get a free room, a free dinner, and maybe even a free show. Of course, to get these comps you have to play the machines. But then, that's what you are doing anyway, so you might as well cash in.

For the slot machine and video poker player, slot clubs have no down side. Slot clubs operate on the same principle as frequent flier clubs. They are designed to encourage you to gamble in their casino by rewarding serious players with various comps. This is done with a computerized player tracking system that monitors each player's activity so that the comps can be awarded in a fair and consistent manner.

The best approach is to determine which casinos you prefer, and then join their slot clubs. This is easy to do—it takes only a few moments to fill out a slot club application. You will also have to show them some form of photo identification to verify your identity. The main purpose of the application is to record your mailing address so they can send discount coupons and information on special promotions. In most casinos you will be given some discounts or comps just for signing up.

After you have signed up, you will be issued a coded card so that the computer can track your playing habits. The more you play, the more points you rack up. These points can then be traded in for a variety of comps. Even if you don't use the card very much, the casino will notify you of slot tournaments and mail special offers to entice you to come in and play.

When you play a machine, be sure to always insert your card so that you can accumulate points. Every slot machine and almost every video poker machine has a card reader that accepts slot club cards. Remember, however, that the card has to be from the casino in which you are playing. When you insert the card, a screen display will greet you by name and may even tell you how many points you have accrued. When you leave the machine, be sure to retrieve your card. If you forget or lose the card, however, don't worry—you can easily get another. In fact, most casinos will honor a request for two cards so that you can play two machines at the same time. Furthermore, you and your spouse can combine your accumulated points by setting up a joint account.

If you are a regular player, the comps from most slot clubs will add 0.1 to 0.5% to the total amount of your wagers, and some will add as much as 1%. Some casinos even offer cash rebates. These comps and rebates are based on the total *action*, which is much larger than the amount you actually risk. Let's say you start with $20 worth of quarters and spin the reels at the leisurely rate of 400 times an hour. After just two hours of play at five coins a spin, you have cycled all 80 quarters through the machine 50 times (400 spins x 2 hours x 5 coins ÷ 80 quarters = 50). Whether you came out ahead or lost the entire $20, you generated $1000 worth of action (800 spins at $1.25 a spin = $1000). Many people do not realize how little money has to be at risk to generate those comps. Be sure to take advantage of the available comps by always using your card.

TEN IMPORTANT TIPS FOR SLOT PLAYERS

1. Be sure to always insert your slot club card. In some casinos, using your card can effectively increase the payback of the machine you are playing by as much as 1%.

2. Play only what your bankroll can handle. When you arrive at a gambling resort, you should first ascertain what denomination of machine you should be playing. To help you determine this, the following table shows how much bankroll is needed for a two-, three-, or five-coin bet in each denomination, assuming eight spins per minute and a 90% payout rate:

	2 COINS	3 COINS	5 COINS
Nickel machine	$5 per hour	$7 per hour	$12 per hour
Quarter machine	$24 per hour	$36 per hour	$60 per hour
Dollar machine	$96 per hour	$144 per hour	$240 per hour

Next, decide how many hours you would like to play over the course of your stay. For example, assume you start with a bankroll of $600 and would like to play an average of five hours a day for three days. That is a total of 15 playing hours. Dividing 15 hours into $600 gives a rate of $40 per hour. Thus, you should not play anything more costly than a three-coin quarter machine. Of course, in actuality, you may win more or lose more than the 90% payback would indicate, but at least you have a reasonable starting point.

3. When you insert coins, be sure you get what you pay for. Like any equipment with mechanical components, slot machines are subject to considerable wear and tear. This is especially true of the coin mechanism. After handling hundreds of thousands of coins, the mechanism will malfunction sooner or later. Your best protection is to observe the glass and the paylines as you insert each coin to be sure the correct sections light up, showing that they are properly activated. If you hit a winning combination that doesn't pay because only two of your three coins registered, you are out of luck. If one of your coins doesn't register, be sure to wave down an attendant or press the CHANGE button and wait for someone to arrive. Don't spin the reels before the situation is rectified.

4. Play one machine at a time. Slot managers know that some people like to play two slots simultaneously, so they often flank a loose machine with tight ones on both sides. At best, you will win from a loose machine only to lose your winnings to a tight one; at worst, you will lose to two tight machines. Two loose machines are rarely placed alongside each other.

5. Never play the machine right next to someone who is winning. If the winner's slot machine is loose, the machines on either side may be tight. Of course, the winner's machine may just be a moderate payer that turned hot, but you don't know that for certain.

6. Stay with a hot machine. Never leave a machine that just paid a big jackpot. By definition, it is a hot machine that could continue to pay out very nicely. Don't abandon the machine unless it has not paid anything for six consecutive spins.

7. Abandon a cold machine. Don't throw good money after bad. If, after six spins, the machine has paid out very little, abandon it. If available, move over to the machine right next to it. Tight and loose machines are often placed side by side.

8. Never leave a machine that owes you money. Sometimes when you hit a big jackpot, an attendant has to make the payoff, or sometimes during a payoff, the machine's hopper runs out of coins. *Stay with the machine no matter how long it takes the attendant to arrive.* Occasionally a machine malfunctions and you can't redeem your credits, or the bill acceptor gets hung and eats your Franklin without giving you credits. *Stay with the machine no matter how long it takes for a mechanic to arrive.* If you leave the machine, you will have trouble claiming what is rightfully yours.

9. Don't forget to press the CASH OUT button. Most machines accumulate credits as you play, and you must press the CASH OUT button to convert the credits into coins. Even if you have just won a hand-paid jackpot, before leaving the machine, press the CASH OUT button and be sure the credit meter reads zero. If it doesn't, call an attendant because the machine may need a hopper fill, or the coin mechanism may be jammed. If you are distracted when you leave your machine and forget to cash out, someone else will get to enjoy your winnings.

10. And finally, remember the cardinal rule of slot play: QUIT WHILE YOU ARE AHEAD, BUT NEVER QUIT *WHILE* YOU ARE WINNING!

MICROPROCESSOR AND RNG

All slot machines today are *microprocessor* controlled. Microprocessor is the term used for the dedicated computer board inside the machine, which is the electronic brain of the game. It is very similar to the computer you may have at home, except that it serves the single purpose of controlling all the functions of the slot machine including the movement of the mechanical reels. In video slots, the screen is similar to the monitor on a home computer, except that it usually has touch-screen capability.

In most gaming jurisdictions, new models and styles of slot machines have to be approved by the local gaming commission before they can be installed. The main concern of the gaming regulators is that the random number generator (RNG) in each machine is operating properly.

The RNG is one of the chips on the internal computer board. It generates thousands of random numbers a second, and each random number sequence defines a specific set of reel symbols. The instant a player presses the MAX BET or SPIN button, the next set of randomly-generated numbers is selected.

The program uses this set of numbers to define the symbol combination that will appear under the payline on the reels or on the video screen.

A fraction of a second after the player hits the button, the program has already determined the final position of the reels—before the reels have even gotten up to full speed. Obviously, the actual spinning of the reels is window dressing since the outcome has already been pre-determined.

By using this scheme, slot machines operate in a totally random fashion, and there isn't anything a player can do to change that. This is true for all currently-approved machines in legal casinos in the United States, whether they have video screens or spinning reels.

SLOT MACHINE PAYBACK

The average amount of money that a slot machine returns to the player after a long period of play is called the **payback**. The payback is stated as a percentage of the amount that the player invested in the machine. If the payback is 95%, for example, you can expect to lose 5% of every dollar that you bet.

Thus, the casino is charging you an average of 5% (over the long run) for the privilege of playing its machine. That is, for every dollar you risk, the casino keeps a nickel. That doesn't sound too bad, but in many cases the charge can be 10%, or even 20%. The only thing that keeps this number from getting completely out of hand is the competition between casinos.

The payback is adjusted by changing a chip in the microprocessor, a procedure generally done at the slot machine factory. The payback usually ranges from 80% to 99%, except in New Jersey where, by law, slots have to pay back at least 83%. Keep in mind that these numbers are *long-term* averages. Machines that are set to the lower end of the range are considered to be **tight**, while those at the upper end are **liberal** or **loose**.

In most major gaming jurisdictions, the average paybacks actually range from around 90 to 98%. Historically, the highest-paying machines have always been in Nevada, where Reno/Tahoe and North Las Vegas are usually in the lead, with downtown Las Vegas not far behind. The average paybacks on the Las Vegas strip run neck in neck with most smaller jurisdictions such as those in Mississippi, Louisiana, and Illinois. Atlantic City, taking advantage of the largest population center in the United States, trails behind by one to two points.

The average paybacks also vary according to the machine denomination. The more you are willing to risk, the more the casino is willing to give back. When a player switches to a higher denomination, the casino makes more money and can afford to give more of it back.

Except for penny games, the nickel games still have the poorest payback, but that is beginning to change. Only a few years ago, the average for nickel payback was less than 90%. Nickel machines have changed dramatically with the proliferation of forty-five- and ninety-credit video games. The average bet per spin on a forty-five-coin nickel game is over a dollar, which makes these games more profitable for the casino than the quarter machines. Consequently, some casinos have been raising the paybacks on nickel games higher than their quarter slots. And before long, it is expected that the average payback for nickel games will exceed the quarter, and maybe even the half-dollar machines.

FINDING THE LOOSEST SLOTS

Unlike video poker machines, you can't look at the payout schedule on a slot machine and tell if it is loose or tight. And when a casino advertises that its slots pay back *up to* 97% or that some of its slots have a "certified" 98% payback, it's difficult to tell which of the hundreds of machines on the floor are the ones advertised. Actually, you can get in the neighborhood, but it's not nearly as precise as finding the best video poker machines. The secret is (as they say in the real estate business)—location, location, location.

Years ago, it was generally known that the best slots were usually located in high-traffic areas—next to the main aisles or near the front entrance—where the greatest number of people would notice the flashing lights and ringing bells of a jackpot winner. Many old-time slot players remember that advice and still seek out machines in those locations. Times have changed, however.

Today, most slot managers place their loosest machines where the greatest number of *slot players* will see and hear them when they pay off. The idea is to motivate the serious slot players so they will keep feeding their machines in the hope that the next big jackpot will be theirs. Consequently, they locate the loose slots next to change booths, on elevated carousels, and anyplace in the center of the slot area where plenty of slot players will notice them when they pay off. Whenever loose slots are placed in a straight row of machines, they are usually one of the first three machines from either end, and never in the middle.

However, not all machines in these locations will be loose because there are always far fewer loose slots than tight ones. In fact, a typical ratio is 5 to 10% loose, 30 to 40% tight, with the remainder being mid-range. The best you can do is find the general area where most of the loose machines are likely to be.

Sometimes the managers also put a few loose slots within sight of the patrons in cafes and coffee shops (but not where the entrance line forms) to encourage players not to dally over their coffee, but to get back to their machines. Keep in mind, however, that tight slots often flank a loose slot machine, even though the machines appear to be identical. This is done to thwart those people who like to play two side-by-side machines simultaneously.

It is also important to know where the tight machines are likely to be placed by the slot manager, so you can avoid them. Wherever people stand in lines waiting to get into buffets or shows, are prime locations for tight machines. Those people will kill time by idly dropping coins into the machines without really expecting to win—and they won't. Because many table-game players are distracted and annoyed by the constant clatter of coins, the areas surrounding the table games (especially baccarat and roulette) are populated with tight machines. The same is true of areas near the sportsbook. In fact, any location where the noise of slot machines would disturb non-slot players is apt to have predominately tight machines.

Finally, you must assume that all slot machines located outside of casinos, such as in convenience stores, grocery stores, laundromats, airports, bars, and restaurants, are very tight. In fact, they are probably the tightest machines in town.

THE SPINNING REEL MACHINES

On the surface, many reel-spinners still look similar to slot machines installed in the early Las Vegas casinos over a half century ago. They have three spinning reels, and some of them still have a pull-handle on the right side, just like the old one-arm bandits. Inside the cabinet, however, they are totally different. They may have mechanical reels, but those reels are driven by electric stepper motors that are fully controlled by a microprocessor. The pull-handle, which used to engage gears and cams that mechanically spun the reels, now simply operates an electrical switch connected to the same circuit as the switch under the SPIN button. Many progressive machines are also reel-spinners, but this section only covers games with a static (unchanging) top jackpot.

Although the variety of spinning reel machines may seem endless, they come in just three main flavors. All other differences have to do with the kinds of symbols used and the amounts of the payouts. Following are the three basic types:

COIN MULTIPLIERS

In most casinos, **multipliers** are very popular machines. Multipliers are single-payline games where the number of coins bet on one spin multiplies the potential payouts. When this mathematical relationship is exact, the game is called a **true multiplier**.

In most games, however, the top jackpot is higher than the multiple when the maximum number of coins is bet. This version is called a **modified multiplier** (see illustration). The purpose of a modified multiplier, of course, is to encourage the player to bet the maximum on every spin. For instance, on most three-coin multipliers, if the top jackpot pays 1000 coins for a one-coin bet, the second coin will pay 2000 coins, but the third coin may pay 4000 coins (instead of 3000 coins), or even 5000 coins or more. Hence, the conventional advice is to always bet the maximum number of coins. However, this is not necessarily good advice, as will be explained in the strategy section.

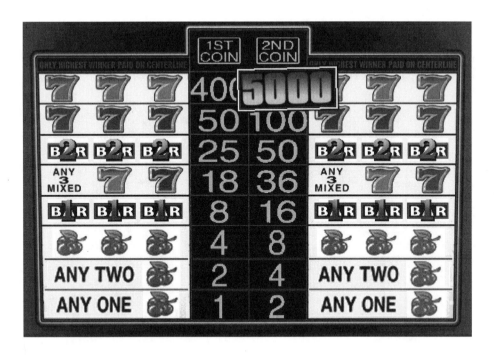

MULTI-LINE GAMES

As you stroll through the casinos, you will notice that there are plenty of reel-spinners with multiple paylines. In the industry, they are called **line games** because the paytable is payline-driven. While a single payline slot machine has one horizontal line across the window, a three-payline machine has two extra horizontal lines, one above and one below the center line. Betting additional coins activates the extra paylines, giving you two additional chances of hitting a winning combination. Although you may activate one, two, or three of the paylines by inserting one, two, or three coins, to qualify for the maximum jackpot benefit, you must play all three coins.

Some machines have five paylines, with two of them criss-crossing the window diagonally, giving you a total of five winning chances (see illustration). These machines take up to five coins, one for each payline, and here again, you must play the maximum number of coins to qualify for the top jackpot. From the standpoint of return on investment, the multi-line slots are perfectly fine machines if you don't mind the higher bankroll requirement.

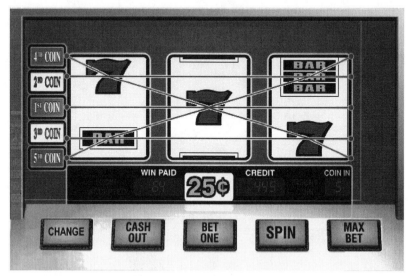

Slot window with five paylines

When looking for a game to play, don't assume all machines with the same name are identical. The IGT game called Triple Diamond comes in several versions that have one, three, five, or nine paylines. Furthermore, the one-payline version comes as a two-coin or three-coin multiplier.

OPTION-BUY GAMES

Option-buy games are usually (but not always) single-payline games that may be called Buy-Your-Pay or Buy-a-Pay, as well as various disparaging names. When you bet more than one coin, instead of multiplying the payout, these machines activate additional winning symbol combinations (see illustration). To get all the possible winning combinations, you must play the maximum number of coins. If you fail to do so, the overall payback of the machine is seriously compromised.

Some three-coin option-buy games can be misleading because the second coin is a multiplier, and only the third coin buys you additional symbol combinations. Therefore, on any game you are considering, study the paytable carefully because if it is an option-buy, you must never bet less than the maximum.

Typical option-buy paytable

People can become frustrated with option-buy games because they fail to read the paytable carefully. They get angry when they bet one coin, hit a winning combination of symbols, and are paid *absolutely nothing*. If it was a multiplier, they would have been paid a reduced amount, but at least they would have won *something*. Most people tend to get upset when they finally hit a winner and then aren't paid. Don't let this happen to you. If you decide to play an option-buy game, be sure you always bet the maximum.

VIDEO VERSIONS OF SPINNING REEL GAMES

The major slot machine manufacturers, such as IGT and Bally, provide some of their most popular machines in either a spinning reel or video format. These are three-reel slots and, except for the format, both versions are identical. They are either multipliers, multi-line, or option-buy machines, so the information in this section applies to the video versions as well as the spinning reel versions. Following are a few examples of slots that are marketed in both formats:

- Blazing 7s
- Double Diamond
- Red, White & Blue
- Sizzling 7s
- Triple Diamond
- White Lightning

SPINNING REEL STRATEGY

When most slot machine players take a vacation at a gambling resort, they allocate a certain amount of money for gambling, known as their **bankroll** or **stake**. Some of the players lose their bankroll by the end of the first day. Some of them are able to stretch their bankroll to the end of their vacation. Some of them come home money ahead. It appears that some people are just lucky and others are not.

This may be true, but if the same people almost always lose and other people almost always win, there must be more than luck involved. The difference is that some people play haphazardly without thinking, while others play thoughtfully and methodically. Is there a thoughtful way to play a seemingly mindless game such as slots? You bet there is—and the following sections suggest some shrewd and intelligent ways to improve your chances of coming out ahead.

STUDY THE GLASS

On a reel-spinner, the paytable (known as the **glass**) is prominently posted above the reels. You should carefully examine this paytable before you actually start to play any machine. You may be surprised to note how different the payouts are from machine to machine, especially how much the top jackpot changes. Two side-by-side machines that appear to be basically identical (say, two-coin, one payline) may have top jackpots of 2500 coins and 10,000 coins, respectively. Although it might seem better to play the one with the highest jackpot, to compensate for that jackpot, it will have fewer small and medium payouts. The overall long-term paybacks of the two machines may, in fact, be very similar.

So which machine should you play? If you select the one with the large jackpot, you can't worry too much about small wins, because you are going for the big one. Just try not to be too disappointed when you don't hit it, because that top jackpot is at least as elusive as a royal flush in video poker. If you select a machine with a smaller top jackpot, your bankroll will last longer and fluctuate less because it will be regularly replenished with small and medium wins. Most players are more satisfied with such a machine.

Finally, before you start to play, check the glass to be sure you didn't inadvertently choose an option-buy game. This type of machine is not always obvious; especially those versions where the option-buy feature only applies to the last coin or credit. If you really do want to play an option-buy game, be sure to read the section below on Multi-Line and Option-Buy Machines.

COIN MULTIPLIERS

Choose a simple machine. The best practice used by many experienced players when selecting a spinning reel slot machine is to stick to the basic three-reel non-progressive machines. This is also the best advice for novice players. To stretch your bankroll, look for two-coin machines with a single payline. By sticking with a single-payline machine, you will know, without studying the paytable, that you are playing either a multiplier or an option-buy game. By betting maximum coins or credits on a two-coin machine, you know that you will always qualify for the top awards. For inexperienced players, this is the safest approach for a minimum investment.

If you find the paytables to be even the slightest bit confusing, heed the above advice. The more sophisticated techniques outlined below require you to fully understand the paytables for the various types of games. If you are looking for more variety, there is nothing wrong with playing the three- and five-coin machines, so long as you have a sufficient bankroll that allows you to always bet the maximum.

Avoid games with high jackpots. Somehow this sounds contrary to what we are trying to do. Don't we want to win the biggest jackpots? Sure, but the chances of being successful are extremely remote. For example, a very popular Bally game is Stars & Bars. One version of this game has a top jackpot of 10,000 coins, but the chances of winning it are 1 out of 262,144 spins. It doesn't take a math genius to figure out that at 400 spins per hour, you would have to play over 655 hours to rack up 262,144 spins.

There is another version of Stars & Bars with a top jackpot of only 1200 coins, for which the chances of winning are much better: 1 out of 32,768 spins. In this case, the lower the payout, the better the chance of winning it.

An examination of the manufacturer's specifications for different models of machines, reveals that this is a general trend. Take a *really* high jackpot, such as the 40,000 coins found on French Quarters (50,000 in some versions). Here the chances of winning the top award are 1 in 2 million spins! This is getting to be astronomical for a non-progressive game. Of course, there is a mathematical reason why the program designers have to do this: to control the overall payback on the machine, these very high jackpots have to be made much tougher to hit.

This leads to the logical and correct conclusion that, most of the time, it is easier to win the top prize in a game with smaller jackpots. Furthermore, to keep the overall payback balanced, many games with modest top awards will compensate by rewarding you with a greater number of small and medium payouts.

Therefore, the best strategy advice is to play those games with the lower jackpots, preferably no higher than 3000 coins. This has another advantage: Most slot players go for machines with high jackpots, so the ones with low jackpots are more likely to be available in a crowded casino.

Bet one coin per spin. *"But everyone says I should always bet the maximum coins to be sure I qualify for the top jackpot. In fact, you just said that a few paragraphs earlier."* Yes, I did. But that advice was for inexperienced players and those who would rather not walk around the casino studying paytables.

I disagree with the advice to bet the maximum when it is given as a blanket rule. You will actually come out ahead by betting only one coin when you play certain machines, such as a true or near-true multiplier with a relatively-low top jackpot (see illustration). This is the case even if you eventually win the jackpot, which is a remote possibility.

Typical true multiplier paytable

Betting a single coin on a three-coin machine cuts your monetary risk to one-third of what it would have been with a maximum bet. Such an approach may also allow you to move to a higher denomination, and higher denomination machines are generally a little looser. Thus, by applying some judgment in selecting your machine, you could get a better overall return by betting only a single coin or credit.

Although true multipliers may be somewhat scarce in some casinos, you shouldn't have much trouble finding a near-true multiplier. There are usually plenty of them around. These are machines where the maximum bet jackpot is only slightly greater than the coin multiple.

The following chart gives some examples of what you should be looking for.

EXAMPLES OF TRUE AND NEAR-TRUE MULTIPLIERS

GAME	COINS	1st Coin	2nd Coin	3rd Coin	TYPE
IGT GAMES					
Double Diamond	3	800	1600	2500	Near True
Purple Passion	2	800	1600		True
Purple Passion	3	800	1600	2500	Near True
Spin Til You Win	2	500	1000		True
Triple Diamond	2	1000	2500		Near True
Triple Diamond	3	5000	10,000	15,000	True
BALLY GAMES					
California Dreamin'	2	800	1600		True
California Dreamin'	3	800	1600	2500	Near True
Diamond Winners	3	1000	2000	4000	Near True
Double Trouble	2	800	1600		True
Triple Gold	2	1000	2500		Near True
Wild Rose	2	800	1600		True

The 1st Coin, 2nd Coin, and 3rd Coin columns show the top jackpot for those games. Lesser payouts for all the listed games are exact multiples of the number of coins bet. Be careful when you check the paytables because some true and near-true multipliers also come in option-buy versions.

MULTI-LINE AND OPTION-BUY MACHINES
Avoid games with high jackpots. Avoiding high jackpots is the same advice given above for multipliers. It applies equally to multi-payline and option-buy games, and the justification is the same as for multipliers.

Always bet the maximum. Both multi-payline and option-buy machines penalize the player for not making a maximum bet, some more than others. Therefore, if you insist on playing these games, always bet the maximum, which in most cases will be two, three, or five coins or credits. If you don't do this, you will be penalizing yourself.

THE VIDEO SLOT MACHINES

The newest and glitziest slot machines on the casino floors display five or six simulated reels on a video screen. Although these games typically have nine to fifteen paylines, there are some with up to forty paylines that zigzag in almost every conceivable direction across the screen. On most machines, a bonus mode appears on a secondary screen when you hit the right symbol combinations. This bonus mode is the only real chance you have to recoup your losses and get ahead of the game.

The most common games have five reels, nine paylines, and encourage you to bet up to five coins per line. Because this adds up to forty-five coins, a maximum bet on a quarter machine costs $11.25 a spin, which is too rich for most players. Consequently, the nickel machines have taken on new popularity. At $2.25 per spin, the maximum bet on a nickel version is all most players are ready to contend with. Yet the casinos continue to display their greediness by putting more and more ten-coin-per-line nickel machines on the main floor. At $4.50 for a maximum bet, these nickel games are competing with the $5 machines in the high-limit area. As you play any of these computerized wonders, keep in mind that when you bet forty-five credits, and the machine noisily announces that you won thirty credits, *you are still losing money.*

Of course, none of this could happen if the nickel machines weren't more convenient to operate than they used to be. The days of buying rolls of nickels from the cashier and feeding them, one at a time, into the machine are gone. Now all you have to do is slip a bill into the currency acceptor and start to play. Of course, when you are ready to cash out, you still have to contend with that little coin bucket. Even this inconvenience is being overcome by machines that spit out credit tickets instead of coins.

BONUS GAMES

Except for the video versions of spinning reel machines, almost all video games have secondary bonus screens that pop up when you hit certain symbol combinations. The bonus screens often require some action on the part of the player, and always result in the award of extra credits. Examples are:

Choose your bonus: Three to five objects appropriate to the game theme appear on the screen. By touching the screen, you select one of them, which then displays the number of credits you have won. An example is Bally's Boxcar Bonus.

Free spins bonus: A set of bonus reels with special symbols and multipliers appears on the screen. When the reels spin, a bonus is awarded for winning combinations, which may include additional bonus spins. An example is IGT's Elephant King.

Match play bonus: A bonus grid with hidden symbols appears on the screen. By touching the screen, you select grid spaces to find matching symbols and multipliers, which determine the amount of your bonus. An example is IGT's The Munsters.

Pick to win bonus: Items that hide bonus amounts are displayed on the screen. By touching the screen, you pick items that reveal bonus credits and multipliers. An example is WMS's Monopoly.

MULTI-GAME MACHINES

This is a configuration where the player has a choice of several different games within a single game machine. Most multi-game machines, such as Bally's Game Maker, include a mix of video slot games and video poker games. The video slot games may be of the bonus and/or banking variety.

VIDEO BONUS GAME STRATEGY

Because the new video games are significantly different than the old spinning reel machines, the best ways to play them are also different. Most video games use entertainment or personality themes to attract players. They may be based on television game shows such as Jeopardy or Wheel of Fortune, or they may be based on board games such as Monopoly or Bingo, or they may be pure inventions such as Reel 'Em In or Filthy Rich. Whatever the case, try not to be influenced by the theme; select a game on its potential first and entertainment value second.

Except for the exact spinning reel emulators mentioned earlier, most video slot machines have the bonus screen feature. To keep it as uncomplicated as possible, the following strategy for bonus games covers only the most common types of machines, which are those with nine paylines and a maximum bet of either five or ten credits per payline (see illustration). If you want to play a game with more paylines, try to apply the same basic principles described below.

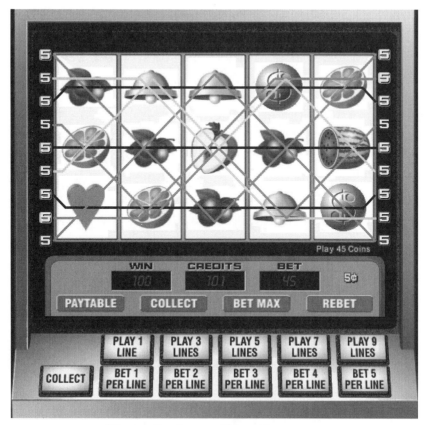

Five-reel, nine-payline video screen

STUDY THE PAYTABLE

Unlike spinning reel machines, the paytables on most video games are not posted on the outside of the cabinet. You must press a button to bring the schedule up on the screen, which may be several pages in length. Consequently, most players never look at the paytable and play the game virtually blind. Unless you are totally unconcerned with playing strategy, this is not a good way to go.

Before you start playing any unfamiliar video games, it is always a good idea to scrutinize the paytable. If nothing else, you should verify that the game is a true multiplier, that is, that the payouts are multiplied by the number of credits bet, and that there is no special payoff benefit for playing the maximum number of lines and credits. Some games give a serious advantage for maximum bets. Avoid these because you lose all flexibility in your playing style.

The other thing to establish is whether the game is a *credits-per-line* multiplier or a *total credits* multiplier. The first type will have a statement on the paytable such as: *All Wins are Multiplied by the Credits Bet per Line*. The second type will say something like: *All Wins are Multiplied by the Total Credits Bet*. Knowing the type of multiplier is necessary for determining the best way to play the game.

A statement such as: *Scatter Wins are Multiplied by the Total Credits Bet*, does not necessarily mean the machine is a total credits multiplier. The statement, which applies only to scatter wins, appears in the paytable of most credit-per-line multipliers as well as total credits multipliers. Since scatter wins are not line dependent, this rule has no effect on the playing method.

STRATEGY FOR CREDITS-PER-LINE MULTIPLIERS

When playing a credits-per-line multiplier, the basic idea is to maximize the credits per line because that maximizes the amount of the payouts. This is done by activating fewer paylines and betting more credits per line. The down side is that with fewer active paylines the win frequency drops. The benefit is that an incremental betting sequence, which varies the credits per line, is simpler, and the bonus payouts are satisfyingly larger.

Start with three paylines. The payline choices on most nine-payline games are one, three, five, seven, or nine lines. Unless you are an old hand, resist the urge to hit the MAX BET button, which can commit you to a bet of ninety credits on some machines! On a nickel machine, that amounts to $4.50 a spin. Even if your bankroll can handle higher denominations, you should stick with the nickel machines until you are very familiar with these games.

To preserve your stake on a credits-per-line multiplier, never start by betting all nine lines. If you start with only one line, however, the pay-outs are so infrequent that you may get discouraged before you win anything. No matter what the machine denomination, it is usually best to start with one credit and three lines.

If you are losing after a dozen spins, try another machine. If, however, you have accumulated some credits, then start betting two credits. If you continue winning, increase your bet to three credits, and so forth. While doing this, you should activate only three paylines. You can play this way in an informal manner, or you can learn the betting sequence in the next section and use a more methodical approach.

Use an incremental betting sequence. With so many choices of pay-lines and credits, you can make a total bet of as small as one credit or as large as forty-five credits. On a ten-credits-per-payline machine, you can make a one-credit bet or a ninety-credit bet. This freedom lends itself to strategies of systematic play that will minimize risk and maximize gain.

One way of doing this is shown by the sequence below. The number of credits bet is slowly increased while the number of lines stays at three. This progression for forty-five credits has many more steps than a common doubling system, and is easy to remember. The amount shown in the last column is the total cost per spin on a nickel machine.

SUGGESTED BETTING SEQUENCE FOR CREDITS-PER-LINE MULTIPLIERS			
Number of Lines	Credits per Line	Credits per Spin	Total Amount
3	1	3	$0.15
3	2	6	$0.30
3	3	9	$0.45
3	4	12	$0.60
3	5	15	$0.75
5	5	25	$1.25
7	5	35	$1.75
9	5	45	$2.25

There are two good reasons for increasing the number of credits per line faster than the number of lines. First, the chance of hitting a scatter pay is the same no matter how many paylines are activated. Second, when you get lucky and activate a bonus screen, the payout is multiplied by the number of credits per line. The number of lines has no effect on the total amount of the bonus.

Apply the betting sequence. The best way to apply the chart is to start at the lowest betting level (three lines, one credit per line). If, on your first spin, you win something (any amount) remain at the one-credit level and stay there until you win nothing. The first time you don't win (which may be the first spin), proceed to the next step by raising your bet to two credits per line.

At the two-credit level, you can take three possible actions:

1. If you win nothing, remain at the two-credit level, and stay there until you have won nothing two times in a row. The rule is that you

remain at any level until you have lost the same number of times *in a row* as the number of credits per line.

2. If you win an amount less than five times your total bet, remain at the two-credit level and restart the loss count in (1), above.

3. If you win an amount greater than five times your total bet, drop back to the one-credit level at the top of the chart and start the sequence over.

Continue working down the chart in this manner until you reach the three-line, five-credit level. If at this point you are losing money, quit or change machines. Resist the urge to increase the number of lines until you are ahead and then be sure to set a loss limit (see the Money Management chapter) to preserve the lion's share of your winnings.

There are now machines with forty or more paylines. When you play one of those, be sure you progress to the maximum credits per line before you start to increase the number of paylines (unless the game is a total credits multiplier). Also, check the paytable to be sure that specific paylines do not have special payout bonuses.

STRATEGY FOR TOTAL CREDITS MULTIPLIERS

With a credits-per-line multiplier, you activate fewer paylines and try to maximize the credits per line. This maximizes the amount of the payouts. The best playing method for total credits multipliers is almost completely opposite to the method used for credits-per-line multipliers.

Start with maximum paylines. With a total credits multiplier, you should always activate the maximum number of paylines and limit the total bet amount by cutting down on the credits per line. There is a good reason for this. Instead of playing three lines at three credits per line, for a total of nine credits per spin, you should play nine lines at one credit per line, for the same total of nine credits. Although the total credits multiplier is the same either way (nine credits), with nine paylines activated, you will hit three times the number of wins. Since the total payout for each win is the same either way, you should maximize the win frequency by activating all of the lines.

Use an incremental betting sequence. Just as for a credits-per-line multiplier, you should try to apply an incremental betting sequence. Since you should always activate all of the paylines, the only betting variability is in the number of credits per line.

The simplest way is to start with one credit per line and incrementally increase it by one credit, say every three spins (you can decide on the exact number). Thus, on a nickel machine, your first bet would be forty-five cents (five cents times nine lines). Increase this bet by one credit when you have three no-wins in a row. Anytime you hit a small win of less than five times your total wager, restart the three-count.

You can also increase the loss count as you increase the number of credits per line. You can make the loss count the same as the credits per line, or if you have a limited bankroll and are really conservative, make it double the credits per line.

The sequence shown below is for a nine payline, five credits per line machine. The number of lines is kept at nine, while the number of credits is increased incrementally. The amount shown in the last column is the total cost per spin on a nickel machine.

SUGGESTED BETTING SEQUENCE FOR TOTAL CREDITS MULTIPLIERS			
Number of Lines	Credits per Line	Credits per Spin	Total Amount
9	1	9	$0.45
9	2	18	$0.90
9	3	27	$1.35
9	4	36	$1.80
9	5	45	$2.25

Whenever you get a payout that is at least five times your total wager, restart the entire sequence at one credit per line. As an alternative, you may want to hold off by one spin before you restart the sequence, just in case you hit back-to-back wins. Waiting for two spins is usually not worthwhile because a big win three times in a row is rare. By restarting the sequence, you will help to preserve the amounts won. If you are fortunate enough to hit some nice bonus payouts, set a loss limit (see the Money Management chapter) and cash in when you reach it.

The above method is only one way of doing this. You should modify the sequence to fit games with more than nine paylines and/or more than five credits per line. You should also modify the overall procedure to fit your own personality so you will be more likely to stick with it. The only part you shouldn't change is the number of paylines. For games that are total credits multipliers, always activate the maximum number of paylines.

STRATEGY BENEFITS

Finally, I should make clear that the betting sequences suggested above do not convey any particular mathematical advantage to the player. They are not a magic formula for beating the system, but they do carry the following benefits that will help to preserve your bankroll, reduce your losses, and help you come out ahead.

1. Applying a predetermined betting sequence forces you to play in a more methodical manner, rather than aimlessly hitting the buttons as fast as you can.

2. This methodical approach reduces your playing speed, which also helps to preserve your bankroll.

3. By starting low and gradually increasing your bet you keep your average betting level down, thus, you reduce your overall investment risk.

4. The betting sequence helps to preserve larger wins by returning you to the lowest betting level.

5. And most importantly, the methodical approach forces you to pay attention to the performance of the game so that you are more likely to stay with it when it is hot and abandon it when it goes cold.

THE BANKING GAMES

These are games in which points, credits, or some form of game assets are accumulated as they are played. They are designed to encourage players to continue playing until they eventually collect the banked bonus. Banking games may also have the paytable features of multipliers or line games.

Although some banking games, such as Piggy Bankin' and X-Factor, are reel-spinners, more and more of them are video games with secondary bonus screens. The best strategy for profitably playing reel spinning banking games is basically the same as for the video versions, so they are treated here as a single category.

Many reel-spinner banking games have a distinctive orange dotmation screen above the reels. To the casual observer, video banking machines appear to be ordinary bonus games, in that a secondary screen is part of the mix. Banking games, however, have an important distinction that puts them in a class by themselves. As the game is played, points or some form of game assets are visibly accumulated by the machine in a "bank." When the bank reaches a certain condition as a result of continued play, these assets are finally paid out in the form of bonus credits.

This feature is designed to entice players to remain at the machine longer than they intended in an attempt to reach the payoff goal. Regardless of this enticement, some players may quit the game (for any number of reasons) before reaching the payoff goal. This leaves the game in a favorable state for any subsequent player who knows how to take advantage of it.

BANKING GAME STRATEGY

Unlike other bonus games, banking games have a unique characteristic that, if taken advantage of, can result in overcoming the normal payback percentage built into the machine. This can happen when a previous player has left a banking machine in a state of increased value, either due to ignorance, a lack of funds, a pressing engagement, or some other reason. Another person, who recognizes the potential value of the machine, can play it to advantage.

The advantage arises when some form of game assets have been saved or "banked" by the machine during a period of previous play. When the machine attains a certain condition or bonus goal as the result of resumed play, the accumulated assets are finally paid out in the form of credits. This will occur even if the resumed play is by a person other than the one who originally accumulated most of the banked assets.

The trick is to recognize when an abandoned machine has reached the point at which continued play will likely be profitable.

SEARCH FOR BANKED CREDITS

Video slot machines that have a banking feature are not always apparent. To the casual observer, most of them just look like ordinary bonus games. The banking feature, however, is described on the paytable (which you can see by touching the paytable button on the screen), and the feature usually becomes apparent when you start playing the game. Therefore, you can eventually find a banking game by walking from machine to machine, bringing up and reading the paytable on each one.

Reel spinning banking machines are a little more obvious. They often have a top box with some type of dotmation graphic display. In any case, I'll save you some time and trouble by listing a number of the most common video and reel spinning banking games in the next section, along with suggestions as to when they have attained a profitable state.

Since the banking feature has been around for a few years, many experienced slot players know the potential value of banking games. Sadly, a few unscrupulous types have used techniques for encouraging a player to leave a machine when it reaches a valuable state. Casinos are aware of this and do not look kindly on such activities.

Keep in mind that it is not good form to look over the shoulder of someone who is playing a banking machine, in the hope that they will abandon the game. Casinos generally don't care who plays their slot machines or who wins the bonuses, but they have been known to bar individuals who harass or annoy other slot players. Before you sit down at a machine, take a moment to assure that the machine has really been abandoned.

When you begin to play, study the paytable and playing directions very carefully. Some banking games get rather complicated in the way the bonuses are banked. You need to know that you are playing correctly, or you may lose the advantage that you started with.

MACHINES TO LOOK FOR

Useful information for playing some of the most popular banking games is provided below. The playing advice is as current as I could make it, but be aware that manufacturers frequently modify their machines and you should try to verify that the game you are considering is the same as the one described. Applying the following suggestions does not guarantee that you will be ahead every time you play an advantageous machine, but only that your long-term average will be profitable.

Bingo: This is exactly like the game using cardboard bingo cards (you do know how to play bingo, don't you?). The video screen displays five reels that represent the five columns on a standard bingo card. Most of the time, the machine plays like any five-reel video game, but every so often a bingo ball appears on one of the columns and the machine will draw a bingo number. This continues until the selected bingo configuration is completed, whereupon a bonus round determines how many credits have been won. Study the paytable to learn how to identify the various bingo configurations.

Bet one credit per spin on one payline if you find a game in which the bingo is at least half finished. Although Bingo has five paylines, the bingo ball does not have to fall on a line to be valid. Cash out when the banked bonus is won.

Boom: This game banks firecrackers and awards the bonus when fifty are accumulated. Although it is a five credits-per-payline, nine-payline game, don't ever bet forty-five credits. *Bet one credit on one payline when* *you find a game with at least thirty firecrackers lined up across the top of the screen.* Cash out when the banked bonus is won.

Chuck Wagons: In this game of racing chuck wagons, if Your Wagon reaches the bonus area before Their Wagon finishes, you collect the banked bonus. The race distance is seventy miles. *Bet maximum credits per spin when you find a game in which Your Wagon has gone at least thirty miles and Their Wagon is at least 25% behind Your Wagon.* Cash out when the banked bonus is won.

Diamond Thief: This is a rather complex three-reel game with the ultimate goal of filling all nine compartments of a case with diamonds, six diamonds per compartment, for a total of fifty-four diamonds. *Bet one credit per spin when you find a game that needs no more than five diamonds to completely fill the case.* Cash out when the banked bonus is won.

Double Diamond Mine, Triple Diamond Mine: In these games, a bonus is paid when ten diamonds are accumulated in any of the three mineshafts. *Bet one credit per spin when you find a game with nine diamonds in one shaft, eight diamonds in two of the three shafts, or at least seven diamonds in each of the three shafts.* Cash out when the game no longer meets any of the above conditions.

Empire, Empire King: In these games, King Kong has to climb the Empire State Building a certain number of stories within a certain time limit. In Empire, the first bonus level is seventy stories; in Empire King, the bonus level is ninety stories. Study the paytable to get the details. *Bet the maximum credits per spin when you find a game with at least twice as many seconds left on the timer as there are stories remaining for King to climb.* Cash out when the distance counter resets to zero.

Fishin' for Cash: This is a fishing version of Double Diamond Mine. Whenever a fish appears on the payline, it is reeled in and piled on one of three stacks. *Bet one credit per spin when you find a game with nine fish in one stack, eight fish in two of the three stacks, or at least seven fish in each of the three stacks.* Cash out when the game no longer meets any of the above conditions.

Greased Lightning: This is a version of Chuck Wagons, where '57 Chevys are raced instead of chuck wagons. *Bet maximum credits per spin when you find a game in which Your Car has gone at least thirty miles and Their Car is at least 25% behind Your Car.* Cash out when the banked bonus is won.

Isle of Pearls: This is a variation of Empire where you go down instead of up. To get the bonus, a pearl diver needs to descend at least seventy feet before time runs out (100 seconds). *Bet the maximum credits per spin when you find a game where the diver has gone at least thirty feet and there are at least twice as many seconds left on the timer as there are feet remaining for the diver to descend.* Cash out when it is obvious that the diver will not reach seventy feet before the time runs out.

Jungle King: This is the opposite of Isle of Pearls, where the Jungle Man needs to climb up a vine a distance of seventy feet within 100 seconds. *Bet the maximum credits per spin when you find a game where there are at least twice as many seconds left on the timer as there are feet remaining for Jungle Man to climb.* Cash out when the distance counter resets to zero.

Merlin: This is another clone of Empire with Merlin trying to reach a castle before time runs out. *Bet the maximum credits per spin when you find a game with at least twice as many seconds left on the timer as there are units remaining for Merlin to travel.* Cash out when the distance counter resets to zero.

Piggy Bankin', Big Bang Piggy Bankin': Piggy Bankin' was the original banking game, and it caused quite a stir among the experts and analysts when this three-reel machine was first introduced. It also established WMS Gaming as a major competitor in the slot machine business. Big Bang Piggy Bankin' is a newer version of the same game.

In Piggy Bankin', whenever you get three blank spaces on the payline, your bet is added to the contents of a piggy bank. Then, when the Break the Bank symbol lands on the right-hand payline, the contents of the piggy bank are yours. *Bet one credit per spin when you find a $1, $2, or $5 game with at least twenty-five credits, or a nickel or quarter game with at least thirty credits in the bank.* Cash out when you break the bank.

In Big Bang Piggy Bankin', you have to get three Break the Bank symbols (or wild equivalents) to win the banked bonus. *Bet one credit per spin when you find a game with at least fifty credits in the bank.* Cash out when you break the bank.

Red Ball: This three-payline nickel machine displays two 3 x 3 matrix squares alongside the video reels. The idea is to fill one of the squares with red balls and the other with black balls. Under each square is a number indicating the amount of the payoff bonus for completing that square. *Bet one credit per line per spin (a total of three credits) when you find a game with at least a twenty under either square or at least a fifteen under both.* Cash out when the game no longer meets the above conditions.

Shopping Spree: This game banks frequent shopper points, and the banked bonus is paid when fifty points are accumulated. *Bet two credits per spin when you find a game with at least thirty frequent shopper points already registered.* Cash out when you win the bonus.

Super 7s: This five-payline game is found on Game King machines, and the banked items are square sevens, that is, each seven is inside of a square. *Bet one credit per line per spin (a total of five credits) when you find a game with at least three square sevens showing.* Cash out when you win the bonus.

Temperature's Rising: The idea is to raise the temperature on a large red thermometer to the bonus level. The temperature goal depends on the particular machine version, but is plainly shown. *Bet one credit per spin when you find a game where the amount of the bonus is greater than the number of degrees needed to "break" the thermometer.* Cash out when the bonus is won.

Triple Cash Winfall: This is a money version of Double Diamond Mine, where coins fall on one of three stacks. *Bet one credit per spin when you find a game with nine coins in one stack, eight coins in two of the three stacks, or at least seven coins in each of all three stacks.* Cash out when the game no longer meets any of the above three conditions.

Triple Diamond Baseball Diamond: Ball players move around the bases as you hit a single, double, triple, or home run on the third reel of this machine. The runs are accumulated and are paid out when you get a home run. *Bet one credit per spin when you find a game with at least twenty-five accumulated runs plus the runs shown over the base runner's heads.* Cash out when the base runners are cleared by a home run.

Wild Cherry Pie, Wild Cherry Bonus Pie: Through a rather convoluted process, a total of fifty-four cherries have to be accumulated in a nine-section pie. *For Wild Cherry Pie, bet one credit per spin when you find a game with at least forty-four cherries in the large pie. For Wild Cherry Bonus Pie, bet one credit per spin when you find a game with at least forty-eight cherries in the large pie.* Cash out when the pie is filled and the bonus is paid.

X-Factor: The X factor is a payout multiplier that starts at 2X and can build as high as 10X. Whenever you choose to use the multiplier, it resets to 2X. *Bet the maximum credits per spin when you find a game with an X factor of at least 6X.* Cash out when the multiplying factor has been used.

MULTI-GAME MACHINES

Nearly all casinos have plenty of multi-game machines on the floor. The most popular are Bally's Game Maker, IGT's Game King, and Anchor's Winning Touch. Each of these machines contains a variety of choices, which usually includes a mix of video poker and video slot games. Some of the video banking games listed above can be found on multi-game machines.

Most of these machines are almost entirely touch-screen driven. Before committing any currency to one of them, you can surf your way through numerous screens to get instructions and paytable information on every game it contains.

In addition to video poker, most of the selections will likely be video bonus games and video versions of reel spinners. Use the playing strategies described earlier for these games. If the menu contains a banking game, by using the suggestions in the previous section, you can determine ahead of time if it is worth playing.

THE PROGRESSIVE SLOTS

In progressive slot machines the top jackpot is not fixed. Progressives are usually part of a linked group of machines, and as the individual slots are played, the jackpot continually grows until someone wins it. After a win, the jackpot is reset to a base value and then begins to grow again. Some players are unaware that there is often a secondary jackpot, which is much smaller than the primary.

Progressive slots are typically two-, three-, or five-coin machines, although some video nickel machines will take as many as forty-five coins. In every case, the maximum number of coins must be bet to qualify for the top prize. Because progressives require a larger bankroll than basic flat pays, they are not recommended for beginning slot players. The looseness or tightness of a progressive machine is entirely dependent on the current jackpot amount, since that determines the overall payback.

Progressive slot machines can be divided into three distinct categories. The categories roughly define how many machines are linked together (if any), and how large the progressive jackpots grow. The playing strategies for all the categories are quite similar.

STAND-ALONE PROGRESSIVES

At one time, all progressive slot machines were stand-alone. That was before someone thought of the idea of linking progressives together to make the jackpot meter tick up faster and higher. Most casinos still have stand-alones, the big difference being that the progressive jackpot is in the thousands of dollars rather than in the hundreds of thousands or millions. Generally you can identify a stand-alone by the lack of a large jackpot meter above the row or carousel. Instead, there is a meter on each individual machine, which doesn't change unless someone is playing the game.

LOCAL PROGRESSIVES

The first linked progressives were groups of machines within a single casino that were connected together so that they all contributed to a common jackpot pool. The size of a particular progressive group may be as small as a half dozen machines or as large as several dozen. Each cluster of machines has a large meter that displays the current value of the jackpot. You can tell it isn't a WAPS (see below) because the jackpot will be in the tens of thousands. If you are not sure, just ask an attendant or a floor supervisor.

WIDE AREA PROGRESSIVE SLOTS (WAPS)

These are the big money progressive machines. In 1986, IGT set up the first citywide linked progressive machines in Las Vegas and called them Megabucks. They were so successful that dozens of wide-area progressive systems have been started since then—the majority being operated by IGT. On most of them, the top jackpot runs into the millions, which accounts for their enormous popularity. The idea of linking hundreds of similar machines within a single gaming jurisdiction such as Nevada or New Jersey has resulted in very high payouts and frequent winners.

The individual casinos do not own the wide area machines. They are installed and maintained by a system operator such as IGT. When IGT sets up a new Megabucks machine, all the casino does is provide the floor space and take its cut of the action. IGT maintains the machine and all associated equipment including the interconnecting telephone lines. They handle all the needed administration and promotional activities, in addition to verifying and paying all the jackpots.

PROGRESSIVE STRATEGY

The vast majority of progressive players are primarily interested in winning the top jackpot. These players consider the smaller wins to be useful only for replenishing their bankrolls so they can stay at their machines for a longer period of time. To support the large progressive jackpots, the machines are programmed so that the medium and small wins occur less often than in non-progressive games. If you have this all-or-nothing mentality, then the progressives are your game.

STAND-ALONE AND LOCAL PROGRESSIVES

If you like the idea of big jackpots but would prefer something less elusive than what the wide area progressives offer, you might be interested in trying a local bank of progressives. If the amount on the progressive meter is less than $100,000, then it is almost certainly a local group, unless it is Bally's Blondie, which has a rather low reset of $25,000. If you are not sure if a particular row or carousel is local or WAPS, ask a floor supervisor. One advantage to playing a stand-alone or local progressive is that the jackpot will be paid in a lump sum.

Look for high jackpots. The only strategy is to find a linked group of machines that is displaying a high amount on the progressive meter. This is not difficult because the present value of the top jackpot is prominently displayed on a large digital sign above each bank of machines, the number continually ticking upward as the players insert coins. If there is a secondary jackpot, it is shown on a smaller meter below the top jackpot sign.

Each time the jackpot is won, the amount on the meter is reset to a base value. Whenever a progressive meter is close to the base amount, it means there was a recent win and the next win is not likely to occur for some time. You should always try to find a group of machines where the meter shows the greatest dollar increment over the reset value. To find out what that reset value is, you will have to ask a supervisor. Just remember that when you play *any kind* of progressive, you must always bet the maximum if you expect to qualify for the big jackpot.

Then there are those individual stand-alone machines with progressive jackpots that are often no higher than many of the non-progressive slots. There doesn't seem to be any valid reason to play these machines. If you do, be sure to find one in which the jackpot has been run up by other players, and bet the maximum.

Bet the maximum coins or credits. No matter what else you might do, when playing a progressive *always bet the maximum*. It is the only chance you have of beating the system. If you don't bet the maximum coins or credits, you cannot win the progressive jackpot—and if you don't have a crack at the top jackpot, the overall payback on the machine will be rather poor. If you don't want to risk that much money, you are playing the wrong machine and you should find one of a lower denomination. Or you shouldn't be playing progressives at all.

WIDE AREA PROGRESSIVE SLOTS (WAPS)

The jackpots on WAPS, which can be a lifestyle-changing amount of money, are seldom won—so seldom that when someone gets lucky, it is always reported in the newspaper. WAPS have to be approached with a totally different attitude; that is, you can't mind blowing your entire bankroll on the infinitesimal chance of hitting a gigantic payday. It's something like playing the state lottery on a continuous basis. And you know what they say about most state lotteries: Your chances of winning the big one are statistically the same whether or not you buy a ticket.

Furthermore, besides feeding a percentage of the receipts to the progressive jackpot escrow account, both the WAPS operator (such as IGT or Bally) and the casino in which the machine is located, take their cut. Consequently, the overall payback to the player is always less than 90%, often much less. For this reason, *I don't recommend playing them.* The odds of winning the progressive jackpot itself are so poor that every time you hit the SPIN or MAX BET button, you are throwing your money down a black hole. How can this be any fun?

For those of you who still insist on playing these machines, be sure you always bet the maximum coins or credits, or you will have a zero chance of winning the top jackpot. Although some WAPS have been known to hit just above the reset amount, I still recommend that you wait until the progressive meter gets at least twice as high. I do hate to encourage you, but I will provide some basic information on the most popular progressives that can be found in most jurisdictions.

Megabucks: The mother of all WAPS, these dollar slots have been around since IGT installed the first ones in 1986. The first Megabucks progressive jackpot was hit on February 1st, 1987 in Reno, Nevada for nearly five million dollars. These machines can be found in most casinos within the major gambling jurisdictions such as Nevada and Mississippi, as well as in Tribal casinos. All the machines in a given jurisdiction are linked to the same huge jackpot pool.

Megabucks is usually a three-coin, four-reel machine, so you have to invest $3 on each spin to qualify for the primary jackpot. Line up the four Megabucks symbols on the payline and you win a multi-million dollar jackpot that is paid out in annual installments. After a win, the primary jackpot is reset to $7 million (in Nevada), and the secondary jackpot is reset to $2000.

In 1990, IGT set up a Megabucks WAPS network in Atlantic City. It never was very profitable for the operators; some analysts blamed the nature of the Eastern gaming market. For many years, in an attempt to improve revenues, IGT did some serious adjusting and fiddling. They changed the number of reels and raised the reset amount, but they could never find the formula for success. In 2002, they finally gave up and shut down the system. In Nevada, however, Megabucks has never been more popular.

Wheel of Fortune: Another IGT success story, this three-reeler is now the most popular of all WAPS. It comes in four denominations, and requires the maximum number of coins to win the progressive, as follows:

> **Quarters** — Three coin max bet and $200,000 reset.
> **Halves** — Three coin max bet and $500,000 reset.
> **Dollars** — Two coin max bet and $1 million reset.
> **Five dollars** — Two coin max bet and $1 million reset.

The top payouts are made in annual installments for all denominations, which is common for IGT machines.

Wheel of Fortune Video: The video version has five simulated reels and is found in most jurisdictions except Nevada. It comes in nickel and quarter denominations.

Betty Boop's Big Hit: This is Bally's most popular WAPS, and it has some unusual features. First, most of the machines are multi-denominational; you feed a bill into the currency acceptor and then decide if you want to play nickels, quarters, or dollars. Second, in one carousel there are usually several theme variations, such as Swing Time Betty, Betty Boop's Double Jackpot, and Betty Boop's Roaring '20s.

To qualify for the progressive jackpot, you have to bet five nickels, three quarters, or two dollars. If you think you can beat the system by betting just five nickels, think again. According to Bally, a player's chances of hitting the top jackpot are eight times better if he bets two dollars than if he bets twenty-five cents. Furthermore, the overall theoretical payback rises as the denomination goes up: 84%, 86%, and 88% for nickels, quarters, and dollars, respectively. After someone hits the progressive, the machines reset to $100,000, and the winner is immediately paid the entire jackpot (less taxes).

Quartermania: As the name implies, this IGT WAPS accepts quarters, although it takes two of them to qualify for the big payoff, which is paid in twenty annual installments. The primary reset is $1 million, while the secondary is restarted at a measly $1000.

Jeopardy: Jeopardy is basically a three-coin quarter machine except in Atlantic City where there are also fifty-cent and dollar versions. This is another IGT machine, so it pays the top jackpot in annual installments.

Jeopardy Video: Jeopardy also comes in a video version. It is a nickel machine with a reset of $100,000. Because you have to bet forty-five credits to qualify for the progressive payout, it is more expensive to play than the non-video three-reel version.

Elvis: This is another popular three-reel IGT game, which sports a bonus feature that plays Elvis tunes. It comes in two denominations with the following specifications:

> **Quarters** — Three coin max bet and $100,000 reset.
> **Dollars** — Two coin max bet and $250,000 reset.

The jackpot is paid immediately on both the quarter and dollar versions.

Millionaire 777s: Right now, this Bally WAPS can only be found in Nevada, but it is so popular that by the time this book is published, it will surely have spread to other jurisdictions. These are dollar machines with a reset of $1 million.

◆19◆
SPANISH 21

A child of the computer age, Spanish 21 is a mathematically-derived variation of blackjack. The term "Spanish" refers to the 48-card deck used in some Spanish card games. It is a regular 52-card deck with the four tens removed. Although, in most respects, Spanish 21 is played just like standard blackjack, the basic strategy is somewhat different.

As a uniquely-designed modification of blackjack, Spanish 21 has liberalized rules and numerous bonuses. The casinos can be so generous because removal of the four tens from the deck gives the house a large advantage. The changes in rules and payouts were designed to attract jaded blackjack players and have made the game popular. The modified rules have considerable appeal. For instance, in standard blackjack, it is always exhilarating to hit a count of 21 on the nose, but it quickly turns into a disappointment if the dealer also hits 21 (resulting in a push instead of a win). In Spanish 21, if both dealer and player have 21, the player wins!

In addition, bonuses are paid for getting 21 with five cards, six cards, and seven cards, and for getting certain three card combinations such as 6 7 8 and 7 7 7. Then there is the super bonus: If you get a suited 7 7 7 and the dealer's upcard is a 7, a bonus is paid to *all* the players at the table. It's no wonder that many blackjack players are migrating to Spanish 21.

Spanish 21 is played on a regular blackjack table. Except for the liberal payoffs, the game appears to be almost identical to standard blackjack, which is what fools some experienced blackjack players. Many of them don't realize that the basic strategy for standard blackjack does not work very well, and that the house edge is higher. To keep from losing your shirt, you have to learn a modified strategy.

Like regular blackjack, the game is easy to learn and play. You are dealt two cards and then take additional cards (hits) one-by-one, trying to get as close to a total count of 21 without going over. When all the players are through taking hits, the dealer does the same by following a fixed set of house rules. If you beat the dealer, you win even odds, and if the dealer beats you, you lose your bet. If your hand has the same numerical count as the dealer (except for a count of 21) it is a tie (called a push), and no money changes hands.

FUNDAMENTALS OF PLAY

THE EQUIPMENT
The implements used for playing Spanish 21 include a half-moon table with stools for the players, several decks of cards, and a dealing shoe. These items are described below.

The playing table: Spanish 21 is played on a table that is essentially identical to a standard blackjack table and is located in the blackjack area. In most casinos it is easy to find because there is an elevated sign at the table identifying the game. The dealer stands at the flat side with a chip rack directly in front of her and a card-dealing shoe to her left.

At each player position there is one betting spot in the shape of a circle or a rectangle. The first player seat to the left of the dealer is called **first base**. This spot is the first hand dealt in a round of play. The last seat to the dealer's right is called the **anchor position**, and is also referred to as **third base**. It is the last player hand dealt in a round.

The felt surface of the table has two game rules imprinted on it. The most common rule is: *Dealer must hit soft 17.* In Atlantic City and some other jurisdictions, this rule is modified to read: *Dealer must draw to 16 and stand on all 17s,* which is a more favorable rule for the player. The second imprinted rule is: *Insurance pays 2 to 1.*

The dealing shoe: Spanish 21 games use six or eight decks of cards, which are dealt from a **dealing shoe**. The shoe is an elongated plastic box into which the pre-shuffled cards are stacked, one end of which has a slot and a finger notch so that the dealer may easily slide out the cards, one at a time.

The shuffling machine: To speed up the game, many Spanish 21 tables are now equipped with an automatic shuffling machine.

The deck: The 48-card deck used in Spanish 21 is standard except that all four 10s have been removed. Removing the 10s effectively reduces the number of ten-value cards by 25%, giving the dealer a major mathematical advantage. Each face card (jack, queen, and king) has a numerical value of ten. In a standard blackjack deck, there are sixteen ten-value cards, while in a Spanish 21 deck (because of the missing tens) there are only twelve ten-value cards. As in blackjack, an ace may be valued one or eleven.

THE PLAYERS' HANDS
A player's initial hand consists of two cards, which may be categorized in the following ways.

Hard hand: This is an initial hand that does not contain an ace and has a total count of more than 11. It is called **hard** because the total numeric value of the hand is fixed and an additional card can cause it to exceed a count of 21. For instance, if the two dealt cards are a 5 and a 9, the hand has a hard value of 14. A third card of 8 or higher will result in busting the hand with a total greater than 21.

Soft hand: This is an initial hand in which one of the cards is an ace. It is called **soft** because the value of the ace can be changed from 11 to 1, to prevent the total count of the hand from going over 21. Whenever the value of the ace has to be changed from 11 to 1 to prevent busting, it becomes a hard hand.

An initial hand with two aces is a special case. Although it may have a value of 2 or 12, the best strategy is to always split the aces into two separate hands.

Pat and stiff hands: A **pat hand** is one that cannot reasonably be improved. Any hand with a hard count of 17 through 21 is considered pat. A **stiff hand** is one that is not pat and can be busted with the addition of a single card. Specifically, any hand with a hard total of 12 through 16 is considered stiff.

Blackjack: A blackjack, also called a **natural,** is a two card initial hand consisting of an ace plus any ten-count card. If the dealer's upcard is an ace or a ten-value card (jack, queen, or king), she peeks at her downcard to see if she has a natural. If she does, the hand is terminated and everyone loses automatically unless they also have a natural. Whenever you get a natural, you win regardless of what the dealer has, and are paid 3 to 2 odds. This is a nice improvement over standard blackjack where, if you match the dealer's natural, it is just a push. In Spanish 21, you will be dealt an average of one natural in about 24 hands. This is not quite as good as standard six-deck blackjack, however, where you can expect to get one natural in about 21 hands

An ace plus a ten-count card constitutes a natural only on the initial two card deal. Any subsequent ace-10 combination, such as might occur as a result of splitting a pair of aces, is not considered a natural. Of course, if you get a total of exactly 21 with certain three card combinations, you will be paid 3 to 2 odds or better (more on that later).

21 Count: If your hand has a count of 21, you win even odds. This is true even if the dealer has 21. The only way you can lose is if the dealer has a natural. There are no pushes on a 21 hand. Additionally, certain card combinations that add up to 21 pay better than even odds, which is covered in the section on payoffs.

Busted hand: When, in the course of drawing additional cards, the total point count of the hand goes over 21, it is said to be **busted**. When that happens, the hand is an immediate loser; the dealer collects the bet and places the player's cards in the discard tray. The dealer's hand can be busted as well; however, since the dealer plays last, if the dealer busts, the busted player still loses.

PLAYER OPTIONS

Once you've examined your initial two cards and determined if the hand is hard, soft, stiff, or pat, you are expected to take some action. A number of different player options are available, all of which are reviewed below. Some actions are communicated to the dealer with hand signals, while others are communicated by simply increasing the initial wager.

Hit: If you are not satisfied with the two card count, you may request additional cards, one by one. This is called taking a **hit**. Indicate your desire to take a hit by pointing at your cards with an index finger. Some players prefer to tap or scratch the felt directly behind the cards. Either way is acceptable. You may hit as many times as you want, so long as you don't go over 21. If the card count exceeds 21, you have busted and your bet is lost.

Stand: When you are satisfied with the card count and don't want any more hits, you may **stand**. Signal your intention to stand by waving your hand over the cards, palm down. You can stand at any time: after looking at your original hand, after taking one or more hits, or after splitting a pair. Standing is automatic if you double down (see below) because you are given just one card and are not allowed to take any hits.

Double down: You may **double down** on any hand by placing another wager up to the amount of your original bet. Do this by placing the new wager alongside your original bet. When you double down, you receive only one additional card from the dealer. Doubling is good strategy when your hand reaches a total of 10 or 11 and the dealer is showing a low card.

In Spanish 21, you may double down on your original two card hand, after you have taken one or more hits, or after a split. However, after doubling down, your hand does not qualify for a bonus. .

Double down rescue: If, after getting a double down card you don't like the resulting hand, you may take back (rescue) the doubled portion of your wager and forfeit your original bet. This can only be done if the hand did not go over 21. Assuming you used proper doubling strategy in the first place, this is not a recommended option.

Split: Whenever you are dealt a pair, you have the option of splitting the cards into two separate hands. Indicate this to the dealer by placing a second wager alongside your original bet. It must be for the same amount as the original bet. Before acting on your signal, the dealer may ask if you intend to double or split. With a pair of fives, for instance, most dealers know that splitting is not good strategy, but doubling may be appropriate.

When it is clear that you are splitting, the dealer will give you two more cards, one on each of your original cards, so that you are now playing two hands of two cards each. In most casinos, if you are splitting aces (which is always recommended), those two are the only cards you will get. For all other pairs, you may hit each of the hands as many times as you wish.

Resplit: If, when you split a pair, one or both of the cards you get from the dealer are the same rank as the original pair, you may split again. This is called **resplitting**. For instance, if you split a pair of eights and get another eight, you can resplit into three hands. In Spanish 21, you may split cards of the same rank up to four times.

Surrender: If you don't like what you see when you are dealt the first two cards, you may **surrender** (fold) your hand and forfeit half of your bet. If you decide to surrender, simply tell the dealer that you are surrendering and she will take half of your bet and toss your cards into the discard tray. Once you take the first hit, you lose this option. You also lose it if the dealer has a natural, in which case you lose your entire bet. Surrender is not offered in Atlantic City. In other jurisdictions, the availability of surrender varies from casino to casino.

Insurance: If the dealer's upcard is an ace, the dealer will call out, "Insurance," and you are offered the opportunity to place an insurance side bet. You do this by putting up to half the amount of your original bet on the layout area marked: *Insurance pays 2 to 1*. If, after peeking at the downcard, the dealer turns up a natural, any insurance bets are paid off at 2 to 1 odds. If the dealer does not have a natural, the insurance side bet is lost. From a player's strategy standpoint, this is not a good wager.

DEALER FUNCTIONS

As a representative of the casino, the dealer manages and controls the Spanish 21 game. She converts a player's money into chips, deals out the cards, collects from the losers, and pays the winners. She also enforces the table betting limits and makes sure that all the players follow the table rules.

Dealing: The cards are dealt out in a clockwise direction, starting from the dealer's left. Every player who has put out a bet is dealt two face up cards. Whenever the player's cards are dealt face up, the player can look, but can't touch—all the card handling is done by the dealer. The dealer also gets two cards, one face up (called the **upcard**) and one face down (called the **downcard** or the **hole card**).

Dealer's playing rules: After all the players have acted on their hands, the dealer turns over her hole card and either stands or hits her hand. She can not double down or split—those are options reserved for the players. Assuming she doesn't have a natural, the dealer has to play her hand according to a fixed casino rule. In most casinos that rule is: *Dealer must hit soft 17*. This means that the dealer must draw to 16 and stand on hard 17. Some gambling venues, including Atlantic City, apply a rule that is more favorable for the player: *Dealer must draw to 16 and stand on all 17s*.

TABLE ETIQUETTE

Experienced blackjack players will find that Spanish 21 is very similar to standard blackjack. If you are new to Spanish 21 and blackjack, just watch what the other players are doing and try to do the same. Should you make a mistake in table protocol, the dealer will politely correct you.

The first thing you have to do is place your wager. Put the chip(s) directly on the betting spot as soon as the dealer has collected all the cards from the previous hand. If you are slow in doing this, you may get bypassed on the deal. Most dealers, however, will simply remind you by pointing at the empty bet circle.

As soon as you see your two cards and the dealer's upcard, make a quick decision as to what action to take. Quickness is especially important if you are in the first-base position at the table, and you don't want everyone staring at you. If you know the strategy well, this should not be a problem.

Remember that you are not allowed to touch your cards or your original bet. The dealer does all the card handling. If you double down or split, never place additional chips on top of your original bet. Always put them alongside.

Don't signal the dealer until it is your turn. Make your hand signals clear so your intentions are not misunderstood. When you are paid off, be sure to pull back the chips or they may become your wager for the next round.

THE PAYOFFS

Naturals, 21 counts, and bonus hands are paid as soon as they occur. Other non-busted player's hands are paid after the dealer has finished playing her hand. If the dealer goes over 21, all non-busted hands (that haven't yet been paid) are winners and are paid off at even odds.

STANDARD PAYOFFS

Natural: When you have a natural, you are paid 3 to 2 odds even if the dealer also has a natural. That is, for a $10 wager, you will win $15 and keep your original bet of $10.

21 Count: If your hand has a count of 21, you win even odds. This is true even if the dealer has 21. The only way you can lose is if the dealer has a natural. There are no pushes on a 21 hand. Certain 21 hands pay better than even odds. This is covered below, in the section on bonuses.

Other Hands: In general, when your non-busted hand has a higher count than the dealer's hand, you are paid even odds. That is, a $10 wager wins an additional $10. When your hand is the same as the dealer's, it is considered a push and no money changes hands. When your count is less than the dealer's, you lose your bet.

BONUSES

Bonus 21. Certain non-doubled 21 hands pay bonuses as high as 3 to 1. The bonuses are always paid except when the dealer has a natural. These bonus hands are as follows:

- A five-card hand with an exact count of 21, pays 3 to 2.
- A six-card hand with an exact count of 21, pays 2 to 1.
- A seven-card (or more) hand with an exact count of 21, pays 3 to 1.
- A three-card hand of a 6, 7, and 8 with mixed suits, pays 3 to 2.
- A three-card hand of a 6, 7, and 8, all of the same suit, pays 2 to 1.
- A three-card hand of a 6, 7, and 8, all of which are spades, pays 3 to 1.
- A three-card hand of all sevens with mixed suits, pays 3 to 2.
- A three-card hand of all sevens of the same suit, pays 2 to 1.
- A three-card hand of all sevens of spades, pays 3 to 1.

The bonuses were carefully designed to get you to take hits that risk busting your hand. To get the bonus for the five, six, or seven card hands, the count has to be exactly 21. You will find that this is not an easy task to accomplish because of the very high probability of busting. If you have the start of a 6 7 8 or 7 7 7 hand and are trying for the bonus, you may have to take a hit when you don't want to.

The following table summarizes the nine bonus hands described above:

BONUS 21 PAYTABLE	
Hand	**Pays**
Five card 21	3 to 2
Six card 21	2 to 1
Seven card 21	3 to 1
6 7 8 Mixed suits	3 to 2
6 7 8 Suited	2 to 1
6 7 8 Spades	3 to 1
7 7 7 Mixed suits	3 to 2
7 7 7 Suited	2 to 1
7 7 7 Spades	3 to 1

Super bonus: When you get a 7 7 7 hand, all of the same suit, and the dealer's upcard is a seven of any suit, you will be paid a super bonus and all of the other players at the table will be paid an "envy" bonus. If you wagered between $5 and $24, the super bonus pays $1000. If you bet $25 or more, the super bonus is $5000. In either case, an envy bonus of $50 is paid to every other player at the table. *The super and the envy bonuses do not pay off if your hand was split or doubled.*

In some casinos the super bonus payoff is handled a little differently. You get $1000 for each $5 bet increment, up to a maximum of $5000 for a $25 bet. For instance, if you wagered $15, the bonus would be $3000. No matter what you wagered, the other players still get their $50 envy bonus.

PLAYING STRATEGY

Like standard blackjack, Spanish 21 is a negative expectation game. There is no playing strategy that will overcome the house edge and make the game profitable for the player. Sure, you can learn to count cards and reduce the house edge, but to swing it to a positive expectation is not easy to do. Spanish 21 was specifically designed to thwart card counters (more on this later). Whether or not you count cards, when playing this game you must use some reasonable strategy or you will lose consistently. The problem is that the basic strategy rules for standard blackjack do not work very well for Spanish 21. Experienced blackjack players should be aware that they have to learn a new set of strategy rules if they expect to last at a Spanish 21 table.

The basic strategy for standard blackjack is fairly complicated. In Spanish 21, the basic strategy is not any simpler, just different. The changes in strategy are mainly due to the 25% fewer ten-value cards in the deck. The bonuses for certain 21-count hands also contribute to the variation in strategy rules.

A simplified strategy was devised for those casual players who would rather not memorize the full basic strategy table. If you are familiar with the basic strategy for standard blackjack, you will find the simple strategy to be similar, yet there are some significant differences.

A SIMPLE STRATEGY

The simple strategy is a condensed and simplified version of the full basic strategy table shown later. True, these strategy rules are over-simplified, but they will keep you going until you have memorized the full basic strategy. Before sitting down at a Spanish 21 game, you should at least try to learn the following rules:

Pair splitting: This is pretty easy to remember. Always split aces and 8s. Never split 4s, 5s, or 10s. Split others when the dealer shows a low card.

Aces are split because 2- or 12-count hands are not good, but hitting just a single ace can often result in a very good hand or even a count of 21. You should always split 8s because 16 is an awful hand, while hitting a single 8 can often result in an 18.

Never split 4s or 5s because hitting an 8-count or 10-count can produce a good hand. Never split 10s, because you don't want to destroy a 20-count hand, which is usually a winner.

Split 2s, 3s, 6s, 7s, and 9s when the dealer shows a low card. This way, you will win on two hands if the dealer busts, which will happen over one-third of the time. Whenever you don't split a pair, it should be played like a normal hard hand.

Soft hands: Even though you can't bust a soft hand, you should stand on a count of 18 through 21 because those hands are hard to improve. For a count of 17 or less, always take a hit.

Hard hands: It is easy to remember that you always stand on hard counts of 17 through 21. It is also easy to remember that for counts of 5 through 9 you always take a hit, because you can't bust.

It may be harder to remember to hit all 12-count through 14-count hands because this is something that isn't done in standard blackjack. In Spanish 21, however, the reduced number of ten-value cards makes it safer to hit such hands. Although it is risky to hit 15-count and 16-count hands, you have to assume that a dealer showing a 7 or higher already has you beat, so you have little choice.

You normally double on a 10 or 11 when the dealer shows a low card. If you have 5 or 6 cards in your hand, however, you should take a hit and go for the bonus.

Insurance: Never take the insurance side bet because the odds always favor the house.

The above rules are summarized in the following chart.

SIMPLE PLAYING STRATEGY FOR SPANISH 21

Pairs	Dealer's Up	Action
A A & 8 8	All	Split
9 9	2 through 9	Split
2 2, 3 3, 6 6, 7 7	2 through 7	Split
4 4, 5 5, 10 10	Do not split — Play as hard hands	

Soft Hands	Dealer's Up	Action
A 7 through A 10	All	Stand
A 2 through A 6	All	Hit

Hard Hands	Dealer's Up	Action
17 through 21	All	Stand
15 & 16	7 through A	Hit
15 & 16	2 through 6	Stand
12 through 14	All	Hit
10 & 11	9 through A	Hit
10 & 11	2 through 8	Double
10 & 11 with 5+ cards	2 through 6	Hit
5 through 9	All	Hit

Never Take insurance

THE BASIC STRATEGY FOR SPANISH 21

Although the simple strategy table works well for most recreational players, when you are ready to exert the extra effort needed to cut the house advantage down to the minimum, you will have to learn the full basic strategy. Although it is similar to the basic strategy for standard blackjack, there are significant differences that should not be overlooked. These differences are mainly due to the 25% fewer 10-value cards in the deck. The bonuses for certain 21-count hands also contribute to the alteration in strategy rules.

The Spanish 21 strategy chart that is shown on the next page was derived from strategy that was originally developed by the late Lenny Frome and subsequently refined by Michael Shackleford. When you apply this chart, keep in mind that a soft hand of more than two cards is one in which the ace is counted as an 11. It is a hard hand if the ace must be counted as 1 to keep from busting.

In most Spanish 21 games, the dealer must hit a soft 17, thus the first chart, designated as Chart 1, is based on that rule. If you are fortunate enough to encounter a game in which the dealer stands on soft 17, apply the rules of Chart 2. Remember to never take the Insurance side bet.

Key to Chart 1 and Chart 2 abbreviations

S = stand   H = hit   P = split pair   D = double down

S4, S5, S6 = stand, except hit if hand has 4, 5, 6 or more cards

D3, D4, D5, D6 = double, except hit if hand has 3, 4, 5, 6 or more cards

F = surrender on first two cards, otherwise hit

Ph = split, except hit if sevens are suited

a = hit if any 6 7 8 bonus is possible

b = hit if a suited 6 7 8 bonus is possible

c = hit if a spaded 6 7 8 bonus is possible

CHART 1 — SPANISH 21 STRATEGY
DEALER HITS SOFT 17

Player's Hand	Dealer's Upcard									
	2	3	4	5	6	7	8	9	Face	Ace
PAIRS										
A A	P	P	P	P	P	P	P	P	P	P
10 10	S	S	S	S	S	S	S	S	S	S
9 9	S	P	P	P	P	S	P	P	S	S
8 8	P	P	P	P	P	P	P	P	P	F
7 7	P	P	P	P	P	Ph	H	H	H	H
6 6	H	H	P	P	P	H	H	H	H	H
5 5	D5	D5	D	D	D	D4	D3	H	H	H
4 4	H	H	H	H	H	H	H	H	H	H
3 3	P	P	P	P	P	P	P	H	H	H
2 2	P	P	P	P	P	P	H	H	H	H
SOFT										
A 9, A 10	S	S	S	S	S	S	S	S	S	S
A 8	S	S	S	S	S	S	S	S	S6	S6
A 7	S4	S4	D4	D5	D6	S6	S4	H	H	H
A 6	H	H	D3	D4	D5	H	H	H	H	H
A 5	H	H	H	D3	D4	H	H	H	H	H
A 4	H	H	H	H	D4	H	H	H	H	H
A 2, A 3	H	H	H	H	H	H	H	H	H	H
HARD										
18 - 21	S	S	S	S	S	S	S	S	S	S
17	S	S	S	S	S	S	S6	S6	S6	F
16	S6	S6	S6	S	S	H	H	H	H	F
15	S4a	S5b	S6	S6	S	H	H	H	H	H
14	H	H	S4a	S5b	S6c	H	H	H	H	H
13	H	H	H	H	S4a	H	H	H	H	H
12	H	H	H	H	H	H	H	H	H	H
11	D4	D5	D5	D5	D5	D4	D4	D4	D3	D3
10	D5	D5	D	D	D	D4	D3	H	H	H
9	H	H	H	H	D	H	H	H	H	H
5 – 8	H	H	H	H	H	H	H	H	H	H

CHART 2 — SPANISH 21 STRATEGY
DEALER STANDS ON SOFT 17

Player's Hand	Dealer's Upcard									
	2	3	4	5	6	7	8	9	Face	Ace
PAIRS										
A A	P	P	P	P	P	P	P	P	P	P
10 10	S	S	S	S	S	S	S	S	S	S
9 9	S	P	P	P	P	S	P	P	S	S
8 8	P	P	P	P	P	P	P	P	P	P
7 7	P	P	P	P	P	Ph	H	H	H	H
6 6	H	H	P	P	P	H	H	H	H	H
5 5	D5	D5	D	D	D	D4	D3	H	H	H
4 4	H	H	H	H	H	H	H	H	H	H
3 3	P	P	P	P	P	P	P	H	H	H
2 2	P	P	P	P	P	P	H	H	H	H
SOFT										
A 9, A 10	S	S	S	S	S	S	S	S	S	S
A 8	S	S	S	S	S	S	S	S	S6	S
A 7	S4	S4	D4	D5	D5	S6	S4	H	H	H
A 6	H	H	D3	D4	D5	H	H	H	H	H
A 5	H	H	H	H	D4	H	H	H	H	H
A 4	H	H	H	H	H	H	H	H	H	H
A 2, A 3	H	H	H	H	H	H	H	H	H	H
HARD										
18 – 21	S	S	S	S	S	S	S	S	S	S
17	S	S	S	S	S	S	S6	S6	S6	F
16	S5	S6	S6	S	S	H	H	H	H	H
15	S4a	S5a	S5c	S6	S6	H	H	H	H	H
14	H	H	S4a	S5a	S4a	H	H	H	H	H
13	H	H	H	H	H	H	H	H	H	H
12	H	H	H	H	H	H	H	H	H	H
11	D4	D5	D5	D5	D5	D4	D4	D4	D3	D3
10	D5	D5	D	D	D	D4	D3	H	H	H
9	H	H	H	H	D3	H	H	H	H	H
5 – 8	H	H	H	H	H	H	H	H	H	H

HOUSE EDGE

Perfect application of Chart 1 results in a long-term house edge of 0.76%. In places such as Atlantic City, where the dealer stands on soft 17, the application of Chart 2 drops the house edge to 0.40%. Thus, Spanish 21 in AC has a slightly lower house edge than an AC eight-deck blackjack game.

CARD COUNTING

As most blackjack players know, a proficient card counter can overcome the house edge and even swing it to his advantage. Ever since Dr. Edward Thorp published his groundbreaking book "Beat the Dealer" in 1962, the casinos have been annoyed to no end that some players can actually get the better of them. If it wasn't for the fact that the increased popularity of blackjack has produced huge profits, the casinos might have introduced drastic rule changes or even eliminated the game entirely. As it was, few players bothered to master the many counting techniques that have been published over the years. In fact, most people play blackjack so carelessly that the casinos never have to worry about losing money. However, the casino industry learned never to introduce a new game that had any possibility of being beaten honestly.

Enter Spanish 21. As a major variation of standard blackjack, it was designed to intrigue blackjack players and, at the same time, thwart any attempts to gain an advantage by counting cards. This goal was fully accomplished. The game's designer even eliminated the possibility of a player cheating by having the dealer do all the card handling.

Yes, you can still count cards, but the count very rarely gets good. When perfect playing strategy is used, the house edge can get as low as 0.4%. With fewer ten-value cards, this is still too high for most expert counters to surmount. In theory, the house edge could be overcome by making very large (and very obvious) bet swings, but this is simply not practical. Your best bet is to stick to the basic strategy and enjoy the game.

CONCLUSION

With its more favorable payoff rules, most blackjack players consider Spanish 21 to be a pleasant change. Some of the annoyances of standard casino blackjack have been eliminated. The big danger is to blackjack players who think they can use the basic strategy that they know so well. The casinos rely on this and have been raking it in. With proper playing strategy, however, the house edge can get as low as for a multi-deck blackjack game with good rules, which is not bad. It allows your bankroll to survive while you wait for that big lucky streak.

◆20◆
SUPER FUN 21

Super Fun 21 is a copyrighted modification of single-deck blackjack that is now found in many casinos. Although this is a single-deck game with rules that appear to be more generous than standard blackjack, the house edge is higher than for most multi-deck blackjack games.

The lures in this game are the many liberal rules. These rules are more than offset, however, by paying only even money on almost all naturals, a fact that has disturbed many long-time blackjack players who are afraid that this may become a trend.

THE RULES

Before playing Super Fun 21, you should be familiar with standard blackjack. If you enjoy playing a version of blackjack with friendly rules, you should consider Spanish 21, which pays 3:2 on naturals and has a lower house edge than Super Fun 21. In either case, you will have to learn a new strategy to play the game well.

Most of the rules for Super Fun 21 are the same as for standard blackjack (see the chapter on Blackjack) except for the following:

- You may double down on any number of cards, even after splitting and hitting.

- You may split pairs up to three times, including aces.

- You may surrender on any number of cards, even after splitting, hitting, or doubling down.

- A hand totaling 20 or less with six cards and without doubling down, is an automatic winner.

- A hand totaling exactly 21 with five cards or more and without doubling down, is an automatic winner and pays 2 to 1.

- A player's natural is an automatic winner.

- A natural in diamonds pays 2 to 1; other naturals pay even money.

PLAYING STRATEGY

On the following page is the complete Super Fun 21 strategy chart. This strategy was developed by Michael Shackleford, who calculated the overall house edge to be 0.94% when perfect playing strategy is used.

Key to chart abbreviations:
S = stand   **H** = hit   **P** = split pair   **D** = double down
S3, S4, S5 = stand, unless hand has 3, 4, 5, or more cards
D3, D4, D5 = double, unless hand has 3, 4, 5, or more cards
F = surrender
F4, F5 = surrender, unless hand has 4, 5, or more cards

SUPER FUN 21 STRATEGY

Player's Hand	Dealer's Upcard									
	2	3	4	5	6	7	8	9	10	ace
Pairs										
A A	P	P	P	P	P	P	P	P	P	P
10 10	S	S	S	S	S	S	S	S	S	S
9 9	S	P	P	P	P	S	P	P	S	P
8 8	P	P	P	P	P	P	P	P	P	P
7 7	P	P	P	P	P	P	P	H	F	F
6 6	P	P	P	P	P	P	H	H	H	H
5 5	D	D	D	D	D	D	D	D	D	D
4 4	H	H	H	P	P	H	H	H	H	H
3 3	P	P	P	P	P	P	H	H	H	H
2 2	P	P	P	P	P	P	H	H	H	H
Soft										
21	S	S	S	S	S	S	S	S	S	S
20	S5	S5	S5	S5	S5	S5	S5	S5	S5	S5
19	S5	S5	S5	S5	D5	S5	S5	S5	S4	S5
18	S3	D4	D4	D4	D5	S4	S4	H	H	H
17	D3	D3	D4	D4	D5	H	H	H	H	H
16	H	H	D3	D4	D4	H	H	H	H	H
15	H	H	D3	D4	D4	H	H	H	H	H
14	H	H	D3	D	D	H	H	H	H	H
13	H	H	H	D	D	H	H	H	H	H
Hard										
18 - 21	S	S	S	S	S	S	S	S	S	S
17	S	S	S	S	S	S	S	S5	S5	F5
16	S	S	S	S	S	H	H	H	F4	F4
15	S5	S5	S	S	S	H	H	H	H	F4
14	S5	S5	S5	S5	S5	H	H	H	H	H
13	S4	S4	S5	S5	S5	H	H	H	H	H
12	H	H	S4	S4	S4	H	H	H	H	H
11	D4	D4	D4	D4	D4	D4	D4	D4	D4	D4
10	D4	D4	D4	D4	D4	D4	D4	D4	D3	D4
9	D3	D4	D4	D	D	H	H	H	H	H
5 - 8	H	H	H	H	H	H	H	H	H	H

◆21◆
THREE CARD POKER

Three Card Poker is a variation of an English game known as Brag. The American version was invented and introduced by Prime Table Games under the nondescript name of Brit-Brag. It was renamed Three Card Poker and is currently being distributed by Shuffle Master. It is a fast-moving game that combines some of the better attributes of Caribbean Stud and Let It Ride. As a result, it is rapidly becoming a mainstay in many casinos, especially in Mississippi where there are more Three Card Poker tables than on the Las Vegas Strip.

Like many other games in this book, Three Card Poker is played on a blackjack-like table. The game is similar to five card stud poker except that you get only three cards and play against the dealer's hand and not against the other players. You have two opportunities to place a direct wager on your hand. In addition, you can make an independent side bet to qualify for a bonus payout.

The game is easy to learn and the playing strategy is very simple. Within the three card constraint, winning hands are based on a variation of standard poker hands. There are no wild cards. Because, like blackjack, you play against the dealer rather than against the other players at the table, the bluffing and normal playing strategies that are used in regular poker games do not apply.

When the game begins, you may put up an initial ante wager and/or place a side bet in the Pair Plus circle. The dealer then distributes three cards to each player and to herself. There are no draws or community cards, so the three card hand you are dealt is all you have to work with. The only decision you have to make is whether or not your hand is likely to beat the dealer. If you think your cards are good enough to win, you may place an additional wager to stay in the running. If you think your hand is a loser, the best move is to fold your hand and lose the ante.

Should your hand be a winner, and the dealer has a qualifying hand (more on that later), you will be paid even odds. If you have a straight or better, you will also collect a bonus. If you placed the independent Pair Plus side bet, you will win a bonus for a pair or better, regardless of whether or not you beat the dealer. These bonus payouts add interest and appeal to the game.

FUNDAMENTALS OF PLAY

THE PLAYING TABLE

Three Card Poker is played on a table that is very similar to a blackjack table and is usually located in or near the blackjack area. In most casinos it is easy to find because there is an elevated sign at the table identifying the game. The table has six or seven player positions around the curved side of the table (see illustration). The dealer stands at the flat side with a chip rack directly in front of her and a card-shuffling machine to her right.

There are three betting spaces at each player position. The circle nearest the dealer, marked PAIR PLUS, is where the bonus side bet may be placed. The center space, marked ANTE, is where your initial bet should be placed. The third space, nearest the player, is marked PLAY. This is where to put the second bet if, after viewing your dealt hand, you decide to continue playing.

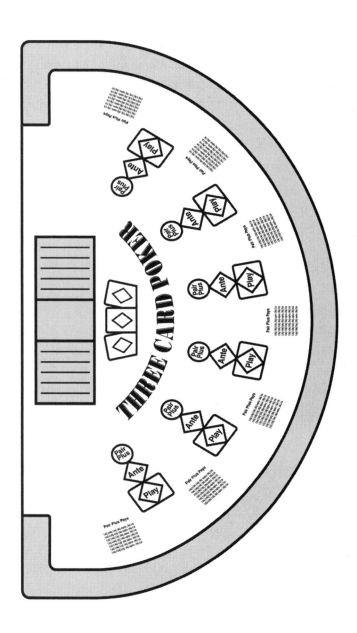

Three Card Poker Table

HOW THE GAME IS PLAYED

The initial goal in Three Card Poker is to get a better three card poker hand than the dealer's. If that goal is met, and the dealer has a qualifying hand, the next goal is to get a hand strong enough to pay an ante bonus. As long as you didn't fold, the ante bonus pays off for a straight, a straight flush, or three-of-a-kind, regardless of whether you beat the dealer or the dealer is qualified. To be **qualified**, a dealer's hand must contain at least a queen, which is explained more fully in the next section. If you placed an optional bet on the PAIR PLUS circle, you're hoping to get a pair or better to win a Pair Plus bonus. This bonus pays off independently of the rest of the game.

At the beginning of each hand, you have to place a wager in the ANTE box, or a wager in the PAIR PLUS circle, or both. You have the option of not putting up an ante and only betting the Pair Plus, but then you are playing against the Pair Plus bonus schedule rather than against the dealer. When everyone has placed his or her ante and / or Pair Plus bets, the dealer distributes three cards face down to each player and to herself. The cards are usually dealt from a shuffling machine that uses a single 52-card deck with no wild cards.

You now have to decide if your hand is good enough to invest more money. If you believe your hand may beat the dealer, you can stay in the game by placing an additional wager. This call bet is put in the PLAY box and must be exactly the same amount as the original ante. That is, if the ante was $10, then the additional wager must also be $10, for a total investment of $20. If you feel that your hand is not good enough to beat the dealer, you can fold and lose the ante. This is done by laying the cards face-down and not placing a play bet. The dealer will then remove your cards and your ante.

Until the dealer turns them over to determine the payoff, you are supposed to hide your cards from the other players. If you do get a glimpse of another player's hand, it could help in making the bet-or-fold decision. This situation will be covered in the section on playing strategy.

After all the players have decided whether to bet or fold, the dealer turns over her cards for everyone to see. If the dealer's hand is qualified, the active player's hands (those who didn't fold) are turned over one by one and the appropriate payoffs are made. The amounts of the payoffs are based on the ante bonus paytable and also depend on whether or not the dealer has a qualifying hand. In addition, if you made a Pair Plus bet, you will be paid in accordance with the Pair Plus paytable. The Pair Plus payout is not affected by the qualification status of the dealer's hand.

If the dealer's hand is not qualified and you did not fold your hand, you automatically win your ante bet at even odds and get back your play bet. In addition, both the ante bonus and the Pair Plus bonus are paid according to the respective paytables.

THREE CARD POKER PLAYING SUMMARY

1. Player folds hand:

- Ante bet is lost.

2. Player raises (makes play bet equal to ante) **and Dealer's hand does not qualify:**

- Ante wins even money and play bet is returned.

3. Player Raises and Dealer's hand qualifies:

- Player beats dealer. Ante and play bets both win even money
- Dealer beats player. Ante and play bets both lose.
- Player ties dealer. Ante and play bets both push.

QUALIFYING THE DEALER

To be qualified, the dealer's hand must contain at least a queen. On average, the dealer is dealt a qualifying hand about 44% of the time. The lowest qualifying hand is Q 3 2, as shown below.

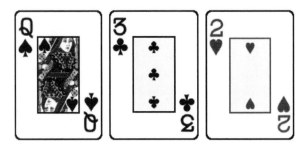

Lowest qualified dealer hand.

When the dealer has a qualifying hand, the game proceeds in a normal manner. That is, you have to beat the dealer's hand to win both the ante and play bets (at even odds). If your hand is a straight or better, you are also paid the ante bonus. If the dealer's hand beats yours, you lose both the ante and the play wagers but, if your hand is good enough, you still win the ante bonus. All ties are pushes in which case no money changes hands.

Whenever the dealer's hand is not qualified, the dealer folds and pays even odds on just the ante bet. The play bet is returned to you and the ante bonus still pays off. In either case, if you made a Pair Plus bet you will be paid according to the Pair Plus bonus paytable.

TABLE ETIQUETTE

Three Card Poker is a fast moving game. To avoid annoying the other players, you should stay alert and try not to hold up the action. Because of the game's simplicity and its uncomplicated strategy, this should not be hard to do.

When you sit down, get some chips from the dealer if you need them and then place your wager. Your bet may be put either on the ante spot or on the Pair Plus circle, or you can put a bet on each. Place your bets as soon as the dealer has collected all the cards from the previous round. Unless you feel very lucky, you should bet the table minimum.

After all the cards have been dealt, look at your three cards and quickly make your bet-or-fold decision. If you decide to fold, toss your cards (face down) toward the dealer. She will place them in the discard stack and remove your ante. If you decide to bet, place the same amount as your ante in the PLAY box and lay your cards face-down next to the bet. Now you are done, and the dealer takes over.

The dealer will turn over each active player's cards, in turn, and make the appropriate payoffs. Dealers do make mistakes; so keep alert to be sure you are getting the proper bonuses.

Tipping, of course, is a matter of personal preference. Instead of tipping a dealer directly, you may prefer to place a bet for the dealer. In Three Card Poker, however, because of the two-tier betting procedure, placing a bet for the dealer is discouraged. If you want to tip the dealer, it is simpler to just toss her a chip.

THE PAYOFFS

THE ANTE BONUS
The ante bonus is paid even if the dealer beats your hand. The ante bonus is also paid if the dealer does not qualify, which is an improvement over Caribbean Stud. If your hand is a straight or better, you are paid a bonus on your ante wager in accordance with the following schedule:

ANTE BONUS PAYTABLE	
Hand	**Pays**
Straight Flush	5 to 1
Three-of-a-kind	4 to 1
Straight	1 to 1

Let's say your ante and play bets are $10 each and you are dealt three-of-a-kind, but the dealer beats you with a straight flush. Because the dealer has a better hand, you lose the ante and play bets; however, you still win a 4 to 1 bonus on the ante bet, which amounts to $40. Your net gain for this hand is $40 - $10 (ante) - $10 (play) = $20. Somehow, I am attracted to a game that pays off even when I have a losing hand!

The house edge for the above paytable is 3.4%. Inevitably, however, greed raises its ugly head and some casinos have modified the original paytable to reduce the payoffs. Some examples of these modified paytables are shown below, along with their higher house edges.

OTHER ANTE BONUS PAYTABLES		
Hand	**Pays**	**Pays**
Straight Flush	4 to 1	3 to 1
Three-of-a-kind	3 to 1	2 to 1
Straight	1 to 1	1 to 1
House Edge	3.8%	4.3%

Of course, you should try to avoid playing at casinos that have less favorable paytables.

THE PAIR PLUS BONUS

The Pair Plus is a side bet that pays according to the value of your hand and is independent of the game itself. An unusual aspect of Three Card Poker is that the Pair Plus side bet can be played *instead* of the main game. That is, if a Pair Plus bet is placed, the ante bet becomes optional. If you placed a Pair Plus bet and are dealt a pair or better, you will be paid according to the following schedule:

PAIR PLUS BONUS PAYTABLE	
Hand	**Pays**
Straight Flush	40 to 1
Three-of-a-kind	30 to 1
Straight	6 to 1
Flush	4 to 1
Pair	1 to 1

Anything less than a pair and you lose the Pair Plus wager (that's why its called *Pair Plus*). On average, you can expect to get a paying Pair Plus hand about once in every four deals. If you don't ante and only place a bet in the Pair Plus circle, you are essentially cutting the dealer out of the equation. The dealer's hand becomes immaterial because you are strictly playing against the Pair Plus bonus paytable.

The house edge for the above paytable is 2.3%. As for the Ante Bonus, some casinos have modified the original Pair Plus Bonus paytable to reduce the payoffs. Examples of modified paytables are shown below, along with their higher house edges.

OTHER PAIR PLUS BONUS PAYTABLES			
Hand	Pays	Pays	Pays
Straight Flush	40 to 1	35 to 1	40 to 1
Three-of-a-kind	25 to 1	25 to 1	30 to 1
Straight	6 to 1	6 to 1	6 to 1
Flush	4 to 1	4 to 1	3 to 1
Pair	1 to 1	1 to 1	1 to 1
House Edge	3.5%	4.6%	7.3%

WINNING HANDS

The poker rankings in Three Card Poker are similar to standard poker except that a triplet beats a straight, and a straight beats a flush. Since the hand contains only three cards, many standard poker hands such as two-pair, a full house, or four-of-a-kind cannot exist. Three Card Poker uses one standard 52-card deck with no wild cards. The value of a hand depends on which of the following card combinations it contains, listed in order from the highest to the lowest:

Straight Flush: Three consecutive cards, all of the same suit. A K Q is the highest straight flush and A 2 3 is the lowest. The odds of being dealt a three card straight flush are 1 in 460 hands. Should the dealer and a player both have straight flushes, the hand containing the highest-ranking card is the winner. If both the dealer and player have identical straight flushes (except for the suit), it is a push.

Three-of-a-kind: Three cards of the same rank. The odds of being dealt three-of-a-kind are about 1 in 425 hands. Should the dealer and a player both have three-of-a-kind, the one with the highest rank is the winner.

Straight: Three consecutive cards of mixed suits. An ace may be either the lowest card as in A 2 3 or the highest card as in A K Q. The odds of being dealt a three card straight are 1 in 31 hands. Keep in mind that in Three Card Poker three-of-a-kind beats a straight. Should the dealer and a player both have straights, the one containing the highest ranked card is the winner. If the highest ranked card in both hands is the same, it is a push.

Flush: Three cards of the same suit, not in sequence. The odds of being dealt a three card flush are 1 in 20 hands. Keep in mind that in Three Card Poker three-of-a-kind and a straight both beat a flush. Should the dealer and a player both have flushes, the one containing the highest ranked card is the winner. If the highest ranked card in both hands is the same, then the second- and third-highest ranked cards are the tiebreakers.

Pair: Two cards of the same rank. The remaining card is unrelated. The odds of being dealt a pair are about 1 in 6 hands. On average, you will be dealt a pair *or better* every fourth hand. The highest-ranked pair wins. If two hands contain pairs of the same rank, then the one with the highest-ranked odd card wins. If all cards are the same rank, it is a push.

Queen-high: A hand that contains none of the above poker hands, but does have one queen. The two remaining cards are unrelated. The odds of being dealt a queen-high *or better* are about 1 in 2.3 hands. That means the dealer will qualify about 44% of the time.

Low Cards: A hand that contains none of the above poker hands, and has mixed cards no higher than one jack. The odds of being dealt a jack or lower hand are about 1 in 3.3 hands. This is a non-qualifying hand for the dealer.

PLAYING STRATEGY

Like most table games, Three Card Poker is a negative expectation game. There is no strategy that will overcome the house edge and make the game profitable for the player. Sure, sometimes a sloppy dealer will inadvertently expose her bottom card, but that does not happen very often (more about that later).

To make your bankroll last as long as possible (until you hit that winning streak), you need to apply good playing strategy. The Three Card Poker player has three basic decisions to make: (1) how much money to ante, (2) whether or not to place the Pair Plus bet, and (3) whether to continue playing after seeing the cards or fold the hand and lose the ante. Each of these three choices will affect how fast you lose your money.

THE PERFECT STRATEGY

For some games in this book, a mathematically perfect or near-perfect strategy is given, as well as a simpler strategy so that inexperienced players can get started quickly. Fortunately, the perfect strategy for Three Card Poker is so easy that only the one version is needed. This is the simplest perfect strategy of any table game requiring player decisions, and consists of the following three rules:

Rule 1: Ante the table minimum. Since Three Card Poker is a negative expectation game, the more you bet, the faster you will lose. The lowest table minimum you are likely to find is $5. Try to play at those tables. The only time to raise your ante is when you clearly hit a winning streak.

Rule 2: The Pair Plus wager is optional. It is called optional because, although it is a negative expectation gamble, the house edge is only 2.3% (for the best paytable). Since you don't get to make any playing decisions, there is no strategy and the outcome of the wager is purely dependent on luck.

Rule 3: Call any hand containing a Q 6 4 or better. Otherwise, fold.
That is, if your hand is a Q 6 4 or better, as shown below, make the play bet.

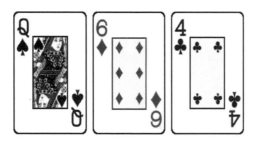

This is the basic call-fold playing strategy, and it couldn't be easier to remember. The next question is: what constitutes a *better* hand. In poker, the best hand is determined by comparing the highest card in each hand, then the second highest, and then the third highest. Thus, Q 7 3 is a better hand than Q 6 4.

PERFECT STRATEGY FOR
THREE CARD POKER

Rule 1: Ante the table minimum.

Rule 2: Pair Plus bet is optional.

Rule 3: Call any hand containing a **Q 6 4** or better. Otherwise, fold.

SEEING OTHER CARDS

As mentioned earlier, the rule is that you are not supposed to show your cards to any other players. Since many players are casual about their card handling, it is sometimes easy to get glimpses of other cards. This, however, is often not very helpful, and can sometimes lead to incorrect strategy decisions.

The general rule is that if you see at least three player's cards that are queen or higher, the dealer is less apt to qualify. You can then risk calling a hand that you would normally fold in hopes of winning the ante.

On the other hand, if you see one of the *dealer's* cards, you can get a significant edge. When distributing the three card stacks from the shuffling machine, an inattentive or inexperienced dealer may expose the bottom card. If you see the dealer's bottom card, you should do the following:

- Dealer's card is a jack or less: Call all hands.
- Dealer's card is a queen: Call with Q 9 or better.
- Dealer's card is a king: Call with K 9 or better.
- Dealer's card is an ace: Call with A 9 or better.

This is a rare situation, but it pays to be prepared. When it occurs, it can give you more than a 3% edge over the house.

CONCLUSION

Three Card Poker is a fun and easy game to play. It pays nice bonuses for the better hands, which pay out even if the dealer does not qualify. It moves along quickly and smoothly and has no rules that are annoying or irritating to the players. Although the speed of play makes the game nice and lively, it also carries with it some danger. The 3.4% house edge on the basic game will grind down your bankroll faster than most table games. However, the game is a pleasant diversion and you might just hit a nice Pair Plus bonus.

◆22◆
VIDEO POKER

Although video poker was introduced in the 1970s, these games didn't become popular until the 1980s. By the 1990s, many slot players realized that video poker had become the most liberal slot game on the casino floors. Consequently, its popularity surged until it became a major segment of the slot machine business.

Video poker is a machine version of a popular form of poker called *five card draw* or, more simply, *draw poker*. In the most common version of video poker, a five card hand is randomly dealt by the machine. The player then gets to discard any or all of the cards in the dealt hand, which are replaced by new ones. Choosing which cards to hold and which to discard to maximize the payback requires correct playing strategy. There are a number of game variations, but almost all of them are based on a one-time replacement of any of the cards in a five card hand.

It is easy to find standard video poker machines that pay back more than 98% and some that pay back more than 100% when perfect playing strategy is applied. Whereas the payback of any particular traditional slot machine is a mystery, this is not true of video poker. Every video poker machine has its complete payout schedule posted on the video screen or on the glass display above the screen. Using this information, the overall payback of that machine can be computed.

Taking full advantage of the potentially high payback in video poker requires two important actions. The first is to find a video poker machine with a payout schedule that provides a high payback. The second is to use the best playing strategy. This chapter will provide the information needed for a player to do both in a simple and effective manner.

FUNDAMENTALS OF PLAY

VIDEO POKER VS. DRAW POKER

Video poker is fundamentally a one-player video representation of draw poker. Aside from the fact that all the action occurs on a video screen, video poker has some significant differences from draw poker. To avoid falling into serious traps while playing video poker, it is important to be aware of these differences. This is especially true for players already familiar with draw poker, since they have likely developed particular playing styles and habits. Although the two games have many similarities, the playing strategies are quite different.

The most important point in video poker is that you are playing alone against a machine with a fixed payout schedule. In table poker, if your hand is better than that of any other player at the table, you win the entire pot. You could win with a very poor hand, or you could lose with a very good hand. To win a hand in video poker, it must simply match one of the hands defined on the posted payout schedule. You don't have to *beat* anyone.

Another important point is that the rank of a winning combination is usually immaterial. That is, three kings pay the same as three deuces, and an aces-up two pair pays the same as any other two pair. And finally, you can't fold your hand, so you draw no matter how bad a hand you were dealt.

Many players who have never seen any video poker strategy information, continue to apply their own draw poker strategy. They do things such as keeping a single ace or face-card (called a kicker) when drawing to a pair. This fools nobody (there aren't any other players to fool) and, although it doesn't change the probability of drawing another pair, it greatly reduces the odds of drawing three-of-a-kind, four-of-a-kind, or a full house. In other words: *Never keep a kicker.*

In the table game a player would normally drop out rather than draw four cards to a single face card. Since dropping is not an option in video poker, holding one face card is frequently done in a jacks-or-better game. For a garbage hand that doesn't even have a low pair or a face card, it is appropriate to draw five new cards. These situations are all covered in the playing strategy tables.

VIDEO POKER — THE GAME

As with slot machines, to activate a video poker machine you must feed it money. A one-dollar bill will give you four credits on a quarter machine or twenty credits on a nickel machine, which you can then play in any desired amount, usually up to a maximum of five credits. While inserting a bill will simply register an appropriate number of credits, dropping in one or more coins will actually start the machine. If you insert five coins or press the PLAY 5 CREDITS button, the machine will deal your initial hand automatically. The following button arrangement is typical, although most of the newer machines now also use touch screens.

CASH OUT	BET ONE CREDIT	HOLD — CANCEL	HOLD — CANCEL	HOLD — CANCEL	HOLD — CANCEL	HOLD — CANCEL	PLAY FIVE CREDITS	DEAL — DRAW

If you insert fewer than five coins or enter fewer than five credits, you will have to press DEAL or DEAL–DRAW to see your initial hand. The machine will then display five cards on the video screen, which constitute your initial hand.

Now, examine the hand carefully to decide which cards you want to save or discard. Do this by pressing the appropriate HOLD or HOLD–CANCEL buttons, which are approximately lined up with the cards on the video screen. On machines with touch-sensitive screens, you can just touch the screen images of the cards that you want to keep. You may hold or discard any number of cards you wish. If you change your mind, press any of the HOLD buttons (or touch the screen) again and the action will be reversed. Sometimes the HOLD buttons don't register correctly, so you should check to see that the word HELD appears by each card you intend to keep. Note that, instead of HOLD buttons, some older machines may have DISCARD buttons, which act the reverse of HOLD buttons.

Should you be so fortunate to be dealt a pat hand, you must be careful not to inadvertently discard any of the cards. Although a few machines have a STAND or HOLD ALL button, on most you have to press all five HOLD buttons. Be certain all five cards in your hand display the word "HELD" before you press DRAW. If you accidentally hold or discard the wrong card, don't feel stupid—everyone does it sooner or later. It usually happens when you are tired or are playing too fast.

When you are ready to draw, press DRAW or DEAL–DRAW and every card that is not held will be replaced with a new card. This is your final hand. If it matches one of the payout combinations, the machine will automatically register the appropriate number of credits. The payout table is located on either a glass panel above the screen or on the video screen itself.

With some modifications, the payout schedule is based on standard poker hands. In games without wild cards, the minimum payout is usually for a pair of jacks (jacks or better) although there are some machines that set the minimum at a pair of tens, a pair of kings, or two pair. For games with deuces wild, the minimum payout is for three-of-a-kind. Many games also pay bonuses for four-of-a-kinds of a specific rank or royal flushes with the cards in a specific order.

When you are finished playing, pressing the CASH OUT button converts the credits on the machine to coins that will be dropped into the coin tray with a loud clatter. You may also press this button anytime between hands. Don't ever forget to press the CASH OUT button when you leave the machine, or someone else will do it for you.

VIDEO POKER — THE MACHINE

Externally, video poker machines appear to come in a great variety of types, styles, and flavors. Internally, however, they are all quite similar. Each one contains a specialized, dedicated microprocessor, along with its memory and support chips that control every aspect of the machine's operation. The major difference between machines is how the microprocessor is programmed.

Whenever a new hand is about to be dealt, the machine shuffles the deck electronically. To assure that the shuffle is done honestly, the poker program in each machine accesses a constantly-running random number generator (RNG) to assure that the 52 cards (53 cards with a joker) in the deck are always dealt out in a random fashion. Fundamentally, the RNG is a program algorithm within the machine's microprocessor that continually generates pseudo-random numbers. To further assure complete randomness, the RNG randomly accesses over a billion different number sequences and typically cycles through them at a rate of more than a thousand per second. Thus, there is no chance that the player can affect the randomness of the deal.

It is the programming of the RNG that is of greatest concern to state gaming regulators whenever a new model machine is being evaluated. They examine the mathematical basis for the algorithm and verify, by testing, that the machine consistently deals random hands. If the deal is random, and the machine payouts are in accordance with its posted schedule, then the player cannot be cheated. As a result, in states that have effective gaming controls (such as Nevada and New Jersey), the chance of encountering a rigged machine is almost non-existent. Unless you are playing in an illegal or uncontrolled gambling hall, you don't need to worry about it.

Once the initial hand is dealt by the machine, it waits for the player to decide which cards to discard. The replacement draw cards are then sequentially dealt out from the random deck when the player presses the DRAW button. The machine then indicates whether or not the final hand is a winner.

VIDEO POKER HANDS

Although the winning hands in video poker are similar to standard table poker, there are some deviations. For instance, in table poker, in a game with wild cards, five-of-a-kind is the highest-value hand. In the vast majority of wild-card video poker games, however, five-of-a-kind is a lower value hand than a royal flush. Following are the most common paying hands in video poker, along with the approximate odds of making the hand after the draw:

Royal Flush: This is an ace-high straight flush with no wild cards. Also called a *natural royal*. For most payout schedules, a royal flush will occur once in 40,000 to 45,000 hands, or a little more often if you sacrifice pat hands to draw to a royal. The cards may appear on the video screen in any order, as below.

Don't be discouraged if you can't seem to get a royal flush; at 40,000 to 1, it can be a long time in coming. One day at the Plaza, a lady sitting next to me hit a royal flush. I glibly muttered, "Guess this is your lucky day." She turned to me and snapped, "And it's about time!"

Sequential Royal: This is a royal flush in which the five cards must appear in ordered sequence on the video screen, as below.

Some machines require the sequence to be right-to-left, that is, with the ten at the right end and the ace at the left end. Using perfect playing strategy, you will make a sequential royal an average of once in four- to five-million hands, so don't hold your breath. An even tougher variation is when the sequential royal has to be in a specific suit, which multiplies the odds by four.

Reversible Royal: Same as the sequential royal except that the sequence can be in either direction, reducing the odds to one in two+ million. Don't hold your breath for this one, either.

Suited Royal: A royal flush of a particular designated suit. If you don't change strategy, this hand occurs one-quarter as often as a regular royal flush, or about once in every 160,000 hands. If the strategy favors the specified suit, then it occurs a little more often.

Joker Royal or Deuce Royal: A royal flush with wild cards. In a joker wild game, the odds of making it are about one in 12,000. In a deuces-wild game, the odds are about one in 600. The cards may appear on the video screen in any order, as below.

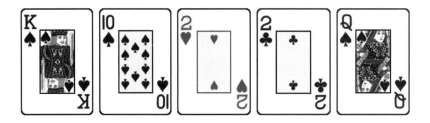

Five-of-a-kind: Five cards of the same rank. Since a standard deck has only four cards of a given rank, one of each suit, this hand necessarily includes at least one wild card.

In some joker wild games, this is the top-paying hand and will occur once in about 11,000 hands; in deuces wild, the odds are one in 300 hands. In deuces and joker wild games, the top-paying hand is five wild cards, which occurs about once in 130,000 hands.

Straight Flush: Five consecutive cards, all of the same suit. When the ace is part of the sequence, it is always low because if it is high, the result is a royal flush. A natural straight flush is typically made about once in 9,000 hands. This improves to once in 1700 hands with a joker, and once in 200 hands with deuces wild.

Four-of-a-kind: Four cards of the same rank, also called quads. The fifth card is unrelated. Quads can be made an average of about once in every 425 hands. In joker poker, the odds drop to one in 120, and the four wild cards in deuces wild drop the odds to once in every sixteen hands.

Since quads is a pat hand in a jacks-or-better game, the conventional wisdom is not to draw the fifth card since there is no way to improve the hand. However, in video poker not drawing a card to four-of-a-kind is a bad habit to get into. If you play both wild-card and jacks-or-better games you might, without thinking, not draw when you are playing with wild cards and miss a potential five-of-a-kind.

Four-of-a-kind (Aces): When four-of-a-kind is limited to a single specified rank, it is usually aces, but may also be kings, queens, or deuces. A high payout for four deuces is typically found in deuces wild games. The odds of making four-of-a-kind of a specified rank are one in 5,000.

Four-of-a-kind (Faces): When four-of-a-kind is limited to three specified ranks, it is often the face cards (jacks, queens, and kings), but more often twos, threes, and fours, as a group. The odds are about one in 2,000.

Full House: Three-of-a-kind and a pair. With no wild cards, a full house occurs once in every ninety hands. In joker poker, the odds are one in sixty-five, and in deuces wild, the odds are one in forty.

Flush: Five cards of the same suit. This hand is made as often as a full house—once in every ninety hands. Joker poker is one in sixty-five, and deuces wild is one in sixty.

Straight: Five consecutive cards of mixed suits. Straights occur about as often as full houses and flushes in non-wild and joker poker games. In deuces wild, however, the chances of making a straight improves dramatically to one in eighteen.

Three-of-a-kind: Three cards of the same rank. The remaining two cards are unrelated. The chances of ending up with trips is about one in fourteen hands. In joker poker, it is one in eight, and in deuces wild, it is one in four. Three-of-a-kind is the lowest-paying hand in deuces wild.

Two Pair: A pair of one rank and a pair of another rank. The fifth card is unrelated. Two pair wins one out of eight hands in non-wild and joker poker games. This is not a paying hand in deuces wild, and is the lowest-paying hand in many joker poker schedules.

Jacks or Better: Two cards of the same rank. They must be either jacks, queens, kings, or aces. The three remaining cards are unrelated. A pair of jacks or better wins about every five hands. In non-wild games, this is usually the lowest-paying hand. In some games, however, the lowest paying hand may be tens or better, kings or better, or a pair of aces.

CHOOSING THE BEST MACHINE

THE HOUSE PERCENTAGE
The average amount of money that a video poker machine returns to the player after a long period of play is called the **payback**. The payback is usually stated as a percentage of the amount that the player invested in

the machine. If, for example, the payback of a game is 98%, then, over the long term, you can expect to sustain a 2% loss on each hand.

The payback of the game also determines the average profit made by the casino, which is called the **house percentage**. For a payback of 98%, every $100 put into the machine will return a long-term average of $98 to the player. The remaining $2 is the casino's profit. Actually, the $98 is an **expectation**. It could be more and it could be less. It is the amount that, statistically-speaking, is *expected* to be returned in the form of winnings over a very long period of time. Over the short term, however, anything can happen.

For any given machine, there are two payback numbers. One is the maximum payback for perfect play. This is the payback of interest to the player. It is the highest possible return when the best playing strategy is used. It is what I have in mind whenever the term "payback" is used in this chapter. To the casino, this payback has only academic interest because it does not directly define the casino's profit.

The other payback is based on the actual recorded return from the machine. It is the one that the casino cares about because it is an estimate of the casino's potential long-term profit on that machine. Since many players do not apply the best strategy or bet the maximum coins, the payback for those players is typically 2% to 4% lower than for perfect play. Thus, if the maximum attainable payback on a machine is 98%, the actual recorded payback will typically be 95% to 96%, leaving the casino with a 4% to 5% profit.

COIN MULTIPLIERS

All video poker machines employ **coin/credit multipliers**. Most machines will accept one through five coins (or credits) for each hand played. The more coins deposited, the higher the payout for each winning hand. The payouts increase proportionally to the number of coins or credits, except that the largest jackpot is significantly higher when five coins are played. Coin multipliers are designed to encourage players to bet the maximum number of coins.

For most winning hands, the payout for five coins is five times the payout for one coin. For the top hand, however, the jackpot payout for five coins is typically sixteen to twenty times the payout for one coin. For example, the payout for a royal flush is typically 250 coins or credits for each coin or credit played. Thus, for two coins played, you would win 500 coins; for three coins, you would win 750; and for four coins, you would win 1000. For five coins, however, instead of winning 1250 coins, you would win 4000 coins. On some machines, you would win 4700 or 5000 coins.

As a result, when fewer than the maximum number of coins are bet, the average long-term payback percentage is reduced by 1% to 2%. For this reason, the strategies presented in this chapter are based on five-coin play. The only exception is for the Second Chance machines described below.

DETAILS OF THE GAMES

Even within a single casino, there can be a bewildering array of different kinds of video poker machines. One way to sort them out is to group them into major categories. Many players come to prefer certain types of machines, which is fine as long as they seek out the best paying machines within that type. Although new kinds of video poker machines regularly appear, the following are the most common in today's casinos:

NON-PROGRESSIVE MACHINES

Jacks or Better: This was the original form of video poker and is still very popular today. The lowest paying hand is a pair of jacks, and there are no wild cards. The payout schedule is based on standard poker hands and, except for a royal flush, the ranks of the cards in a given hand are immaterial. That is, four deuces are worth the same as four queens, and a king-high straight is worth the same as a five-high straight. These machines come in a variety of paybacks from fair (95-96%) to good (97-98%) to excellent (99-100%).

Two Pair or Better: The name tells the tale. The lowest paying hand is two pair. The best of these machines has a pretty good payback of 98%, but there are also versions that pay only 94%. You will often find two-pairs machines scattered among the jacks-or-better machines; the casinos take advantage of the fact that some players don't seem to know the difference.

Bonus Quads: Bonus machines are basically jacks-or-better machines that offer bonus payouts for specified four-of-a-kind (quad) hands. These non-progressive machines, including double, double-double, and triple bonus varieties, have extra-high payouts for certain quads such as four aces, four face cards, four eights, etc. To compensate for these bonuses, the payouts on some standard hands are somewhat reduced and, in one case, the lowest payout is changed from jacks-or-better to kings-or-better. As a group, these are the best paying machines in Nevada with paybacks in the range of 98% to 100%. Accordingly, they have become the most popular types of video poker machines around. The versions found in Atlantic City and along the Mississippi, however, only pay about 94% to 98%.

Bonus Royals: This is a small category of non-progressive bonus machines that, instead of quads, have extra-high payouts for certain royal flushes. Most of these games pay back in the range of 98% to 100%, but depend on some jackpot combinations that occur very rarely, such as a sequential royal flush.

Joker Wild: This game uses a 53-card deck in which the joker is a wild card. The joker can be substituted for any other card in the deck. In most cases, a royal flush with a joker (called a **joker royal**) does not pay as well as a natural. Many players are attracted to joker poker, despite the fact that in many versions of the game the payback is only fair. Although there have been a few machines out there that pay as high as 101%, most of them pay in the range of 94% to 97%.

Deuces Wild: As the name suggests, in this game the four deuces are wild cards. In all cases, a royal flush with deuces (called a **deuce royal**) pays much less than a natural because it is (typically) eighty times easier to make. All other hands, however, pay the same with or without deuces. Although the lowest-paying hand is three-of-a-kind, many versions of deuces wild have an excellent payback of 98% to 101%. However, you need to be careful; there are some that pay only 94% to 96%.

Deuces and Joker Wild: Five wild cards in a 53-card deck results in a very lively game with over half the hands being potential winners, although they are mostly pushes. If you can find one, the deuces and joker wild machines have an excellent 99% payback in Nevada casinos, but the versions found along the Mississippi pay only about 93%.

Double Joker: Two wild jokers in a 54-card deck, with two pair being the lowest-paying hand. So far, this game has only been available in Atlantic City. There are two almost identical versions: one has an excellent payback of 100%, while the other pays less than 98%.

PROGRESSIVE MACHINES
Progressive Jackpot: A progressive jackpot network is a group of machines that are electrically connected to a common jackpot pool. As people play the machines, a small percentage of the money paid in by the players is diverted to the jackpot pool, which continues to grow until someone wins it. The jackpot is then reset to a predetermined

minimum value and the growth cycle repeats itself. Each player is competing against the other players on that network, and each time coins are inserted, the jackpot gets a little larger.

A progressive network may consist of a bank of a dozen machines with a jackpot that rarely exceeds a few thousand dollars. The winning progressive hand is usually a natural royal flush, so the chance of hitting the jackpot in such a small localized network is not unreasonable. Local banks of progressive machines can be found for many varieties of games including original jacks or better, bonus quads, bonus royals, deuces wild, and joker wild.

If the machine is part of a city-wide or state-wide network that interconnects hundreds of other machines, the winning progressive hand is always a very rare combination such as a sequential royal flush. Consequently, the jackpot pool can reach lifestyle-altering levels. The chance of winning that jackpot is almost as small as the chance of winning the Power Ball lottery.

Many progressive players do not care about the overall payback of the machine, since they are only interested in the main jackpot. Until the jackpot gets quite high, the long-term payback for wide-area network games is only fair—and the short-term payback is never very good.

DOUBLE DOWN STUD

Double-down stud is not another version of draw poker, but is loosely based on the game of five card stud poker. Since double-down stud requires little skill and has a simple playing strategy, it will be fully covered in this section. This game has not really caught on, probably because the long-term average payback is less than 98%.

You begin playing by inserting one to ten coins—the tenth coin doubles the payout for a royal flush. Four cards are dealt face up, and you are given the option of doubling your original bet before the fifth card is dealt. When you make your choice, the fifth card is exposed and the machine pays in accordance with the following chart:

DOUBLE DOWN STUD FIFTH CARD PAYOUT SCHEDULE		
Winning Hand	**1 coin**	**10 coins**
Royal Flush	1000	20,000
Straight Flush	200	2000
Four-of-a-kind	50	500
Full House	12	120
Flush	9	90
Straight	6	60
Three-of-a-kind	4	40
Two Pair	3	30
Pair of: J, Q, K, or A	2	20
Pair of: 6, 7, 8, 9, or 10	1	10

If you insert ten coins, the payout for a royal flush is increased to 2000 per coin. The best playing strategy is to double when you have the following situations:

- Any paying hand, from a pair of sixes on up.
- A possible royal flush.
- A possible straight flush.
- A possible flush.
- A possible straight (open-ended).

Do not double on a pair smaller than a six. Do not double an inside or single-ended straight. Remember, this is not draw poker so you do not get to discard any unwanted cards. You just get to see the fifth card after making the doubling decision. This game is only described here in the interest of completeness. It is not recommended, but you may want to try it as a diversion from the draw poker games.

NOVELTIES AND ODDITIES

Many video poker machines contain stratagems to help you lose your money a little faster. Some of these ploys kick in after your final hand is displayed and give you another opportunity to win more or to lose what you have already won. Although most of them have no effect on the basic playing strategy, each one will be described so you can decide whether or not you want to play along.

Multi-Hand: The first multi-hand video poker game, called **Triple Play**, is an interesting variant in that it isn't quite what it appears to be. The player is dealt three hands at once from three different decks, but only one hand is exposed. The exposed hand is played in a normal manner and when the draw occurs, the same cards that were held appear in the other two hands. Each of the three hands then gets replacement cards dealt from its respective deck. Thus, if you start off with a good hand, you will have three good hands, but if you have a bad hand, you will have three bad hands.

From the standpoint of mathematical probability, this is exactly like playing three different machines simultaneously. The fact that the three hands always have the same held cards somehow adds an exciting flavor. This is often a multi-game machine from which the player may select one of several standard versions of bonus quads or deuces wild. To get all three hands dealt, at least three coins or three credits must be played. To qualify for the maximum jackpot payout, however, fifteen coins (or credits) must be played—5 for each hand. This accounts for the popularity of the nickel version.

There are now four-, ten-, fifty-, and 100-hand machines available. You can play any number of hands on any of them, but even on the penny version of the 100-hand machine, to qualify for the maximum jackpot on all hands costs $5. Of course, if you play only a single hand in any of these games, it acts like a normal video poker machine.

Double or Nothing: On a few video poker machines, whenever you get a winning hand, you are given the option of risking the entire payout on a double-or-nothing bet. If you press the YES button, five new cards appear on the screen, four down and one up. You may then select one of the four face-down cards. If it is higher than the first face-up card, the payout is doubled; if it is lower, you lose your winnings, and the game is concluded. A tie is a push, and is replayed. You may continue the doubling-up game as many times as you wish—until you lose.

Although this turns out to be a very fair even-money proposition, it is not recommended. Statistically, the probability of losing is cumulative, so that if you try to double more than one time in succession, your *overall* chances of winning rapidly decrease. On the first try, the chance of winning is 50%, on the second, it is 25%, on the third, it is 12.5%, and so on. Like any repeated double-or-nothing proposition, you will eventually lose your money.

Double Card: Some jacks-or-better video poker machines deal from a 53-card deck where the extra card is a **doubling card**. No, it is not a wild card. When it appears in a winning hand, it doubles the payout. Although at first glance it seems like a good deal, whenever the double card appears, it effectively reduces your five card hand to a four card hand. The doubling card actually interferes with any winning hand that requires five cards such as a straight, flush, or royal flush. If you get a four-straight or a four-flush and the fifth card is a double, you should discard the double. Better yet, you should discard this game.

Second Chance: On some video poker machines, you are given the option of taking a sixth card whenever your final hand, after the draw, is one that could be improved to a straight or better. The sixth card is dealt from the remaining cards in the same randomly-shuffled deck that was used for the original hand. A new payout schedule appears on the screen showing the possible winning hands for that particular situation. For instance, if your final hand is two pair, the new schedule will show a payout for a possible full house. This payout is not necessarily the same as the original payout schedule, but is set so that the overall payback with the sixth card is about 97%, which is usually less than the overall payback of the machine.

If, after the draw, you have a possible straight or better, the back of a sixth card will appear on the screen and the SECOND CHANCE button will illuminate. To accept the option, press the button. You may now insert one to five additional coins (or credits), regardless of how many coins you originally bet. The machine will expose the sixth card and automatically select the best five out of the six cards

The main advantage to second chance is that you can change the value of your bet in midstream. Therefore, the best initial approach is to play one coin at a time and use the recommended strategy for the posted payout schedule. Only activate the second chance option if you draw four cards to a royal. Then insert five coins (or credits) to maximize the jackpot and go for the sixth card.

Progressive Second Chance: This is another version of second chance that has a separate progressive jackpot for royal flushes. The option kicks in when you have four cards to a royal flush. It can raise the overall payback of the machine to well over 100%, even when the jackpot is at its lowest level. You are allowed to drop in five coins, even if your original bet was only a single coin. Be sure to do that. Progressive Second Chance is definitely a worthwhile gamble.

VIDEO POKER STRATEGY

After the initial five cards are dealt out, it is up to the player to decide which cards to hold and which to discard. This decision is the only control exercised by the player and is a significant factor in the outcome of the game. Therefore, it is important to apply the correct playing strategy when making the hold/discard decision.

There are many good descriptions of the perfect mathematical strategy for drawing cards in video poker, but most of them over-complicate the problem. For instance, a portion of the strategy for jacks-or-better is often given as:

Four Card Outside Straight Flush	Draw 1 card
Two Pair	Draw 1 card
Four Card Inside Straight Flush	Draw 1 card

What this means is that drawing to an outside straight flush is preferential to drawing to two pair, and that drawing to two pair is preferential to drawing to an inside straight flush. This strategy is absolutely correct. However, a possible straight flush and two pairs cannot occur in the same hand, so the strategy can be simplified by saying:

Four Card Straight Flush	Draw 1 card
Two Pair	Draw 1 card

which is mathematically identical to the more complicated version. In fact, one can also say:

Two Pair	Draw 1 card
Four Card Straight Flush	Draw 1 card

without fear of contradiction. Since both hands are mutually exclusive, it doesn't matter in what order they are listed in the strategy table. This is typical of the simplifications used in this section.

Simplification was sometimes attained by rounding to the second decimal place in the probability calculations for some of the dealt hands. When compared with most published strategies that are based on very precise numbers, the difference in real-world play turns out to be negligible.

To apply the mathematical strategy with absolute accuracy takes considerable concentration, which is simply not possible for most people. With all the distractions in a typical casino, trying to use a complicated strategy can easily result in inadvertent playing errors that reduce the overall payback. The simplified strategy presented here will reduce such errors.

BASIC STRATEGY RULES

To assure that you are getting the highest return from a video poker machine, a certain amount of playing discipline must be used. The following basic rules have to be followed to assure that the best strategy is effectively applied:

Play the Maximum Coins: Last year, while waiting for somebody, I was killing time by idly playing a jacks or better machine, one quarter at a time. When my friend appeared, the machine had five credits showing, so I hit the PLAY 5 CREDITS button, just to be done with it. To my amazement, I was dealt three high spades and made the royal on the draw. The payout was 4000 coins ($1000), or the equivalent of 800 coins per quarter. Had I continued to play one quarter at a time, the payout would have been only 250 coins, or a measly $62.50. The moral to this story is to play the maximum coins (usually five), unless you have a very good reason not to.

The one consistency in all video poker machines is that the per-coin payout for the highest hand is always enhanced when the maximum number of coins (or credits) is played. Although there are situations where single-coin play is advisable (such as Second Chance machines), the following playing strategies are based on five-coin play, unless otherwise noted.

Many recreational players find that dollar machines deplete their bankroll too quickly. Therefore, if you feel uneasy playing for $5 a hand, move to a quarter machine. If you insist on playing fewer than the maximum coins, be aware that the long-term payback will be reduced by 1% to 2%—and much more if you hit an early royal, as I did. However, there is one caution: If you move from a quarter machine to a nickel machine, be sure that the payout schedule is the same. Although there isn't much variation in schedules between quarter, dollar, and five-dollar machines, most nickel machines have significantly poorer payout schedules.

Never Hold a Kicker: A kicker is an unmatched card held in the hand when drawing replacement cards. Some video poker players hate to discard an ace, even if keeping it doesn't improve their hand. This is a throwback to the table game where such strategy is sometimes appropriate. In video poker, however, holding a kicker is disastrous because it significantly reduces the chances of improving a hand. For instance, on a full-pay jacks-or-better machine, keeping a kicker with a high pair reduces the overall payback by over 1.5%. If you are dealt a low pair, discarding two instead of three cards reduces the payback by almost 4%. Don't do it.

Stick to the Strategy: Do not try to outguess the strategy table. The table is based on mathematical probabilities and your hunch is not. Occasionally you may guess correctly, but over the long run, the strategy table will serve you well. If you don't like the idea of breaking a straight or a flush in order to draw one card to a possible royal, you may be playing the wrong game.

Do not depend on your memory: Take this book or copies of the strategy tables into the casino and refer to them frequently. Until you are familiar with a particular version of video poker, don't depend too much on your memory. After you have played a particular game for a while, you will get to know the strategy by heart.

PAYOUT SCHEDULES AND STRATEGY TABLES

The following sections provide payout schedules and strategy tables for six basic varieties of video poker:

JACKS OR BETTER
BONUS AND DOUBLE BONUS POKER
DOUBLE DOUBLE AND TRIPLE BONUS POKER
DEUCES WILD
JOKER POKER – Kings or better
JOKER POKER – Two pair

Selecting the Best Machine: In each section, a selection of abbreviated payout schedules is shown for that type of game, which is followed by the strategy table. The house edge is given for each payout schedule so that you can decide whether or not it is a game you want to play. Following is an example of a complete payout schedule.

JACKS OR BETTER					
Credits Bet	1	2	3	4	5
Royal flush	250	500	750	1000	4000
Straight flush	50	100	150	200	250
Four-of-a-kind	25	50	75	100	125
Full house	9	18	27	36	45
Flush	6	12	18	24	30
Straight	4	8	12	16	20
Three-of-a-kind	3	6	9	12	15
Two pair	2	4	6	8	10
Jacks or better	1	2	3	4	5

To save space and make comparisons easier, the schedules shown in the following sections show only the 1-credit columns. These are the columns you should examine and compare when selecting your machine. Except for the 5-credit royal flush payout, the other columns are simply multiples of the 1-credit column. The payback percentages given are for perfect strategy and 5-credit play.

Applying the Playing Strategy: After selecting your machine, turn the page to the strategy table for that type of game. The strategy table lists all possible hands in the order they should be played. After the initial five cards are dealt, work your way down from the top of the strategy table until you find a match and then draw the indicated number of cards.

You do not have to consult the strategy table for every hand that is dealt. For most hands, the correct strategy is obvious. The main purpose of the table is to resolve conflicts when there is more than one way to logically play a hand. For instance, what do you do if you are dealt a pat flush that includes a four card royal? What about a four-flush that includes a three card royal? And once you have learned these things, remember to recheck the strategy table whenever you play a new type of game.

JACKS OR BETTER — PAYOUT SCHEDULES					
Royal Flush	250	250	250	250	250
Straight Flush	50	50	200	40	50
Four-of-a-kind	25	80	30	20	80
Full house	9	8	8	9	8
Flush	6	6	8	6	5
Straight	4	4	8	4	4
Three-of-a-kind	3	3	3	3	3
Two Pair	2	1	1	2	1
Jacks or Better	1	1	1	1	1
Payback	99.5%	98.5%	98.5%	98.3%	97.4%

JACKS OR BETTER — PAYOUT SCHEDULES					
Royal Flush	250	250	250	250	250
Straight Flush	50	50	50	50	50
Four-of-a-kind	25	80	25	20	25
Full house	8	7	7	7	6
Flush	5	5	5	5	5
Straight	4	4	4	4	4
Three-of-a-kind	3	3	3	3	3
Two Pair	2	1	2	2	2
Jacks or Better	1	1	1	1	1
Payback	97.3%	96.3%	96.2%	95.5%	95.0%

The paybacks shown above are for schedules with a Royal Flush 5-credit payout of 4000 credits. For schedules paying 4700 credits, increase the payback by 0.3%. For 5000 credits, increase the payback by 0.5%.

JACKS OR BETTER STRATEGY TABLE

Dealt Hand	Draw
Royal Flush	0
Straight Flush	0
Four-of-a-kind	0
Full House	0
Four Card Royal Flush	1
Flush	0
Straight	0
Three-of-a-kind	2
Two Pair	1
Four Card Straight Flush	1
Pair J, Q, K, or A	3
Three Card Royal Flush	2
Four Card Flush	1
Pair 2 through 10	3
Four Card Outside Straight	1
Three Card Straight Flush	2
Four Card Inside Straight (3 or 4 HC)	1
J A, Q A, or K A (same suit)	3
J Q K (mixed suits)	2
10 J, 10 Q, or 10 K (same suit)	3
One or Two High Cards	3-4
Mixed Low Cards	5

BONUS OR DOUBLE BONUS POKER — PAYOUT SCHEDULES

Royal Flush	250	250	250	250	250
Straight Flush	100	50	50	50	50
Four Aces	200	80	80	80	160
Four – 2s, 3s, or 4s	40	40	40	40	80
Four – 5s through Kings	25	25	25	25	50
Full House	12	8	7	6	9
Flush	8	5	5	5	6
Straight	5	4	4	4	4
Three-of-a-kind	3	3	3	3	3
Two Pair	1	2	2	2	1
Jacks or Better	1	1	1	1	1
Payback	99.4%	99.2%	98.0%	96.9%	96.5%

BONUS OR DOUBLE BONUS POKER — PAYOUT SCHEDULES

Royal Flush	250	250	250	250	250
Straight Flush	50	50	50	50	50
Four Aces	160	160	160	160	160
Four – 2s, 3s, or 4s	80	80	80	80	80
Four – 5s through Kings	50	50	50	50	50
Full House	10	9	9	9	9
Flush	7	7	6	7	6
Straight	5	5	5	4	4
Three-of-a-kind	3	3	3	3	3
Two Pair	1	1	1	1	1
Jacks or Better	1	1	1	1	1
Payback	100.2%	99.1%	97.8%	97.7%	96.5%

The paybacks shown in the previous page are for schedules with a Royal Flush 5-credit payout of 4000 credits.

BONUS OR DOUBLE BONUS POKER STRATEGY TABLE	
Dealt Hand	**Draw**
Royal Flush	0
Straight Flush	0
Four-of-a-kind	0
Full House	0
Four Card Royal Flush	1
Flush	0
Straight	0
Three-of-a-kind	2
Two Pair	1
Four Card Straight Flush	1
Pair J, Q, K, or A	3
Three Card Royal Flush	2
Four Card Flush	1
Pair 2 through 10	3
Four Card Outside Straight (1 to 3 HC)	1
9 10 J (same suit)	2
Four Card Outside Straight	1
Three Card Straight Flush	2
J Q K A (mixed suits)	1
Two Card Royal Flush	3
J Q K (mixed suits)	2
One or Two High Cards	3-4
Mixed Low Cards	5

DOUBLE DOUBLE OR TRIPLE
BONUS POKER PAYOUT SCHEDULES

Royal Flush	250	250	250	250	250
Straight Flush	80	60	100	80	50
Four Aces	240	400	240	240	240
Four – 2s, 3s, or 4s	120	80	120	120	120
Four – 5s through Kings	50	50	50	50	75
Full House	9	7	8	8	10
Flush	5	5	5	5	7
Straight	4	4	4	4	4
Three-of-a-kind	3	3	3	3	3
Two Pair	1	1	1	1	1
Jacks or Better	1	1	1	1	1
Payback	99.6%	98.9%	98.7%	98.5%	98.5%

DOUBLE DOUBLE OR TRIPLE
BONUS POKER PAYOUT SCHEDULES

Royal Flush	250	250	250	250	250
Straight Flush	50	50	50	50	50
Four Aces w/ 2,3,4	400	400	400	400	400
Four – 2s, 3s, or 4s w/ A,2,3,4	160	160	160	160	160
Four Aces	160	160	160	160	160
Four – 2s ,3s, or 4s	80	80	80	80	80
Four – 5s through Kings	50	50	50	50	50
Full House	10	9	9	8	6
Flush	6	6	5	5	5
Straight	4	4	4	4	4
Three-of-a-kind	3	3	3	3	3
Two Pair	1	1	1	1	1
Jacks or Better	1	1	1	1	1
Payback	100.1%	99.0%	97.9%	96.8%	94.7%

The paybacks shown above are for schedules with a Royal Flush 5-credit payout of 4000 credits.

DOUBLE DOUBLE OR TRIPLE BONUS POKER STRATEGY TABLE

Dealt Hand	Draw
Royal Flush	0
Straight Flush	0
Four-of-a-kind	0
Three Aces	2
Four Card Royal Flush	1
Flush	0
Straight	0
Full House	0
Three-of-a-kind	2
Four Card Outside Straight Flush	1
Pair Aces	3
Four Card Inside Straight Flush	1
2 Pairs	1
Pair J, Q, or K	3
Three Card Royal Flush	2
Four Card Flush	1
Four Card Outside Straight	1
Pair 2 through 10	3
9 10 J (same suit)	2
J Q K A (mixed suits)	1
Three Card Straight Flush	2
Two Card Royal Flush	3
J Q K (mixed suits)	2
One Ace	4
Four Card Inside Straight	1
One or Two High Cards	3-4
Mixed Low Cards	5

DEUCES WILD PAYOUT SCHEDULES

Natural royal	250	250	250	250	250
Four – Deuces	200	500	200	400	500
Deuce royal	25	25	25	25	25
Five-of-a-kind	15	15	16	16	12
Straight Flush	9	8	10	11	8
Four-of-a-kind	5	4	4	4	4
Full House	3	3	4	3	3
Flush	2	2	3	2	2
Straight	2	2	2	2	2
Three-of-a-kind	1	1	1	1	1
Payback	100.7%	100.2%	99.7%	99.6%	99.2%
Natural royal	250	250	250	250	250
Four – Deuces	500	200	200	200	200
Deuce Royal	25	20	25	20	20
Five-of-a-kind	15	12	15	15	12
Straight Flush	5	9	9	9	9
Four-of-a-kind	4	5	4	4	4
Full House	3	3	4	4	4
Flush	2	2	3	3	3
Straight	2	2	2	2	2
Three-of-a-kind	1	1	1	1	1
Payback	99.1%	98.9%	98.9%	98.0%	97.1%

The paybacks shown above are for schedules with a Royal Flush 5-credit payout of 4000 credits.

DEUCES WILD
STRATEGY TABLE

No Deuces	Draw
Natural Royal Flush	0
Four Card Royal Flush	1
Straight Flush	0
Four-of-a-kind	1
Full House, Flush, or Straight	0
Three-of-a-kind	2
Four Card Straight Flush	1
Three Card Royal Flush	2
Three Card Outside Straight Flush	2
One Pair (discard second pair)	3
Four Card Outside Straight	1
Four Card Flush	1
Three Card Inside Straight Flush	2
Two Card Royal Flush	3
Assorted Cards	5

One Deuce Hand	
Royal Flush or Five-of-a-kind	0
Straight Flush	0
Four-of-a-kind	1
Four Card Royal Flush	1
Four Card Straight Flush	1
Full House, Flush or Straight	0
Three-of-a-kind	2
Three Card Royal Flush	2
Three Card Straight Flush	2
One Deuce	4

Two Deuce Hand	
Royal Flush or Five-of-a-kind	0
Straight Flush	0
Four-of-a-kind	1
Four Card Royal Flush	1
Two Deuces	3

Three Deuce Hand	
Royal Flush or Five-of-a-kind	0
Three Deuces	2

Four Deuce Hand	
Four Deuces	1

JOKER POKER (KINGS OR BETTER)
PAYOUT SCHEDULES

Natural royal	400	400	400	400
Five-of-a-kind	200	200	200	200
Joker royal	100	100	100	100
Straight flush	50	50	50	50
Four-of-a-kind	20	20	17	15
Full House	7	6	7	8
Flush	5	5	5	5
Straight	3	3	3	3
Three-of-a-kind	2	2	2	2
Two Pair	1	1	1	1
Kings or Better	1	1	1	1
Payback	100.7%	99.1%	98.1%	98.0%

JOKER POKER (KINGS OR BETTER)
PAYOUT SCHEDULES

Natural Royal	400	400	400	400
Five-of-a-kind	200	200	200	200
Joker Royal	100	100	100	100
Straight Flush	50	50	50	40
Four-of-a-kind	20	15	20	20
Full House	6	7	5	5
Flush	4	5	4	4
Straight	3	3	3	3
Three-of-a-kind	2	2	2	2
Two Pair	1	1	1	1
Kings or Better	1	1	1	1
Payback	97.6%	96.3%	96.0%	95.5%

The paybacks shown above are for schedules with a Royal Flush 5-credit payout of 4000 credits. For schedules paying 4700 credits, increase the payback by 0.3%. For 5000 credits, increase the payback by 0.5%.

JOKER POKER (KINGS OR BETTER) STRATEGY TABLE

No Joker	Draw
Natural Royal Flush	0
Straight Flush	0
Four-of-a-kind	1
Four Card Royal Flush	1
Full House or Flush	0
Three-of-a-kind	2
Four Card Straight Flush	1
Straight	0
Two Pair	1
Three Card Royal Flush	2
Pair King or Ace	3
Four Card Flush	1
Pair 2 through Q	3
Three Card Straight Flush	2
Four Card Outside Straight	1
Two Card Royal Flush	3
A and/or K	3-4
Assorted Cards	5

JOKER POKER (KINGS OR BETTER) STRATEGY TABLE

Joker Hand	Draw
Royal Flush or Five-of-a-kind	0
Straight Flush	0
Four-of-a-kind	1
Four Card Royal Flush	1
Full House or Flush	0
Four Card Straight Flush	1
Three-of-a-kind	2
Straight	0
Four Card Flush (1 or 2 HC)	1
Three Card Royal Flush	2
Three Card Straight Flush	2
Pair King or Ace	3
Four Card Outside Straight	1
Four Card Flush	1
Joker	4

JOKER POKER (TWO PAIR) PAYOUT SCHEDULES

Natural Royal	500	500	500	100
Five-of-a-kind	100	100	100	400
Joker Royal	50	50	50	100
Straight Flush	50	50	50	100
Four-of-a-kind	20	20	20	16
Full House	8	10	8	8
Flush	7	6	7	5
Straight	6	5	5	4
Three-of-a-kind	2	2	2	2
Two Pair	1	1	1	1
Payback	101.6%	99.4%	98.6%	97.2%
Natural Royal	500	500	500	100
Five-of-a-kind	100	100	100	400
Joker Royal	50	50	50	100
Straight Flush	50	50	50	100
Four-of-a-kind	20	25	20	15
Full House	8	8	8	6
Flush	6	5	6	5
Straight	5	4	4	4
Three-of-a-kind	2	2	2	2
Two Pair	1	1	1	1
Payback	96.4%	95.6%	93.6%	93.3%

The paybacks shown above are for schedules with a Royal Flush 5-credit payout of 4000 credits. For schedules paying 4700 credits, increase the payback by 0.3%. For 5000 credits, increase the payback by 0.5%.

JOKER POKER (Two pair)
STRATEGY TABLE

No Joker	Draw
Natural Royal Flush	0
Straight Flush	0
Four Card Royal Flush	1
Four-of-a-kind	1
Full House, Flush, or Straight	0
Four Card Straight Flush	1
Three-of-a-kind	2
Two Pair	1
Three Card Royal Flush	2
Four Card Flush	1
Four Card Outside Straight	1
Three Card Straight Flush	2
One Pair	3
Four Card Inside Straight	1
Three Card Flush	2
Two Card Royal Flush	3
Three Card Outside Straight	2
Two Card Straight Flush	3
Assorted Cards	5

Joker Hand	Draw
Royal Flush or Five-of-a-kind	0
Straight Flush	0
Four-of-a-kind	1
Full House or Flush	0
Four Card Royal Flush	1
Four Card Straight Flush	1
Straight	0
Three-of-a-kind	2
Three Card Straight Flush	2
Four Card Flush	1
Four Card Straight	1
Three Card Outside Straight	2
Joker	4

GLOSSARY

Ace — The highest-ranking card in poker. May also be used as the lowest card in an A 2 3 4 5 straight or straight flush. In blackjack and Spanish 21, an ace may be valued either 1 or 11.

Ace high — A hand of mixed cards that contains one ace.

Ace kicker — A lone ace that is held (usually with a pair), when drawing replacement cards. Not a recommended strategy in video poker.

Aces up — Two pair, with one of the pairs being aces.

Action — The total amount of money bet. Win or lose, the same dollar bet fifty times, constitutes $50 worth of action. The basis used for awarding comps.

Advantage — *See* **House advantage**.

Aggregate limit — The maximum payout in any one game or hand.

American wheel — A roulette wheel containing 38 ball pockets, numbered 1 through 36, plus 0 and 00, using the American number sequence, and having a betting layout that uses English terminology. Also called a double-zero wheel.

Anchor position — *See* **Third base**.

Ante — In poker, the chips put into the pot before the initial deal. In Caribbean Stud, Deuces Wild Hold'em Fold'em and Three Card Poker, the initial wager.

Any craps — A one-roll wager that the next number on the dice will be a 2, 3, or 12.

Any seven — A one-roll wager that the next number on the dice will be a 7.

Back counting — The act of counting cards as a spectator without actually playing.

Back line — *See* **Don't line**.

Ball — A small ball, which is spun around the ball track of a roulette wheel. The ball is usually white and has a diameter of about 13/16 inch.

Ball deflector — An oblong deflector in the bowl below the ball track of a roulette wheel, designed to increase the random motion of the ball after it leaves the track and before it lands in a pocket. A typical wheel has either 8 or 16 deflectors. Also called canoe stop because most deflectors are shaped like tiny upside-down canoes.

Ball track — The circular groove inside the rim of a roulette wheel bowl where the ball spins. Also called track or race.

Bank — (a) Money on the table that is used by the dealer to pay winning bets. (b) The casino or the game operator. (c) Any person who covers all the bets in a game.

Banker's hand — One of the three wagers in baccarat.

Bankroll — The total amount of money that a player has allotted to a gambling session.

Bar — A common symbol on slot machine reels.

Bar 12 (or 2) — A rule that is printed on a craps layout in the don't pass and don't come areas. It means that during a come-out, the 12 (or the 2) is a push for don't bets.

Basic strategy — The best long-term playing decisions in blackjack for a person who is not tracking or counting cards.

Behind the line — An odds bet after a point is established in craps.

BET MAX button — Pressing this button registers a maximum credit bet, (whatever it might be for that slot machine), and automatically spins the reels. On some machines, this button is marked PLAY MAX CREDITS.

BET ONE button — Pressing this button will register in the machine as a one-credit bet. It is the same as putting one coin into the slot, which is an alternative. Pressing the button a second time, will register as a two-credit bet, and so forth. On some machines, this button is marked BET 1 CREDIT.

Betting interval — In table poker, the period during which each player has the right to bet, raise, or drop out.

Betting right — Betting with the dice; that a pass bet will win.

Betting wrong — Betting against the dice; that a don't pass bet will win.

Biased wheel — A roulette wheel that repeatedly favors a certain number or group of numbers, instead of being random.

Big 6 — An even money bet in craps that a 6 will be rolled before a 7.

Big 8 — An even money bet in craps that an 8 will be rolled before a 7.

Big bertha — A giant slot machine with eight to ten reels, often placed near the entrance of a casino to lure potential slot players. Not a good machine to play.

Bimodal bias — A type of roulette wheel bias that favors two separated numbers or two contiguous groups of numbers.

Black bet — An even-money bet on the eighteen black numbers on a roulette wheel.

Blackjack — In blackjack and Spanish 21, a hand consisting of an ace and a ten-value card. Also called a natural.

Blacks — Black casino chips with a value of $100 each.

Blank — A stop on a slot machine reel with no symbols. A few machines give a minimum payout for three blanks.

Bleeder — A paranoid casino supervisor who worries about players winning. Also called a sweater (one who perspires).

Blower — A mechanical air-driven device for randomly mixing and dispensing keno balls. Formerly called a goose.

Bluff — In table poker, trying to convince other players in a poker game that you have the winning hand, when you probably don't.

Bonus game — A slot machine in which certain symbol combinations cause a bonus mode to appear on a secondary screen.

Bowl — The outside part of a roulette wheel that houses the revolving wheelhead. The bowl contains the circular ball track. Also called rim.

Box Numbers — The boxed numbers 4, 5, 6, 8, 9, and 10 on a craps layout, which are used to mark the point, and to position the place, come, and buy bets.

Boxcars — A slang term for a dice roll of 12.

Boxman — The supervisor of the craps table who sits between the two inside dealers.

Break — *See* **Bust**.

Bug — A restricted joker that may be used only as an ace or a wild card to fill a flush, straight, or straight flush.

Burn card — A card removed from the top of the deck after a shuffle, and placed in the discard tray.

Bust — To exceed a count of 21 in blackjack or Spanish 21. Also called break.

Buy bet — A craps wager that is similar to a place bet, but is paid at correct odds, for which the casino charges a 5% commission.

Buy-a-pay game — Another term for an option-buy slot game.

Buy-in — (a) An exchange of a player's currency for casino chips. (b) The amount of money a player gives the dealer for the chips.

Buy-your-pay game — Another term for an option-buy slot game.

Cage — Short for cashier's cage, where casino chips may be exchanged for cash and other financial transactions may be consummated.

Call bet — A verbal wager with no chips on the table.

Caller (baccarat) — The dealer who controls the operation of the game.

Caller (keno) — The keno employee who announces the winning numbers as they are drawn.

CANCEL button — A button on a video poker machine that resets all the hold buttons and allows the player to make new hold/discard choices.

Cancellation system — See **Labouchere system**.

Candle — The light on top of a slot machine cabinet that indicates the machine denomination and signals for an attendant when you press the CHANGE button.

Canoe stop — *See* **Ball deflector.**

Catch — Each number on a keno ticket that matches one of the drawn numbers.

Card counter — A person who mentally keeps track of which cards have been played, so as to determine which cards remain in the unplayed portion of the deck.

Card mechanic — A skilled dealer who uses sleight-of-hand to cheat.

Carousel — A group of slot machines, usually surrounding an elevated change booth.

CASH OUT button — A button on a video poker or slot machine that converts credits to coins. This button is sometimes marked CASH/CREDIT or COLLECT.

Cash ticket — A printed paper coupon that can be redeemed for cash or inserted in another ticket-equipped game machine.

Casino advantage — *See* **House edge.**

Casino host — The casino employee who caters to the needs of high-stakes players.

Casino manager — The head honcho for all gaming operations.

Center bet — *See* **Proposition bet**.

Change booth — A booth set up to convert a player's paper currency to coins or coins to currency.

CHANGE button — Pressing this button on a slot machine summons the change person. You should also press the button whenever something seems to go wrong with the machine. This button is often marked SERVICE.

Change person — The casino employee who roams the slot machine area and makes change for the players.

Chasing losses — Raising the betting level in an attempt to recoup losses. Not a recommended procedure.

Check or cheque — Alternate term for Chip that is commonly used by casino personnel and professional gamblers.

Checkracker — An additional dealer who assists the roulette dealer by picking up and stacking used chips. Also called a mucker.

Cherry — A common symbol on slot machine reels.

Chip — A gaming token with an imprinted value that is used in place of real money at various table games in a casino. Chips may be redeemed for cash at the issuing casino. Also called house check, casino chip, or value chip. The terms Chip and Check are used interchangeably.

Clocking — (a) The collecting and recording of winning numbers to see if a roulette wheel exhibits any bias. (b) Any study of a wheel to see if it has non-random characteristics.

Cold hand, Cold dice — Dice that consistently don't pass, resulting in a losing streak for pass bettors and a winning streak for don't bettors.

Cold machine — A slot machine that is paying less than its expected payback.

Color change — A change in the denomination of chips.

Color up — To convert small denomination chips to chips of a larger denomination.

Column bet — A bet on one of the three long columns on the roulette layout. Each column contains twelve numbers and pays 2 to 1.

Combination bet — Any bet in roulette where a single chip or a single stack of chips crosses a line and covers more than one number.

Combination ticket — A keno way ticket in which two or more way groups are combined to form additional wagers.

Come bet — A bet with the dice that is made after the come-out roll.

Come-out roll — Any dice roll made before a point is established.

Commission — The percentage charged by the casino against certain winning hands in table games such as craps and baccarat. A commission is typically 5% of the amount won.

Comp — Shortened term for the complimentary rewards, such as rooms, meals, or show tickets, given to regular players.

Contiguous number group — A group of numbers on a roulette wheelhead that are directly adjacent to each other.

Corner bet — A combination roulette bet covering four numbers. Also called a square bet.

Correct odds — The true mathematical odds that a bet will win or that an event will occur. Also called true odds.

Crap-out — To throw one of the craps numbers on the come-out roll.

Craps — The name of the game. Also, the term used for the numbers 2, 3, or 12.

Craps-eleven — A combination of an any-craps bet and a one-roll bet on 11.

Credits — Instead of paying out coins, most modern slot machines keep track of winnings in the form of credits that can be converted to coins by pressing the CASH OUT button. The accumulated credits can also be played.

Crew — The four or five casino employees who staff a craps table.

Croupier — The French term for a dealer.

Crown marker — *See* **Win marker**.

CSM — An acronym for Continuous Shuffling Machine. This device speeds up a card game by eliminating shuffling delays.

Cut card — A special card, usually solid in color, used to indicate how far down to deal the deck.

Cylinder — *See* **Wheelhead**.

D'Alembert system — An even-money betting system in which the bet is increased by one unit after every loss and decreased by one unit after every win. Also called a pyramid system.

DEAL button — A button on a video poker machine that directs it to deal the next hand.

DEAL–DRAW button — A button on a video poker machine that combines the functions of a deal button and a draw button.

Dealer — The casino employee who operates or helps to operate a table game.

Dealing shoe — An elongated plastic box into which pre-shuffled cards are stacked. One end of the box has a slot and a finger notch so that the dealer may easily slide out the cards, one at a time.

Dealer signature — The characteristic way a particular dealer spins a roulette ball.

Denomination — The minimum coin or credit value required to play a video poker or other slot machine. The most popular denominations are nickel, quarter, and dollar.

Deuce — The two-spot card.

Deuces wild — All four deuces in the deck are designated as wild cards. See Wild card.

Dice — The two plastic cubes with one through six spots on the six sides, that are used to play craps and other dice games.

Discard — A card that is not held when drawing replacement cards.

Don't come bet — A craps bet against the dice that is made after the come-out roll.

Don't pass bet — A craps bet against the dice that is made prior to the come-out roll that the dice will not pass.

Don't pass line — The area on the craps layout where a don't pass bet is made.

Double down — In blackjack and Spanish 21, to double your bet and receive one additional card. Also called double.

Double Exposure — A variant of blackjack where both dealer cards are dealt face up.

Double odds — An odds wager made at double the amount of the original craps bet.

Double zero — One of the two green numbers on an American roulette wheel, the other green number being zero.

Double-street bet — *See* **Line bet**.

Double-zero wheel — *See* **American wheel**.

Downcard — A card that is dealt face down.

Dozen bet — A bet on the first, second or third dozen numbers on the roulette layout. These numbers are 1-12, 13-24, 25-36, and each dozen pays 2 to 1.

Draw — The action in draw poker or video poker during which cards are drawn from the deck to replace those that have been discarded by the players. In blackjack and baccarat, adding cards to a hand.

DRAW button — A button on a video poker machine that directs it to draw replacements for all the cards that were not held.

Draw poker — A game of closed poker in which there is a one-time opportunity to replace unwanted cards in the player's hand with new cards drawn from the deck.

Drop — The total money a gaming table takes in during one shift.

Drop box — A locked cash box under a gaming table into which the dealer inserts money received from the players.

Duplicate ticket — *See* **Outside ticket**.

Easy way — A roll of a 4, 6, 8, or 10, where the numbers on the dice are not paired.

Edge — A statistical advantage. Usually the casino's advantage.

En prison — When the winning number is zero, any player who made an even-money outside bet has the option of either losing half the bet or allowing the entire bet to be held over (imprisoned) for the next spin. This rule is applied to French roulette wheels at most European casinos. See Surrender.

English wheel — Any roulette wheel with only a single zero and an English-language betting layout.

Even bet — An outside bet on the 18 even numbers on a roulette wheel. Zero and double zero are not considered even numbers.

Even money — A wager that pays off at 1 to 1 odds, if it wins. That is, if a $10 bet wins, the original bet is returned along with an additional $10. Also called a flat bet or even odds.

Expectation — The average amount that may be won or lost in a particular game over an extended period of play. Also called expectation of winning.

Face-card — A jack, queen, or king. In blackjack and Spanish 21, all face cards count as 10.

Face-down cards — Cards that are not exposed.

Face-up cards — Cards that are exposed for all to see.

Field bet — A one-roll craps wager that the next roll of the dice will be a 2, 3, 4, 9, 10, 11, or 12.

First base — The end seat at a gaming table, to the dealer's immediate left, which is the first hand that is dealt and played.

Five-number bet — A combination bet covering the numbers 0, 00, 1, 2, and 3 that can only be made on an American roulette wheel. It is known as a sucker bet because it pays only 6 to 1 and gives the house a 7.89% edge.

Five-of-a-kind — Five cards, all of the same rank. Since a standard deck has only four cards of each rank (one in each suit), this must include a designated wild card such as a deuce or a joker.

Flashboard — A lighted number display that shows the results of the current keno game.

Flat bet — *See* **Even money**.

Floor person — A floor supervisor.

Floor supervisor — A pit supervisor who reports to the pit boss. This person watches dealers to assure that all losing bets are collected, winning bets are correctly paid, and nobody is cheating.

Floorman — A politically incorrect term for floor supervisor.

Flush — Five cards of the same suit.

Fold — In card games, to throw in your hand and drop out of play. This action forfeits any wagers made up to that point.

Four straight — Four of the five cards needed for a straight.

Four card royal — Four of the five cards needed for a royal flush.

Four-flush — Four of the five cards needed for a flush; four cards of the same suit.

Four-of-a-kind — Four cards of the same rank.

French wheel — A roulette wheel containing 37 ball pockets, numbered 1 through 36, plus 0, using the French number sequence, and having a betting layout that uses French terminology.

Frets — The metal separators forming the numbered pockets in a roulette wheelhead.

Front line — *See* **Pass line**.

Full house — Three-of-a-kind and a pair.

Gaff — A cheaters device or technique.

Gaffed wheel — A rigged roulette wheel that has been altered to favor the house.

Garbage hand — A hand of no potential value that does not even contain a low pair.

Glass — The posted chart on a slot machine showing the winning symbol combinations and the payouts.

Goose — *See* **Blower**.

Green numbers — The zero and double zero on a roulette wheel.

Greens — Green casino chips with a value of $25 each. Also called quarters.

Hand — The cards held by the dealer or a player. In craps, the series of dice rolls from one come-out to the next come-out. Also called a game, a round, or a shoot. Sometimes these terms are used to describe the entire time a shooter has possession of the dice.

Handpay — A jackpot payoff or a cashout that is made by an attendant rather than by the machine.

Hard hand — In blackjack and Spanish 21, a hand that either does not contain an ace or the ace can only be valued as 1, without going over 21.

Hardway — A roll of 4, 6, 8, or 10, where the numbers on the dice come up as a pair, e.g., 2+2, 3+3, 4+4, or 5+5.

Hardway bet — A craps bet that 4, 6, 8, or 10 will be rolled as a hardway before the easy way appears or before a 7 appears.

High card — The highest card in a hand. In jacks or better video poker, a jack, queen, king, or ace.

High number bet — An even-money bet on the 18 high numbers on a roulette wheel.

High pair — In jacks-or-better poker or video poker, a pair of jacks, queens, kings, or aces. In Let It Ride, a high pair also includes the ten.

High roller — A gambler who plays for high stakes.

Hit — In blackjack and Spanish 21, a request for another card.

HOLD button — One of five buttons on a video poker machine that designates a card to be held (not discarded) when the draw occurs. Also, HOLD-CANCEL button.

Hole card — In stud poker and poker-like games, a card that is dealt face down. In blackjack and Spanish 21, the dealer's face down card.

Hop bet — A craps bet that a particular dice combination will come up on the next roll.

Hopper — The container inside a video poker or slot machine that holds the coins used to pay off wins or a cashout.

Horn bet — A simultaneous one-roll craps bet on the 2, 3, 11, and 12.

Hot hand, hot dice, hot roll — Dice that consistently pass, resulting in a winning streak for pass bettors and a losing streak for don't bettors.

Hot machine — A slot machine that is paying more than its expected payback.

House — The casino, the bank, or the game operator.

House edge — The difference between the actual odds and the payoff odds, usually stated as a percentage, which is the mathematical edge the house has over the player. Also called casino advantage, house advantage, house percentage, or P.C.

House numbers — The 0 and 00 numbers on the roulette wheel, which do not pay off on outside bets.

House odds — The amount the house pays a winning bet, usually stated as an odds ratio such as 2 to 1. Also called odds paid or payoff odds.

House percentage — *See* **House edge**.

Inside bet — A straight-up or combination bet placed directly on the numbers on the roulette layout, including zero and double zero.

Inside dealer — The craps dealer who stands next to the boxman and handles the bets at his end of the table. Sometimes called a standing dealer.

Inside numbers — In craps, the place bet numbers 5, 6, 8, and 9.

Inside straight — Four of the five cards needed for a straight with a gap between the lowest and highest cards. The gap can be filled with a card of only one rank, or a total of four possible cards.

Inside ticket — A keno ticket marked by a player and used to place a bet. Also called an original ticket.

Insurance — In blackjack and Spanish 21, a side bet on whether or not the dealer has a blackjack when an ace is showing.

Jackpot — The largest payout on any particular machine. Also, any big win with a large payout.

Jacks or better — A game in which a pair of jacks is the lowest-paying hand.

Joker — An extra card in the deck that is designated as a wild card. See Wild card.

Juiced wheel — A gaffed roulette wheel that is controlled by electro-magnets.

Keno writer — A keno employee who takes bets, generates outside tickets, and pays winners.

Kicker — An unmatched card held in the hand when drawing replacement cards. Not a recommended strategy in video poker.

Labouchere system — An even-money betting system in which the first and last numbers in a betting line are canceled after every win and the amount of the bet is added to the betting line after every loss. Also called a cancellation system.

Lammer — A small plastic disk with an imprinted number or word. In roulette, it is used by the dealer to keep track of the value of a player's chips. In craps, it is used to keep track of the status of bets. Also called a button.

Lay bet — A craps wager which is the opposite of a place bet, made by a don't bettor and paid at correct odds, for which the casino charges a 5% commission.

Laying odds — An odds bet made by a don't bettor in craps.

Layout — The imprinted surface of a gaming table displaying the various bets.

Le partage — Similar to the en prison rule, except that the player loses half of the bet and doesn't have the option of letting it ride. Applied in the United Kingdom. See Surrender.

Lemon — A common symbol on slot machine reels.

Limit — *See* **Table limit**.

Line — Short for payline.

Line bet (roulette) — A combination bet on the six numbers in two adjacent rows, that pays 5 to 1. Also called six-number bet or double-street bet.

Line bet (craps) — *See* pass bet.

Line game — Another term for a multiple payline slot game.

Loaded dice — Crooked dice that have been weighted so that certain numbers are favored.

Local progressive — Similar progressive slot machines, usually in a bank or carousel, that are linked together within a single casino.

Loose machine — A slot machine programmed for a higher than average long-term payback.

Low number bet — An even-money bet on the 18 low numbers on a roulette wheel.

Low pair — In video poker, any pair that does not pay. In jacks-or-better, low pairs are 2 through 10. In table poker, a pair too small to open the betting.

Marker — A casino IOU which permits a player to obtain chips against previously-established credit or money on deposit.

Martingale system — An even-money betting system in which the bet is doubled after every loss and is reduced to the initial bet after every win. Also called a doubling system.

Maximum — *See* Table limit.

Mechanic — A skilled dealer who uses sleight-of-hand to cheat.

Minimum — The smallest bet allowed at a table.

Miss-out — *See* Seven-out.

Mucker — *See* **Checkracker**.

Multi-Game machine — A slot machine in which the player has a choice of several different games, usually including video poker.

Multiple payline game — A slot machine that has more than one payline. Wagering more coins or credits activates the added paylines.

Multiplier game — A slot machine in which the number of coins or credits wagered multiplies the amount of the payout.

Natural (baccarat) — An initial hand consisting of 8 or 9 points.

Natural (blackjack) — An initial hand consisting of an ace and a ten-value card. Also called blackjack.

Natural (craps) — A 7 or 11 rolled on the come-out resulting in a win for pass bettors. Craps dealers use the term to mean any number that results in the immediate resolution of the pass bets at the come-out (2, 3, 7, 11, or 12).

Neighbors bet — A straight-up bet on one roulette number plus additional straight-up bets on adjacent numbers (on the wheelhead).

Nickels — *See* **Reds**.

Odd bet — An even-money bet on the 18 odd numbers on a roulette wheel.

Odds — The ratio of the number of ways to win versus the number of ways to lose.

Odds bet — A craps bet that is paid at the correct odds, which can be made on a pass, don't pass, come, or don't come bet after a point is established.

Odds paid — *See* **House odds**.

Off — A designation that a craps bet on the layout is temporarily not working.

On — A designation that a craps bet is working.

One-armed bandit — An old slang term used for slot machines, indicating that the payouts were very poor.

One-roll bet — A craps bet that is resolved by the next roll of the dice.

Open-ended straight — Four cards in sequential rank that can become a straight if a card is added to either end. The straight can be completed with a card of either of two ranks, or a total of eight possible cards. Also called an outside straight.

Option-buy game — A slot machine in which additional winning symbol combinations are activated by betting the maximum number of coins or credits.

Original ticket — *See* **Inside ticket**.

Outside bet — A roulette bet on any of the options outside of the main number field, that pay 1 to 1 or 2 to 1.

Outside numbers — The place bet numbers 4, 5, 9, and 10 on a craps layout.

Outside straight — Same as an open-ended straight.

Outside ticket — A ticket generated by a keno writer to provide a player with bet verification. Also called a duplicate ticket.

P.C. — Gambler's abbreviation for percentage. See **House edge**.

Pair — Two cards of the same rank.

Pass — In craps, a winning decision for the dice: either a pass on the come-out or a made point.

Pass bet — A craps wager with the dice that is made prior to the come-out roll that the dice will pass. Also called a line bet or a pass line bet.

Pass line — The area on the layout where a pass bet is made. Also called the front line.

Past posting — A late bet placed or a bet increased after the results of a game or event are known.

Pat hand — A good hand, that does not require a draw or a hit. In blackjack, it is an unbusted hand with a total count of 17 or higher.

Payback — The total long-term winnings as a percent of the total amount bet.

Payline — A line across the window in front of the slot machine reels that shows where a winning symbol combination has to be aligned for a payoff. Some games have several paylines.

Payoff — The amount paid out by the casino for winning.

Payoff odds — *See* **House odds**.

Payout — Same as payoff.

Paytable — A chart, usually above the reels of a slot machine or the screen of a video poker machine, showing the winning combinations and the payout amounts. On a video machine, the paytable may be displayed on the screen by pressing the PAYTABLE button.

PAYTABLE button — Pressing this button on a video game brings the paytable to the screen. Sometimes this button is marked SEE PAYS.

Pit — The area behind a group of gaming tables that is restricted to casino employees.

Pit boss — The supervisor who is responsible for the tables in a specific pit or gaming area. The pit boss reports to the shift manager.

Place bet — A craps bet that a particular place number will be rolled before a seven. The place numbers are 4, 5, 6, 8, 9, and 10.

Player's hand — One of the three wagers in baccarat.

Pocket — One of the numbered recesses in the roulette wheelhead into which the ball may land.

Point — In craps, one of the numbers 4, 5, 6, 8, 9, or 10, when rolled on the come-out.

Press — To increase a bet, usually by doubling it.

Progressive jackpot — A dynamic top jackpot that grows larger by pooling a fraction of each wager as the games are played.

Proposition bet — Any of the craps wagers in the center of the layout. Also called a center bet or a prop bet.

Purples — Purple casino checks with a value of $500 each.

Push — A tie between a player and the casino in which no money changes hands. Also called a standoff.

Pyramid system — *See* **D'Alembert system.**

Quads — Another term for four-of-a-kind.

Quarters — *See* **Greens.**

Race — *See* **Ball track.**

Random number generator (RNG) — The RNG is one of the chips on the internal computer board of a slot or video poker machine. It generates thousands of random numbers a second, and each random number sequence defines a specific set of cards or reel symbols. An RNG is also used in some keno games.

Rank — The ordinal position of each card within a suit, determining its value. The lowest rank is the deuce and the highest is the ace. In a straight or a straight flush, an ace may also be used as the lowest card.

Red bet — An even-money bet on the 18 red numbers on a roulette wheel.

Reds — Red casino chips with a value of $5 each. Also called nickels.

Reels — The side-by-side rotating wheels displaying various symbols on the outside rims in a slot machine.

Regular ticket — The simplest and most common keno ticket with a single bet on one group of numbers. Also called straight ticket.

Rigged wheel — A roulette wheel that has been modified to favor either the house or the player. See Gaffed wheel.

Right bettor — A craps player who bets that the dice will pass by making a pass or a come bet.

Rim — *See* **Bowl**.

Roll — A throw of the dice.

Roulette chip — A gaming token with no imprinted value, used at roulette tables to avoid bet confusion by assigning each player a different color. Roulette chips have no intrinsic value and must be cashed in at the table that issued them. Also called color check, wheel check, or nonvalue chip.

Row bet — *See* **Street bet**.

Royal flush — A ten, jack, queen, king, and ace, all of the same suit.

Runner — A keno employee who brings marked tickets to the keno writers from players in other locations, and returns outside tickets to the players.

Scatter symbols — Symbols that result in a slot payoff when they appear anywhere in the reel window.

Scorecard — A card with a matrix of printed squares provided at a baccarat table for keeping track of the winning hands, used by players who like to bet on trends.

Secondary screen — A bonus screen on a video slot machine that is initiated by certain symbol combinations.

Seconds dealer — A card mechanic who specializes in dealing the second card from the top of a deck.

Separators — *See* **Frets**.

Sequential royal flush — A royal flush in which the five cards are displayed on the video poker screen in rank sequence as: 10 J Q K A or A K Q J 10, depending on how the particular machine defines it.

Seven-out — The roll of a 7 after a point is established in craps and before the point is repeated, causing pass bettors to lose and don't bettors to win. Also called a miss-out.

Shift boss — The top manager during the course of a single work shift.

Shill — A casino employee who gambles with house money to stimulate interest in a game. Also called a prop.

Shoe — *See* **Dealing shoe**.

Shooter — The player who is rolling the dice.

Showdown — The point in a table poker game when the hands of all active players are exposed and compared to determine who wins the pot.

Side bet — An optional second bet at a table game.

Silver — Casino chips or tokens with a value of $1 each.

Single odds — In craps, an odds wager made for the same amount as the original bet.

Single-ended straight — Four of the five cards needed for a straight in a sequence that is open at only one end. Specifically: A 2 3 4 or J Q K A. The straight can be completed with a card of only one rank, or a total of four possible cards. Also called inside straight.

Single-number bet — *See* **Straight-up bet**.

Single-zero wheel — A French or English roulette wheel. A 37-pocket roulette wheel that does not have a double zero.

Six-number bet — *See* **Line bet** (roulette).

Slot floor — The area of a casino designated for slot machines.

Slot manager — The top manager for the slot department of the casino.

Slot mechanic — The casino employee who is responsible for maintaining the proper mechanical and electronic operation of the slot machines.

Snake eyes — A slang term for a dice roll of 2.

Soft hand — In blackjack and Spanish 21, a hand containing an ace that can be valued as either a 1 or 11 without going over 21.

SPIN button — Pressing this button starts a slot machine by causing the reels to spin, but only after coins are inserted or credits committed. On some machines, this button is marked SPIN REELS.

Spinning reel machine — A slot machine with actual mechanical spinning reels, although the reels are now computer controlled.

Split — In blackjack and Spanish 21, to divide a pair into two separate hands.

Split bet — A combination bet in roulette covering two numbers.

Spot — A marked number on a keno ticket.

Square bet — *See* **Corner bet**.

Stack — A pile of 20 roulette chips.

Stake — Another term for bankroll.

Stand — In blackjack and Spanish 21, to not draw any more cards.

STAND button — A button on a video poker machine that automatically puts a hold on all five cards.

Standoff — *See* **Push**.

Stickman — The craps dealer who moves the dice around with a dice stick and controls the center bets.

Stiff hand — A hand that is not pat and can be busted with a single hit. In blackjack and Spanish 21, it is a hand with a total count of 12 through 16.

Stop — The position of a slot machine reel when it comes to rest. A reel may stop when a symbol is under the payline or when the blank space between two symbols falls under the payline.

Straight — Five cards of consecutive rank, with mixed suits.

Straight flush — Five cards of consecutive rank, all of the same suit.

Straight ticket — *See* **Regular ticket**.

Straight-up bet — An inside bet on any single number in roulette, including zero and double zero. Also called single-number bet.

Street bet — A combination bet in roulette on the three numbers in one row. Also called row bet.

Substitute symbol — *See* **Wild symbol**.

Suit — The name of one of the four families of 13 cards that make up a standard deck. The four suits are spades, hearts, clubs, and diamonds.

Surrender (blackjack) — In Spanish 21 and some blackjack games, an option to drop out of play before taking a hit in return for forfeiting half the original wager.

Surrender (roulette) — Identical to the le partage rule. For even-money outside bets, the player loses only half the bet when the winning number is zero or double zero. This rule is applied in Atlantic City on double-zero wheels only.

Sweater — *See* **Bleeder**.

Symbols — The pictures of various objects that appear on slot machine reels.

Table limit — The largest bet allowed at a table, which may be increased for a high roller. Also called limit or maximum.

Taking odds — An odds bet made by a pass-line or come bettor in craps.

Third base — The end seat at a gaming table, to the dealer's right, which is the last hand that is dealt and played. Also called anchor position.

Three-of-a-kind — Three cards of the same rank.

Tie bet — A wager on a tie hand in baccarat and other games.

Tight machine — A slot machine programmed for a lower than average long-term payback.

Toke — Short for token, a gratuity given to the dealer.

Top box — An illuminated box above the reels or video screen of a slot machine that displays the game theme and/or additional bonus features.

Touchscreen — A video screen where you can touch an object to select it.

Triplet — Another term for three-of-a-kind. Also called trips.

True odds — *See* **Correct odds**.

Twenty-one — Another term for the game of blackjack.

Two pair — Two cards of the same rank and two cards of another rank.

Unit — The size of a basic bet that is used as a standard of measurement.

Upcard — A card that is dealt face up.

Value chip — *See* **Chip**.

Video machine — A slot machine in which the spinning reels are simulated on a video screen.

Visual tracker — A person who, by watching a spinning roulette ball and its relationship to the rotating wheelhead, tries to predict into what group of numbers the ball is likely to fall. Also called a tracker.

Way ticket — A keno ticket combining two or more wagers by indicating two or more groups of numbers on a single ticket.

Wheel check — *See* **Roulette chip**.

Wheel signature — The characteristics of a particular roulette wheel. This includes any bias traits, it's location in the casino, it's orientation on the table, and any physical distinctions (such as make, model, marks and scratches) that would help to identify it at a future time.

Wheelhead — The central rotating piece within the bowl of a roulette wheel that carries the numbers and the ball pockets. Also called cylinder.

Wide Area Progressive Slots (WAPS) — One of a large number of similar progressive slot machines that are linked together over a wide geographic area such as a city or a state.

Wild card — A card, such as a joker, that may be designated as any other card to improve the hand, even if that card already appears in the hand. For instance, a hand containing four kings and a wild card would be considered five-of-a-kind.

Wild symbol — A symbol that can substitute for any other symbol on the reels of a slot machine. Wild symbols can combine with other symbols to produce a winning combination, and often include a payout multiplier. Also called substitute symbol.

Win marker — The object that a dealer places over the winning number on a roulette layout to identify the winning chips. Also called crown marker.

Window — The glass area in front of the reels of a slot machine where the payline and the symbols are viewed.

Working — A term indicating that a bet is currently active.

Wrapped royal — A sequential royal flush that can begin with any card and proceed in either direction, such as Q K A 10 J. Also called wrap-a-royal.

Wrong bettor — A player who bets against the dice by making a don't pass or a don't come bet.

Yo, yo-leven — In craps, the stickman's verbal term for the number 11, to avoid confusion with the number 7.

Zero — (a) One of the two green numbers on an American roulette wheel, the other number being double zero. (b) The only green number on a French or English roulette wheel.

DOYLE BRUNSON'S SUPER SYSTEM
A COURSE IN POKER POWER!
by World Champion Doyle Brunson

CONSIDERED BY PROS THE BEST POKER BOOK EVER WRITTEN

This is the classic book on every major no-limit game played today and is considered by the pros to be one of the best books ever written on poker! Jam-packed with advanced strategies, theories, tactics and money-making techniques - no serious poker player can afford to be without this essential book! Hardbound, and packed with 605 pages of hard-hitting information, this is truly a must-buy for aspiring pros. Includes 50 pages of the most precise poker statistics ever published!

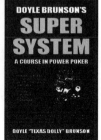

CHAPTERS WRITTEN BY GAME'S SUPERSTARS

The best theorists and poker players in the world, Dave Sklansky, Mike Caro, Chip Reese, Bobby Baldwin and Doyle Brunson, a book by champions for aspiring pros - cover the essential strategies and advanced play in their respective specialties. Three world champions and two master theorists and players provide no-nonsense winning advice on making money at the tables.

LEARN WINNING STRATEGIES FOR THE MAJOR POKER GAMES

The important money games today are covered in depth by these poker superstars.

You'll learn seven-card stud, draw poker, lowball, seven-card low stud (razz), high-low split (cards speak) and high-low declare; and the most popular game in the country today, hold'em (limit and no-limit). Each game is covered in detail with the important winning concepts and strategies clearly explained so that anyone can become a bigger money winner.

SERIOUS POKER PLAYERS MUST HAVE THIS BOOK

This is mandatory reading for aspiring poker pros, players planning to enter tournaments, players ready to play no-limit. Doyle Brunson's Super System is also ideal for average players seeking to move to higher stakes games for bigger wins and more challenges.

To order, send $29.95 by check or money order to Cardoza Publishing

WIN MONEY AT BLACKJACK! SPECIAL OFFER!
THE CARDOZA BASE COUNT STRATEGY

Finally, a count strategy has been developed which allows the average player to play blackjack like a pro! Actually, this strategy isn't new. The Cardoza Base Count Strategy has been used successfully by graduates of the Cardoza School of Blackjack for years. But now, for the first time, this "million dollar" strategy, which was only available previously to those students attending the school, is available to you!

FREE VACATIONS! A SECOND INCOME?

You bet! Once you learn this strategy, you will have the skills to **consistently win big money** at blackjack. The longer you play, the more you make. The casino's bankroll is yours for the taking.

BECOME AN EXPERT IN TWO DAYS

Why struggle over complicated strategies that aren't as powerful? In just **two days or less**, you can learn the Cardoza Base Count and be among the best blackjack players. Friends will look up to you in awe - for you will be a **big winner** at blackjack.

BEAT ANY SINGLE OR MULTIPLE DECK GAME

We show you how, with just a **little effort**, you can effectively beat any single or multiple deck game. You'll learn how to count cards, how to use advanced betting and playing strategies, how to make money on insurance bets, and much, much, more in this 6,000 word, chart-filled strategy package.

SIMPLE TO USE, EASY TO MASTER

You too can win! The **power** of the Cardoza Base Count strategy is not only in its **computer-proven** winning results but also in its **simplicity**. Many beginners who thought card counting was too difficult have given the Cardoza Base Count the acid test - they have **won consistently** in casinos around the world.

The Cardoza Base Count strategy is designed so that **any player** can win under practical casino conditions. **No need** for a mathematical mind or photographic memory. **No need** to be bogged down by calculations. Keep **only one number** in your head at any time. The casinos will never suspect that you're a counter.

DOUBLE BONUS!!

Rush your order in now, for we're also including, **absolutely free**, the 1,000 and 1,500 word essays, "How to Disguise the Fact that You're an Expert", and "How Not to Get Barred". Among other **inside information** contained here, you'll learn about the psychology of the pit bosses, how they spot counters, how to project a losing image, role playing, and other skills to maximize your profit potential.

As an **introductory offer to readers of this book**, the Cardoza Base Count Strategy, which has netted graduates of the Cardoza School of Blackjack **substantial sums** of **money**, is offered here for **only** $50!

To order, send $50 by check or money order to:
Cardoza Publishing, P.O. Box 1500, Cooper Station, New York, NY 10276

POWERFUL POKER SIMULATIONS
A MUST FOR SERIOUS PLAYERS WITH A COMPUTER!
IBM compatibles CD ROM Windows 3.1, 95, and 98, ME & XP - Full Color Graphics

Play interactive poker against these **incredible** full color poker simulation programs - they're the absolute **best** method to improve game. Computer players act like real players. All games let you set the limits and rake, have fully programmable players, adjustable lineup, stat tracking, and Hand Analyzer for starting hands. MIke Caro, the world's foremost poker theoretician says, "Amazing...A steal for under $500." Includes free telephone support. **New Feature!** - "Smart advisor" gives expert advice for every play in every game!

1. TURBO TEXAS HOLD'EM FOR WINDOWS - $89.95 - Choose which players, how many, 2-10, you want to play, create loose/tight game, control check-raising, bluffing, position, sensitivity to pot odds, more! Also, instant replay, pop-up odds, Professional Advisor, keeps track of play statistics. Free bonus: Hold'em Hand Analyzer analyzes all 169 pocket hands in detail, their win rates under any conditions you set. Caro says this "hold'em software is the most powerful ever created." Great product!

2. TURBO SEVEN-CARD STUD FOR WINDOWS - $89.95 - Create any conditions of play; choose number of players (2-8), bet amounts, fixed or spread limit, bring-in method, tight/loose conditions, position, reaction to board, number of dead cards, stack deck to create special conditions, instant replay. Terrific stat reporting includes analysis of starting cards, 3-D bar charts, graphs. Play interactively, run high speed simulation to test strategies. Hand Analyzer analyzes starting hands in detail. Wow!

3. TURBO OMAHA HIGH-LOW SPLIT FOR WINDOWS - $89.95 -Specify any playing conditions; betting limits, number of raises, blind structures, button position, aggressiveness/passiveness of opponents, number of players (2-10), types of hands dealt, blinds, position, board reaction, specify flop, turn, river cards! Choose opponents, use provided point count or create your own. Statistical reporting, instant replay, pop-up odds, high speed simulation to test strategies, amazing Hand Analyzer, much more!

4. TURBO OMAHA HIGH FOR WINDOWS - $89.95 - Same features as above, but tailored for the Omaha High-only game. Caro says program is "an electrifying research tool...it can clearly be worth thousands of dollars to any serious player. A must for Omaha High players.

5. TURBO 7 STUD 8 OR BETTER - $89.95 - Brand new with all the features you expect from the Wilson Turbo products: the latest artificial intelligence, instant advice and exact odds, play versus 2-7 opponents, enhanced data charts that can be exported or printed, the ability to fold out of turn and immediately go to the next hand, ability to peek at opponents hand, optional warning mode that warns you if a play disagrees with the advisor, and automatic testing mode that can run up to 50 tests unattended. Challenge tough computer players who vary their styles for a truly great poker game.

6. TOURNAMENT TEXAS HOLD'EM - $59.95

Set-up for tournament practice and play, this realistic simulation pits you against celebrity look-alikes. Tons of options let you control tournament size with 10 to 300 entrants, select limits, ante, rake, blind structures, freezeouts, number of rebuys and competition level of opponents - average, tough, or toughest. Pop-up status report shows how you're doing vs. the competition. Save tournaments in progress to play again later. Additional feature allows you to quickly finish a folded hand and go on to the next.

GREAT POKER BOOKS
ADD THESE TO YOUR LIBRARY - ORDER NOW!

TOURNAMENT POKER by Tom McEvoy - Rated by pros as best book on tournaments ever written, and enthusiastically endorsed by more than 5 world champions, this is a must for every player's library. Packed solid with winning strategies for all 11 games in the World Series of Poker, with extensive discussions of 7-card stud, limit hold'em, pot and no-limit hold'em, Omaha high-low, re-buy, half-half tournaments, satellites, strategies for each stage of tournaments. Big player profiles. 344 pages, paperback, $39.95.

OMAHA HI-LO POKER by Shane Smith - Learn essential winning strategies for beating Omaha high-low; the best starting hands, how to play the flop, turn, and river, how to read the board for both high and low, dangerous draws, and how to win low-limit tournaments. Smith shows the differences between Omaha high-low and hold'em strategies. Includes odds charts, glossary, low-limit tips, strategic ideas. 84 pages, 8 x 11, spiral bound, $17.95.

7-CARD STUD (THE COMPLETE COURSE IN WINNING AT MEDIUM & LOWER LIMITS) by Roy West - Learn the latest strategies for winning at $1-$4 spread-limit up to $10-$20 fixed-limit games. Covers starting hands, 3rd-7th street strategy for playing most hands, overcards, selective aggressiveness, reading hands, secrets of the pros, psychology, more - in a 42 "lesson" informal format. Includes bonus chapter on 7-stud tournament strategy by World Champion Tom McEvoy. 160 pages, paperback, $24.95.

POKER TOURNAMENT TIPS FROM THE PROS by Shane Smith - Essential advice from poker theorists, authors, and tournament winners on the best strategies for winning the big prizes at low-limit re-buy tournaments. Learn the best strategies for each of the four stages of play–opening, middle, late and final–how to avoid 26 potential traps, advice on re-buys, aggressive play, clock-watching, inside moves, top 20 tips for winning tournaments, more. Advice from McEvoy, Caro, Malmuth, Ciaffone, others. 160 pages, $19.95.

WINNING LOW LIMIT HOLD'EM by Lee Jones - This essential book on playing 1-4, 3-6, and 1-4-8-8 low limit hold'em is packed with insights on winning: pre-flop positional play; playing the flop in all positions with a pair, two pair, trips, overcards, draws, made and nothing hands; turn and river play; how to read the board; avoiding trash hands; using the check-raise; bluffing, stereotypes, much more. Includes quizzes with answers. Terrific book. 176 pages, 5 1/2 x 8 1/2, paperback, $24.95.

WINNING POKER FOR THE SERIOUS PLAYER by Edwin Silberstang - New edition! More than 100 actual examples provide tons of advice on beating 7 Card Stud, Texas Hold 'Em, Draw Poker, Loball, High-Low and more than 10 other variations. Silberstang analyzes the essentials of being a great player; reading tells, analyzing tables, playing position, mastering the art of deception, creating fear at the table. Also, psychological tactics, when to play aggressive or slow play, or fold, expert plays, more. Colorful glossary included. 288 pages, 6 x 9, perfect bound, $16.95.

WINNER'S GUIDE TO TEXAS HOLD 'EM POKER by Ken Warren - This comprehensive book on beating hold 'em shows serious players how to play every hand from every position with every type of flop. Learn the 14 categories of starting hands, the 10 most common hold 'em tells, how to evaluate a game for profit, and more! Over 50,000 copies in print. 256 pages, 5 1/2 x 8 1/2, paperback, $14.95.

KEN WARREN TEACHES TEXAS HOLD 'EM by Ken Warren - In 33 comprehensive yet easy-to-read chapters, you'll learn absolutely everything about the great game of Texas hold 'em poker. You'll learn to play from every position, at every stage of a hand. You'll master a simple but thorough system for keeping records and understanding odds. And you'll gain expert advice on raising, stealing blinds, avoiding tells, playing for jackpots, bluffing, tournament play, and much more. 416 pages, 6 x 9, $24.95.

THE CARDOZA CRAPS MASTER

Exclusive Offer! - Not Available Anywhere Else)

Three Big Strategies!

Here It is! **At last**, the **secrets** of the **Grande-Gold Power Sweep**, **Molliere's Monte Carlo Turnaround** and the **Montarde-D'Girard Double Reverse** - three big strategies - are made available and presented for the **first time anywhere**! These powerful strategies are designed for the serious craps player, one wishing to bring the best odds and strategies to hot tables, cold tables and choppy tables.

1. THE GRANDE-GOLD POWER SWEEP (HOT TABLE STRATEGY)

This **dynamic strategy** takes maximum advantage of hot tables and shows you how to amass small **fortunes quickly** when numbers are being thrown fast and furious. The Grande-Gold stresses aggressive betting on wagers the house has no edge on! This previously unreleased strategy will make you a powerhouse at a hot table.

2. MOLLIERE'S MONTE CARLO TURNAROUND (COLD TABLE STRATEGY)

For the player who likes betting against the dice, Molliere's Monte Carlo Turnaround shows how to turn a cold table into hot cash. Favored by an exclusive circle of professionals who will play nothing else, the uniqueness of this strongman strategy is that the vast majority of bets **give absolutely nothing away to the casino**!

3.MONTARDE-D'GIRARD DOUBLE REVERSE (CHOPPY TABLE STRATEGY)

This **new** strategy is the **latest development** and the **most exciting strategy** to be designed in recent years. **Learn how** to play the optimum strategies against the tables when the dice run hot and cold (a choppy table) with no apparent reason. **The Montarde-d'Girard Double Reverse** shows how you can **generate big profits** while less knowledgeable players are ground out by choppy dice. And, of course, the majority of our bets give nothing away to the casino!

BONUS!!! Order now, and you'll receive **The Craps Master-Professional Money Management Formula** ($15 value) **absolutely free**! Necessary for serious players and **used by the pros**, the **Craps Master Formula** features the unique **stop-loss ladder**.

The Above Offer is Not Available Anywhere Else. You Must Order Here.
To order send ~~$75~~ $50 (plus postage and handling) by check or money order to:
Cardoza Publishing, P.O. Box 1500, Cooper Station, New York, NY 10276

VIDEOS BY MIKE CARO
THE MAD GENIUS OF POKER

CARO'S PRO POKER TELLS

The long-awaited two-video set is a powerful scientific course on how to use your opponents' gestures, words and body language to read their hands and win all their money. These carefully guarded poker secrets, filmed with 63 poker notables, will revolutionize your game. It reveals when opponents are bluffing, when they aren't, and why. Knowing what your opponent's gestures mean, and protecting them from knowing yours, gives you a huge winning edge. An absolute must buy! $59.95.

CARO'S MAJOR POKER SEMINAR

The legendary "Mad Genius" is at it again, giving poker advice in VHS format. This new tape is based on the inaugural class at Mike Caro University of Poker, Gaming and Life strategy. The material given on this tape is based on many fundamentals introduced in Caro's books, papers, and articles and is prepared in such a way that reinforces concepts old and new. Caro's style is easy-going but intense with key concepts stressed and repeated. This tape will improve your play. 60 Minutes. $24.95.

CARO'S POWER POKER SEMINAR

This powerful video shows you how to win big money using the little-known concepts of world champion players. This advice will be worth thousands of dollars to you every year, even more if you're a big money player! After 15 years of refusing to allow his seminars to be filmed, Caro presents entertaining but serious coverage of his long-guarded secrets. Contains the most profitable poker advice ever put on video. 62 Minutes! $39.95.

Order Toll-Free 1-800-577-WINS or use order form on page 527